HOWE LIBRARY
COLLEGE &
USIC

D0891642

Madame de Staël, Novelist

Madame de Staël. Isabey. Musée du Louvre, Cabinet des Dessins. (Photo from Réunion des Musées Nationaux, Paris.)

HOWE LIBRARY
SHENANDOAH COLLEGE &
CONSERVATORY OF MUSIC
WINCHESTER, VA.

Madelyn Gutwirth

Madame de Staël, Novelist

THE EMERGENCE OF THE ARTIST AS WOMAN

University of Illinois Press

URBANA   CHICAGO   LONDON

Publication of this work was supported in part by a grant
from the Andrew W. Mellon Foundation.

© 1978 by the Board of Trustees of the University of Illinois
Manufactured in the United States of America

"Lamentation" from Denise Levertov, *The Sorrow Dance*.
© 1966 by Denise Levertov. Reprinted by
permission of New Directions Publishing Corporation.

Library of Congress Cataloging in Publication Data

Gutwirth, Madelyn.
Madame de Staël, novelist.

Bibliography: p.
Includes index.
1. Staël-Holstein, Anne Louise Germaine Necker,
Baronne de, 1766–1817—Fictional works.   2.   Women—
France—History—18th century.   I.   Title.
PQ2431.Z5G87   843'.6   78–5836
ISBN 0–252–00676–3

PQ
2431
.Z5
G87
1978
843 St13g

Gutwirth, Madelyn.

Madame de Staël,
novelist

HOWE LIBRARY
SHENANDOAH COLLEGE &
CONSERVATORY OF MUSIC
WINCHESTER, VA

. . . la gloire elle-même ne sauroit être pour une femme qu'un deuil éclatant du bonheur.

GERMAINE DE STAËL

. . . the crooked roads . . . are the roads of genius.

WILLIAM BLAKE

13.50 Goldberg 10·31·80

IN MEMORY OF MARGARET GILMAN

CONTENTS

ILLUSTRATIONS

Preface

This is a work of feminist criticism. By that I mean that it is an effort to add to our knowledge and understanding of the emergence of female self-consciousness in literature.

The bias here is clear. In studying the works of a woman author whose fiction is focused on the effects of love and genius upon woman, I have wished to understand and explain, in much greater detail than other critics have wished to do, the quality of and the reasons for Mme de Staël's preoccupations as these may be adduced in French culture and society and in her life. What we have here is an attempt to rehabilitate a social and personal *Weltanschauung* now largely lost to us, but not, I think, without intrinsic merit or influence, both of which have become obscured.

In 1952, when the late Margaret Gilman of Bryn Mawr College, knowing my feminist tendencies, suggested Mme de Staël's novels to me as a possible dissertation subject, I was distinctly annoyed. I was a rather prissy young woman, and the lascivious reputation of *"la trop célèbre"* (all I knew of her except what one reads in manuals of literary history) was not such as to entice me: my own view of feminism at the time carefully eschewed sexual gaudiness. It seemed to me, in my supreme ignorance, that hers was a figure of little substance, undeserving of my ardor to work on a writer of genuine literary worth. But nevertheless I began to read *Corinne*. From my superior vantage point of 145 years later and a continent away, the novel made me smile. It moved me, as well, and I began to see much in it that I thought had not been clearly stated before. *Delphine* only deepened the feeling of discovery, but the full extent of the protest that I felt to be the inherent value of these works could be expressed only guardedly in that time and circumstance. A ponderous dissertation was duly written and accepted, thus apparently closing the episode—but never for me.

I knew that matters had conspired to thwart my realization

of the kind of work on Mme de Staël's fiction that it deserved. I was only too aware that the initial response of others to an attempt to reassess these works might prove to be much like my own original reaction—a dismissive shrug of the shoulders.

That was before the women's movement was reborn. As it gathered momentum, my hopes rose—and so did my fortunes. In 1971–72 I was given an American Council of Learned Societies grant to pursue work on this book. The impetus that all the many women's caucuses and discussions on women writers I have eagerly attended since they began gave to my mind and spirits is incalculable, and for that I thank those of my colleagues who showed me—to my intense relief—that mine were shared, not solitary, concerns.

The somewhat unorthodox manner in which this study is constructed arises from this history. Much of the analytical material on the works themselves was in the dissertation, but it is here drastically revised in presentation and emphasis. The initial biographical material has undergone similar expansion. Moreover, I have dug more deeply into social, intellectual, and literary history to establish a proper framework for the reevaluation of the novels, the questions they treat, and the manner of their composition. Accordingly, in the Prologue I have begun by presenting a general overview of woman's place in the eighteenth century and a discussion of the meaning of the phenomenon of the novel for women to set the scene for Mme de Staël's own novelistic era, that of Revolutionary France. Chapter 1 sketches in a spiritual biography of Mme de Staël's youth and gathers together some of the facts of her background. Chapter 2 goes at length into her earliest fictional efforts in an attempt to establish the themes that preoccupied her and her habitual strategies of arraying them. In Chapter 3 various kinds of background materials—historical, biographical, and literary—are used to prepare the ground for the extensive discussion of *Delphine* to be found in Chapter 4. There follow three chapters on *Corinne:* 5, a set of origins; 6, an essay on the style of the work; and 7, an interpretation of its themes and substance.

The final chapter is frankly polemic. It begins by treating the last, slight, fictional works and the ending of the author's life, goes on to assess the various types of influence the novel *Corinne* has had, traces a history of the novelist's reputation in literary criticism, and ends by attempting an integration of the Corinne myth into an understanding of the historical evolution of woman's self-conception.

Mme de Staël's fiction is not autonomous and is not treated here as separable from her fantasies: rather, the life and the work each speak to the other and have been employed to illuminate one another. However, it is fiction that is the center of this study and its reason for being.

A word about language. After a good deal of regretful cogitation (for a French teacher) over the accessibility of my study to the kind of reader, quite possibly ignorant of the French tongue, who might be interested in a work of feminist criticism, I decided to put the whole of the book into English. All translations from a French source not otherwise credited are my own. Mme de Staël's writing style itself is not sufficiently arresting to override such a decision, but I hope it will be understood that the exact quality of the works is somewhat betrayed by the alteration of language in the discussion to follow.

I acknowledge with gratitude my debt to the American Council of Learned Societies for granting me a fellowship in 1971–72 and to my college, West Chester State, for giving me leave at that time for this work. The friendship of Simone Balayé, who knows and understands Mme de Staël best of all, has given me heart, and I thank her warmly for her kindness and encouragement. The Haverford College Library has sheltered and fed my curiosity for a quarter century: my affection for it and for its courteous and helpful staff is accordingly very great. I acknowledge with pleasure the skilled collaboration of Mildred Hargreaves in preparing the text. To Sarah Gutwirth, who assisted me in typing the manuscript, I give loving thanks. As for Marcel Gutwirth, who has supported and subsidized my work (both morally and financially), I must express not only gratitude, but my deep admiration.

I hope that some of my own surprise and excitement in the results of bringing together some previously unexploited avenues of approach, like that of the Revolutionary context and the situation of a woman novelist, will be shared by readers: may they participate, too, in the elation, winning out over whatever defeats Mme de Staël was constrained to suffer, attendant upon a systematic, circumstanced reconstruction of works so palpably ambitious and courageously conceived, whatever their imperfections.

PROLOGUE

Eighteenth-Century Fiction
and Woman's Place

A chaste young woman never read a novel.

ROUSSEAU

The novel is born in the same moment as the spirit of revolt and it transposes to the aesthetic plane a similar ambition.

CAMUS

We entered the salon. Next to Madame Necker's armchair was a little wooden stool upon which her eleven-year-old daughter was seated, obviously obliged to hold herself very erect. Scarcely had she taken up her accustomed place when three or four elderly personages approached her . . . one of them . . . engaging in conversation with her just as if she were twenty-five years old. This man was the Abbé Reynal; the others were Messieurs Thomas, Marmontel, the Marquis de Pezay, and the Baron Grimm.[1]

After dinner, many more people arrived. Each one, as he approached Madame Necker, would say a word to her daughter, pay her a compliment, or make a witty remark. . . . She replied to them all with ease and grace; the company took delight in alternately attacking, embarrassing, exciting this young imagination that already displayed such brilliance. The very men who were most celebrated for their wit were the ones most apt to draw her out. They asked her to tell them about her readings, suggested new ones to her, and gave her a taste for study by hearing out what she knew and what she did not know.[2]

When in the eighteenth century, a girl-child is born, she is not received into the family in joy. The home is not a place of feasting at her

---

1. Jean-François Marmontel (1723–99)—French novelist and moralist, author of *Contes moraux* (1756) and *Bélisaire* (1766); Antoine-Léonard Thomas (1732–85)—literary abbé, author of the *Essai sur les éloges* (1773) and *Essai sur le caractère, les moeurs et l'esprit des femmes* (1772); Alexandre-Frédéric Jacques Masson de Pezay (1741–77)—graceful salon figure and minor litterateur; Friedrich-Melchior, Baron von Grimm (1723–1807)—literary critic and essayist, associated with Mme d'Epinay and Diderot.

2. Quoted by Charlotte Julia van Leyden Blennerhasset, *Madame de Staël et son temps*, 3 vols. (Paris: Westhausser, 1890), I, 183–84.

coming; her birth gives her parents none of the exultation of a triumph: it is a blessing that they accept in a spirit of disappointment.[3]

As we juxtapose the account of her childhood salon life with the opening phrases of the Goncourts' study of women in the eighteenth century, the contrast between the common lot of womankind and the exceptional career of Germaine Necker, who is known to us as Mme de Staël, is bound to strike us as flagrant. It will not suffice to accept the disparity, as is so often done in the case of this woman, as one of nature's anomalies. It is only when we peer more closely at this scene that we become capable of discerning the lineaments both of the uniqueness of this destiny and of its kinship with the spirit of its times.

It is a commonplace of our thinking about eighteenth-century life in France that we very nearly believe women to have dominated its society.[4] This is a myth that flatters the complacency of both sexes: the females in their pleasure at being able to believe that once upon a time they were, whatever their subsequent status, able to command; the males in that it assures them that, in their generosity, they once did, in fact, allow this turn of events to go as far as nature could take it. Such a belief was common even when the Goncourts wrote their work, in 1862, and no doubt it was to disabuse the public of this popularly held notion that they chose to open it with so unkind and yet so true a remark on the birth of a daughter to that time. Of course the eighteenth century was *not* dominated by women. In asserting this, we can do no less than try to clarify this statement, so at issue with the belletristic cliché, with some remarks on the actual condition of women in that period.

---

3. Edmond and Jules de Goncourt, *La Femme au XVIIIe siècle* (Paris: Didot, 1862), p. 1.

4. It was "the most truly feminine century in our history." Jean Larnac, *Histoire de la littérature féminine en France* (Paris: Editions Kra, 1927), p. 139. Jean Starobinski puts the situation in perspective: "Woman reigns (she is led to believe she reigns). This is to say that the promise of pleasure floats about her being. For those few who are mistress of themselves, who reign over a salon, how many others are there who are treated as objects: shut up in convents, married off against their will, made conquests of by trickery." *L'Invention de la liberté* (Geneva: A. Skira, 1964), p. 55.

The first observation might be that the exception proves the rule. The core of truth that is distorted by this misapprehension of the real balance of society is that a small caste of extraordinarily energetic and intelligent women, rich and well placed, had indeed extended the limited but dynamic influence over the social and intellectual life of the nation that the salon had won in the previous century. But the existence of these women was considered a derogation from the rule of social inequality: the leaders of the salons were all brilliant and delightful exceptions, and few of them rejected so flattering an assessment of themselves even though it might implicitly deny to them, and certainly to the rest of their sex, a basic human equality. These women, in the elegance of their manners, in the grace of their persons, bewigged, trussed, powdered, painted, and bejeweled, seductive, politic, and amusing by turns, have sometimes been considered, not without justification, an ultimate expression of French refinement. That they achieved this status by internalizing their consecration as supreme objects— objects curious, amazing, and comely (or, if precocious children like Germaine Necker, wondrous nearly mechanical dolls)—is difficult to deny, when they are placed, not in a context removed from history as "famous women throughout the ages," but rather within their own social history and that of the major thought of their time.

That there is a heightened *interest* in women in the eighteenth century cannot be denied. "Society does not cease in the least to be 'androcentric'; man remains the norm: but as such, he is thought to be known, and therefore less interesting, emitting a feebler magnetic charge." Literature, dominated by men of imposing stature, fictionalizes this reality and so we find that "bourgeois myth constantly superimposes an imaginary gynocentrism upon a real androcracy."[5]

The idea of female domination over Enlightenment society runs through that period itself. In Montesquieu's *Lettres persanes* Rica writes, ironically to be sure, from Paris to his friend Ibben back in Ispahan: "People complain in Persia that the government is controlled by two or three women: it is much worse in France,

5. Pierre Fauchery, *La Destinée féminine dans le roman européen du dix-huitième siècle* (Paris: Armand Colin, 1972), pp. 9, 835.

where women generally govern, and not only assume wholesale all control of authority, but even divide among themselves the retailing of it" (cvii).

Montesquieu, like Mme de Staël who followed him in this as in much else, tied the increase in women's freedom to the principle of monarchy and the life of the court which he saw before him. Women, in their love of propriety, thought Montesquieu, encourage stratification and hierarchy, but court life, combining social order with social life and movement, is liberating to them. He was perplexed by the significance of the increased and illicit (because sanctioned neither by law nor by long-established custom) participation of women in social affairs he witnessed under the loosened social and political framework that came to replace the Sun King's overlong reign, under the Regency and then in the licentious era of Louis XV. Court and city life in the seventeenth century had granted to more women a larger role in social life than they had before dreamed of under more purely war-oriented regimes. Mme de Staël tried to account for this: "The influence of women is necessarily very great when all events occur in salons, and all character is revealed in words; in such a state of affairs, women are a power, and what is pleasing to them is cultivated. The leisure that the monarchy allowed to most of the distinguished men in all spheres was necessarily very favorable to the increased importance of pleasures of the mind and of conversation" (*Litt.* i, xviii). The perception of the power of language as a power accessible to women, binding them to men by thought and discourse, is one that recurs frequently in Mme de Staël's works.

What we find here in Montesquieu and Mme de Staël may be thought of as a kind of wish fulfillment (for her) and a fear fulfillment (for him). Whenever it is said that the influence of women was "very great," only an augmented degree of female influence can be safely inferred, for active participation in society on the part of women has always been perceived as menacing to the received social order, a usurpation. Hence it has taken on the aspect of an oversized and aberrant threat whenever it has appeared, no matter what the dimensions of its actual nature. It was the fuller participation of women in social life, with its consequence of a relative feminization of manners and at least the appearance of feminine dominance in the setting of mores, that made the eighteenth century appear to drift to the distaff. But this drift was never to receive basic approval: it remained an epiphenomenon of taste and style, without consecration in law or in education. Montesquieu writes of women (*L'Espirit des lois*, XIX, xii) that "in the countries where they live with [as opposed to being segregated from] men, the desire they have to please, and the desire that one has to please them, make one continually change in manner. The two sexes are spoiled; each of them loses its own distinctive and essential quality; something arbitrary creeps into what was absolute, and customs change daily." In other words, in social intercourse at least, women's similarity to men was becoming so manifest as to unsettle, though still not so great as to alter materially the foundations of existing sexual arrangements, which were predicated upon absolute disparity.

It is significant that already in 1748 with *L'Esprit des lois* Montesquieu could find that the sexual order was in such disarray, long before ideas of sexual equality had achieved any sort of consensus in any important segment of society. Woman, thanks to the salon, had begun the process of evolving for herself some sort of assured and vital place in the social structure of the time; yet the core of the ordinary life of society remained by and large, as the events of 1789 were to prove, tragically unaffected by libertarian ideas. Women's legal disability achieved perhaps its ultimate point with the passing by the Parlement de Paris in 1731 of article nine of the *Ordonnance des donations*, which stripped them formally of equality before the law. There was no class, party, or group that espoused the cause of women, and yet, because of the new exposure of women to currents of thought and the acuity of political debate throughout the period, the question of feminine equality was more and more written about, both affirmatively and negatively, until the year before the Revolution, when discussion of it reached a paroxysm of intensity.[6]

---

6. For the source of details given here, see the excellent summary of the subject, to which I am much indebted, by David Williams, "The Politics of Feminism in the French Enlightenment," in *The Varied Pattern: Studies in the 18th Century*, ed. Peter Hughes and David Williams (Toronto: A. M. Hakkert, 1971). See also the exceedingly complete documentation of Jane Abray, "Feminism in the French Revolution," *American Historical Review*, 80, no. 1 (Feb., 1975), 43–62.

During the first half of the century there were as many works that share Bocquel's view concerning *La Supériorité des hommes sur les femmes* (1744) written by women as by men, and the popular *Advice of Father to Daughter* by the Marchioness of Halifax, favoring men, was translated into French (to be read in aristocratic circles) in 1756. What remains for us the most celebrated attack upon women's pretensions to equality is found in Rousseau's *Emile,* his treatise on education, Book V, which is a succinct presentation of a widely shared view, one prevalent in all classes of society, though perhaps presented here with more vigor than polite society would have wished it to be. "The entire education of woman must be relative to that of man. To please him, to be useful to him, to raise him when he is little, to take care of him when he is grown, to counsel him, to console him, to make his life cozy and agreeable, these are the duties of woman in all times and they must be taught her from childhood on. . . . Woman was created to yield to man and to bear even his injustice." Of course Rousseau remains the most paradox-ridden of the great eighteenth-century French thinkers. One might easily reproach him, using his own weapons, for his absolute injunction to women that they "please": in his own *Discourse on the Origin of Inequality among Men* he had argued with some cogency that it is the very need *to please* that society enforces upon men which enslaves them. Naturally, he had no thought of applying this insight to women.

Rousseau's expressions of scorn for women, though they did not go unanswered by other polemicists, were met either with a masochistic accord or with a silent puzzlement on the part of his hordes of female admirers. And the Republic of Men Only, which is his ideal, was to be, certainly in respect to the other sex, the republic to which the men of 1789 would also adhere.

Diderot, that worldling, who scarcely suffered from the same degree of terror of women as Rousseau, appears friendlier toward them, sympathizing with them in their sexual exploitation by men. If he does so, as a critic rightly maintains "without enthusiasm," the explanation is probably to be found in his own affection for the seductive, the pleasing, all that the eighteenth century held out in the way of an enticement to women to convince them that theirs was a power above the mere political or economic. This was, after all, the most elegantly erotic period of modern European history.

Diderot's view of woman is therefore unbalanced by his sensual delight in her, and his perception of her is largely limited to the interpersonal sphere. In his biologically oriented outlook, woman is governed by her organs, her senses, but one part of her outranks all others in his hierarchy: "Woman bears within her an organ capable of terrible spasms that take possession of her and arouse . . . all sorts of phantoms in her imagination. . . ." The mechanisms of this single terrifying organ have the most irresistibly far-reaching consequences upon female character. Elsewhere we see him write, "Never is that wound nature made in you altogether healed. . . . The woman who has been hysterical in youth becomes devout with advancing years; the woman who keeps some energy into later years was hysterical in her youth. The head still speaks the language of the senses, even when they are stilled. Nothing is more contiguous than ecstasy, vision, prophecy, revelation, fiery poetry, and hystericism."[7] This side of his vision, even when tempered by the gift of poetry and prophecy, seems to bear some imprint of the ancient male image of woman as terrifying castrator.[8] But Diderot is ambivalent and seeks a way of making this fearsome temptress approachable, since approach her he will. "It is above all in the passions of love . . . that women astonish us, as beautiful as Klopstock's seraphim, as terrible as Milton's devils."[9] Diderot's essay on women was written, in all haste and emotional intensity, as a reply to the Abbé Thomas's careful, dull, and equitable treatise on Le Caractère, les moeurs et l'esprit des femmes (1772)—that same Abbé Thomas who was an habitué of Mme Necker's salon, her good friend, and one who often interrogated her daughter. Wittily but cruelly alleging that Thomas's book is a hermaphrodite having neither the nerve of man nor

---

7. Denis Diderot, *Correspondance,* ed. Georges Roth, 5 vols. (Paris: Editions de Minuit, 1955–59), III, 113.

8. For further elucidation of this male psychic fear, see H. R. Hays, *The Dangerous Sex: The Myth of Feminine Evil* (New York: Putnam, 1964).

9. Denis Diderot, "Essai sur les femmes," *Oeuvres complètes,* ed. Jules Assézat and Maurice Tourneux, 20 vols. (Paris: Garnier, 1875–77), II, 252. The following Diderot quotations also appear in this essay.

the softness of woman, Diderot rapidly jettisons the Abbé's patient arguments and tumbles forth his own confused but genuine convictions. The passionately inspired image he evokes to combat the hermaphrodite is one shared, of course, in a far more dilute form, by a culture that saw women as beings apart from the mainstream of male civilization, and somewhat alien to it. The angel-devil, dark-light syndrome that Diderot claims to detect in the female character is a permanent dichotomy of the literature on women, the very one which becomes dominant for the Romantic movement. In the preoccupations he sees as central to women (and which surely have been central to their self-conception), their passionate loves, amorous and maternal, he represents them always as possessed—by lovers, by natural powers, or by powers of darkness. "No man ever sat, at Delphi, upon the sacred stool. The role of Pythia is appropriate only to a woman. Only a female brain could become exalted to the point of truly having the presentiment of a god's approach, of becoming distraught, disheveled, foaming at the mouth and crying out: 'I feel you, I feel it, here he is, the God!' and of really repeating his discourse." Diderot can imagine the oracle only as a woman possessed by a (male) spirit. In seeming agreement with this view, Mme de Staël's Corinne, who will be compared (following Virgil) to the Cumaean Sibyl, is described vividly at the end of her novel in a way that will recall Diderot's hysterical evocation of oracular intensity. But Diderot's facile attempt to see only woman as an empty vessel into which the god pours meaning, a meaning she alone is equipped to utter, would not have been shared by Victor Hugo, and was not shared, apparently, by Moses, Jesus, or Mohammed.

This melodramatic attitude toward women, tinged but not dominated by fear, contrasts sharply with the cool, clear-sighted, worldly, and controlled *mot*, so typical of the age, expressed in Diderot's formula: "If you hear a woman speak ill of love, and a man of letters exclaim his scorn for public esteem, say of the first that her charms are fading, and of the second that his talent is waning." Eloquent exponent of the emotional clichés of his period (though, happily, not the intellectual ones), Diderot's remarks illustrate the paradox of woman in his time: she must be tame and worldly, dominated by the need to maintain and heighten her charms, in other words, she must be enslaved to love; in all her relations divorced from the sexual realm or in her withdrawal from a belief in love, following upon betrayal, or in later life, she will be seen—and very likely will see herself—as alien, unreasoning, frightening, or all three.

There is scarcely any writer who exceeds Diderot in a gift for the unforeseen. He ends his brief essay on woman with a totally unexpected and curiously generous remark: "When they possess genius, I believe it makes a more original stamp upon them than on us." It is an unwarranted, unsupported statement, perhaps intended as gallant atonement for the harshness of the preceding pages, which certainly might prove enough to dampen the aspirations of any ardent young female reader, but it lends support to a concession we will find again and again in this era: some few women may be allowed their superiority, so long as their genius is acknowledged to be exceptional. However, womankind must draw no special conclusions from the existence of these paragons.

Such limited concessions were utterly useless to the mass of women, of course. The *philosophes* did not waste any deep cerebration upon them, preferring not to do battle with authority on this particular ground. Even Voltaire, upon occasion so courageous in defense of the weak, was distressingly ambivalent in his positions concerning women. Adhering with a conviction and dedication greater than that of any other tragic author of his period to the conventions of the classical (especially the Racinian) drama which gave dramatic preponderance to women, he created in such works as *Mérope* and *Zaïre* (this one of the favorite works of Mme de Staël) heroines possessed of singular strength and virtue; but he was equally, and increasingly with age, drawn to the other pole of representation of women in French letters, the *gaulois*, that wench-loving, reductive style of treating women alternately as sexy prey or as terrifying crones—an inheritance that goes back to the thirteenth century's Jean de Meung, at the least.[10] In the *Encyclopédie* (1751–), the article "Femme"[11] at least theoretically recognizes woman's equality, but only under the aegis of the man,

---

10. It is far from my intent to reduce Voltaire's complex of views here to a simplistic formulation. I wish only to indicate the tortured quality of Voltaire's understanding of "le sexe," and leave it to others to delineate its workings.

11. Allegedly written by the Chevalier de Jaucourt.

within marriage; the unmarried woman has no standing whatever and is a sort of pariah whose chief asylum is the convent. Indeed, retreat from an antagonistic world became a fairly popular recourse for those disaffected women who could afford it. Any claim on the part of women to an existence apart from men, divorced from their support, was implicitly denied, considered beneath notice. As to civil rights, so little did most women feel they deserved them, notwithstanding the efforts of advocates of equality, that Mme de Genlis would claim these in 1790 only for widows, who would thereby merely replace their husband's franchise.

In the high society of the first half of the century, marriage, despite its bestowal of status upon the wife, was the merest absurdity. Marriage, conferring instantaneous rank or money, or instantaneously and permanently denying them to young women, lost most of its prestige and moment right after the wedding. It was a rare and courageous individual indeed who admitted to anything so ridiculous as amorous inclination toward the spouse. By the end of the century, spurred by Rousseau's moralistic *Nouvelle Héloïse,* a contrary cult, that of virtue, arose. After 1770 conjugal and maternal love became not merely admissible, but, for some, moral imperatives. As Mme de Genlis put it, "A woman needs support. She can win esteem only by the exercise of a peaceable and stainless virtue." The admirable Manon Phlipon who was later to become the eloquent Mme Roland of the Revolution, wrote in youthful wistfulness in 1774 about her ideal, like that of Rousseau's Héloïse once passion has passed, of devoting her life to the intimate pleasures of home, of making her husband happy or raising children in an atmosphere of devotion and courage. This ideal of enlightened domesticity, so socially acceptable, would have a prestige that far outstripped the attractions of the superior woman, although we see them endlessly set at variance with each other, as if it were somehow obvious, despite the lack of any overt acknowledgment to that effect, that the admission to nearly full status of a few women of wit and position did in fact deeply undermine the structures of society. Laclos wrote to his wife: "The greatest service you can give to your daughter is to water her soul with your generous sensibility. It is by one's wits that one may shine, but it is through one's feelings that one loves and is loved; the first procures but a vain glory, whereas the other makes us capable of the sole true happiness it is given us to enjoy. . . ."[12] We all need *sensibilité*, men and women, Laclos seems to be saying, but for a daughter, all else is beside the point. Furthermore, if you shine, you may be rewarded with a little vainglory, but will you be truly loved? The general opinion would be, if you were a woman, certainly not.

The Idea of Woman in the Rising Genre

What part had the novel played in the evolution of this idea of woman? For the larger part of the eighteenth century, this bastard art form was deemed to be a frivolous genre, destined to be read by an audience of which women were increasingly a part—a delightfully wicked pastime. Marking the eclipse of the prestige of religious training in society, a thinly disguised libertinism was frequently its major component. A "natural" morality, replacing the churchly one, preached the ideal of "sincerity" in human, and especially amorous, relations and held that pleasure being natural, abstinence is error, a pointless frustration of nature's exquisite sensual design.

The newer morality of pleasure was not unaccompanied by anxiety.[13] The search for happiness has two major enemies: an *ennui* in privation, which becomes a fathomless spiritual dejection comparable to death itself; and the pleasure-hating opinion of society *en bloc*, which relentlessly harries and undermines the happiness of the few individuals privileged to possess it. But the pursuit is endlessly renewed no matter the often tragic consequences.

In political theory the assertion of the right to happiness came as a confirmation of the right to freedom. The antislavery cause received important impetus from the new appreciation of this right, as well as from a growing sense of the universality of human nature.

---

12. Quoted by Albert Marie Pierre de Luppé, *Les Jeunes Filles à la fin du XVIIIe siècle* (Paris: Champion, 1925), p. 14.

13. Robert Mauzi, *L'Idée du bonheur au XVIIIe siècle* (Paris: Armand Colin, 1960), p. 23 and *passim*, gives this interpretation of the underside of the pursuit of happiness.

What gives greater rein to freedom and pleasure combined than love? Love is the sole great adventure of the novel and both male and female novelists do it tiresome and abundant homage. It is the absolute in the service of which the lover illustrates his value.

The heroine is a pure unsullied girl. She burns with a mysterious malaise that will gradually be diagnosed as the need to love passionately. (Prurience is not the least of the pleasures the eighteenth-century novel has to offer.) Love for her will either reform the more experienced—sometimes libertine—hero, or else merely confirm in him a moral perfection he already possesses. Abstraction of plot and character are matched by abstraction of language. The names of places, whether exotic or local, Orenoco or Mondoville, as of characters—Adélaïde, the Marquis of Orfeuil—are standard. Heroines are "fair," "gentle," "charming"; heroes "handsome as the sun." Nature is "majestic," "grand," "great," and "wild," though not dangerously so. When in nature, kindred souls commune. This common coin of novelistic wealth, so simplistic as to annoy or amuse us, is nonetheless essential to recall.

Despite its evident weaknesses, this was the very period in which the novel gained preponderance as a literary form, even though the quarrel over its legitimacy moved ferociously on, its conservative opponents waging an outraged rearguard action against it. As Georges May has so illuminatingly written, the enemies of the novel were often recruited from the ranks of male supremacists who scorned the unitary preoccupation of the novel with love as evidence of moral decadence and a softening of the French nation's virile fiber. Rousseau is significantly to be ranged with the theological opposition to both women and novels, although in typical self-contradiction he created the most striking heroine and the foremost novel of the century in France. The danger the novel presented, as the Catholic clerics saw it, was no less a one than gynocracy. "If novels wish her [woman] to dominate over mankind, and for her to reign over civil society, what is left to complete the ruination of modesty? Honors that belong only to the Deity are lavished here on earth, or a form of worship that resembles it. Novels do not refuse her such homage."

The Reverend Porée exclaimed in outrage that instead of the formula "fear has created gods," a substitute, thanks to the novel, might replace it, to wit: "love has created goddesses." In 1755 the Abbé Jacquin asked, rhetorically, "What is indeed lacking in these novels but temples and altars to complete the apotheosis of woman?"[14]

In fact, the function of the novel, as Pierre Fauchery has noted, was to "celebrate the dream world realm of woman. In solemnizing the great moments of her life, it withdraws from her the dull weight of dailiness and pulls her toward the heaven of myths, into the orbit of her *destiny*."[15] Presumably, its subversion lay in the notion that she had a destiny.

A less outspoken position than that taken by the antinovel, antilove faction was one of playful condescension, typified in Voltaire's statement that the novel amuses women by "dealing with the only thing that interests them." According to this argument, the novel is a frivolous genre appropriate to the childish creatures women are.[16] Such a scornful, dismissive attitude was actually far more difficult to combat, both for novelists and for women, than those frankly misogynistic attacks that were patently prejudiced.

In the wake of Mlle de Scudéry's and Mme de La Fayette's successes, the novel was looked upon increasingly as a "feminine" form. Bayle had written already in his *Dictionnaire historique et critique* (article "Virgile") that "our best French novels have for some time been written by young ladies or women," although a list of 344 novelists published between 1700 and 1750 is, according to Georges May, illustrated by the presence of only forty-three women. Whether or not more novels were or were not actually

---

14. These quotations and much of the material on woman and the novel question are from Georges May's *Le Dilemme du roman au XVIIIe siècle* (Paris: Presses Universitaires Françaises, 1963), chapter "Feminisme et roman," p. 210.

15. Fauchery, *La Destinée féminine*, p. 10. The section of Fauchery's work called "Le Destin féminin et les morales" (pp. 46–49) further elaborates the climate of novelistic creation with regard to women.

16. Georges May says that this view was not automatically indicative of misogyny. I would disagree.

written by women than by men, the fact that women wrote them at all was enough, in the eighteenth century, to feminize the activity.

Of course, the writing of novels offered incredible opportunities to women, in numbers unprecedented in all of history, to scrutinize and defend themselves for the first time and even, in a few hardy cases, to attack. This it is that explains their increased use of the pen: the excitement of being able to read and write about love (decreed as their sphere) from what they considered their own point of view. The tremendous success of Mme Ricco-boni's works reveals the truth of this, if nothing else does. Her *Fanni Butlerd*, authorized, to be sure, by that male creation Clarissa Harlowe, writes to her treacherous lover in accents that ring with an angry, articulate authenticity male authors, even ostensibly staunch supporters of women like Richardson or Laclos, could only counterfeit: "And who are you, men? Where do you find the right to fail to observe with a woman those standards you impose among yourselves? What law of nature, what convention of the state ever authorized such an insolent distinction? What, your word simply given, engages you solemnly to the lowliest of your fellows, and your repeated oaths do not tie you to the woman you have chosen!"[17]

We find numerous examples of generous impulse toward women among eighteenth-century male novelists: Racine is their progenitor in his unflagging and superb penetration of the motives of the female characters, both noble and ignoble, in his tragedies. Modernizing his approach, Marivaux, in whose drama women rival and often surpass their men in wit and enterprise, was the author of a "feminist" play, *La Colonie* (1729), which, raising the question of the parity of women with men, failed signally to win an audience in his lifetime.[18] Richardson, Prévost, Crébillon, and Laclos present us with women characters who possess zest and passion such that sometimes their heroes will indeed engage, at

---

17. Marie-Jeanne Riccoboni, *Lettres de Mistriss Fanni Butlerd . . .* (Paris: Humblot, 1759), pp. 202–3, near the end of Letter CXVI.

18. Leo Spitzer, in "A Propos de *La Vie de Marianne*," *Romanic Review,* XLIV (1953), 122, thought he had found in Marivaux's novel "*the glorification of the feminine principle in human thought.*" Italics his.

least momentarily, in that abject worship of the sex so dreaded by the theological fathers.[19] With those products of a masculine imagination *Clarissa Harlowe* and *Pamela* setting the pattern, the novels of the period present women essentially as victims of society. The female novelists explore and heighten this state with particular flair. Their altogether natural espousal of such a pose is dangerously buttressed, however, by the moralistic tendencies that all novels possess, in greater or lesser degree, in this era.

Amoralism is the other face of moralism. A sentimental bourgeois heart beats in the disabused amoral breast of Diderot. Rousseau, who sought for himself the crown of morality in ostensibly defending marriage, presents in his *Nouvelle Héloïse* the most enticing and extended defense of illicit love ever penned. The root of the problem is that as the century progressed sensibility became confused with morality: passionate feeling, if expressed in a highly civilized mode with grace and nuance, makes us forgive the Rousseau of *The Confessions,* for example, his pettiness, his jealousies, his betrayals. This moral-amoral byplay, present already in the novels of Richardson, was to be more intense as the century unfolded.

Despite the proliferation of works by female authors, there is no single feminine novel during this century that appears to rival in importance the *Princesse de Clèves* of the preceding one. Of course, Mme de La Fayette's novel is the prototype of the feminine novel that follows, but her heroine's moral nobility, her tact, and her visible breeding were not really imitable. What *was* imitable was simply suffering through the passion of love, and this came to be the imperative of the novel: the female victim of a wicked society that allows masculine exploitation of feminine weakness, ignorance, or innocence became a rigid stereotype.

Far worse from the standpoint of the emergence of a genuinely new female novel were the actual strictures, social and educational, by which society tamed the minds of women who then considered themselves to be nothing but enticing, powerless victims. The only revolt possible to them, given the nature of their bonds,

19. May thinks of Crébillon's *Les Egarements du coeur et de l'esprit* (1736–38) as a feminist work.

would have to have been a revolt of the mind. The English Aphra Behn,[20] through the odd circumstances of her nearly unique life, had been able to imagine a heroine free of the constraints on acts and emotions that society enjoined upon other women, conventions that are paid obeisance by novelistic amoralist and moralist alike. For them, men *or* women, heroines must be yielding creatures, often foolish in their frailty, absurdly delightful when they pretend to gravity, and they must *never* have preoccupations other than love. Any lapse from this rule is stigmatized with the ultimate anathema: the character is "not feminine." Ridicule rains down upon such freaks. The woman novelist often takes her revenge by creating heroes who are as vapid, stereotyped, and love-oriented as the women are generally portrayed as being.[21]

Whatever exaltation of woman we find in the novel is, therefore, but the prelude to her domestication by sex. In the world of the eighteenth-century novel, women are required both to yield to love and to seem to resist it, the choice to be made on the basis of sensibility alone; no truly feeling young woman could resist outright her suitor's pleas of undying passion. *Schadenfreude* is a large element in the consecrated reaction to her fall. "Sex so fascinating, having so great a sway over our own, uniting so many different charms to seduce us, that is where a single slip will lead you!" exclaims a male novelist. He goes on, "If Eustasia had absolutely rejected all opportunities of meeting with Léonce, she would have taught a lesson to that longing which was to produce her misfortunes as well as her errors."[22] She is an amiable schoolmistress whose pupil suffers from a hopeless behavior problem for which she will be punished.

Georges May, following Max Ascoli, ties feminism to the

20. Aphra Amis Behn (1640–89), British dramatist and novelist, author of *Oroonoko*. She is another of those women authors who "had a great strength of Mind and Command of thought, being able to write in the midst of Company, and yet have her share of the conversation." From Charles Gildon's foreword to Behn's *Novels*, ed. Charles Gildon, 2 vols. (London: F. Clay, 1722).

21. See Philippe Séjourné, *Aspects généraux du roman en Angleterre de 1740 à 1800* (Aix-en-Provence: Orphys, 1966), p. 307.

22. François-Thomas-Marie de Baculard d'Arnaud, *Eustasia, histoire italienne*, 2 vols. (Paris: André, 1803), I, 18.

right to passion and the defense of the novel in which this right is so forcefully expressed. In this view, a radical approach to sexuality is construed as favorable to the flowering of women's rights. Even on the sensual plane, however, such a stance did not necessarily work to free women from the confines of convention. Although it cannot be denied that it had a hand in their awakening, the preoccupation with love served to ensconce them even more firmly in the hold of the moral-immoral dichotomy. In inevitable reaction against the proclamation of the rights of passion, a spate of moralizers descended to smite this show of fire where, it must be presumed, only a chaste discretion ought to have prevailed. "I ought never to have so blinded myself to the duties imposed, doubtless by God himself, upon my sex," cries the miserable, guilty, pregnant Eustasia.[23] Woman's moment of glory in love leaves her chastened by an ashen guilt.

The question must be raised: what was the context for women of this sensual "liberation"? The eighteenth-century ethos was far too crippling to the spirit of freedom in woman to allow her, except in a handful of cases, to enjoy a sensual discovery which, in any case, without effective contraception, lay beyond the confines of emotional comfort. The chimera of an overt sensual awareness was, to be sure, an explosive force that may have heightened the sense of repression woman endured socially, economically, and creatively. But the novel gave only minimal expression to these extra-amorous needs. The best that could be done for woman in this atmosphere was to help her accept love as an adored calamity. This the novel did.

An enlightened woman like Mme de Lambert is not fooled. "Le genre faible est voué au sexe faible—The weaker genre is meant for the weaker sex" argue the opponents of the novel. In catering precisely to the weakness of women, their abject need to please, the novel helped maintain them in it. A heroine writes to her lover from whom she is separated: "I rejoice in the delicious confidence of knowing I please the one I love . . . but it can never make me forget that it is to you that I owe all you deign to approve of in me. As a Rose draws its brilliance from the rays of the Sun,

---

23. Arnaud, *Eustasia*, I, pp. 28–29.

so are the charms you find in my spirit and feelings the gifts of your luminous genius; nothing is mine but my love for you."[24] Zillia wants no personal identity. Mme de Lambert rejects such a selfless ideal: in her study on the education of young women, she cautions that novels must not have a preponderant role in the development of girls, but she accepts them, notwithstanding, as part of a wider, serious education, including the sciences.

Nevertheless, it must be admitted that the novel, when important, has ever been on the frontier of the unspeakable, and that the rise to preeminence of the previously platonized and sublimated passions of sex gave women, because they were its object, a reflected glory they were quick to exploit. The exploitation had to be covert, however, and vestiges of hypocrisy hung on to women's writings. How could it have been otherwise? Only consider the true situation of women authors: "People may accept a love of letters in a man," wrote Mme de Lambert, "but they will not forgive it in a woman."[25] She begins her *Réflexions nouvelles sur les femmes* (1727) with this comment: "For some time novels written by women have been appearing and their works are as amiable as their persons; one could scarcely give them more praise. Some, instead of examining their felicities, have sought to cover them with ridicule. This ridicule has become so redoubtable that people fear it even more than they do dishonor."[26]

She then elucidates, with some cogency and bite, the dilemma of women in her own society:

But what is odd is that in forming [women] for love, we prevent them from its practice. We ought to make up our minds: if we are interested only in their being pleasing, let us not forbid them the use of their charms; if you wish them to be rational and witty, don't abandon them when they are endowed with these traits only. But we ask of them a combination and a manipulation of these qualities it is difficult to seize or to reduce to any sort of golden mean. We want them to have minds but to hide them; check their progress and stop them short of any new achievement;

---

24. Françoise d'Issembourg d'Happencourt de Graffigny, *Lettres d'une Péruvienne* (Amsterdam: aux dépens de la Cie, 1761), p. 11.

25. Quoted in G. May, *Le Dilemme du Roman*, p. 233.

26. Anne-Thérèse de Marguenat de Courcelles Lambert, *Réflexions nouvelles sur les femmes* (Paris: F. Le Breton, 1727), p. 103.

they scarcely find a way of taking flight before they are called back by what we call custom. Fame, which sustains all efforts of the mind, is refused them. We deprive their minds of any object, any hope; we debase them and, to use a term of Plato's, we clip their wings. It is certainly surprising if they still have any left.[27]

A destructive ridicule was apt to fall upon even the most distinguished female accomplishment; in fact it might fall more heavily upon the most distinguished. The power of ridicule did not weaken as the century progressed: on the contrary, at its end it was fortified by a fountain of moralism. That combination of mockery and moral outrage Mme de Lambert alludes to has ever been the entire arsenal in the masculine attempt, seconded by servile women, to discourage feminine achievement. Each woman who takes up the pen is compelled, in an attempt to combat its withering influence, to elaborate a defense, be it that her work is innocent use of leisure hours, or the use of a talent discovered by merest chance, or that, grandly but unselfishly, it will result in nothing less than the improvement of the species. For the expansive nature and spacious ego of Mme de Staël, the last and least modest of these claims will also be the least hypocritical.

Female Aspiration: The Aborted Revolution

The rejection of female intelligence was such that it had made even the decidedly superior Mme d'Epinay, writer, protector and friend of Diderot and Rousseau, mistress of Grimm, turn against the development of all talent in women:

The most learned of women has not and cannot possess any knowledge but the most superficial. I contend that a woman is not able, by reason of her being a woman, to acquire any knowledge extensive enough to be useful to her kind, and it seems to me that it is only in such knowledge that one can take pride. To make useful application of knowledge, of whatever sort, one must link practice to theory, for otherwise one has but highly imperfect notions. How many are the things it is forbidden women to approach! All that pertains to the science of administration, of politics, of commerce, is foreign and forbidden to them: they cannot nor must they be involved in them, and these are the sole great means by which culti-

---

27. Anne-Thérèse de Marguenat de Courcelles Lambert, *Lettres sur l'éducation d'une jeune demoiselle* (Paris: Louis, 1811), p. 128.

vated men can truly be useful to their fellows, to the state, to their nation.[28]

Her disillusionment is all too evident. Women are cut off from useful work through their defective education which robs them of precise knowledge of the physical world and imprisons them in the nebulous aura of *sensibilité*. Work useful to one's fellow creatures is what she appears to crave, but at her level of the social scale useful work is not that of shoeing horses, or even of building bridges, but that of manipulating power through commercial or political activity. Her inability to envisage such a role for herself or for any other woman, given the prejudices of the time, probably dictates her rather spiteful conclusion that women simply cannot do such things. Clearly, we are very far removed indeed from Montesquieu's playful contention that the women were controlling everything.

If the rights of the superior woman are suspect and their exercise bound to be penalized by a resultant reduction in the consideration of her as a feeling, feminine being, how much more suspect will the education of less exalted women, lacking the alibi that God has given them irresistible gifts, appear? The Abbé Wandelaincourt wrote in 1782 that the time of woman's education should be "shorter, less serious, and less intensive than that of men; the study of the arts and sciences must be presented to her simply as a relaxing and agreeable pastime."[29] As may be inferred also from Mme d'Epinay's remarks, inroads had been made in increasing woman's cultivation, to which these strictures were reactions. Women of the leisure classes now learned to read, but their culture was chiefly ornamental. The Abbé Galiani carried this idea to a logical conclusion: he thought that women should become learned, but in "their own language—poetry"!

It is because women largely accepted the premises, repeated universally and monotonously all around them, that a woman's life must be circumscribed by her emotions that the propagandists

---

28. From a letter to the Abbé Galiani, quoted in Luppé, *Les Jeunes Filles*, p. 2.

29. See Luppé, *Les Jeunes Filles*, pp. 141–42.

for women's rights had so little in the way of ideological success in a period when every kind of political freedom was in constant question. Tracts were not lacking; those advocating the cause of women were indeed more numerous than those of their opponents.[30] "The feminists," writes Fauchery in summation, "often go as far as possible in their affirmation of the equality of the sexes and of the theoretical rights of woman. But . . . they show themselves to be timid and evasive in their application of them."[31] What the apologists for women appear to have achieved was a sort of compromise with public opinion in the sense that they had created an atmosphere in which while it might no longer have been acceptable to be outspokenly and unequivocally against them (although Rousseau pulled this off admirably) neither could further claims on their part be advanced. A public consensus pervaded with an insistence on the fulfillment of the feminine duties and *bienséances* successfully repressed any concerted expression of female rights of the kind we find expressed in d'Alembert's eloquent reply of 1759 to Rousseau's letter on *Spectacle*. What, asked d'Alembert in his caustic way, might the cause be for that dearth of worthy women that Rousseau had asserted: could it lie, perhaps, in "the debasement and the kind of slavery into which we place women; the limits we set upon their mind and soul; the meaningless chatter, humiliating for them and for us, to which we have reduced our dealings with them, as if they had no minds to cultivate or were not worthy of doing so? Finally, the futile, I might almost say murderous education that we provide for them, without allowing them any other; an education which teaches them nearly nothing except sham, to have no feeling that they do not stifle, no opinion that they do not hide, no thought that they do not disguise?"[32] Despite the sting and bite of truth in d'Alembert's

---

30. They follow the lead of the rigorously argued tracts of François Poulain de la Barre, *De l'Egalité des deux sexes* (Paris: Jean Du Puis, 1673) and *De l'Education des dames pour la conduite de l'esprit dans les sciences et dans les moeurs* (Paris: Jean Du Puis, 1674).

31. Fauchery, *La Destinée féminine*, p. 548.

32. Jean Lerond d'Alembert, "Lettre à J. J. Rousseau citoyen de Genève," in *Oeuvres complètes*, 5 vols. (Paris: Belin, 1821–22), IV, 450.

several pages, the most unequivocal political statements on behalf of women on the eve of the Revolution were to be Condorcet's, published in 1788 and 1789.

Condorcet, too, advanced the view that education was the prime cause of the evident gap in the achievements of the two sexes, saying that "a species of constraint put upon the strength and the mind of woman by public opinion as to what custom deems acceptable, from childhood on, and *especially at that point where genius begins to unfold,* must harm their progress in every sphere."[33] He urgently asked his fellow revolutionaries that women be given equal rights with men by the Revolution and begged them to answer his arguments not with jokes and mockery, but by a valid rejoinder. Such a rejoinder never came.

Although this is not the occasion to trace the fate of the feminist movement in the Revolution, we must nevertheless see clearly that the moment of reckoning of the have-nots could not leave women as a class unmoved: whether or not they openly espoused the principle of women's rights, and few of them ever did so, millions of Frenchwomen must have hoped secretly that their rights would be recognized, wholly or in part, when the Rights of Man were published, or at least soon afterwards. This was not the case. "Most often pity took the place of a good conscience; and on this score, as on many others, the Constituent Assembly cruelly disappointed the expectations of women: children of their time, their last word on the emancipation of this sex is perhaps that of Mirabeau who declared that the role of woman is to 'chain to her feet all the strength of men through her irresistible power of weakness.' "[34] Despite this sentimental prejudice, Olympe de Gouges, a feminist activist hoping to capitalize on revolutionary opportunity, actually published her *Déclaration des droits de la femme et de la citoyenne* (1791?). A number of women tried to join the political clubs, but the effect of this was only that women were soon officially disbarred from their membership.

---

33. Marie Jean Antoine Nicolas Caritat de Condorcet, *Lettres d'un bourgeois de New-Haven à un citoyen de Virginie (Mazzei), sur l'inutilité de partager le corps législatif entre plusieurs corps* (Paris: A. Colle chez Froullé, 1788), p. 286. Italics mine.

34. Fauchery, *La Destinée féminine* pp. 48–49.

When the women then formed clubs of their own, *Les Amies de la Vérité* and *Citoyennes révolutionnaires,* the convention specifically abolished them, thus effectively closing off for more than a century any evolution in women's political status.[35]

The effect upon the women of Germaine Necker's generation, young in 1789, must necessarily have been most acute of all: their entire future lives might have been led as free citizens. The repression of that hope is the premise with which this book begins.

---

35. The rights actually granted to women by the Revolution were that "to the same education as that of boys insofar as is fitting to their sex," with special emphasis on "sewing, weaving, and the domestic labors appropriate to their sex," and the suppression of the right to inheritance by the oldest male child alone, thus granting female and younger male children a right to share in patriarchal booty. See Larnac, *Histoire de la littérature féminine,* p. 157.

CHAPTER 1

"La Curchodine"

> . . . Ogboinba was an extraordinary child. She
> understood the tongues of birds and beasts, trees, and
> even the blades of grass. She prophesied and performed
> things strange and wonderful, and her name became a
> byword on every lip.
>
> AN IJAW STORY
(NIGERIA)

> In all things, what reassures us is superiority; and what
> we must fear are all those defects that meagerness of
> soul brings in its path.
>
> GERMAINE DE STAËL

The Sources of Singularity

That odd scene, so often evoked, of the little Anne-Louise
Germaine Necker already presiding over a salon at eleven must
prompt us to examine the mother at whose side she sat, already
emulating and rivaling her.

Madame Necker had been born Suzanne, later to be known as
"la Belle Curchod," in 1739. The only child of the pastor of a
village in the country of Vaud, she was raised by him to be both
a moral and, for her time, a learned woman, whose competence
in classical Latin, for example, would be significantly greater than
that of her daughter. Her devoted father died while Suzanne was
still unmarried, abandoning mother and daughter to a relentlessly
genteel poverty.

Although Mme de Staël would later claim that her mother
had no part whatever in her being, there is a clear presentiment of
both Germaine and Corinne in a sketch of Suzanne as a young
woman, surrounded with students and *beaux esprits* who would
read her their word portraits and dissertations. They called themselves Céladon or Sylvandre and would declaim their works at her
feet, conceiving for her sake a new *Carte du Tendre*[1] where they

---

1. Mme de Staël would later be dubbed *"La Curchodine,"* or chip off the

would set, amidst the stormy sea of Sentiment, the island of Themira; Themira was, of course, none but Mlle Curchod.

Despite her bereavement, Suzanne was to find an abundance
of friends and protectors; a particularly faithful and interested
friend was the Pastor Moultou whose children she was hired to
tutor. With Moultou she would visit Voltaire at Ferney and meet
Rousseau, who found her a lively and attractive young woman.
Edward Gibbon, the future historian of the *Decline and Fall of the
Roman Empire*, during his visit to Switzerland, was another
litterateur to be drawn to the charms of this tall, graceful, honey-
haired Latinist. So smitten was he that he wished to marry Suzanne, and for five years their union seemed an intermittent possibility; but Gibbon *père* rejected his son's seriously entertaining a
union that was so socially and financially unprepossessing, and
with a suspicious foreigner, to boot. Compelled by this disappointment to earn her way as a governess, Suzanne Curchod displayed
the phlegm which was the mask she wore in public to hide the
violent spasms of *sensibilité* she suffered in private. Her whole
life long she would seem to the world a cold and aloof woman,
even when giving displays of those "deep feelings" every refined
young woman was supposed, in those days, to show. Her suitor,
Gibbon, made reference to what he deemed to be her artifices. Of
a performance of *Zaïre*, which they attended together, he wrote:
"During the interesting portions . . . she sobbed to the point of
attracting all eyes to her. Yet when she removed the handkerchief
from her face, one saw only a fresh, joyous countenance showing
no trace of tears. How that girl plays at sensibility!"[2] Less studied,
perhaps, but no less melodramatic were Suzanne's hysterical scenes
of despair when her mother died. Their relations had indeed been
strained, but the bereaved daughter could not rid herself of the
guilty obsession that she had made her mother's last days unhappy,
and this idea was to remain with her, stubbornly poisoning her

---

maternal block, in mock tribute to the blue-stocking qualities she inherited from
her mother. The *Carte du Tendre* is a map: Madeleine de Scudéry, seventeenth-
century author of *l'Astrée* and publicist of Preciosity, that elaborate game of
manners, invented this imaginary realm of amorous sentiment which was its
game board. Initiates assumed conventional pastoral names.

2. Pierre Kohler, *Madame de Staël et la Suisse* (Paris: Payot, 1916), p. 26.

emotions for some time. Something related to the death of her parents gave her a morbid fear of her own decay, which would later dictate those odd funerary arrangements of the Neckers: they were embalmed in alcohol.

On coming to Paris at the invitation of a fellow Genevan, Mme de Vermenon, the penniless young woman improved her situation dramatically. At Mme de Vermenon's house, she met that lady's own suitor Jacques Necker, a young Genevan who had come to Paris fourteen years before and who had already become rich at thirty-two. In choosing this comely newcomer over Mme de Vermenon, Necker reclaimed her from the prospect of a life of poverty and nonentity, and it was in this light that she would always see him. Shortly after their marriage in 1764, she wrote to a friend: "I am wed, my dear, to a man who is the most lovable of mortals. . . . These days I no longer see anything but my husband in all of nature; all my tastes, all my feelings are related to him; I only take notice of other men insofar as they resemble him more or less. . . ."[3] Mme Necker's will to conjugal success is evident here, and it was a resolve she would never abandon; it remained the cornerstone of her being, and would strongly mark her daughter's. The way she viewed herself with regard to her husband could be wittily stated: "People constantly address to me all the praise they bestow upon M. Necker; I resemble one of those portraits of an absent king towards which one turns on ceremonial occasions. M. Necker is so absentminded when you speak to him of himself that I *must* represent him; but it is, as it were, merely as a picture."[4] His picture, his shadow, his second: this is the role assumed with such overwhelming enthusiasm by Suzanne Necker that it would make many suspect her of a desire for domination of which she was by no means incapable, but which was certainly foreign to her conscious designs.

The kind of counsel she was to give to women is totally rooted in the conventions of her enlightened bourgeois Protestant milieu —that first generation of Rousseau's Swiss readers into which she

3. Gabriel-Paul Othenin d'Haussonville, *Le Salon de Madame Necker*, 2 vols. (Paris: Calmann-Lévy, 1882), I, 112–13.

4. Suzanne Curchod de Nasse Necker, *Mélanges extraits des Manuscrits de Mme Necker*, 3 vols. (Paris: Charles Pougens, 1798), II, 106.

was born. "We must make ourselves necessary to those we depend on and continually strive to please them. With patience and gentleness one can take hold of the hand that holds our chains, and then they no longer weigh so heavily upon us. . . . We must make men happier for what they do for us than in what they do for themselves. They must be made to rejoice more in soul, mind, and all their being when once they have abandoned them all to us."[5]

In the light of her will to union, it is a bit surprising that she should persist in seeing that there were chains that must somehow be dissolved from consciousness. In the transaction of marriage, Suzanne exacted a perfect submission in return for her own total obeisance. Her behavior within marriage remained exceedingly egalitarian: she was still Themira, queen over her salon and her home; Necker was her king, truly chosen. In contrast, her attitude toward women and marriage in principle remained unegalitarian and traditional. She wrote to a male friend, " 'Women,' you say, 'are always the cause of all evil and all good in this world'; this *mot* persists in displaying some animus against the female sex; *it* scarcely merits the compliment you pay it: only the exceptional ones have the strength of great vice or virtue. Consider rather that nature has given them their faults so as to exercise your virtues: we have nothing of our own; our whole existence is but relative."[6] A disabused view of the world was Mme Necker's: it reflects what we should have called, not too long since, wisdom.

And what of Jacques Necker, that "original" of which Suzanne was but the portrait? Born in Geneva in 1732, son of a fairly distinguished writer on jurisprudence of German origin, Jacques was the younger brother in a family whose elder son, Louis, two years older than he, was singularly gifted and would become a mathematician of note. After pursuing acceptable but unremarkable classical studies, Jacques Necker was placed in a banking house where at first he manifested no interest whatever in finance, and, sent to Paris at eighteen he by no means changed overnight. Though at twenty he still thought of himself as a writer of comedies, he later began seriously to earn the Genevan banker Vernet's respect

---

5. S. Necker, *Mélanges*, I, 110.
6. S. Necker, *Mélanges*, Letter to Mxxx, n.d., II, 161–62.

for his competence so that at the older man's retirement in 1762 Necker, then only thirty, received from him a sum of money that allowed him to found, with Thélusson, the bank which was soon to become the greatest in France.

The hallmark of Necker's banking skill was that he engaged in daring commercial speculation of considerable scope and apparent probity. The court of Louis XVI, shivering on the brink of ruin, was compelled to appeal to his bank for financial aid and, in 1773, Necker published an *Eloge de Colbert*—a work in praise of the guardian of Louis XIV's treasury—which nakedly revealed his own ambitions to be Finance Minister. Consequently, he was galled when Turgot received the finance post, not he. As financial chaos grew more acute, some began to *demand* that Necker finally be given the charge as minister. The impediment to this course, despite his high qualifications and palpable interest in the post, was that Necker was deemed undesirable because of his Genevan origin and, what was worse but inseparable from the fact, his Protestant faith. At long last he was appointed *contrôleur* in 1777. Although he was granted the powers of Finance Minister, as a Protestant he was still not admitted to the council of state.

Necker's performance in the finance post has naturally given rise to innumerable evaluations and counter-evaluations by historians of the outbreak of the Revolution. What seems clear is that his brilliant stratagems of borrowing funds gave the nation an unwarranted illusion of recovery for a time. It is generally agreed that despite a generous and even elevated sense of the common good, he lacked the will and decisiveness to give reality to his ideas.

Removed from power, his insistence on replying to attacks upon his conduct in public life in his *Compte rendu* of 1784 led only to his being exiled by a *lettre de cachet*. In 1788, Necker again was asked—as a last resort—to return to the ministry, and this time with what amounted to the power of Prime Minister. In August of 1788, when he returned, it was in a general spirit of jubilant popular acclaim, for he was expected to operate a miracle, that of circumventing imminent disaster.

The perceptive, intelligent Mme Necker, despite her often-repeated incantations of adulation ("M. Necker is certainly a man of genius; but he has no right to any pride in it . . . nature created him as he is"), was known to make some sharper observations also concerning her husband: "He pursued glory and praise in the same way as hunters do who neglect and scorn their prey once it has fallen at their feet." Paris saw the Neckers as avidly ambitious parvenus, somewhat grotesque and outlandish. Voltaire and Condorcet called the couple "the Envelopes" after a supposed *mot* of Necker's to the effect that principles should be put in an envelope of thought. His ponderous style, so little resembling Parisian quicksilver, was Necker's outstanding characteristic: he took himself with utmost seriousness, but noticed others rather less. In fact, in the brilliant and successful salon Suzanne Necker established first in the rue Michel-le-Comte, then in the rue de Cléry, and finally in the rue Bergère, Necker was an often silent and remote observer, and even an occasional napper. The company of Grimm, Diderot, Thomas, Reynal, Marmontel, Mme Geoffrin, and Buffon kept him only intermittently interested; he was the very model of the banker of caricature who nods at the opera. But it was his pomposity that was his ultimate flaw. His was a pomposity so great that it encompassed his family. His wife and daughter shared with him, in his mind, the standing of a privileged race, but he demanded of them always that they be worthy of him.[7]

Mme Necker did nothing to discourage her husband in his exaggerated notion of his own worth. As far as one can tell from her public pronouncements, she seems to have idolized him, and she gave herself up entirely to his dreams of glory. Fighting off her shyness and her distaste for the worldly life, she launched their salon to enhance his reputation. But as we understand her better we see Suzanne's illusionless, caustic self occasionally bursting through the screen of propriety, as in her letter to a close friend where she tells him, though in a chaffing way, exactly what in all probability she really felt about her husband: "Imagine the most humorless fellow in the world so positively delighted by his own superiority that he doesn't even notice mine; . . . confounding the clever with the dullards because he feels himself always to be

---

7. This, at any rate, is Constant's view of the Necker family as reported by Pierre Jolly, *Necker* (Paris: Les Oeuvres françaises, 1947), p. 27.

somewhere on a mountaintop whose height makes him see as diminutive fools all who are beneath him because, he says, they make so striking a contrast with his own sublime genius. . . ."[8]

Even though this letter, written in Necker's presence, was supposedly intended for his "improvement," it would have given some relief to those who during their lifetime were irritated by the ostentatious shows of affection and mutual adulation to which the Necker family tirelessly gave themselves. Without our wishing to make an allegation of hypocrisy (they believed utterly in these protests of devotion and admiration), we see that in intimacy Suzanne's relations with her husband were a mix of affection and salient criticism. The dry, critical, judgmental side of her attitude toward her husband probably played its part in alienating Germaine, who fully identified herself with that myth of the perfect Necker so tenderly fostered by Suzanne herself.

Anne-Louise Germaine was born on April 22, 1766. Before her birth, her mother was beset by obsessive fears of death. She felt sure she would leave her child motherless and restlessly looked about for an appropriate stepmother. Despite her Latin and her friendship with those great propagators of information, the *Encyclopédistes,* she had scarcely any understanding of the workings of physiology and gave birth for the first time at thirty-three years of age in an ignorance as total and superstitious as that of any woman of the Dark Ages.

I confess that my terrified imagination fell far short of the truth. For three days and nights I suffered the tortures of the damned, and Death was at my bedside, accompanied by his satellites in the shape of a species of men who are still more terrible than the Furies, and who have been invented for the whole purpose of horrifying modesty and scandalizing nature. The world *accoucheur* still makes me shudder. . . . The revolting details of childbirth had been hidden from me with such care that I was as surprised as I was horrified, and I cannot help thinking that the vows women are made to take are very foolhardy. I doubt whether they would willingly go to the altar to swear that they will allow themselves to be broken on the wheel every nine months.[9]

---

8. Mme Necker, in Haussonville, *Le Salon,* I, 24.

9. J. Christopher Herold, *Mistress to an Age: A Life of Madame de Staël* (New York: Bobbs-Merrill, 1958), p. 23.

The child, born under these traumatizing circumstances, would be an only child; its being only a girl, therefore a permanent and ineradicable reproductive failure (although of course never acknowledged as such), was deeply felt. There were to be two important consequences of this fact: the first of these was that the ambitious Mme Necker, regarding her daughter as a failure of her own as well as an unwelcome rival, adopted a posture of emotional remoteness from her that increased and became more bitter with time. Her relations with her own mother had been poor, which left her emotions with regard to her maternity even more unsettled. The second consequence was that, spurning the express instructions about the education of young girls, in his *Sophie,* of the Rousseau she so abundantly respected, she would write: "I am raising my daughter not like Sophie, but like Emile, and so far her true nature is more amiable and honest than any artifice can be."[10]

Mme Necker, in her piety toward Rousseau, would never even have thought of taking open issue with him explicitly on this score, but we can see in her rebellious decision a determination that her daughter would be raised to be *as good as a man.* The deep ambivalence of her mother's unconscious play of feeling toward Germaine's femininity would generate a parallel ambiguity in the daughter's own ideas on the subject. We have observed that Mme Necker's spontaneous affective life was deeply inhibited. Rent by the conflict between her resentment of her daughter and a rigorous sense of maternal duty, she would not prove to be the best of models for Germaine's passage to a confident sense of womanhood.

Suzanne Necker has been too much maligned as a mother, however. "The charms of childhood did not much appeal to Mme Necker: she had dominated nature too long to have kept much in the way of instinct."[11] Such barbs are moralistic and futile,

---

10. Haussonville, *Le Salon,* II, 26.

11. Albertine Necker de Saussure, "Notice sur le caractère et les écrits de Madame de Staël," in Anne-Louise Germaine Necker de Staël, *Oeuvres complètes,* 17 vols. (Paris: Treuttel et Würtz, 1820–21), I, xxi. This text is referred to hereafter simply by volume and page number of this edition of the *Oeuvres complètes:* lowercase Roman numerals will indicate that this prefatory essay is being cited. In the case of the novels, textual references, following the policy estab-

especially in view of the fact that Mme Necker appears to differ little from the other mothers the Goncourts speak about at that period:

> The souls of children do not flourish at their mothers' knees. Mothers are unaware of those caressing bonds that tie the child a second time to the one who has borne them and which develop friendship in a daughter for the sake of the mother's old age. The maternity of that time knows nothing of the intimate family habits that give children a confident gentleness. It maintains about itself a hard, severe aspect which it jealously guards; it believes its role to be that of maintaining a sort of dignity bordering on indifference. So it is that the mother appears to the little girl a fearsome power; an authority she fears to approach. Timidity seizes her; her attempts to show affection, thwarted, turn inward; her heart is closed off. Fear comes in where respect should have been.[12]

These lines were not written with the Necker family in mind, and yet they seem utterly germane to Suzanne Necker's practices as a parent.

If Mme Necker was under the illusion that her daughter was being raised "like Emile" she was indeed wrong, as one of her cousins was moved to note at the time. She looked anxiously for signs of the dawning of reason in her child and no sooner had the girl spoken her first sentences (she spoke late!) than the mother reported she had started to give her religious and moral instruction. We see that the Pastor of Crassier's rigorous training was a far stronger influence than the veneer of Rousseauesque verbiage would lead us to believe. The sharp and cultivated mind of Suzanne Necker conceived of education only in the loftiest of terms, both intellectual and moral, but her ideas and her actions were often at odds. Germaine profited enormously from her gifted mother's range of reading and acquaintance, even as she suffered from her inconsistency. A peculiar mixture of coolness and tension, of emotional remoteness and iron control, of concern and self-love, went into Suzanne Necker's maternal makeup. They are visible in a letter she wrote to her husband when, at puberty, Germaine's development was particularly stormy:

lished by other Staël scholars, will be to part and letter (*Delphine*) and book and chapter (*Corinne*) to facilitate access to other editions.

12. Goncourt and Goncourt, *La Femme au XVIIIe siècle*, pp. 6–7.

For thirteen of the most beautiful years of my life, in the midst of many other unavoidable cares, I practically never lost sight of her; I cultivated her memory and her mind by reading the best books. . . . I walked with her, read with her, prayed with her. Whenever her health faltered, my anxiety and solicitude doubled the physician's zeal and I have learned since that she would often exaggerate the coughing spells she was prone to so as to luxuriate in the excesses of my tenderness toward her; lastly, I ceaselessly cultivated and embellished all those gifts she had received from nature, believing that this would be of profit to her soul, and my own self-love was bound up in her.[13]

Family relationships were obviously in a highly strained state for this self-defense to have been written, and the ultimate polarization of father and daughter against the mother was already complete. Her case is feelingly presented, but we see in it her obvious failings. Stress was placed upon the education of the mind and the soul, but not of the emotions. Her defensive stance perhaps made Suzanne exaggerate the care she had lavished on her child, but in her insistence she certainly gives the appearance that this care was given grudgingly. Her compulsive child's demands evidently sprang from some real or imagined need denied.

We observe in passing Suzanne's revealing remark that if one becomes too angry with children "who prefer an open and caressing air" one only alienates them, but we are arrested by her ability to write and to publish this: "To descend into the depths of our heart and to perceive that we have ceased to love those who were dear to us is the kind of misfortune that frightens us and obliges us to keep on our guard more than ever."[14]

Since she never lost her love for her husband, it may well be that it is of her daughter that she is speaking. What could have happened of such severity as to place Suzanne so consciously and unwaveringly at odds with her own daughter? The Rousseauesque educational regime was one calculated to confuse an impressionable, emotional child: it gave her the illusion and some of the realities of freedom, of romping in the woods dressed in Grecian fashion, not eternally trussed up in confining clothing, of some botanizing and random talk; but it also gave her a rigorous and im-

---

13. Haussonville, *Le Salon*, II, 55–56.
14. S. Necker, *Mélanges*, II, 53–54.

perative moral code that made her condemn her freedoms as wicked and lazy excesses. The combination was disastrous to the gifted and unstable girl. When Germaine was eleven, Mme Necker, despairing of her bad habits and moodiness, imported from Geneva a highly intelligent and talented companion for her, Mlle Huber, who later recalled her effusive meeting with the Neckers' over-wrought daughter. Clearly in desperate need of affectionate companionship, the child overwhelmed her with greetings, asked if she went to the theater frequently, and promised that they should write to each other every morning. That Germaine was being raised apart from other children and in a milieu that constantly pushed her into interests and a capacity to express herself far beyond those of others of her age was plain to the newcomer.

Mme Necker believed that in exposing her daughter's mind to the *philosophes* she would be giving her an unparalleled educational opportunity. This was undoubtedly true, and without this immersion in the salon there would have been no Mme de Staël.[15] The audacity of such permissiveness paid enormous dividends in the daughter's sense of competence within society, an absolute anomaly for a woman in her time. One can certainly argue with the wisdom of this view from the standpoint of the child's psyche, however. How could she have been unaware of the effects such over-stimulation would have upon the spirited, quick-minded, emotional girl? Perhaps it was an overwhelming pride in her extraordinary daughter that led Suzanne to use her for her own ends, beyond the child's strength. Germaine's constitution promised to break, and the famed Doctor Tronchin advised that she be exiled

---

15. David Glass Larg, *Madame de Staël: La vie dans l'oeuvre (1766–1800)* (Paris: Champion, 1924), p. 5, wrote: "Intellectual superiority aside, it was already bad for this young girl to acquire the habit of being surrounded by a permanent court of gentlemen, even old ones, and also of believing that this is how the world was, that it was quite natural that it should render her homage and not pay attention to anything else but herself." And, "It was not without concern that Mme Necker saw her daughter acquire the habits and demands of a *grande dame* without her having passed first through the beneficent school of need." Larg is irritated by the child's *folie des grandeurs* that became the woman's. Yet, patently, without the absurdity of such *démesure* there would in all likelihood have been no call upon her to become what in fact she did become.

to their country home at Saint-Ouen and given childlike occupations. By that time, however, the damage had been done.

"It is only with difficulty that I can resolve to write to you," wrote Germaine from the country. "If I felt worthy of your lessons, I would fully enjoy doing homage to you with my progress . . . but when I have nothing to offer but shame and the distress of always falling back into the same faults, my pen falls from my hands, I fall prey to discouragement and sadness . . . it makes me blush to speak to you only of my faults; why can't I tell you rather of victories I have won over myself? Ah! Mama, my dear Mama, correct me."[16] Suzanne's incapacity to make her aware of anything about herself but her defects and shortcomings forced Germaine into this obsequious pose, but just beneath this shell we can virtually detect an acceptance by her of the refractory role. She was close to taking pleasure in being her mother's wayward daughter.

In her letters to her and in her reply to Albertine Necker de Saussure, a cousin and friend, who had complimented her on her daughter's distinction of mind—"it is nothing, absolutely nothing next to what I wished to make of her" (I, xxiv)—Mme Necker showed little but an ill-concealed disappointment in her child, an expression of her enraged inability to mold so exuberant a temperament as Germaine's. Yet their characters, in essentials, were not by any means as antithetical as they seem. An emotional and headstrong (but repressed) self-made and self-contained woman, Suzanne preached to her daughter the message of the time: to abandon unreason and to gain self-mastery. This state is not one attained by fiat, however, and her mother's incessant disapproval hardened the headstrong daughter into a posture of revolt. Her mother's moralism would leave permanent traces even upon the apparently liberated Germaine, who long, long into her adult life bore an immense sense of guilt and shame for having so much gall as to be herself.

In accordance with what Freud would term natural inclination, the child turned toward her father in early adolescence. Ger-

---

16. Haussonville, *Le Salon*, II, 38–39.

1. *Germaine Necker at Fourteen*. Carmontelle. Chateau de Coppet. Courtesy of the Count d'Haussonville.

maine had discovered that her mother was too involved with her husband ever to grant her more than a secondary place in her heart.[17] What course could be more obvious, the mother's love once despaired of, than to turn to the sole object of her love and win him to herself? That she succeeded is strongly suggested by Mme Necker's morose remark: "Women of charm are not always incapable of serious thought; often this very grace can be a close link with man or things: so it is that a young person ingratiates herself better into the graces of an old man than a grave and severe woman."[18] The two women engaged in a fierce rivalry of devotion to Necker in which accusations of inadequate fealty were a common weapon. We see the duel emerge in what we perceive in hindsight as the grotesque match with William Pitt the younger proposed for Germaine by her ambitious parents. M. and Mme Necker's marriage had been a love match, but they were richer and more powerful now and willing to take no chances with their valuable Germaine, even though arranged marriages were at that time coming into disrepute. Germaine, they felt, must marry a Protestant and someone who would enhance Necker's position in France. In this light Pitt appeared to them a great catch; but not so to Germaine. She had no wish to leave Paris and its society, which to her were the sun and the moon of her world. She feared the relative retirement that she knew English society forced upon women. She disliked Pitt. The Neckers were forced to see their plan ended. Surely no couple would have been more ill matched than the arch-conservative enemy of the Revolution and the liberal Mlle Necker with her radical personality. But a year later, when Mme Necker was very ill, she preyed still on the subject, writing her daughter:

I would have wished you to marry Mr. Pitt. I would have liked to place you in the bosom of a husband of great character; I also wanted a son-in-law

---

17. An index of Mme Necker's hysterical possessiveness and of the endurance of this family posture can be found in this quotation by Haussonville from her last letter; she refers to her husband as one "whom I would like to nourish with my blood, who has so captivated my power of loving here on earth that *no one else can come near my heart."* *Le Salon,* I, 299. Italics mine.

18. S. Necker, *Mélanges,* III, 287.

to whom I could confide the care of your poor father, and who would understand the value of this charge. You have not wished to give him that satisfaction. Very well, all is forgiven if you give back to your father and to yourself all that I expected from that union. Multiply yourself to produce the distractions that England, the standing of a son-in-law, and his consequent occupations would have given to your father. Wherever he may go, follow him; live in his house. . . . Give yourself over to your good nature; you will only make mistakes if you stray from it. . . . Oh my child! Your character is not formed; your head frequently leads you astray; take religion as your guide. . . . On earth I lived only for your father, for you were but a part of him for me. Well then, now you must take my place by his side. You will become a wife and a mother . . . teach your husband and children that upon this earth your father must be the center of everything for them.[19]

Mme de Staël's subsequent life is a startling enactment of all these injunctions. Not merely did she give her family and all those around her to understand that her father was the first among men, not only did she live in his house at Coppet, though sometimes unwillingly. What appears more striking is that she did what her mother intended cruelly to suggest she could never do: she multiplied herself, employed herself, spent herself in producing for her father more distractions and achieving by her own efforts more to give him pride in her than any mere son-in-law could ever have done. This stratagem of Mme Necker's was a remarkably effective means of combating the rivalry between them for Necker's affections by embracing it and forcing Germaine's love to take the form of a maternally imposed duty. Whenever she departed from a strict adherence to this filial piety, the daughter would feel uneasy, for instance when, ever in need of distraction, she left her father at Coppet while she went to Paris or on some other voyage. Her mother's role as her conscience is confirmed by Germaine's reply to a tactless remark once made to her in company: "Your father seems to care for you more than your mother," to which she replied, "My father thinks more in terms of my present happiness and my mother of my future happiness."[20]

Although Jacques Necker was a gayer and more loving parent to Germaine than her mother, he was by no means uncritical of

19. Haussonville, *Le Salon*, II, 56–57.
20. Haussonville, *Le Salon*, II, 48.

her. "I owe to my father," she declared, "the frankness of my character and my naturalness. He unmasked all affectation and it was at his side that I acquired the habit of believing that people saw right into my heart."[21] Certainly her mother also constantly called Germaine sternly back to naturalness and honesty, but there was a flattering reassurance in her father's attitude toward her that made her heed his admonitions even where her mother's tense preachments had failed.

If Necker tended to cajole and spoil his daughter, on the whole, there is one vital respect in which he refrained from doing so: he did not approve of her writing and obviously mocked, chided, and even moralized at length about it. He would call her "Master Holy-Desk"[22] when he caught her scribbling, as she did from early adolescence, her little plays, poems, and stories. He did not actually kill off this need of hers, but so loved a parent could not be altogether without influence. "My father is right," wrote the nineteen-year-old in her diary. "How little are women cut out to follow the same career as a man! To struggle against them, inciting in them a jealousy so different from that which love inspires! A woman ought not to have anything of her own and should find all her pleasures in those she loves."[23] Here is the first overt statement of the very problem that was to become central to her creative life and the core of her novels.

Monsieur Necker in fact disapproved of all women pursuing independent forms of self-expression. That battle had already been fought in the case of his wife, who naturally enough in that time and place, being intelligent and learned, had had some literary pretensions of an altogether appropriate order: she had planned, and had actually begun, some sketches on a work dealing with the cleric and educator Fénelon. When Necker discouraged her from proceeding with it, this became the source of some friction between them. Though she pretended, in the following letter, to be willing to abandon everything for her husband, clearly she was too stung to be willing to do so without concrete return:

---

21. Haussonville, Le Salon, II, 48.
22. "Monsieur de Sainte-Ecritoire."
23. Haussonville, Le Salon, II, 48.

It seems to me, my dear, that I have never loved you as I do now. . . . I no longer feel that I exist except through you. . . . After all this, do you dare reproach me for my love of letters? It is nothing but the remains of a habit that I feel it valuable to maintain because of my liveliness of spirit and because of the void I fall into when you are away. But this reproach is becoming too frequent . . . and so I want to make my conditions with you; from the moment that you renounce the East India Company forever, I promise you, if you should demand this, that I will give up Fénelon and even the idea of taking up the pen ever again on any other subject, and I hope with all my soul that the sacrifice I ask of you does not cost me any more than the one I make to you. . . . As for myself, I feel that I have but one soul and it is yours. I must love you or die.[24]

Necker's monstrous self-centeredness would not brook any rival concern on his wife's part, even that of so modest a project as the Fénelon study: it was enough that her interest was real and that it was directed outside the domestic circle for it to be condemnable. The wife, although she couches her "bargain" in the obsequious language of domestic courtesy, is clearly being made to act against her inclinations. She turns this disregard for her wishes into a willed self-sacrifice, thus preserving her self-respect and giving her a martyred position from which to barter with her husband. That very traditional ideal she asserts here of an impassioned feminine selflessness so perfect that it becomes self-sacrifice was passed on intact to Germaine, whose unrealized ideal it was to remain.

When Mme Necker finally did publish, long afterward, her *Mélanges*, her husband thought fit to have her include in it a highly laudatory verbal portrait of himself that she had written, so that her book remained under his aegis. He could not really allow her to do something altogether outside his orbit. Germaine, too, was to write a *portrait* of Necker, even in this tourney of praises competing with her mother for his favor: mother and daughter were each reduced by domestic necessity to hiding their literary efforts behind a flattering paean to the household god. In so doing, not only did they pander to him, but what is far more grave and, in Germaine's case consequential, they pandered to their own ideas of themselves.

---

24. Haussonville, *Le Salon*, II, 9–10. The East India Co.—Necker's farsighted but costly and engrossing speculations in the New World were *his* pet project.

"This taste for writing was not encouraged by M. Necker and he could only forgive it when a decided superiority manifested itself, for he did not naturally like women authors," wrote his niece. This distaste meant that the person Germaine loved most in the world found her original literary penchant "unfeminine." Absurdly enough, it was this attitude of his, plus the rush of events, that probably made her turn from literature, her first love, to politics—an area generally deemed even less "feminine" and in which the public's venom against notorious women was likely to be unbridled. But politics was her father's world and she could enter it by playing a more socially acceptable role as mistress of a salon.

Necker, for all his affection, was able to sustain Germaine only in her personal trials, not in her aspirations to achievement and power. These had to be fed, once the flattering vanity of her childhood precocity was past, entirely from within. It is her cousin who again gives us an enlightening bit of information:

As Monsieur Necker had forbidden his wife to write, through fear of the idea of interrupting her when entering her room, Mlle Necker, who did not wish to draw down upon herself such a prohibition, had accustomed herself to writing, as it were, on the fly; so that always seeing her standing, or leaning on a corner of the mantelpiece, her father could not have dreamed that he was making her leave off from any serious work. She always so much respected this little weakness of Monsieur Necker's that it was only after his having long been gone that she had in her room even the minimum of writing arrangements. Finally, when *Corinne* had made a great splash in foreign countries, she said to me: I would really like to have a big desk; it seems to me I have the right to one now." (I, cccxviii–ix)

It seems scarcely to be believed that this woman could have written what she did—pamphlets, tracts, treatises, novels—often under such covert circumstances, while scarcely according even to herself the dignity of being a "serious" writer.[25] The methods of composition thus acquired could not have been very fully thought through. In fact, we know that Mme de Staël, even after Necker's death, generally wrote quickly and at a small remove

---

25. Fanny Burney, Mme de Staël's English contemporary, suffered the parallel indignity of writing only *sub rosa*, by night, to keep *her* father from knowing her to be that shameful thing—a female writer. Miss Burney probably never dreamed that the self-assured and high-living Germaine, whom she met in 1794, suffered personal agonies just like her own.

from her circle, to whom she read her finished papers, and that she would not start to work until she held a rather fully conceived plan in her mind. That these working arrangements, with their resultant negligences or airiness of style, were dictated by her inner conflicts over her authorship is not an idea easily dismissed, as we understand her need not to incur her father's disapproval, a disapproval which a part of her espoused. The battle to accept in herself what her father reproved was fought within her mind and spirit and erupts in the fiction.

When Mme Necker died in 1794, Germaine's rivalry was over. Verbally, the bond between father and daugher was an openly incestuous one. After his death in 1804, it seemed that only in proclaiming her love for him could she be solaced. "I was to lose," she wrote, "my protector, my father, my brother, my friend, he whom I would have chosen to be the only love of my life if fate had not cast me in a generation other than his" (xvii, 105). The frustration she felt in the excess of her love sometimes bursts out in such exclamations as this: "It is sometimes a cruel thing to love a man older than yourself so deeply; not to be able to do anything about the invincible necessity that would someday separate you: to break your soul against this barrier; to feel that he would like to live with you, like to love you, and to be able to draw from his breast nothing but this life that troubles you, this life that devours you so as [sic] to share at least some of it with him" (xvii, 118–19). As Benjamin Constant observed, words seemed to fail her when she wanted to express what she felt for him. We certainly sense her bafflement; it is even more pronounced in those passages in which she seems close to blasphemy: "Oh my God! Forgive your weak creatures if their hearts which have loved so much can imagine in heaven only the smile of a father who will receive them into your heavenly courts" (xvii, 74).

She conveys something more of the quality of her feelings when she writes, "The feebleness of age along with his strength of soul and wisdom of spirit . . . his deep feelings constantly coupled with melancholy ideas imparted to my father I know not what halo of the future, a sort of premonitory cloud which often caused in me a feeling of love, an impression like that a young man might inspire in me if he were the victim of a threatening consumption . . ." (xvii, 103). This "halo of the future" made him younger to her than her contemporaries.

In this love impossible of fulfillment, we find the prototype of Mme de Staël's very idea of the lover. Her partners in life would be too weak (Narbonne, Ribbing, Constant), too young (Souza, Barante, O'Donnell), too young and ill (Rocca) to offer full partnership in love. She would find some satisfaction in them because of her capacity for a ministering, if not maternal, kind of love. No other love bond could really be compared to her towering passion for her father: all were doomed to fail, by virtue of the biased nature of the implicit comparisons she would always make. It was her mother, she noted ruefully, who had as her mate *"l'être unique."* A partial explanation of her preference for young men can be understood in this light: the fatality of the generations, exemplified in the decay and death of her beloved father, had a special keenness of meaning for her. She would somehow hope to call up in the hearts of young men some of that loving reverence she had always felt for him.

Once, as Germaine was dancing with her fiancé, Staël, Necker cut in on them, saying he would show the younger man how to dance with a woman one was in love with. Germaine was surprisingly clear-sighted about this ambivalence of theirs, even in this diary entry at age nineteen:

Why is it that I sometimes discover faults in his character which are harmful to the gentle intimacy of our lives? Is it because he wants me to love him like a lover while he speaks to me like a father; because I want him to be jealous of me like a lover while I act like a daughter? Is it the struggle between my passion for him and the inclinations natural to my age, which he wants me to sacrifice completely, that makes me unhappy? . . . we do not love each other to the point of excess, and yet we come so close to it that I cannot bear the idea of anything reminding me we have not reached it yet. Of all the men in the world it is he I would have wished for a lover.[26]

In playing at being both father and lover, in accustoming her to a perfect and unfailing affection, Necker gave Germaine an insatiable

---

26. Herold, *Mistress*, pp. 45–46.

need to possess it. Engaged in the vain search for a perfect love, even during her father's lifetime, she was dogged by the shadow of a happiness known, but known to be impossible. Necker, sharing her sorrow, had once said to her, "Why was I not born your brother? I would protect you all your life" (XVII, 118).

Mme de Staël, out of the fullness of her affection, strove throughout her lifetime to subordinate herself and her own reputation to her father. In the same way as after his death she would spend much time and energy in writing the panegyric *Private Life of Monsieur Necker* (*Vie privée de Monsieur Necker*) and the ambitious *Considerations upon the Principal Events of the French Revolution* (*Considérations sur les principaux événements de la Révolution française*), which were dedicated to reestablishing his tarnished political reputation, so during his years of life she tried to efface herself to give him more importance. A Genevan visitor who dined at Coppet provides us with a glimpse of Mme de Staël's manner in speaking of their lively dinner-table discussions together. "Mme de Staël had great superiority of aptness, ease, and eloquence over her father in these literary or philosophical debates. But, as she was about to make her final thrust, a filial shyness took hold of her and as if frightened by the success she was about to obtain, she let herself appear to lose track of the argument and, with an inimitable grace, left to her opponent the glory of victory. But this opponent was her father, and he was the *only one* to whom she ever accorded such an advantage."[27]

Whether he was the only one or not, he was the crucial one. To Germaine her father was man writ large, a demigod that woman, no matter how superior, needed to propitiate. She would ever be profoundly loving to him. Had he not loved and believed in her when her skeptical mother had refused to take her expressions of feeling as real? She would love him to the full for this goodness, and so would accept being, even want to be, outshone by him in public for his sake. But her love for her father was to make her wretched, too, for in order to please him she tried to rein in her aspirations and feelings, and these would erupt, in his life-

---

27. Frédéric de Chateauvieux, as quoted by Kohler, *Madame de Staël et la Suisse*, p. 298.

time, in her juvenilia, in *Delphine*, and, most eloquently only after his death, in *Corinne*.

The long search for a "proper" match that had gone on since Germaine was barely nubile was ended on January 14, 1786, when she was married in the chapel of the Swedish Embassy in Paris to Eric-Magnus, Baron de Staël-Holstein, the Ambassador. It was a marriage of expediency. To be sure the Baron de Staël was handsome, not unintelligent, and fairly liberal in his views; he was also a Protestant, a nobleman, and the holder of an assured and important diplomatic post. As a prize certainly he was less brilliant than Pitt, but in marrying their daughter to him the Neckers managed both to strengthen their political position and to allow their daughter to remain in Paris, as she insisted upon doing, addicted as she already was to the life of the city and to her part in it. The unpromising aspects of the marriage were Staël's well-known rakish habits and, more gravely, the incompatibility of character of the couple. In temperament and intelligence they were quite ill attuned: she was tempestuous and he phlegmatic. At the outset, Staël, who was her senior by seventeen years, showed little inclination to alter his life for Germaine's sake, while she undertook her duties as wife and ambassadress with zeal. Later on in their marriage, when her affections were decidedly engaged outside the home, Staël seems to have become genuinely fond of Germaine, but by then her inclination to return his esteem had evaporated.

She herself, being a woman, could not occupy any official position except that of wife of the Swedish Ambassador; but this did not prevent her behaving spontaneously as a political figure in her own right, in a way that no 20th century woman, however emancipated (and no man, for that matter), could hope to emulate. That she was a person of great ability and drive goes without saying; but her talents were reinforced by a social confidence so complete that she was not even aware of it....[28]

Her marriage had the exhilarating effect of liberating her from the incessant criticism of her parents. Only the estate of matron could give a woman any sort of freedom in the eighteenth century.

---

28. John Weightman, "Madame de Staël," *Encounter*, XLI, no. 4 (Oct. 1973), 48.

The concerns of a household, a log of the Parisian political scene she kept for the king of Sweden, a group of early works of fiction, a first pregnancy that ended in June, 1787, in the birth of a daughter Gustavine (named for the king), and the care of the ailing infant who did not long survive filled the early years of Mme de Staël's marriage.

In addition, she often entertained in place of her ailing mother, and the salon of Mme Necker was rapidly replaced by the salon of Mme de Staël. Already there was something about her that set her apart from the other women of charm and eloquence who held their court in Paris. How can we explain her unwonted universality of interests, her intense alertness? One commentator tried: "Foreigner and Calvinist, she does not submit with the same degree of rigor to the constraints the French Catholics place upon women. What is more, from her earliest years, her mother consecrated her to a great destiny."[29]

This famous portrait of the Germaine of the year of her marriage, by the suave, aging Guibert, gives us a vivid sense of the young woman's vitality, and of her impact upon her world:

Zulmé is but twenty, and she is the most celebrated of the priestesses of Apollo; she is the favorite of the god. . . . Out from among that group of sacred maidens, one suddenly emerges: my heart will never forget her. Her large black eyes shone with genius; her ebony hair fell about her shoulders in waving curls; her features were pronounced rather than delicate; one sensed in them something above the destiny of her sex. Thus would one be compelled to depict the Muse of Poetry or Clio or Melpomene. "Here she is, here she is!" everyone exclaimed when she appeared, and no one dared breathe. I listen to her, I look at her with delight; I discover in her features charms that are above beauty's. What life and variety play upon her face! What shadings in the tone of her voice! What perfect accord between thought and expression! She speaks, and if her words fail to reach me her inflections, her gestures, her look suffice for me to understand her. Should she be silent for a moment, her last words still resound in my heart, and I find in her eyes what she has not yet said. Should she cease to speak altogether, then the temple resounds with applause; her head falls modestly, her long lashes cover her fiery eyes and the sun remains veiled from our view. (I, xxxiv ff.)

A stunning performer in society, both amazing and amusing, causing ripples of excitement and applause in her audience, Ger-

---

29. Larnac, *Histoire de la littérature féminine*, p. 175.

maine could not help falling under the influence of such incense. This portrait would have an effect upon her far beyond her twentieth year: we will see it in her stories of *Mirza* and *Zulma*, we will find the priestess of Apollo in *Corinne*, and we will meet with the idea of a destiny "above that of her sex" in her every act and work.

A final episode must crown this summary of major influences on the unfolding of Mme de Staël's mind and spirit. Necker had again become Finance Minister in August, 1788, and, at his return, had found scarcely 500 thousand pounds left in the treasury. All the resources of his financial skills were employed to fill this appalling gap, and funds were raised to provide against the emergency. However, in political matters, ever enslaved to his wish to conciliate and be above all factions, he took refuge in a compromising inertia. The French king had already decided before Necker's return that the Estates General were to be convened,[30] and in May, 1789, they did in fact meet, becoming in June, after some struggle, the National Assembly. On July 11, having casually supped at home, Necker and his wife, under the pretext that he had a headache, went out "for a walk." Their little outing took them far afield: they ended up in Brussels. The Finance Minister had been exiled by the king in punishment for his support, even wavering as it was, for the principles of allowing a doubling of their votes to the Third Estate and of turning the three estates into a single assembly. M. and Mme de Staël followed her parents to Brussels. La Fayette had predicted to Necker that if he were exiled thirty thousand Parisians would bring him back to Versailles. The actual occurrence was far more dramatic. On July 12 the news of Necker's exile stirred an insurrection in Paris; on July 13 the National Assembly declared that he bore with him its esteem and regrets; on July 14 the Bastille was taken by the populace; and on July 15 Necker's return was decreed by a badly frightened king and court.

The Necker party was near Basel on July 20 when news came to them of the minister's recall. As they returned, all along their path crowds of admirers thronged around their carriage, women knelt, men and children shouted and waved. All greeted him as a

---

30. Mme de Staël leaves a vivid memoir of their opening in the *Considérations sur les principaux événemens de la révolution française.*

savior. Along their route, Germaine and her father were showered with "palms, crowns, music. Men harnessed themselves to their carriage, amidst the cries of joy of the whole throng. M. Necker and his daughter, although moved to the point of tears and somewhat embarrassed by this excess of honor, entered into the spirit of it."[31] Two hundred thousand Frenchmen acclaimed them as they came into Paris on July 30. Speaking of this glorious return, the daughter would write twenty-five years later, "Alas! It was I more than any other who took pleasure in it for him; it was I who was inebriated [by the affection of the people]; it is I who ought to feel grateful for those days, whatever the present bitterness of my life. . . ." This day was the high point of Mme de Staël's whole existence, what she termed "the last prosperous day of my life," the day after which all the others could hold no comparable joyous intensity.

The extremity of her exaltation befitted an age that celebrated *sensibilité* as the greatest good.

There is but a very small number of women who have had the joy of hearing a whole people repeat the name of the object of their affections. . . . All those glances which seem for one moment to be animated by the same feelings as your own, those numberless voices resounding in your heart, that name that rises into the air and seems to come back from heaven after passing through the acclaim of the earth . . . all the mysteries of nature and society adding their sum to the greatest of all mysteries; that of love— a love perhaps filial, perhaps maternal—but in any case, love; and our soul succumbs to emotions too powerful for it to endure. (xvii, 59–60)

Unable to bear such a degree of excitement, she fainted. "When I came to, I felt as if I had reached the boundaries of the possibility for happiness. I did not imagine, however, that this moment of happiness was to be the last of my life. . . (xvii, 59–60).

The delusion, for it can only have been a delusion, that no happiness ever touched her again persisted stubbornly. Her rhapsody is an expression of that taste for the absolute in happiness which this fantastic episode was to leave with her. It was only natural that she should equate her happiness and her father's success with a spirit of doom, for that brief glory was all too soon

---

31. Arthur Auguste Beugnot, *Mémoires du comte Beugnot, ancien ministre (1783–1815)*, ed. Albert Beugnot (Paris: Dentu, 1889), p. 134.

followed by his downfall and by the vicissitudes of her own political fortunes.

The feeling of happiness that she found, in 1789, through a universal adulation of the object of her love was to undergo a curious transposition. Although she unquestionably rejoiced on that day in her father's triumph, the ecstasy she experienced vicariously through him was such that she came to covet it urgently, in her own right.

CHAPTER 2

Writing Out

> What tedium. And I call that playing. I wonder if I am
> talking yet again about myself. Shall I be incapable to
> the end, of lying on any other subject?
>
> SAMUEL BECKETT

There are many reasons why Germaine took to writing apart from the sheer emulation the literary milieu evoked in the gifted girl. A more personal cause for that literary penchant so early shown was solitude: she was in serious want of companionship. If "to write is to split oneself in two," it was a strategy she employed to feel less alone. But the most signal aspect of her turn to writing lay in its being somehow an attempt to cope with that waywardness on which her mother had harped so much. At first, in adolescence, she wrote to chastise herself, to impress her parents and herself with her moral seriousness. The resulting threads of self-castigation crossed with self-justification are woven into most of what she was to write thereafter.

Notwithstanding their underlying, their unvarying character of profound apologia, her works would never be products of intense deliberation, but rather reflections of the state of her spirit at the time of their writing, pieces of herself. Seized by an inability to be distracted by the world outside herself, she would say, "I don't understand what I'm reading and so I must write" (I, ccxi). Writing was an act that appeased. Once written, a work became quite meaningless to her, and she would almost never reread it. When once someone quoted to her some lines of her own she was heard to remark: "Truly, did I write that? I'm delighted. It's marvelously put."

Characteristically, despite her recurrent melancholia and her filial piety, Mme de Staël was always driven onward in time. Duclos had written that "sensitive souls have more existence than the others." Mme de Staël's restless and impressionable nature insured that present and future time would never fail to attract her more than the past. She was concerned with the past only for what it could contribute to the future; she spoke of the future only in poetic terms and lived only in the present, imperatively. Her works, once a part of her own history, were dead for her. She had not a shred of idolatry concerning them, though she was by no means devoid of authorial vanity. They were but a portion of her unfolding life.

A kindred sense of wishing to capture her impressions *sur le vif*, live, as well as an impatience to be off to less onerous pleasures, is reflected in her habits of composition. She tells us that "going back over my thoughts, coldly changing the expression of a feeling is so painful a task for me that its outcome must inevitably reveal the effort it cost" (XVII, 133). In her first works of fiction she was least willing to subject herself to any prolonged and arduous effort: later she was to work much longer and harder, but essentially in this same careless style.

There is much coquetry in her attitude toward composition, but it is a coquetry dictated by apprehension, the same anxiety that made many of her sister authors claim, as we have noted, that their works were simply casual diversions, mere playthings no one could possibly feel called upon to attack.

The ebullient, ambitious young woman who set out to write fiction in 1786 had more complex creative problems than she knew, fortunately. Her early works were apparently all written in that state of sublime artistic unself-consciousness that lasted as long as she did, but that was to regress in time. Not, let it be understood, that there was ever any lack of a consciousness of self, but that the relation of self to others, to novelistic convention, and to the conventions of society remained confused. Mme de Staël, some have claimed, could see no barriers to her self; from the first she subsumed the world and its inhabitants under her own ego in her fiction.[1] This problem of the relationship of self to others, it seems to me, is more complex and less absurd than such a formulation

---

1. This is essentially the position of David Glass Larg in his two works, *Madame de Staël: La Vie dans l'oeuvre (1766–1800)* (Paris: Champion, 1924) and *Madame de Staël: La Seconde Vie (1800–1807)* (Paris: Champion, 1928).

implies. The question, as it always presented itself to her, was: what frontier of the self is it allowable to expose in fiction? How much authentic strength or vulnerability may the heroine—Germaine's pioneering alter ego in the world—display, and in what spirit? The fictional framework itself is interwoven with these revelations and concealments. What she would have wanted to confront directly in fiction was the impact of a quirky, outlandish, gifted, irrepressibly active young woman like herself on the world, but in these early works we see her attempting to avoid this subject in many ways as she tries to write like a normal lady writer and accept the prescribed norms of fiction. However, we also see her rebellious incapacity to do so cropping up and unbalancing these "harmless little fictions." It is primarily in the depiction of the heroines, as we might expect, that her attempt to be a "good girl" novelist fails most blatantly.

These tales reflect Germaine's own strategies of mediation with respect to her femininity. To her conscious mind, society could not be at fault if she felt peculiar: she embraced its idea of woman and of love with an unquestioning, even an abundant enthusiasm. But in her stories she displayed her sense of innocence at her gaucherie, her anguish over her own incapacity to fulfill the ideal, and even her frustrated will to power, her sheer need to employ her torrential energies.

The early works are not to be spoken of in strict chronology with any particular profit, in part because their chronology is not absolutely established. Four of them may be divided into two very distinct categories, the worldly and the individualistic; the other two, verse plays, stand out against the tales as special cases in form, but they too may be assimilated into these categories.

The first of these special cases is *Sophie, ou les sentiments secrets*, a play in verse which has been dated 1786. Since she derived her notions of theater from the rather pompously rhetorical neoclassical Voltairean drama, it was natural enough for the young author to attempt alexandrine verse; we see also that from the very first her pretension to becoming a dramatic poet was illustrative of her will to step out beyond the confines of the "feminine" novel form and to aspire to the "masculine" empyrean of the tragic poets.

Verse was for her an unfortunate choice, though no doubt it provided her with useful literary practice: the musical Mme de Staël,
who could sing so truly, had a leaden idea of poetry. It is not that
her lines failed to scan, for instance:

> L'espoir dans le printemps couronne l'avenir;
> Mais quand nos jeunes ans commencent à nous fuir,
> Cessant de désirer les jours qu'on doit attendre,
> Vers l'éternelle nuit le temps semble descendre;
> Plus de bonheur pour nous.
>
> (XVII, 217)[2]

it is rather that the verse is labored and pedestrian, the syntax
visibly twisted for rhyme and rhythm's sake and not heightened by
imagery of any distinction.

Sophie is a curious mélange of theatrical and novelistic conventions. Its unique quality is its virtually naked autobiographical
plot, a plot more akin to the novel in 1786 than to the stage. In it
the young orphan, Sophie, falls in love with her guardian, the distinguished Sainval, a man already married and the father of a
family. Though Sainval returns Sophie's passionate attachment,
he virtuously hides his feelings, but his secret is accidentally discovered by both Sophie and by the countess, his wife. There are
then lengthy explanations, during which Sainval and his wife
sing the praises of marriage, though perhaps only to keep up their
spirits, after which Sophie nobly departs. Sophie is then courted by
Milord Henri Bedford. She proudly spurns his suit even though, a
pathetically solitary figure, she has no place to go after leaving
the Sainval home. Sainval, his wife, and Sophie are clear depic-
tions of Necker, his wife, and his daughter. If this were not sufficiently plain in the scheme of the play, the adulation Sophie and
the countess bestow upon Sainval is so unmistakably Neckerian
as to provide full certification.

---

2. Roughly:

> In springtime hopes adorn the future's way;
> But when young years begin to fleet away,
> Deprived of ardor for the day's advent,
> Time makes to night eternal its descent:
> No more of joy for us.

A fictional transformation of the reality of Germaine's love for her father, *Sophie* is alone among Mme de Staël's fictions to have no life separate from autobiography, and it is the least successful of all her artistic efforts. Nonetheless, she has already achieved something that arrests our attention. Writing, in the tradition of *La Princesse de Clèves*, a tale of renunciation of love, she combines this with elements reworked from *La Nouvelle Héloïse*, but now making a heroine rather than a hero the marital interloper. Even within the tight conventions that governed her choice of a plot, Mme de Staël could not prevent her Sophie from becoming the instigator of the romantic action. "Now, without anyone's explaining very clearly why, the most important character of the three is Sophie. No one dreams of sending her off to play with her toys. On the contrary, the older characters show her an extraordinary deference: even their remonstrances are marked by the utmost respect."[3] Her critic, Larg, underlines the obvious self-aggrandizement. This self-absorption, scarcely so exceptional or unforgivable in a twenty-year-old writer, is also profitable. In *Sophie* she analyzes her own nature, her childhood, her unreasonable love for her father, and her rivalry with her mother and tries to settle these difficult scores in the compass of her own young spirit. At the same time she strives to distill from this incestuous brew an ideal figure with which to identify herself: that of a young woman possessed of a spontaneous, childlike grace, but marked with melancholia. Her lover, Sainval, says of her:

> Her solitary childhood days so sad,
> Impressing her whole person as they had,
> Deprived her of all hopes of finding joy.
> Too soon, perhaps, her heart found its employ.
> For that she'll suffer, though her charms but grow;
> For who can match the graces she can show?
> She keeps about her in the spring of life
> A candor seldom seen in childhood's strife;
> And in the impulse of so pure a soul
> We learn to see, to know how nature's whole.
>
> (XVII, 207)

3. Larg, *La Vie dans l'oeuvre*, p. 34.

This fantasized Sophie is, in her tragic awareness, more arresting to us than are the actions of the "real" character in the play. Striving to raise her own illicit passion in imagination to a nearly Phèdresque pitch, Sophie cries out, accusing her lover:

> Yes, cruel one, you know my need of you!
> To leave you now my heart must take its cue.
> I am importunate, and cannot die:
> Oh! Why should you have tied me so to life?
> Had poor Sophie made your existence strife?
> You saved her but to cause her greater pain,
> To crush her heart, you made it beat again.
>
> (XVII, 226)

Mme de Staël thus tries to raise her struggle out of the realm of the unutterable, to write its nightmare quality out of her existence, but in so doing she transmutes her unholy passion into a permanent malediction. "Je vous suis importune, et je ne puis mourir—I am importunate and cannot die" could have been Mme de Staël's motto; it was to be her theme in all her love affairs to come and in her novels and stories. Sophie shows us how she herself decreed, from within, this amorous destiny. The same accents of despair and anger that we find later on are present, only slightly more conventionalized, from the start.

The conventional qualities of the tales of *Pauline* (1785) and *Adélaïde et Théodore* (1786) seem to us even more pronounced, for they are less personal works than *Sophie*. Nonetheless, this verse play belongs with them to that portion of Mme de Staël's fiction in which she stresses the effect of opinion upon the heroine rather than that of the heroine upon opinion. In all of these, the social scene is more central to the work than the woman herself, who appears as its pawn.

With the tale of *Pauline* we enter the arena of amorous vulnerability. The locale of this prose fiction is the tropics, an obvious and stylish choice. The heroine, like all Mme de Staël's heroines—and like herself (she did not flinch before this identification!)—has been *badly brought up*. "Pauline had an amiable and sensitive nature . . . but the best nature will give way before the first impressions of society, if principles are not there to protect it" (II, 268). At the age of thirteen she is married, of course by fiat, to a Monsieur de Valville, who is more protector than mate. A marriage of this sort had evident precedents in social convention and in literature, but it had a more personal meaning for Mme de Staël, for its acceptability enabled her to further explore her feelings for her father. After having spoiled his charge by his paternal affections, Monsieur de Valville fails his "wife" (in name only) by running off. The stock villain of *Pauline,* Meltin, seeing that he cannot have her for himself (she finds him utterly repugnant) nevertheless finds a way to ruin her by encouraging her amours with a shallow but seemly youth named Théodore, who seduces her and then goes off to France. Pauline takes his loss sorrowfully, though we discern some of Mme de Staël's budding perception as she remarks: "Perhaps one might have noticed that she exaggerated her feelings so as to lessen her error in her own eyes . . ." (II, 272). In any case, Mme de Staël shows clearly her personal vision even in this poorly wrought tale, in that it is at least as much Pauline's strange and displaced strength of character as Meltin's diabolical urging that drives Théodore off: she is so passionately involved that she swears she will die if he leaves her.

Meltin is like Lovelace. "No one had less respect for women than he. . . . However he passed for an honest man because he was perfidious and cruel only to women" (II, 275). He finally forces the abandoned girl to give in to him, whereupon she learns that Théodore and her absent husband have both died, the latter serving at least some function by making her rich. Théodore, remorseful, had confessed his transgressions to a certain Mme de Verseuil, who now takes it upon herself to save Pauline. "Still so young and having so little complicity in your soul with those errors which others have led you into, how can you believe they might not be amended?" (II, 282–83). The "essentially" pure and innocent girl goes to France with Mme de Verseuil and lives a new childhood, is re-educated (or educated), and interests herself only in study and the nourishment of the spirit. Though she has rigorously steeled herself to be indifferent to romance, during one of her brief forays into society, to care for a sick aunt, she arouses the interest of a young count, Edouard de Cerney. The ravishingly lovely Pauline, foreshadowing those irresistibles Delphine and Corinne, is saved from a crush of admirers by Edouard, a singular young man whose chief characteristic is "a great austerity of principles. He had been raised by a scrupulously virtuous father." Here is our first glimpses of the rigid young hero, a prototype of the Léonce and Oswald of the novels, and here too we meet a second father, seemingly split off from the indulgent one, whose principles destroy the life of the child.

Mme de Verseuil's role is, like that of Mlle d'Albémar in *Delphine* or of Oenone in *Phèdre,* to goad the lovers to their ruin. Even knowing Edouard's repugnance to marriage with any girl who has had an "impure past," she encourages them to marry. They are happy until that time when, after the birth of their son, Edouard meets Meltin, who reveals Pauline's past to her husband. Enraged, Edouard kills Meltin in a duel and returns to his wife, still loving her but unable to forget the past. Tormented by her plight, Pauline falls into a fever and dies, leaving Edouard to raise their child.

In this apparently altogether conventional tale, Mme de Staël begins to set forth her special themes. The first and most important of these is the perfidy of man toward helpless woman. Neither new nor presented here with any great novelty, it is a subject that she, like Mme Riccoboni, will never exhaust. An exemplary goodness and openness to experience on the part of woman clashes with the relative wickedness, weakness, or rigidity of all the men in her life. Another favorite preoccupation we find here is the impossibility of marriage without perfect mutual faith and candor, the rarity of which makes a good marriage for any of her characters an unusual outcome indeed. In Pauline and Edouard we find the dichotomy Germaine will adhere to in all of her fiction: the gentle, bright heroine, the spirit of compromise and mobility, and the rigid, self-disciplined, and demanding hero, who incarnates unbending principle.

Though the story is told in a pedestrian manner, illumined by some flashes of insight, the narration is brisk. These early stories, in their lack of pretension, are better written in the sense that they are simply easier to read than the tortured long novels. Characterization is already the author's domain of greatest competence; description, the least. Not marked by that easily demonstrable relevance to her own life we find in her other tales, this particular one lacks inner conviction; it is too derivative and empty and owes too much to the plight of Clarissa, the purity of Julie, and the plottings of Lovelace and Valmont. The genuine dilemma we sense being posed is that of the intelligent but ill-guided, emotionally vulnerable young woman who is made to pay for her passing weakness through the perfidy or the unbendingness of men she should have been able to trust. *Pauline* sets the problematic of Mme de Staël's attempt to find authenticity and a voice of her own in a social framework. Ill educated, trapped in social conventions, this protagonist is ill equipped to obey the decrees of the severe and unjust ethic of the double standard unfalteringly. Pauline is in no way a superior heroine, in terms of either character or gifts. She is a human cipher; her only fault lies in her falling victim to a sensibility which, we are bright enough to recognize, is but a virtue lightly disguised.

The tale of *Adélaïde et Théodore* is even more steeped in the affairs of society than was Pauline's. For this reason we may think of it as an embryonic *roman de moeurs* and a first intimation of *Delphine*. Like the later work, it gives us some small sense of the author's worldly self—epigrammatic, witty, and penetrating. For it she created a set of portraits done with a fine flourish, but her characters, cleverly drawn as they are in their fixed poses, have great difficulty in moving and living.

The plot is complicated and mechanical and so sentimentally contrived that it is outside the realm of belief: it is genuine fantasy spun out of the novelistic conventions. The heroine Adélaïde has been raised by a certain Mme d'Orfeuil who has purposely educated her on what would be Emma Bovary's convent fare: novels and God. "Adélaïde loved her deeply; together they read novels, together they prayed to God, they were exalted and touched by the same things and Adélaïde's young soul was in constant turmoil" (II, 229). The young Germaine, released from her mother's domain at last, having suffered personal unhappiness, is looking back, perhaps, on the botanizing, readings, and prayers her mother made her share in to deride them bitterly.[4] The sensitive, impres-

---

4. This critique could be seen to apply as well to Rousseau's education at the hands of his father.

sionable girl is forced to marry a rich prospect, an old man: as in Germaine's own life, "son roman de bonheur était détruit—her romance was over." Two years go by and she learns to live, seeking the diversions of society, but feeling arid and hopeless at heart.

Adélaïde is beautiful, delicate, and blond, as Delphine will be. Mme de Staël here toys with a heroine who is physically unlike herself, but yet her spiritual twin. Such heroines represent the "cool," "fair" side of Germaine. For the social plane to take precedence over the psychological the heroine must be suitably lovely and must not betray any marked distinctions of person or character except the conventionally approved ones, which she must possess in superabundance. Adélaïde has every virtue and always treats her tedious husband with consideration. He is not insensible to her kindness and rewards her by dying, leaving her rich and free.

She first hears of Théodore de Rostain on a visit to the country. Théodore, a young man dominated by his mother, the Princesse de Rostain, is, like Adélaïde, supposed to be endowed with all the virtues of mind and conduct. Although Mme de Staël tries desperately to make Théodore a hero of warmth and passion, even she can never really believe in him. We see this first in her descriptions of Adélaïde and Théodore. Adélaïde she describes as follows: "A soft and delicate visage, blond hair, a dazzlingly white complexion, and a romantic and tender expression made a contrast with her extreme liveliness, but also covered her whole person with a combination of modesty and sensibility that forced one to take an interest in her" (II, 232–33). When we first see Théodore, "he appeared before her: his face was noble and interesting, all his manner had grace and dignity" (II, 236). Noble and interesting though he may be to the author, we are scarcely fascinated by so abstract a character. Placed beside the hackneyed but lively Adélaïde, he looks like a negative.

After some resistance, Théodore finally confesses his passion, but Adélaïde's own aunt opposes their union, telling her she is so changeable and light-headed that any lover of hers would ultimately come to doubt her fidelity. But Adélaïde, being in love, pleads she will be constant. Théodore then confides to her that he has a jealous heart that could never survive the merest shadow over his bliss.

In this tale it is the mothers who impede love's transports.

Théodore's opposes the union, refusing the couple money, but when Adélaïde affirms that her fortune will suffice, they take one of those depressingly solemn private vows of marriage so current in the fiction of the time, Adélaïde swearing before God that "it is sweet to give" her life to her lover.

Adélaïde's uncle, a man "so light-headed that one could not get him to pay attention to anything for the whole of a quarter of an hour, even if it were to save him half his fortune . . . " (II, 228), implores her to come to Paris. They go to the wicked metropolis, only to meet up with the temptations of the city. Her marriage still secret, Adélaïde is treated in society as a rich and beautiful widow; she is lionized and fully enjoys it: "she did not love Théodore any the less, but she united to this feeling a taste for society . . . she dedicated her success to him, but she wished to have it . . . she would not have been able to live without Théodore, but she could be amused when he was not there" (II, 247). Again the conventional plot fades away and the genuine problem emerges. Adélaïde is decidedly novel in her desire not only for sociability but also for notoriety and social acclaim. She wishes to "dedicate" her success to Théodore: that is, she would like him to bask in the satisfaction of being loved by a woman so accomplished and admired, just as any woman would, ostensibly, reflect in contentment the glory of her man. However, as she is capable of obtaining the gratification of applause and finds within herself no natural urge to suppress her *élans*, she feels quite innocent in continuing to enjoy herself.

Troubled by her behavior, Théodore hides his feelings from her. His fault, since this is sure to end badly, will be in having kept his resentment to himself. In an elaborate subplot, Adélaïde compromises herself for the sake of a friend, and Théodore, ignorant of the exculpating details, leaves for his regiment. When Théodore writes to her finally that he is pondering suicide, Adélaïde sends Mme d'Orfeuil to him to explain her apparent betrayal, but asks her, strangely, to remain silent concerning the child she is expecting. "If he rejects the mother, both mother and child must perish." Visibly, there is not much spirit of self-sacrifice in Adélaïde. Mme de Staël, significantly, appears to put a price on motherhood. Théodore does forgive her, and they are reunited in the most melodramatic of scenes, as the fainting heroine is brought before the dying hero. She consents to live only to bear their infant. Théodore could not be so cruel as to ask her to live without his love. Love is the absolute: no one could reasonably be expected, in these stories, to admit that life could be lived without it. After the birth of the child, Adélaïde takes opium, asks her mother-in-law to forgive her for the sorrows "caused by my guilty frivolity," and dies.

Coming to life only in rare patches, the tale falls victim to its own banality of style and substance. The heroine, an immature projection of self, is simply too adorable; the hero has but one flaw, his reticence: both are absurdly idealized, although the heroine tends to possess a trifle more lovable human frailty than does the hero. They stand as innocents, isolated from a world of conflicts and bad impulses. Adélaïde becomes addicted to worldly pleasures only as a result of Mme d'Orfeuil's poor educational philosophy. Having no real autonomy, Mme de Staël argues in good liberal fashion, she can have no guilt. She is forgiven her frivolous tastes not only because they are "imposed," but also because "her sensibility, goodness, and openness were so unvarying, and her faults, to which she readily confessed, served to console those who envied her, while giving her friends an ever-amusing and welcome topic for gentle mockery" (II, 232).

A constant feature of Mme de Staël's fiction, which offers evidence of her immersion in the dialectic of love and self-love, is her use of scenes of public adulation of the heroine. In *Adélaïde et Théodore* Parisian society greets Adélaïde not merely with passive pleasure, but with positive applause. Such applause, which was actually bestowed upon various individuals in social gatherings at the time but is now unheard of, would have astonished Mme de Staël's contemporaries far less than it does us. One critic argues, "Not only does Adélaïde like to dance, which would be only normal, she also likes to shine in conversation, which is perhaps a bit less so. But she needs a husband to support her in this, and this is not normal at all."[5] In Mme de Staël's inversion of the traditional male-female pattern, the heroine becomes the ambitious

5. Larg, *La Vie dans l'oeuvre*, p. 52.

one and her lover is without ambition. Théodore will say, "Most men are concerned with fame or fortune; I will never be unhappy but for one cause alone; I draw all my strength from my heart: it is by that I live or die" (II, 241). In this, Mme de Staël appears to exaggerate perhaps, but she only reflcts a rejection of heroism, one we later encounter in René and Adolphe, who find even love beyond their strength.

Beneath the eighteenth-century object lesson the old conflict still remains. Adélaïde is spirited and has a personality, but the author tries to hide it behind a tinsel facade of conventional feminine charms. In terms of the creation of a new heroine, Adélaïde is a decided regression from Mirza, with whom we have yet to deal: Mirza's tragedy will be presented to us as arising from a psychic disability, whereas we are at a loss to admit that Adélaïde has a soul. Yet despite Adélaïde's plaster-saintlike ways, wrath erupts even here, in the business of the child. The heroine, so apparently light-hearted, is deeply embattled in her struggle to be herself, to be able to enjoy the successes her beauty and wit bring her without losing her lover's allegiance. The child is but a pawn. Théodore can be a father only if he accepts Adélaïde as she is. If he rejects her, she herself does not want to be a mother. In fact, of course, she has no interest in the child at all—first she threatens to die before it is born, and then she lives until its birth only to fulfill the oath sworn to Théodore. For Adélaïde, amazingly, self-love comes first. Love, it is here argued, can be present only where there is self-love. Adélaïde is unmasked: she is not Other, not *ewige Weib*: she actually has an ego that others ignore at their peril. That is the unutterable truth this superficially mild tale tells us.

> . . . whatever I do else but learning is full of grief,
> trouble, fear, and whole misliking unto me.
>
> LADY JANE GREY

The second of Mme de Staël's verse plays, *Jane Grey* (1787), brings us to the second class of her fiction, that in which the heroine's own soul, rather than society, becomes the stage of conflict.

Germaine's use of the martyred intellectual princess as heroine is significant, even though it is Jane's situation rather than her mind that she exploits in her treatment. She claims to have been about the same age as Jane, seventeen, when she began to write her play and asserts that "her youth encouraged my own."[6] An exemplary, exalted spiritual life was paired with a high and tragic destiny in Lady Jane. This Protestant saint was a natural model for the young Germaine, having "the birth of a princess, the learning of a clerk, the life of a saint and the death of a malefactor."[7] In Jane Grey she had discovered a true embodiment of her ideal: her unique position, above that of other women, and her learning were qualities with which Mme de Staël readily identified. Strong in her gifts, able to speak Italian, French, Greek, and Latin and to debate theological questions intelligibly with learned doctors, strong too in her faith, Lady Jane was nonetheless to become a discarded pawn of political forces that cared nothing for her value as an individual, but viewed her solely in terms of her relation to the throne.

The outstanding difference between the historical Jane and Mme de Staël's is that while the real Jane Grey looked with indifference upon Guilford Dudley, the son of the Earl of Northumberland whom she was forced to marry, the fictional Jane is presented as an enthusiastically happy young bride.[8] "I cherish this passion that virtue allows me," Staël has her Jane say, making her sound more like the passionate Germaine than the composed cousin of the king. Like Germaine, Jane has not only a love of study:

---

6. Larg dates it from her twenty-first year, but the inception of the idea and her work on the play may have been earlier.

7. I. A. Taylor, *Lady Jane Grey and Her Times* (London: Hutchinson, 1908), p. 325.

8. Nicholas Rowe's play *Jane Grey*, which dates from the early eighteenth century and inspired Mme de Staël's, had already romanticized Jane's feelings for Guilford and his for her, but in nothing like the sentimentally exalted fashion in which Mme de Staël treated their relations. Rowe's play was primarily a Protestant tract celebrating Jane's unwavering fidelity to God.

> I love above all else things of the mind,
> They charmed my solitude of yore and made it kind;
> I love them still; they calm within my heart
> Those tremors that the love of bliss doth start . . .
>
> (XVII, 132)

but a love of love that is even more intense. Dudley and Jane are sent together in ecstatic communion to the block, the bridegroom saying to Jane, she the center of all the action, universally loved and admired:

> Affixed upon my love, my drunken glance
> Will dull within my heart love's dissonance.
> To love, I do believe, casts out all pain,
> In man's own heart's recess all evils reign;
> The love that he evokes fills all his need.
> Ah! How much passion's flame my heart does feed
> It raises all my soul to heights so fine
> That fears this day are mixed with rapture's wine.
>
> (XVII, 198)

The Jane Grey of history presumably was sustained by faith and personal courage rather than by love. Her only moment of weakness before dying was caused by the sight of the corpse of her dead husband, whose execution had preceded hers. Mme de Staël alters this historical circumstance to her own ends. It is Jane who must precede Dudley in death, thus offering to him the spectacle of her sacrificial gesture. This Jane becomes, like the author, an exhibitionist of grief.

However, Mme de Staël is not so simple. It is not purely the somewhat fallacious pretext of the sacrifice of young love, and more particularly the young bride, that interests her in Jane's story. Her courage and faith ("Lord, into thy hands I commend my spirit") attract her also, and despite Germaine's own youthful adoration of love, she almost ashamedly sets it aside at the last:

> Together let us sing to Heaven our praises,
> Let faith a saintly courage set ablaze,
> To love's famed powers we tend to trust too much.
>
> (XVII, 198)

Jane Grey expresses the amorous and the spiritual sides of Mme de Staël's nature. For her these are not separable, but sides of a coin: the spiritual is but the ultimate form of sensibility. In the young woman love has decidedly the stronger hold, but even then it is never totally divorced from the notion of spiritual force. As she grows older, the purely spiritual will appeal to her more directly.[9]

The element that links the spiritual with the sensual, even in the "social" works, is that of self-sacrifice. As if to validate Helene Deutsch's shaky hypothesis concerning the basic masochism of woman, Mme de Staël glories, fictionally, in the self-destruction of her heroines. "Death for love is, for Mme de Staël, the apotheosis of a woman's life."[10] When the wicked Northumberland is himself about to die, he scornfully asks Jane: "You wish that I in your own sex's way / Should, pale and trembling, yield to terror's sway?" Jane replies in sibylline fashion, "Ah! these same weaknesses do make me strong." That is, the habit of suffering that women are constrained to espouse gives them a Christlike strength.

> If I have learned to bear in peace my fate,
> What matter it when death my life abate?
> When sorrows swell our strength to bear our woe
> We bless the courage that from heaven doth flow.
>
> (XVII, 194)

This work, which may have been written when Mme de Staël had come to realize that her marriage was a failure, is, like those that follow, a sheer indulgence in tragedy, a bath of hopes deceived and joys unrealized, and an emotional celebration of the happy marriage she did not have. *Jane Grey,* despite the presence in it, common to all Staël's fictions, of feminine self-love and of

---

9. For a discussion of the change in her valuation of the role of love over her lifetime, see my article "Mme de Staël, Rousseau and the Woman Question," *PMLA,* 86, no. 1 (Jan., 1971), 100–109.

10. Larg, *La Vie dans l'oeuvre,* p. 38. Helene Deutsch's two volumes, *The Psychology of Women: A Psychoanalytic Interpretation* (New York: Grune and Stratton, 1944–45), were for many years the only extensive treatment of the subject. An orthodox Freudian, Deutsch held that female nature was basically masochistic.

sacrificial love, is unique in that it is devoid of conflict. Jane is the only one of Mme de Staël's heroines who is at one with herself in her tragic destiny. Death for love's sake, met here more than halfway, is, to be sure, gloried in as the greatest act of a woman's existence. But her death must be looked on in this way: if, in order to know the absolute, the transcendent, she has no other course but to die an untimely death, this such a woman will do.

Staël's severe and sarcastic critic Larg writes, "Already without wanting to do so, she speaks of herself, speaks of nothing but herself."[11] Although we may be permitted to wonder if she is alone in this peculiarity, or even whether, ultimately, it is true, we perhaps do better to admit this: she is always the stone thrown into the pool and her fictions are the concentric circles of that impact. If this is so, it is because her being has a stonelike weight, a density, a problematic, heavy, tortured quality. Her self is an impediment to all her attempts to live: her strengths, her energy, her ebullience, her powers of mind and of soul, that fatally unfulfilled capacity to live, are all negative gifts, because she is unable to channel their very plenty into the rigid, compassed frame prescribed by custom for woman. *Jane Grey* is Germaine's attempt to evade the paradox of her being by a fictional flight to an epiphany of passionate self-sacrifice. It did not work. The qualities of character she repressed in inventing the saccharine enthusiast that is her Jane had to return and have their say.

The two remaining early works are the most original ones precisely in their expression of otherwise repressed and condemnable conflicts.

After her marriage to Eric-Magnus, as we have seen, Germaine frequently entertained in the place of her ailing mother, and the salon of Mme Necker soon became the salon of Mme de Staël. The brilliance, vivacity, and warmth of the daughter were recalled in Guibert's word portrait, cited above, of the young Germaine as Zulmé: "Zulmé is but twenty, and she is the most celebrated of the priestesses of Apollo; she is the favorite of the god. . . . "[12] This

---

11. Larg, *La Vie dans l'oeuvre*, p. 40.
12. Quoted in full on page 46.

description, among the first of many we have of Mme de Staël, gives us, despite its artifices, a sense of her quality, the unique impact of her being. Such encomia could scarcely fail to move her: in fact, we shall see her incorporate elements of Guibert's characterization into her persona, both actual and fictional.

The tales of *Mirza* (1786) and *Zulma* (1797) are both cast in a fashionably exotic, escapist form: understandably, a non-French context helped Mme de Staël achieve greater emotional freedom from the social constraints she habitually felt weighing upon her. It was always in foreign places that she set her most successful fictional surrogates.

Mirza is a fascinating work, a real precursor of the work of maturity. In it the third person narration is abandoned in favor of the immediacy of the first person: an "outer" story is related by an anonymous narrator, and an "inner" tale told by the wretched lover-villain himself, Ximéo.

In his travels, the anonymous "outer" narrator comes upon a sorrowful couple. Ourika, the wife of Ximéo, chief of a Haitian tribe, has been "gifted with the true charms of her sex, all that is delicate and graceful": she is gentle, yielding, and feminine. Astonishingly, Ximéo speaks perfect French, and when the narrator remarks upon this, he replies, "One still keeps some rays of light about one after having lived at an angel's side." Then he tells his story.

He was engaged to wed Ourika, whom he loved, when, out hunting one day, he was led afar by the sound of "une voix de femme, remarquable pour sa beauté," singing, significantly, of freedom and of the horror of slavery. Finally he came upon Mirza, singer of the song. She was a daughter of the Jaloffes, a people at war with Ximéo's own tribe. Mirza was "not beautiful, but her noble, balanced figure, her enchanting eyes, her lively visage left nothing to be desired in her person for love" (II, 228). Guibert's portrait of Germaine wafts its emanations through this conception. Ximéo goes on: ". . . I managed to express my astonishment to her over her song; it grew when I learned that she had composed the words I had just heard." An old Frenchman who had retired among the Senegalese had taught her. Mirza told him, "I learned the French tongue, I read some of their books, and I divert myself by meditating alone here in these mountains." Unlikely and ludicrous though these words may seem, they express the author's aspiration, through her heroine, to a lofty self-image. Mirza stretches credulity only a little more than Corinne will, and already there is a remarkable inner consistency which makes one almost believe in this self-dramatized, far-fetched, curiously endowed heroine. "At each word she said, my curiosity increased; this was no longer a mere woman, it was a poet I thought I heard speaking: and never have the men among us who give themselves up to the gods seemed to me so full of a noble enthusiasm." Mirza is a heroine who escapes the yoke of her subordinate sex by virtue of a transcendent quality that cannot be contained by the ordinary exigencies of life.

Ximéo thought he merely admired Mirza and so would be doing no offense to Ourika in seeing her. She taught him all she knew, with tireless patience and goodness. How could the love of Ourika, a mere woman, compare to that of a siren? Ximéo finally confessed to her his love: " 'Mirza . . . take me into the world by telling me you love me, open the heavens so that I may ascend there with you.' In listening to me she became troubled and tears filled her beautiful eyes in which, until that moment, I had seen only the look of genius" (II, 214).

Why did Ximéo love her? Because with her he would be able to scale the heights. This is a Platonic love, not the love of simple, needful humanity, but it is so in a reversal of the Pygmalion-Galatea myth: instead of man awakening woman into life, lifeless stone as she was, woman refashions man to her desire. With his "take me into the world," Ximéo assumed the stance usually assigned to women, who are supposed to find their reality in their lovers.[13] But Ximéo was ultimately in bad faith—men do not so lightly abandon themselves—even though he truly believed himself to be subjugated by Mirza. He falsely told her no one had any claims upon him, and they loved each other without reserve for two months. Shame then seized Ximéo, and all the "reasons" of

---

13. The heroine of Mme de Graffigny's *Lettres d'une Peruvienne* is less disquieting. Zillia, who has been tutored by her lover to make her more his equal, asks, ". . . if it were not for the desire of pleasing you, should I have been able to abandon the tranquility of ignorance for the painful effort of study?" She has done so solely in an effort to merit his esteem.

society and of duty that would impel him to leave Mirza and that he had so ecstatically forgotten for the spell of his enchantment came flooding back: "I trembled as I thought to what excess her heart could love; yet my father would never have called any Jaloffe woman his daughter." So Ximéo, though promising to return to Mirza, went home and wed Ourika, whose soft beauty and tears he could not resist. When the time of his supposed return to Mirza came, he went to her and offered her his friendship. Her reply? "Your friendship . . . barbarian, can you offer such a sentiment to a soul like mine? Come, rather give me death."

Now torrents of unabated misery are released. The betrayed muse will punish her lover with everlasting grief. When Ximéo begged her not to hate him, Mirza replied, "Hate you! . . . Have no fear of it, Ximéo; there are hearts that know only love, and whose passions can turn only against themselves" (II, 218). By an act of will hatred is transmuted into sorrow. Mirza consents to live on only to take care of the old man who had brought her up.

Overcome by remorse, Ximéo went into battle hoping to merit Mirza's esteem. Gravely wounded, he was then taken prisoner. When white men came to choose slaves from among the captives, Ximéo, about to be taken, looked up to see Mirza, radiantly beautiful, saying to his captors, "Suffer me to be enslaved in Ximéo's place." The reader recalls what this meant to her, for it was a haunting chant of freedom that she was singing when Ximéo first heard her; but Mirza cries, "I will not find slavery debasing, I will respect the power of my master . . . Ximéo must cherish life; he is loved!" Ximéo could not but refuse such a sacrifice, but Mirza insists. Finally, the governor, as touched by Mirza's heroism as the reader is supposed to be, steps forth to set them both free. Ximéo has scarcely thanked him when he comes upon Mirza at the foot of a tree. In a strange reversal of moods, she tells her lover, "Your very presence turns that blood that once boiled for love of you to ice; passionate souls know only extremes." After this far from loving statement she pierces her heart with an arrow and dies. Ximéo moans, "Oh God, you who suspended my life in that moment, have you given it back to me only to better avenge Mirza by torturing me with sorrow?" In fact the nature of Ximéo's life after Mirza's death is worth closer scrutiny.

... I enclosed within a tomb the sad remains of a woman I love now that she is no more. . . . There in solitude, as the sun goes down, when all of nature darkens and shares my mourning, at the time when the silence of the world allows me to hear only my own thoughts, then it is that, prostrate upon her tomb, I feel the full measure of misfortune, all her sorrows . . . . I think I see her, but never does she appear to me as "an angry mistress." I hear her console me and comfort me in my pain. As doubt assails me at the fate awaiting us after death, I respect the memory of Mirza in my heart, and fear that if I killed myself, I should be destroying all that remains of her. (II, 226)

Now Ximéo's life belongs utterly to Mirza. The author is constrained to say that Mirza never appeared to him as angry, though we know that she must have been, but rather as a consoling angel. Mirza must be absolved of any taint of the sin of vengeance and Ximéo must bear a thousand times the weight of her tragic existence. We may marvel at the extent, beyond even that of the tearful conventions, to which hero and heroine glory here in remorse and sorrow. This is a constant of Germaine de Staël's fiction, and can be documented by an entry in her journal: ". . . the wrenching pains of sorrow are caused by reminiscences of final goodbyes, and what heart would wish to spare a sense of regret to him who is most dear? We may seek to console all our other friends, but how could we wish to be loved less by the object of a passionate attachment! The only time one is entitled to self-interest is in having an affection that primarily transports one's own existence into that of the beloved."[14]

This is a very enlightening observation displaying the acuteness with which Mme de Staël scrutinized her own heart in its throes of passion and dismay. But her hallmark emerges in this story: it is the stubborn rejection, at the core, of the role of *other*, in spite of all the feminine masochistic trappings. The very existence of this "one occasion" on which it is right to express one's will to control the beloved spoils the entire system, revealing as it does the falseness of demanding a surrender to love so total it can never be realized.

Mirza and Ximéo's love, in fact, is posed in terms, doubtless unconsciously by the author, of maximum probable failure. All

14. Haussonville, *Le Salon*, II, 69.

along, in the very fabric of the narrative, we are made to see Ximéo, man-the-betrayer, as bereft and abandoned; Mirza is subject, he object. It is she who teaches Ximéo the value of freedom to which she, as woman, ought not even to be privy, according to the dictates of the times. Mme de Staël wants Mirza's gifts, which are the very stuff of her freedom, to *constitute* her beauty, to be construed by Ximéo as attractions, in the way a woman, within the conventions, would be expected to be drawn naturally to a bard, a warrior, a free spirit. It is she who initiates their relationship (all but sexually), who seizes his soul in spite of him, who instructs him. What does he, in turn, have to offer her? Again, it is what woman has traditionally been held to offer man: fidelity. That is all. Originality, initiative, freedom: all are hers.

Mme de Staël shows us how this dream of freedom of Mirza's is doomed. Love's laws enslave her, by decreeing that Ourika is more of a woman than she and so more worthy of the love of a man, and then by making Mirza pose as weak and betrayed when she is wrathful and vengeful. All that Mirza is as autonomous subject makes it impossible for her to play at being object, and yet this she must do if she wants love, even after death. The price of love for a woman with a sense of self is seen not as a mere problem of self-betrayal, but as absolutely incommensurable, unthinkable, impossible. And the anger that this view of the situation arouses remains, though the pose of resignation is ceaselessly, tiresomely evoked, unappeasable, never to be assuaged.

Hence we have a problem at the very core of Mme de Staël's being which impinges also upon her style, ruining it for grace or balance. Even at this early stage, despite the force of her vision, the attempt to say something genuine about the female ego in a society and within literary conventions utterly opposed to her statement by their very terms—psychological, familial, linguistic, stylistic, novelistic—creates unbearable tensions on all levels. She persists in remaining within the *conte* framework, and her tale has the force of some real passion, but the character of Mirza cracks the framework and the slight story, the shadowy other characters, cannot bear the stress. Deeply conservative in her emotions, though free in her ideas, Mme de Staël will never suspect until *Corinne* that a new form might be needed to serve her purposes.

But the general failure of style, far less apparent in her non-fiction than in her fiction, must be related to the emotional impasse of wishing to represent an innovative conception of woman in a milieu wholly uncongenial to her. Mme de Staël, when she wrote *Mirza*, could conceive of a new woman, but not of a new world.

Then, within the treatise on the *Passions* (1797) we find the story *Zulma*, its title obviously deriving from Guibert's tribute, a "fragment" of a tale originally intended to show the ravages of love. Mme de Staël theorized that this passion "could possess all its conceivable power only in a creature whose soul was wild, but whose mind was cultivated: for the faculty of judgment adds greatly to the experience of pain when that faculty has in no way diminished the power of feeling" (II, 347).

Zulma's story, *"which more than any other is part of my soul,"*[15] portrays, again, the scenario of the fatality of love in Mme de Staël's life. The resemblance of *Mirza* to *Zulma* may well amaze us. In both ·we find the old theme of love betrayed, which was played out repeatedly by Mme de Staël in her life as in her works. Mistress of Louis de Narbonne at the time of the Revolution, she had worked indefatigably, as only she could, to advance his political prestige, only to be discarded from his affections after his exile to England. *Zulma* is the mirror of her dismay.

Zulma's story is a trial, a self-defense, the inner narrator finally becoming the betrayed woman herself. A native of the Orenoco region, she is accused of the murder of a certain Fernand. At first impassive, she is moved to give her account most eloquently when the body of her dead lover is brought before her.

Fernand, also a native but one who had been raised in Spain, later returns to the Orenoco bringing with him a polish found nowhere else in their primitive vales. "In this land, where no distinctions among us are consecrated by the laws, he seemed to create in his own person a royalty of genius . . ." (II, 331). He takes notice of Zulma and teaches her, making her—reversing the *Mirza* formula—Galatea-like, his creature and his love. In her simplicity she asks him why, if love gives as much happiness as it is supposed

---

15. From Mme de Staël's introduction. Italics mine.

to, it is not the rule of the universe. He cannot answer her, but promises to love her always. Fernand goes off to battle, three times returning victorious. When he has been wounded by a poisoned dart, Zulma sucks the poison from his wound, feeling no sweeter joy can come to her than to risk her life for his. Fernand then takes leave of her for a few days and during this time, while she is walking in the woods, she sees him at the feet of young Mirza. In an unthinking moment of jealous wrath, she shoots her arrow and Fernand falls. Pleading her innocence in the name of the love she has lived, she explains, "I live so powerfully in my own being that to be shown another is beyond my endurance . . . " (II, 345–46). So she ends her story. After eight days of deliberation the tribunal changes her death sentence to an acquittal and her family is saved from dishonor, but Zulma pierces her heart with an arrow and dies. The *crime passionnel* has been vindicated once more.

In recalling her love, Zulma says, "I felt that in the depths of my soul there was such a power of love as ought to dominate him, and that a man so passionately loved could not think himself free." Fernand may be cultivated, noble, and handsome, but he is also morally weak, accused of treachery in war, and perfidious in love. Despite all his cultivation, again he does not matter save as the object of Zulma's love. It is she who is a tower of strength, of brilliance, of bravery. She has all the virtues he lacks: he is lukewarm and wavering; she is passionate and steadfast. Heroism has become heroine-ism. Unhappily, the autobiographical picture is largely true. Narbonne was, compared with Mme de Staël, an attractive cipher, and despite the calumnies of her enemies who claimed she had no conscience, she suffered agonies at having sacrificed her reputation to save him and to build his political career. *Zulma* is a directly self-justificatory work. In it she defends herself by calling upon the name of love, the flame and origin of the moral world which lifts man "above the laws and opinions of men," and accuses her faithless lover.

Ironically, the monumental egocentricity of Zulma's character is unwittingly revealed, dampening her plea and making one at first forgive, at least a little, the lover whom she considers to be her vassal in love. "I love so powerfully in my own being . . . " is not only an example of Mme de Staël's sometimes peculiarly confused expression: it is also a clear indication that she does not perceive the outside world as outside, to be dealt with rather than absorbed in even so capacious an ego as her own. The world, she felt with a sense of panic, should understand her genuine breadth, grasp her love and her gifts, and fit into her needs. The men she chose to love should comprehend the power of her love, and this by itself ought to be sufficient to make them love to the same degree. But the world simply regards Zulma's claim to status as a subject being as irrelevant, and this baffles her, reduces her to incoherence; failing utterly to comprehend the order of a world that denies her so radically, her verbalization of her sense of exclusion becomes its opposite, a statement of her self as absolute. Mme de Staël's relative linguistic perplexity in expressing the claims of her heroines is marked by this dialectic of the taboo placed on the free expression of the female ego.

What interests us about *Zulma* is the symbiotic relationship it bears both to the *Mirza* of her youth and to the later *Corinne*. While the setting and mood of these works differ, all are exotic tales in which are set forth the triangular relations between a passionate lady and a pure one vying for the affections of a weak hero. It is ever the passionate lady whose point of view is espoused. This is, of course, the *Phèdre* pattern.[16]

Mirza and *Zulma*, related in the first person, create a far greater dramatic impact than the other two tales, told in the third person. This factor alone would seem insufficient to explain the charge of immediacy of these tales as compared with the others. *Delphine,* which as an epistolary novel employs the first person, will be far surpassed in intensity by *Corinne*. The differences in the effects of the four tales must be attributed to the author's inability to cope with the creative problems presented by a large canvas, with the protagonists pitted against society, as in *Pauline, Adélaïde et Théodore* and, later, *Delphine*. When love and society are faced off against each other, the author's confidence seems to wane and

---

16. I have discussed the relation Mme de Staël's *Corinne* bears to Racine's *Phèdre* in an article, "Mme de Staël's Debt to *Phèdre: Corinne,*" *Studies in Romanticism,* III, no. 3 (Spring, 1964), 161–76, but visibly this is a scheme already espoused in the earliest fictions that remains the enduring embodiment of Mme de Staël's vision of love.

she cannot sustain a strong dramatic focus. Where the characters are few and the love intrigue uncluttered, all other elements being made subsidiary to it, as in *Mirza, Zulma,* and *Corinne,* Mme de Staël's force comes through to the reader.

The seeming quantum leap from these slim tales to the ponderous novels is primarily one of quantity, although such a considerable increase, in truth, becomes a qualitative matter. The virtually obsessive themes of *Delphine* and *Corinne* are at work in their inventor's mind long before her active life and her apprehensions about attempting major fiction have waned sufficiently for her to work with such amplitude.

Fiction is a form of play, in which the author rearranges, recreates the *données* of experience, both "real" and "imaginary." But play, as we know, is serious business, or at least an activity far from negligible. In play we juggle with our perceptions, seeking, finding, and keeping intelligibility, or thrusting it away as unsatisfactorily boring or limiting. But an author is necessarily limited by his or her own spirit, by its freedoms and by its obsessions. Mme de Staël's obessions are bound up with experiences of love and of freedom.

Sophie is the exorcism in fantasy of parental ghosts; *Jane Grey* her paean to married love. *Pauline* and *Adélaïde et Thédore* are attempts to find accommodation between her heroine surrogates and society. In *Mirza* she gives her first overt, awkward expression to her essential struggle to be a "new" woman, that is herself, without sacrificing the satisfactions of love, and in *Zulma,* the tale "closest to her heart," in a gesture of cosmic despair she pours out her wrath upon man and the world that will not let her know love's deepest fulfillment—that of unconditioned acceptance.

CHAPTER 3

Delphine—Backgrounds

Advice to Women: Aspire only to those virtues peculiar
to your sex, follow your natural modesty, and think it
the greatest commendation not to be talked of one way
or another.

PERICLES

Traumas

My dear Mama,

I need to write to you. My heart is heavy, I am sad, and in this vast
house that only a little while ago held all that is dear to me, that bounded
my world and my future, I see no more but a desert. For the first time I
noticed that the space was too big for me, and I ran off to my little room
so that my view could contain the emptiness that surrounded me. This
momentary emptiness makes me tremble over my fate. You find within
yourself, dear Mama, many consolations, but I find in myself only you.[1]

I passed through a crowd of those who were having perhaps the gay-
est moment in their lives, whereas I was not sure that death did not lie
before me . . . ; wandering about thus, disguised, and in the utmost extremity, extraordinary feelings took hold upon me; I was afraid of my
solitude in the midst of the throng; of my existence, invisible to the eyes
of others, since none of my actions could be attributed to me. It seemed
to me that it was my phantom that walked among the living, and I could
no more conceive of the pleasures that activated them than if, from the
bosom of death, I had been contemplating earthly concerns. I sought
among all these figures, whom I perceived as if in a cruel dream, a single
man, a single being who still truly existed for me and could make my
impressions in all their strength and bitterness real to me. I passed silently
in the midst of dances and outbursts of pleasure, and bore in my soul all
that nature can inflict in the way of sorrow, without uttering a cry, without obtaining from anyone a sign of compassion. (IV, XXXVII)

---

1. Anne-Louise Germaine Necker de Staël, *Correspondance générale*, ed.
Béatrice Jasinski, 5 vols. (Paris: Pauvert, 1962–   ), I, pt. 1, p. 6.

The bond that underlies the plea of the child and the plea of Delphine, the heroine of the thirty-six-year-old novelist, is a continuum of anguish springing from a sense of isolation. A nameless terror and sorrow mark Germaine de Staël's sensibility in a manner far too insistent to be dismissed as the Wertheresque posturing from which it borrows its rhetoric. If it is true that for Mme de Staël "the absence of those she loves is felt as a mutilation,"[2] we are driven to ask the nature of that mutilation. Why do we find, from first to last, this obsessive fear of solitude, of emptiness?

The image, in the passage from *Delphine*, of the self invisible to others whose reality, meeting no confirmation from another being, becomes doubtful, is echoed in the little girl's call of distress from a solitude too large, menacing, and overpowering to her ego. The roots of this recurrent reactional neurotic symptom are lost in the early childhood of Anne-Louise Germaine Necker and can never be known with certainty. She has communicated to us quite clearly, however, that it was from her mother that she sought recognition, love, support—all that we presume the child requires to develop a confident self-image. Of these she felt deprived in adequate measure to insure that in later life her response to any threat of affective privation would not be that of a glorious, assured woman of letters but rather that of an emotional pauper.

The mother-child relationship, insofar as it is the bond charged with providing narcissistic confirmation to the child, is held to be less successful with girl children than when there is sexual differentiation. Mothers of daughters have frequently been observed to enact their roles dutifully, but without that "profound love" they give to their sons. Girl children, perhaps because deprived of this "natural" advantage, are more precocious in seeking their own narcissistic confirmation—through performance of response, smile, speech. In consequence of this lack, they invest their whole being with the narcissistic demand for approval. "Woman lives in and by love, and having been deprived at the start . . . she will project

---

2. Simone Balayé, "Absence, exil, voyages," in *Madame de Staël et l'Europe, Colloque de Coppet, July 18–24, 1966* (Paris: Klincksieck, 1970), p. 230. (Book hereafter referred to as *Colloque de Coppet*.)

her ill-integrated, unstructured narcissism upon her relationships with her partners, and in a sense her whole life will merely be the story of this projection, of her successes (always partial and fleeting) and of her (inevitable) failures."[3]

Whether this depth-psychology portrait is at the origin of, or is merely, as I believe, a response—albeit a profound one—to the depreciation of the female, the result is recognizably the pattern of female affective life we know: the search for confirmation through love, with its insistent call for assurance of worth from others. Germaine Necker's hunger for approval was apparently founded in the clash between her intense nature and the remote, dutiful affection of her reproving mother. That trauma of separation anxiety which was expressed in her childhood letter and whose effects never left her (we know she remained unable to stand departures or sentimental ruptures, even with friends, let alone lovers) presupposes an early and repeated experience of abandonment. It is the capital of feeling invested by her in such fears that strikes us as singular. There is more than a little of a continued primacy in Germaine of infantile narcissism, of a need for the kind of oceanic, unitary feeling of security the infant craves from its mother and that Germaine incessantly and vainly seeks from her perplexed lovers. A corollary of this powerful strain of enduring primary narcissism is the hurt amazement she exhibits when her belief in her own thoughts and feelings is not shared. Demonstrably, the unassuageable character of her loving long antedates her love affairs. It is the precondition of her emotional life, as visible already in her early letters as in *Jane Grey* and *l'Histoire de Pauline.*

In contrast to what we at first believe when we come into contact with Mme de Staël's need for adulation—that it is a function of an absurd delusion of grandeur—we find rather that when, as in Guibert's tribute, she is accorded mythic status as priestess of Apollo, she seizes upon this inflated image for lack of a more solidly grounded one. She is in a sense bought by her own publicity,

---

3. Bela Grunberger, "Jalons pour l'étude du narcissisme dans la sexualité féminine," in *La Sexualité féminine,* ed. J. Chasseguet-Smirgel (Paris: Payot, 1964), p. 120 and *passim.* Grunberger's is obviously a view that, rooting the woman's psyche in her actual experience, pulls away from the stricter Freudian attempt to account for a "sense of mutilation" by ascribing it to castration anxiety.

having no rooted and secure sense of self out of which she might have smiled at it. The overwhelming insecurity of her emotional life reveals that she is deluded by grandeur, *faute de mieux.*

The eternal problem of the young was posed for Germaine: how to assert herself? What mode could she assume that would be her own? The core of that basic disorderliness in multiple aspects of her existence—her toilette (we recall her fatal dishevelment—she tripped and tore her hem as she was presented at court), her improvised habits of letter writing and only slightly more systematic habits of work, the disorder of her friendships and loves —is to be found in the ambivalence with which she met all demands and expectations. Her inspired solution was to be "natural," spontaneous, to meet every person and event as if unforeseen and to throw herself into experience with naïve enthusiasm. In this the ideological bias of her upbringing seconded her. The liberal premises of Rousseau's educational theories gave her a freedom even of movement—and certainly of thought—little enjoyed by other children of her time. In fact the combination of affective parental neglect (her "adoring" father had little to do with her in childhood), material comfort, and permissive theory and practice, encouraging in her precocity of response and independence of judgment, make Mme de Staël remarkably similar to children of the mid-twentieth century. Even more pertinent to ourselves, presaging the dilemma of the modern woman, are the contradictions inherent in granting to this girl child, even as we do following the Neckers' example, intellectual freedom, while withholding from her emotional and spiritual freedom.

But her unappeasable need to be loved, her cult of spontaneity and naturalness, clashed with a third factor that seems to speak to us less: that of a respect for propriety. The court and the Parisian society that so attracted Germaine were ruled over by a public opinion unregulated by any principle save that of wit and special interest, but whose sentences had, nonetheless, the impact of legal decrees. The morality of society was the same in that day as in this: it was the morality of success. A line of behavior that deviated successfully (quietly) from convention was accepted, but the same behavior would be viciously ridiculed if it caused any overt reaction, any comment or ripple in the *status quo.* Yet, deep as was

Mme de Staël's awe of and dependency upon society's good opinion, propriety was not for her a matter of society's decrees alone. God's laws had their share in her scheme of values. Her internalized version of conjugality was a far cry from the practices of her time or of our own. Marriage in the aristocracy, we recall, far from compelling sexual exclusivity, actually licensed a decorous diversity of sexual partners. Her Genevan bourgeois family was, in its professions, radically out of step with its milieu. What reinforced Germaine's rigid emotional adherence to a marital ideal was her sense of outrage that her (to her) cool mother should have enjoyed in all its plentitude the conjugal love that the warm daughter coveted, that of Jacques Necker.

Narbonne and Jealousy

The Viscount Louis de Narbonne was a man Mme Necker, perhaps sensing her daughter's penchant for, had specifically warned the young married woman not to receive. Of noble lineage, sometimes even reckoned to be a bastard son of Louis XV, Narbonne was handsome, well-educated, quite witty and able, and gracefully aristocratic in bearing and manner—all surface embellishments that had great prestige for Germaine. Protected at court by the king's Aunt Adélaïde, Narbonne, in his early thirties, was sufficiently well known as a libertine charmer to cause Mme Necker to worry about her susceptible young daughter's heart and reputation. No counterweight of admiration or affection for the colorless M. de Staël could prevent Germaine from flinging herself with abandon into the first great love affair of her life, an affair that was to last five years and would generate two children and an indelible emotional scar.

In retrospective bewilderment, like Mme Necker we may find this love a foredoomed folly. The princely spendthrift had, all in all, little except ambition in common with that rich "foreign" bourgeoise, the Swedish Ambassadress. As the English novelist Fanny Burney would later put it unkindly, they appeared ill assorted as a couple, he being comely, she not. Events, kinder than nature, seconded Germaine in her search for a lover. It was in the period following Necker's recall to power, while she basked in the reflected glory of his popularity, that Mme de Staël bound Narbonne to her, choosing him from among a selection of gallants including Mathieu de Montmorency, Alexandre de Lameth, and Talleyrand. Twenty-two years old and as immature sentimentally as she was salon-wise, quick-witted, and well-spoken, Germaine loved Narbonne unreservedly and unabashedly, saving the sensibilities of no one. Following Necker's withdrawal, hungry to play a role in affairs in her own turn, she entertained members of all the political factions in the days of ferment between 1789 and 1792, knew everyone, and tried to know everything. She plotted and schemed "naturally," not to any precise political end but as an expression of her total personality, her feelings and ideas blended, as always, together. Starting from a position on the political left, she influenced Narbonne to turn in this direction, but as the Revolution moved leftward, though maintaining her position of principle as a constitutionalist, she became a centrist. Through their joint efforts, Narbonne became Minister of War at the end of 1791. Marie-Antoinette wrote resentfully to Fersen, ". . . what glory for Mme de Staël to have the whole army . . . to herself!"[4] Narbonne's ministry lasted only three months: the revelation of the king's treachery made it ever plainer there could be no constitutional monarchy under Louis XVI. France in the end became a dangerous place for Narbonne and he fled to England. Mme de Staël, wretched and anxious over their separation, after harboring many friends and aiding them to escape, finally made her own reluctant way, seven months pregnant, to the home of her parents in Switzerland. There she gave birth to her second son and Narbonne's, Albert, in November, 1792. In January, 1793, she went off to England and Narbonne, undeterred by parents or children, driven by her passionate need not to be divided from the object of her love.

The four months of exile in England with Narbonne, Talleyrand, and Alexandre d'Arblay remained in Mme de Staël's spirit as an oasis of peace in a turbulent life and agitated times, for when she returned to Switzerland her suffering began in earnest. As Narbonne wrote less and less often, her correspondence became more and more despairing, incoherent, and violent.

---

4. Anne-Louise Germaine Necker de Staël, *Lettres inédites à Louis de Narbonne*, ed. Béatrice Jasinski (Paris: Pauvert, 1960), p. x.

I live only for you in this horrible world; I swear to you that were this bond to be broken, in that very instant my whole existence would be annihilated, and then this horrible revolution that accustoms us to death so well would at least do me the service of snuffing out that physical instinct that survives moral desperation. My love, my only love . . . you alone are happiness, repose, life. I do not know how to express what passes beyond all known feelings, and I fear having displeased you by the very excess of my feeling for you.[5]

In terms not unlike those we have seen used by Mme de Graffigny's Zillia, and that remind us of the love tradition that goes back to the original Héloïse, Mme de Staël had invested her entire being in her love for Narbonne. She could not believe, much less accept, that his commitment to her was so different from hers to him. She disregarded what blatant signs there were; the fact, for example, that so prudent was he that he did not speak to her in his letters even impersonally of their children. By March of the year following her return to Switzerland, her emotions were strained beyond endurance by waiting for letters that came only intermittently, by feverish bursts of absurd plan making, by her mother's illness and her parents' reproaches. This letter of March 12, 1794, is a testament to her torment of spirit in seeing the valedictory of their love. In the midst of her regrets, though, we distinguish her distillation of a personal meaning from her suffering and the sign of her astonishing capacity to find a knot of integrity within to preserve her:

Never have you more truly loved me! Ah! Do not tell me that. Let me think there was a time in our life when I was more dear to you. What would I have done with my youth, with all the devotion in my nature, if this cold sentiment that scarcely merits the name of honest dealing were to be the only prize I had ever obtained? . . . But what of me? What of me? Do you flatter yourself that I will have so different a standard in judging your conduct and in judging mine? When I left last year I also had a fortune, an existence, a family to pacify. I risked it all. I haven't lost anything because the same character that knows how to give itself entirely is able to dominate all that surrounds it, and because intense feeling comes to be respected even by those whom it hurts, and because there is no evil except in half-plans, semi-attachments, half-opinions, all that the uncertainty of your mind and soul make you adopt by turns. . . . I miss you more than France,

5. Staël, *Lettres inédites*, p. 203.

more than all the illusions of my life. I miss you with torrents of tears: twenty times I have interrupted this letter to kiss your portrait with cries of sorrow. But I know you are lost to me.[6]

"France," "all the illusions of my life"—Narbonne represented all of this to Germaine, as well as the hope of that perfect love which she needed to believe possible because it would compensate the imperfection of herself. With Narbonne's defection her juvenile aspirations and part of her courage also abandoned her. The prestige of Old France, of the aristocracy, of power and influence, all waned for her with her hopes of keeping him. But of course most of all his betrayal confirmed what would be confirmed simply too often in her life: that she was not worthy of the ultimate devotion she was prepared to bestow. Narbonne withheld from her precisely that primary acceptance she craved from him too insistently, as she knew.

In that same month, March, 1794, Germaine wrote her recalcitrant lover: "My mother nearly died in the night of a dreadful suffocation; she asked for me and said: 'My daughter, I am dying of the suffering your guilty and public liaison has caused me; you are punished for it by the treatment your lover has given you; it is his behavior that is breaking off what my prayers had not succeeded in making you give up. It will be through the care you take of your father that you will obtain my forgiveness in heaven. Do not say anything. Leave. I have no strength to quarrel at this moment.' "[7] Narbonne had been Germaine's revolt. By taking not merely a lover, but so eminent, so Catholic, so showy a one; by

---

6. Staël, *Lettres inédites*, pp. 241–43. Mme de Staël was not indulgent to others in similar extremity. To her husband's repeated expressions of suspicion and his protests over her behavior, she responded: ". . . the demon of jealousy, of self-love and of love disturbs you all too much. . . . Reflect but a moment upon me. See what impression this continual tempest that troubles my life must make upon me. What heart could resist such perpetual torment? The most passionate of lovers end by separating when they cause each other unhappiness, and you would like a bond that is merely sincere and gentle to resist shocks that would uproot the oak tree? Certainly [our affection] might be rekindled, but I am too candid to show you a fondness I do not feel." *Correspondance générale*, I, pt. 2, pp. 356–57.

7. Anne-Louise Germaine Necker de Staël, *Choix de lettres de Madame de Staël 1766–1817*, ed. Georges Solovieff (Paris: Klincksieck, 1970), p. 403.

pressing his claims to power so openly that she became the scandalous butt of both royalist and radical pamphleteers; by abandoning her children and pursuing him to the ends of the earth (England), she had found all the ways of injuring her proper mother's sense of right. But the mother was not defenseless, and in such scenes, of which there were not a few, she prodded the seemingly dormant sense of guilt in her daughter. "The fear of losing her never fails to make me forget all the pain she has caused and will cause me," she wrote of her mother.[8] Emotional blackmail was a technique Mme de Staël learned at her mother's knee.

> Woman, awake; the tocsin of reason resounds throughout the universe. Nature's powerful sway no longer is hedged about with prejudice, fanaticism, superstition and lies. The torch of truth has dissipated all the clouds of stupidity and usurpation. . . .
>
> OLYMPE DE GOUGES

Woman, Politics, and Revolution

Despite the flurry of interest in civil rights for women exemplified by Condorcet's treatise, by the admission of women to some of the political clubs and their creation of some of their own, and by the agitating activities of such radical women as Olympe de Gouges, Théroigne de Méricourt, and Rose Lacombe, Mme de Staël took no part in, and seemingly no notice of, this effervescence. Her own political efforts were indirect—that is, taken under the cover of, or in the name of, men. They were, however, sufficiently indiscreet—she had a conscience, but no shame—to be not merely noticed but celebrated. And being a woman taken notice of in political life meant to be slandered: "A woman, however little well known she may be, is always too well known in her own lifetime," wrote the revolutionary journalist Prudhomme in his radical paper, *Révolutions de Paris*. An evident supporter of this view was

---

8. *Correspondance générale*, I, pt. 2, p. 379. Béatrice Jasinski claims that Mme de Staël and her father favored an honest break with Staël, whereas Mme Necker held against it, out of a fear of scandal.

Rivarol. Reputedly one of the wittiest men of his time, perhaps jealous of Mme de Staël's rival reputation in this regard, he "dedicated" his *Petit Dictionnaire des grands hommes de la révolution* to her, saying that a list of the great men of the time was nothing but a list of her adorers.[9] "All France knows that it owes its greatest defenders to you, and that in seeming to sigh upon your knees, they could in fact only be smouldering with love of country. . . . It was written, Madame, that even to your lovers, all would be free in France and you have abetted this great destiny absolutely. . . ."[10] Even though she considered herself well above the other overtly political women in terms of social position—the circle of power to which she had entrée—and far above the lowly devices of women assembling together and petitioning for themselves, Mme de Staël was unable to prevent herself from being stewed together with them in the antifeminist pot. It was primarily as a woman that her political enemies could harm her, vilifying her either through allusions to her presumed lovers or by guilt-by-association with militant women.

A product of the real mob, not of that small, mannered, institutionalized mob, the salon, Théroigne de Méricourt did not adhere to Prudhomme's proposition that men are the natural representatives of women. Of Belgian origin, *la belle Liégoise* was a newcomer to the Parisian scene. She had distinguished herself by speaking eloquently in the streets and at the Jacobins' club, asking for a consultative (not a deliberative) voice for women in their discussions. This position was already a clear retreat from the earlier egalitarian *Request of the Ladies to the National Assembly* (1789), which asked for full equality with men. "You have destroyed all the ancient prejudices, but you allow the most ancient and the most general of all to survive, that which excludes from all positions, dignity, and honor, and especially from the right to sit among you, half the inhabitants of the kingdom. You have broken the scepter of despotism . . . and every day you suffer it that thirteen

---

9. We have here an early intimation of a view of her that is echoed in 1958 in the title of Herold's biography, *Mistress to an Age.*

10. Antoine de Rivarol, in Rivarol and Louis Champcenetz, *Petit Dictionnaire des grands hommes de la révolution* (Paris: Au Palais royal, De l'imprimerie nationale, 1790), pp. iv, v.

million slaves bear the chains of thirteen million despots."[11] But Théroigne's more modest request was also refused. When she tried to form an auxiliary of women in this club, she was stopped by the men, who argued that they needed "to find their houses in order when returning home."[12]

Théroigne, according to legend, was an eccentric and impressive figure, young and energetic, wearing a large-brimmed, enormously plumed Henri IV hat, pistols at her waist, and a saber at her side. Even though a number of her pronouncements expressed wider political demands than those for women only, these were not fruitful, and she drew far more attention when she pleaded to be allowed to form a troop of armed Amazons.[13] "Should men lay sole claim to the right to glory? We too wish to stake our claims to a civic crown and to the honor of dying for a freedom which is perhaps dearer to us than it is to them. . . ."[14]

This armed militant was a far cry from the model of womanhood the revolutionary left proposed: Cato's daughter Portia, Brutus's wife, who "put her pride in discretion and did not seek *in any way to rival in glory* those whose heart and destiny she shared."[15]

A caricature circulated in Paris, described in the counterrevolutionary journal *Le Petit Gautier* of February 19, 1792, depicts Théroigne and her followers: "She represents a detachment of the principal sluts who have played a prone role in the revolution. These ladies exhibit themselves to the emperor's troops to make them break ranks. . . .[16] The lady Théroigne shows them her *république*, Mesdames Staël, Dondon (Charles de Lameth), Sillery, Condorcet each show their Villette. . . . We see the army going off to its downfall."[17] Mesdames de Staël, Sillery, Lameth, and Condorcet

---

11. Léon Abensour, *Histoire générale du féminisme des origines à nos jours* (Paris: Leroux, 1923), p. 451.

12. Léopold Lacour, *Les Origines du féminisme contemporain: Trois femmes de la Révolution: Olympe de Gouges, Théroigne de Méricourt, Rose Lacombe* (Paris: Plon-Nourrit, 1900), p. 265.

13. It is striking that then as now, as with the supposed "bra-burners," a gynocratic *threat* (women as angry and violent) is automatically centered upon in the popular mind from out of a welter of feminist claims.

14. Abensour, *Histoire générale du féminisme*, p. 194.

15. Lacour, *Les Origines*, p. 204. Italics mine.

16. The verb *débander* which means literally to "uncock." The pun cannot be retained in translation.

17. Lacour, *Les Origines*, p. 272. This scurrilous image, showing Théroigne

were all known constitutionalists, but by no means of the same exact stripe. This "political commentary" gives us an idea of the nature of the attacks directed upon Mme de Staël as upon others, but she was easily the most celebrated and indecorous of the lot. Such polemics against specific women came also from the left: the author of the *Correspondance littéraire secrète* wrote that concilia- tion was made more difficult because "several women are playing a role in this great quarrel. They are Mme Condorcet, Mme Canon, Mme Staël [*sic*], Mlle Théroigne."[18] These women were in fact all opposed to Robespierre, but why their opposition should have been deemed remarkable or more harmful than anyone else's, or why they should have been lumped together, is explainable only in terms of the general misogyny and of suspicions concerning the pretensions to influence of women. It is certainly noteworthy that one specific feature of the slander from the right, the imputation of plot or associations among women, was accepted wholly by the left. The right remained more personally vindictive, however; the left, more moralistic and proscriptive toward women in general.

François Suleau, scurrilous antirevolutionary publicist, at- tacked such women as Théroigne and Mme de Staël, both of whom, high- and low-born together, were for him *phrynés*—that is, women who, like the Greek courtesans, lived an irregular life, who used "the tyranny of their charms, the seductiveness of their graces, the liveliness of their minds" to the end of "political in- fluence."[19] Suleau made "Talleyrand" write of his intimate devo- tion to the Baroness and had him say that if "the destiny of France

---

(who had no known lovers) exhibiting her sex, is also one of the earliest depic- tions of Mme de Staël as a man-woman, for the Marquis de Villette, whose *moeurs* were suspect, had branded himself definitively as less than a man by making a public defense of the rights of prostitutes and illegitimate children.

18. Lacour, *Les Origines*, p. 272.

19. François Louis Suleau, *Journal* (Paris: Niewied sur le Rhin; and Paris: rue de Seine, 1791–92), pp. 29, 31. Now, it is evident that the virulence of revolution- ary polemics was by no means confined to scurrilous attacks on women. The *Actes des Apôtres* regularly "ridiculed its adversaries by mocking their physical infirmities, their real or suppositious marital misfortunes, alterations in their pri- vate or public life, insisting especially on any possibly pornographic or scatologi- cal aspects." Pierre Albert and Fernand Terrou, *Histoire de la press française des origines à 1814* (Paris: Presses Universitaires Françaises, 1969), p. 476. Nonetheless, the precise flavor of the abuse directed at Mme de Staël illuminates the response to the world that we find in her work.

was once attached to the maidenhead of a girl from Lorraine, the Genevan had proven there was more than one way to save an Empire."[20] In mocking La Fayette, whom he abominated, Suleau advised him that he deserved to be crowned, for his betrayal of the monarchy, with flowers from "the bouquet of [Mme de Staël's] virtuous mother. . . . Leave to Mme de Staal [sic] the care of choosing your laurels; since you wish to be covered with infamy, it is not to subaltern prostitutes that you should give the composition of your garland."[21]

Over and over in these polemics Mme de Staël's name is associated with that of Théroigne de Méricourt, even though there is no known record of any such tie. Clearly such a link was not really needed for a convenient association of ideas to spring up: women who mixed in public affairs must be public women, and they could only be plotting together to contest the supremacy of masculine power prerogatives. That there was no real kinship whatever between the opportunist militant Théroigne and the humanistic opportunist Mme de Staël did not matter. Neither would be spared in the outburst of misogyny occasioned by their surfacing to occupy themselves with public concerns and hence occasioning public notice. A historian who sought diligently to find a single "serious response" of the sort solicited by Condorcet in his defense of the rights of women was able to produce only one article in which the place of women was treated without mockery: in it women were reproved for having been unable to bear "that imposing and masculine spectacle" of decapitations and heads mounted on pikes, and so, it therefore concluded, "the agitations of the rostrum are not at all appropriate to the female sex."[22]

If this were to be the moral, Théroigne de Méricourt's fate provided an exemplary echo of it. She was to provide the occasion of the slaughter of her slanderous enemy Suleau by the mob at the Tuileries on August 10, 1792, as she accosted him in that public place and remonstrated in her rousing way against him, taking him

20. Suleau, *Journal*, "Les Pâques de M. Suleau," p. 11.

21. Suleau, *Journal*, I, "Introduction," p. 21.

22. Alphonse Aulard, "Le Féminisme pendant la révolution française," *La Revue Bleue*, Mar. 19, 1898, p. 362. (Quoting from *Révolutions de Paris*, Feb., 1791.)

by the collar. There was a coda even to this atrocity. Having understood that the Jacobins would not respond to her claims for
women, Théroigne turned from Robespierre to the moderate Brissot, but after she had made a public appeal on Brissot's behalf on
May 31, 1793, the Jacobin women, enraged by her "betrayal," attacked her as she walked about the Terrasse des Feuillants. There
they whipped her and raised her skirts as if in a mime of one of
the most scurrilous masculine attacks launched against her (that of
the *Petit Gautier cartoon*)[23] (see Plate 2). Strange to say, it was
Marat, no friend to militant women, who intervened to save her
from a fate that threatened to parallel Suleau's exactly. As it was,
her political fortunes were at an end, for she succumbed to madness
in 1794. One of her last semilucid acts was to write a letter to
Saint-Just in which she insisted, "I must absolutely be respected,
for there are no means of debasing me that are not used against
me."[24] Théroigne's story—like that of Hypatia of Alexandria—
reminds women at what cost they may presume to full humanity.

Thus ended the brief association in the public mind of
Théroigne with Mme de Staël. However, in our attempt to comprehend Mme de Staël's spirit we cannot dismiss the effects such im-
putations of "suspicious connections," her contamination by them,
may have had upon her. Her moral dilemmas could only be exacerbated by the nature of the hatred arrayed against her, with
its multiple layers of resentment against a rich, sexually adventurous, intellectual, and political woman. One effect was the awakening in her of a consciousness of a whole new order of problems she
had been quite indifferent to heretofore, and an identification with

---

23. Michelet (*Les Femmes de la Révolution*, ed. Pierre Labracherie, Pierre
Dumont, and P. Bessand-Massenet [Paris: Hachette, 1960]), an excellent source
for mythic interpretation, repeats the tale that she was attacked by men and
that her subsequent madness was instantaneous. His version is repeated by
Lamartine and by the Goncourts, but the police record, according to Lacour (see
Les Origines, p. 203), does not appear to support this. Without further docu-
mentary evidence, we are made to ascribe this act to the women, but whether
they were actually goaded to their violence by men or whether they acted "on
their own," they played out a male form of rage to women by undressing their
female victim and making her out a harlot. Lacour is not sentimental about
Théroigne's madness and even posits a possible venereal cause for it.

24. Lacour, *Les Origines*, p. 306.

2. This engraving of "a woman of standing being whipped for having spat upon M. Necker's portrait" in the year 1789 shows us that Théroigne de Méricourt's adventure was not unique. Artist unknown. Bibliothèque Nationale, Cabinet des Estampes.

other women emerged with which she would grapple repeatedly, though rarely satisfactorily, in all her remaining works. Setting herself above her sex was her preferred posture. This solution alone, allowing her personal realization, did not call into question the basic power arrangements in a society that sometimes seemed so congenial to her as to be her playground. But Revolutionary society was evolving new forms and rejected the role she had expected to play—the preponderant role of the aristocratic woman—that of broker, by virtue of her sexual powers and graces, to society. While doing so, the Revolution proposed no alternative role except a punitively sober return to private life. Olympe de Gouges pleaded prophetically with the women, asking: "Oh women, women, when will you cease to be blind? What are the advantages you have gained from the Revolution? A more marked scorn, a more overt disdain. Through centuries of corruption you have reigned only over men's weakness. Your reign has been destroyed; what then is left to you? The conviction of the injustice of men."[25] As she was sent for her rebellious clairvoyance to her execution in 1794, she is said to have declared: "Fatal desire for fame, I wanted to be something." Germaine de Staël also wanted to "be something." How was a woman to manage her desire for fame, if she had one, in a time that demanded great shows of character but was so determinedly uncongenial to them as they appeared in women?

The full measure of this paradox is to be found in the article of the newspaper *Le Moniteur* commenting upon the career of Mme Roland ("Liberty, what crimes are committed in thy name!"), the Girondists' remarkable writer and orator, after her execution in November of 1793:

The Roland woman, a wit with great pretensions, miniature philosopher, queen of a moment, surrounded by mercenary writers she gave suppers for, distributing favors, positions, and money to them, was a monster in every sense. Her scornful posture toward the people and the judges chosen to represent them, the prideful stubbornness of her responses, her ironical gaiety, and that firmness she paraded before one and all in her passage from the Palace of Justice to the Revolutionary Square prove that no painful memory preoccupied her. Nonetheless, she was a mother; but she sacrificed

---

25. Marie Olympe de Gouges, *Déclaration des droits de la femme et de la citoyenne* (Paris, [1791?]), p. 12.

nature in wanting to rise above herself; the desire to be learned led her to a forgetfulness of the virtues of her sex, and this forgetfulness, always dangerous, ended up by causing her to perish on the scaffold.[26]

If Mme Roland, whose virtue, unlike Mme de Staël's, was not so seriously in question, had lost her claim to veneration as a mother in trying to be more than a woman should be, what of Germaine de Staël?

Before she had taken leave of Narbonne and returned to the Continent from England, Mme de Staël had written a cryptic page in which she referred less obliquely to her reputation than was her wont: "Although my name has often been pronounced in those political libels that for years have slandered all whose names might be known in France, I have consistently refused to defend myself, either out of pride or because hatred even of the most reprehensible kind has the power to frighten young and gentle souls, or because a character that is genuine and artless cannot consent to see itself misconstrued." Consequently, she set herself to the writing of a work devoid of party and national interests, the *Passions*. "I do not know," she continued,

whether the political ideas I have been presumed to have will be injurious to the judgment that will be made of this work; however, I cannot believe that in a country like England anyone would imagine that the opinions of a few young women could be placed in the category of causes for a revolution that the ages have prepared and that twenty-four million men willed, of a revolution whose value remains, though sullied with each passing day by the most atrocious inhumanity. I do not know whether the defects or the qualities of a woman could find a place in any part of such a history; he who would believe in her influence has traced the progress of the French Revolution nowhere but in the balls and soirées of Paris.[27]

This odd page is the only direct confrontation of slander. It combines a sage perspective with some deference and some scorn. Of course she is mainly in the right: her influence on the course of events was, especially as compared with her notoriety, exceedingly small, and the direct effect of women upon the Revolution was certainly restricted. Yet there is more than a little disingenuity

---

26. Quoted by Eugène Géruzez, *Histoire de la littérature française pendant la révolution* (Paris: Didier, 1881), p. 157.

27. *Choix de lettres*, pp. 220–21.

in her near-disclaimer to holding an opinion and her pretense to being, *qua* woman, an entirely private person, devoid of any political—that is to say dangerous—ideas.

Love, Guilt, and Sense of Self

The unstable and unenviable place of women in her society is the backdrop of Germaine's desperate attempt to fuse Louis de Narbonne's fate with her own, to provide herself with an emotional fortress from which to act, an asylum to which to repair. As the major women who openly sought an active role in the reborn state were destroyed one by one, the more fortunate and less courageous Mme de Staël was able to escape such ravages. But she could not escape the condition of women in her time, whatever her privilege, and this condition, even on the emotional plane to which she had withdrawn "willingly," as she thought, was a torment. Having absurdly and credulously believed she could keep her shallow but comely lover, follow him to exile, start anew, and put the vital disaffection of her *mariage de raison* behind her, she was compelled to move on, to recognize her own inability to forge a life on anything akin to her own terms, to know impotence deeply, no matter what her individual and even her worldly powers: "I . . . am good only for giving my life, for serving others far more than pleasing them, for giving myself to another far more than for captivating him."[28] Accept though she might the system where women's empire is to please, she was, even within it, a loser whose aspect and character were not natural attractions but rather repelled masculine devotion. Her virtual mania to be of service to everyone and her seemingly abject willingness to accede to a lover's demands reflected her anxious fear of rejection.

Narbonne remained away so long that, anxiety, guilt, and wrath mounting, Germaine finally found a reassuring alternative to her anxiety in the attentions of young Adolphe, Count Ribbing,

---

28. *Correspondance générale*, II, 269. Jean Starobinski speaks cogently, in confirmation of her language here, of Mme de Staël's mode of loving as "an expansive impulse, a devotion, a generous gift [of self] indissolubly linked with a capture" of the beloved, an attempt to recreate and hold a primal harmony. See "Suicide et mélancolie chez Madame de Staël," *Colloque de Coppet*, pp. 244–45.

the Swedish regicide exile, an appealingly romantic figure to her. Ribbing was handsome in the style that most attracted her, of proud, military, aristocratic refinement, and his intense suit was flattering balm to her dejected hopes. In fact, when Ribbing replaced Narbonne as lover, she invested him as well with her displaced hopes—of divorce and remarriage, of establishing together with him a political career in Paris. Yet she suspected, even at the outset, that his love would prove as doomed as the earlier one: "No, my Adolphe—even in his relations with a woman—can be no ordinary man. He must be truer, more faithful than anyone so that there should be no discord in so harmonious a character." The very intensity of her grasping at love, her fear of a rejection that meant chaos to her, even here when still young and desired, was a common element in the tendency of her lovers, no single one of whom had anything like a similar gift to hers for sustained passion, to withdraw. In her attempt to seal Ribbing's love through a sense of his conquest, she significantly portrayed herself as his trophy in an obviously sexual image: "Yes, I love you, and you doubt it no longer. There has been combat, you have triumphed, and I am the victor's chariot. Our roles are exchanged, but treat me gently in my new slavery. You do not know what bond you have contracted . . . and you have seen how constant is my heart.[29] Ah, if for so long it refused to let itself love only you, who will detach it from you?"[30]

Clinging to her need for a sense of feminine self-renunciation in love, she was, willy-nilly, more lucid than she had been. When writing to Ribbing about her dying mother's good fortune in ending her life within her husband's embrace, she foresaw herself dying alone: "When the first glow has passed, you will remember my wrongs: and all my feeling for you, and all the expression I give to it, will but remind you of them. . . . Ah! I love you, but I know neither the risk nor the happiness of an illusion."[31] Even this was not entirely true. Much as she foresaw the ending of their love, she

---

29. She had resisted Ribbing for months, hoping Narbonne might relent.
30. Anne-Louise Germaine Necker de Staël, *Lettres de Madame de Staël à Ribbing*, ed. Simone Balayé (Paris: Gallimard, 1960), pp. 80–82 (Apr. 29, 1794).
31. *Lettres à Ribbing*, pp. 87–92 (May 3, 1794).

could not prevent herself from indulging her habit of delusion. "She slid toward more republican opinions out of love for Ribbing, out of desire to find a regime of freedom where she would be allowed to live openly with him and where he himself would find a career worthy of his talents."[32] She needed to believe in the permanence of her feelings, even as she knew them to be transitory.

Implicit in such an immensity of value placed upon love and upon the lover is the relative devaluation of self. It was not by chance alone that Mme de Staël felt herself compelled to take another lover while her mother lay felled by mortal illness. In the face of her mother's ultimate betrayal—by death—and her reiterated rejection of Germaine's behavior coupled with her admonitions to return to a straight path, flight into the promised land of passion proved virtually unavoidable, but the web of death and this trumped-up love left her dejected and alienated. In writing to Ribbing of the massacre of so many she had known, she expressed the link that this personal mood had with the parlous temper of the time: "How can I flatter myself that I can live and be happy, even in seeing you? How have I deserved a lot so different from theirs?"[33]

The converse of her sense of her nothingness was that megalomaniacal delusion that replaced it—that she was remarkable, unique—a view in which she was to continue to be sustained by a band of sycophants and by her loving father. His support above all was to be providential, for it permitted her to surmount the recurrent, nullifying suicidal trend in her nature.

Already, in September, 1794, she had met Benjamin Constant, of whom she wrote to Ribbing that he was "not too distinguished a figure, but singularly witty." By October she reported that he had fallen in love with "your Minette."[34] Constant, unlike Ribbing and Narbonne, never appealed a quarter as much to Germaine's senses as to her mind: she confided to a friend very early in their acquaintance, "I feel that this man would inspire me with an in-

---

32. *Lettres à Ribbing*, p. 20 (from the Balayé introduction).
33. *Lettres à Ribbing*, pp. 87–92 (May 3, 1794).
34. She was called Louise in childhood, but Minette was the name by which Mme de Staël was known to her intimates in adult life.

vincible physical antipathy."[35] Despite the well-documented hysterical scenes in which he indulged, threatening to die if she would
not love him, Constant's physical charm was simply too effaced for
her more heroic tastes. Far into the year 1795 she put Benjamin off
continually, hoping Ribbing would still fall in with her desires.
When March, 1796, came she pleaded with him either to join her
or to tell her he loved her no longer. Already deeply involved with
Mme de Valence, Ribbing did the latter.

Constant's continuing unsatisfactoriness is further evidenced
in Germaine's unrequited passion, in 1795, for the truly gifted and
touching Chevalier François de Pange, a dedicated revolutionist
despite his aristocratic origin, with a thoughtful, questing intellect.
Author and printer, Pange was a reserved man, in precarious health.
A month before his death in 1796, Mme de Staël wrote him that he
was "the only man who has made me understand that it was possible to love without expecting as much in return."[36] The double
disappointment of Ribbing's abandonment and her inability to
make herself lovable to Pange gave Constant his opportunity. He
alone, whom she loved less, was prepared to go to Paris and play
the game of politics with her. For behind the facade of love the need
to play a larger role always lurked. Love and power were inex-
tricably linked together for her. In her years with Benjamin this
link would be sundered.

Politics and Literature

Women had finally been denied all rights of participation in
the political clubs in 1793. In March, 1795, the Convention told
them categorically that they should stay home. Two months afterward, in May, 1795, Germaine and Benjamin reached Paris. Published there just in advance of their arrival was the pamphlet *Reflections on Peace Addressed to M. Pitt*, which she and Benjamin
had worked out together, a political project designed to consolidate
revolutionary gains by a program of peace. The first among the

---

35. See Herold, *Mistress*, p. 155.
36. Quoted in Herold, *Mistress*, p. 171. Their love affair has been touchingly
reconstructed by the Countess Jean de Pange, descendant by marriage of Pange
and by birth of Mme de Staël, through her daughter's line. See her *Madame de
Staël et François de Pange* (Paris: Plon-Nourrit, 1925).

ambassadors to have resumed diplomatic relations with the French Republic, M. de Staël was again in favor, and his wife's salon resumed its importance as a place where people of the most divergent views could meet and where politics was the bread and meat of the assemblage. Mme de Staël, as before, acted as angel, maecenas, second, but this time it was via Constant's reputation rather than Narbonne's that power was wielded—with the heartening difference that the man on whose behalf she acted was at last her intellectual peer. Although hounded by left and right alike—France, she said, was a "democratic republic where one risks being stoned if one is not for the aristocrats"[37]—Germaine and Benjamin worked harmoniously as a team in the years before Napoleon's rise. A temperamental team it was surely, but capable of writing tracts and planning strategy together. They argued their cause of constitutionality separately with zeal, courted and cajoled those in power, and very nearly succeeded: Benjamin became a tribune under the Consulate, only to be, as Germaine put it, "creamed off" in Napoleon's purification of his critics in 1802. So far did they succeed, in fact, that the Convention, and later the Consul, came to regard them, and more specifically Germaine, as a threat. She was constrained by him to repair to the charming lakeside Swiss château of Coppet that meant nothing but annihilation to her, representing as it did enforced exile from the vital milieu of her life that was Paris—"The Universe is France; outside it there is nothing. . . ,"[38] she asserted. There again, as in her previous exile, she was to return to literature, ever a poor second choice, resorted to when she was frustrated in her active life, no doubt because introspection terrified her. Her work on the *Passions* was, withal, a political act in the sense that it was intended to prove that she was *not* a political animal.

When Mme de Staël wrote her *Delphine*, then, it was by no means as if she were simply a "lady novelist" like Mme de Duras, Mme Cottin, or Mme de Krüdener. To the crime of her amorous irregularities she had added that of having presumed to have ideas worthy of enactment and of scheming, *like a man,* to see that they

---

37. Herold, *Mistress*, p. 175.
38. Herold, *Mistress*, p. 168.

were realized. Even in her withdrawal from the political scene, she had dared to write serious, *ergo* "masculine" works on the *Passions* and now *On Literature* (1800), a far more pondered and ambitious book that was taken into serious account by both friends and foes. Had not Goethe himself translated her *Essay on Fiction:* he and Schiller taken great interest in the *Passions*? She was therefore a natural butt not only for the misogyny of those men so inclined, but also for resentful women, of whom there were not a few in a system which repressed all significant forms of feminine enterprise. The "monstrous outflow of wrath and slander against her, dating from 1789"[39] went on. The *Quotidienne* in 1797 printed this cruel portrait: "Mme de Staël, born devoid of grace, with no nobility, has not compensated for this lack by the least effort of her own. Her bearing has no dignity, her tone no distinction, her gaiety no nuance, her aspect no appeal. Her conversation is peremptory, her dress careless, her look brazen, her amorous leanings depraved . . . there is not the least measure either in her ideas or in their expression. . . ."[40] The newspaper *Le Peuple* continued the battle late into the nineties: "It is not your fault if you are ugly, but it is your fault if you are an intriguer. You know the road to Switzerland. Take it with your Benjamin!"[41] Bertin d'Antilly had contradictory advice; in 1797 he exhorted her, "Sweden claims you. Your conjugal duties await you." The *Ami des lois* was not slow to express its exasperation (July 8, 1799): "No extraordinary event ever occurs in Paris without Mme de Staël being mixed up in it. She has played a scandalous part in all the calamitous periods of the Revolution. She is a crow who sometimes comes to perch in the Tuileries, sometimes in the Luxembourg, and who always announces something sinister by her croakings. One ends up chasing her off and she incessantly finds some means of coming back."[42]

---

39. André Le Breton, *Le Roman français au 19e siècle, Ière Partie: Avant Balzac* (Paris: Boivin, 1901), p. 120. I gratefully acknowledge my debt to Le Breton's discussion of *Delphine* for leading me to explore the influence of slander upon Mme de Staël more deeply.

40. No. 468, le 18 Thermidor, an V (Aug. 5, 1797), "Variétés," p. 16.

41. Quoted by Françoise d'Eaubonne, *Une Femme témoin de son siècle* (Paris: Flammarion, 1966), p. 19.

42. As quoted by J. Viénot in his edition of Mme de Staël's *Des Circonstances actuelles qui peuvent terminer la Révolution* (Paris: Fischbacker, 1902), pp. lii-liii.

Amazingly, considering her daring, Mme de Staël had the thinnest of skins. As a writer, every time she took pen in hand it was with trepidation, and, as a novelist, in writing the "kind of confession" she took the novel to be, so much the more, for she would inevitably reveal vulnerabilities her public would avidly seize upon. "Of all literary works, novels are the ones that have the most judges," she began her preface to *Delphine*, trying to ward off the ready-to-pounce, parrying their thrust by her demonstration that she knew what they were about. Nearly no one feels incompetent, she wryly noted, to judge a novel. She also professed her fear that she might have written a bad novel; much of literary criticism would reply that her fears were fully justified. Souriau, for example, wrote:

Delphine belongs to that collection of celebrated works of which we know nothing but the title. We rediscover in it, with no pleasure, reminiscences of *Clarissa Harlowe*, or *La Novelle Héloïse*, of *Werther* especially, for one might say without too much severity that Delphine is a female Werther. Its style itself has something exotic about it, say her contemporaries: they find it resembles German translated into French (Bardoux). One of her "compatriots"[43] goes farther: recognizing that in general Mme de Staël wrote badly, he confesses that she wrote her *Delphine* especially badly (Kohler). [44]

We are in the presence of a novel that has aroused a good deal of hostility, both at the time of its appearance and since: that it aroused great admiration in her contemporaries has left succeeding generations quite unmoved.

Like *Werther*, of course, *Delphine* was written under the sign of sensibility. Events, Mme de Staël explains in her preface, interest her only insofar as they teach something about the human heart. She will have the courage to be open, as people in a wicked and closed society feel they cannot be. "Let us not . . . esteem novels unless they partake of the nature of a confession wrested from those

---

43. The disingenuous attacks upon Mme de Staël's language, and therefore upon her, as being un-French belong to the melancholy saga of French xenophobia. See, on the struggle of this Parisian to establish her nationality, Simone Balayé's essay, "La Nationalité de Mme de Staël," in *Humanisme actif. Mélanges d'art et de littérature offerts à Julien Cain*, 2 vols. (Paris: Hermann-Spes, 1967), I, 73–85.

44. M. Souriau, *Histoire du romantisme en France* (Paris: Spes, 1927), p. 116.

who live and will live" (v, xl). She speaks of the novel as explaining via our nature the mysteries of our destiny, and in answer to those who would call her deluded to believe in love, in ethics, in the soul she cries feelingly, "What would you have us put in their place?" Life, so fleeting, can teach us less about lasting truth than does fiction. The only species of imagination she truly credits in her conception of the novel is the moral imagination, that "force which ever tends toward the truth" (v, xlviii). Her openly didactic effort will be bent to appealing to this Rousseauesque inner voice. As to her style, she claims to have tried to steer it between the shoals of commonness and artifice: What she strives for is *"le naturel."* She condemns the French novel of her time for its "sterility, coldness, and monotony," and it is rather to the English novel that she has looked for an antidote.

In apparent recognition of her own defensiveness, she says she does not know whether her remarks will be construed as an apology or a critique of the "correspondence" she is about to publish, but she dares to hope that its own characters will be the center of her readers' attention rather than any political consideration. In a sort of apostrophe that prefigures Stendhal's *To the Happy Few*, she reveals that hers is a gamble directed over the Consul's head. "I believe that those writers who, wishing to express what they deem good and true, defy all-too-predictable judgments, must choose their public." They address themselves to that part of France that is silent but enlightened, to the future rather than to the present, perhaps to a more reflective foreign audience, but she summons such nonconformist writers as herself to recall the scornful words of Virgil to Dante as they cross the circle of the mediocre whose lives were lived out in a passion of hatred:

> Fama di loro il mondo esser non lassa,
>
> . . . .
>
> Non ragionam di lor; ma guarda e passa.
>
> The world has not kept even the memory of their names.
>
> . . . .
>
> Let us not stop to speak of them; but look and pass on.

A defiant enough beginning for her novel, whose famous epigraph, drawn, significantly, from her mother's *Mélanges,* "Un homme doit savoir braver l'opinion, une femme s'y soumettre— A man must be able to defy convention, a woman to submit to it," also arouses the reader's curiosity, introducing as it does the work of a woman one might otherwise have imagined to be rather grandiosely unsubmissive.

CHAPTER 4

Delphine—The Failure of Nostalgia

... liberty and chivalry entice her equally.
CHAMISSO

It was not for her writings or her convictions that she had been attacked: "They attacked her where she was vulnerable, her foibles, the miseries of her life, her imprudences, her failures, her tactlessness, her noisily advertised sentimentalities, her thirst for success, her dance, her turban, her court of wits, the parade of her cicisbei and the supposed prodigality of her favors."[1] Is it the woman in herself that Mme de Staël defends in *Delphine?* While that may be, in it she also takes up the defense of woman herself. "It will take me many years to completely repress my heart," she wrote a friend, adding, "I am continuing my *novel* and it is the story of the destiny of women presented in various ways."[2] Perhaps it was to show herself womanly that she wrote this complex novel, but its basic function was to defend her very being, which had been called into question. Although on many counts this is a defensive work, by a dialectical process we can perceive that it is also an offensive and, in some ways, a courageous one. And, as a study of woman in aristocratic society, it is a novel of exploration. It was said that not since *La Princesse de Clèves* had such a worldling of a woman written about society.

Written in 1801–2, *Delphine* is set in the period from April, 1790, to September, 1792. The significance of this era in Mme de Staël's personal life—that of her love for Narbonne—gives the novel its specific emotional and political coloration. Sainte-Beuve justly found it a work that hearkened nostalgically to the graces of pre-Revolutionary aristocratic existence. It looks backward for

---

1. Albert Sorel, *Madame de Staël* (Paris: Hachette, 1890), as quoted by André Le Breton, *Le Roman français*, p. 122.
2. Letter 136, to Mme de Pastoret, *Choix de lettres*, p. 181.

its very form: "*Delphine* . . . belongs to the great series of novels-in-letters derived from *Clarissa Harlowe* with the extenuating circumstance that it is the last."[3] Mme de Staël's novelist contemporaries, like Restif de la Bretonne and Mme de Genlis, had discarded the often clumsy epistolary conception of the novel. Mme de Staël instead sought it out, insisted upon it. Were not the *Nouvelle Héloïse* and *Werther* letter-novels, exemplars of that form? But Le Breton, in some ways the most lucid of her critics, finds far inferior models to have served her by providing her with scenes of unbearable melodramatic absurdity. He thereby abstracts, as is so often the case with our fawning treatment of the acknowledged "greats," Rousseau's and Goethe's own pre-Romantic excesses of rhetoric and action.

Some Sentimental Conventions

It is not amiss, in setting the mood of *Delphine,* to evoke the climate of expression in which Mme de Staël moved and had to find her own voice.

In the *Nouvelle Héloïse* Julie writes to her lover Saint-Preux of her marriage: "At the very moment when I was prepared to swear eternal fidelity to another, my heart still swore an eternal love to you, and I was led to the temple like an impure victim who sullies the sacrifice in which it is immolated.

"At the church, upon entering it I felt the kind of emotion I had never known. I know not what terror came and seized my soul in this simple and august place, filled with the majesty of Him who is served there."[4]

Mme de Staël will use identical elephantine ironies and will be equally attracted by the sensual charge of criminal love. She will be no less preachy than Rousseau and will share his diffuse religiosity. Her language will suffer from a similar pomposity— "majesty," "impure victim," "simple and august," "eternal love"— and generality, a groping for precision not arrived at—the "I know

---

3. Charles-Augustin de Sainte-Beuve, "Dix-neuvième Siècle, Madame de Staël," in *Les Grands Ecrivains français,* ed. Maurice Allem (Paris: Garnier, 1932), p. 51.

4. Jean-Jacques Rousseau, *La Nouvelle Héloïse,* ed. René Pomeau (Paris: Garnier, 1960), p. 332.

not what's," the "kinds of." But she will be less moralistic and ultimately less obsessive than Rousseau.

From Goethe, Mme de Staël borrows a cornerstone of *Delphine*: the sense of the mystery of human nature or, as Goethe has it, that the heart of man is inexplicable. "Oh, how unpredictable is the human heart!" cries Delphine. Goethe embodies this mystery in a hero who is, much as her heroine will be, pretentiously, inexhaustibly, lovable: "I am already very much known and beloved by all the common people here, particularly the children," writes Werther. Like Delphine, he is prone to bouts of sensibility and self-indulgent toward his adulterous impulses. He experiences himself as guiltless but, even as Delphine is moved to do, at moments he feels some small doubt about the wholeness of his innocence. "Surely I am innocent; yet perhaps not entirely so. . . . My heart is like a sick child; and like a sick child I let it have its way." Yet he gives way to remorse: "I know I should be blamed for it." Werther, like Delphine, in fact wallows in grief to a point of extreme pleasure, and his conception of love is identical to that of Mme de Staël's heroine. It was his departed beloved, he pines, who "made me all that I am capable of being."[5] Yet, much though Delphine may be a feminine Werther, the novel *Delphine* is by no means a feminine *Werther*.

Mme de Staël enormously admired William Godwin's novel *Caleb Williams or Things as They Are*, which had appeared in 1794. Should we be tempted to see Mme de Staël as extraordinarily doloristic, or possessed of a unique persecution mania, it is rectifying to read the first paragraph of that novel.

My life has for several years been a theatre of calamity. I have been a mark for the vigilance of tyranny and could not escape. My fairest prospects have been blasted. My enemy has shown himself inaccessible to entreaties and untried in persecution. My fame, as well as my happiness, has become his victim. Everyone, as far as my story has been known, has refused to assist me in my distress, and has execrated my name. I have not deserved this treatment.[6]

---

5. Johann von Goethe, *The Sorrows of Werther* (London: Blake, 1825).

6. William Godwin, *The Adventures of Caleb Williams; or Things as They Are* (London: Richard Bentley, 1849), p. 1.

François-René de Chateaubriand, with whom Mme de Staël was equated in their lifetime (and is still, in literary history) is now universally considered a far greater novelist than his female contemporary. We have only to examine some paragraphs of his *Atala* (1801) to find numerous rhetorical parallels between the two. His heroine, who had sworn to her dying mother to remain chaste, is increasingly tortured by this vow in her love for Chactas and takes poison to avoid her inevitable betrayal of it. She cries out to her lover and the missionary, "Now that I am to be engulfed by eternity . . . at this moment of joyfully seeing my virginity devour my life—even so . . . I bear off with me a regret at not having been yours! . . . 'My daughter,' interrupted the missionary, 'your sorrow leads you astray. This excess of passion to which you give yourself is rarely justified, it does not even exist in nature; and in this sense . . . [it is] something vicious in the heart.' " The missionary then tells Atala she might have been forgiven a lapse from her vow of chastity. " 'It is too late . . . ,' she cried. 'Must I die at the moment I discover I might have been happy! . . . Today, what bliss I would enjoy, with a Christian Chactas . . . consoled, reassured by this august old man . . . forever . . . !'"[7]

Mme de Staël shares with Chateaubriand the pre-Romantic addiction to the apostrophe. She will, though in a different spirit, similarly enjoy titillating the reader's senses in the play of passion and chastity in her novel. Naturally, fatal love is an ideal for both, despite the lip-service, here Catholic, there Protestant-Deist, that is paid those tedious tyrants sanity and regularity. Chateaubriand's moralism is—if not greater—at least as pronounced as Mme de Staël's. And melodrama provides for both the essential ambience of the novel.

A last apposite sample of mood and convention in the period from 1790 to 1810 is the statement of a young widow who offered herself and 40,000 pounds of income to Robespierre, saying, "You are my supreme divinity. I know no other on earth but you. I look upon you as my guardian angel and wish to live only according

---

7. François Auguste René de Chateaubriand, *Oeuvres complètes*, 27 vols. (Paris: Ladvocat, 1826–31), XVI, 97–99.

to your laws."[8] Here is the flavor of the master-slave mentality as it was assumed by some women of exalted nature and the inflated terminology in which it was licit to express it. In this excess of self-abasement we find the very model of the time's conception of female love, that with which Mme de Staël grapples in her novel.

As a novel, *Delphine* is utterly a creature of the social and literary conventions that spawned it. It makes no pretense to being anything else. In fact, it wills itself to be as conventional as possible. It is this tidal pull of society that draws the heroine inexorably to it, even as she is seemingly tossed off by its swirling eddies, that is the novel's medium. And society here is a force, an uncontrollable, irrational, destructive, counter-natural force.

Delphine: The Story

The young widow of the old and wealthy M. d'Albémar, Delphine has been raised, like her author, in accordance with the *philosophes*' ideas, to trust her heart, which is exceedingly kind, and her mind, which is liberal. She lives a contented life as lioness of an aristocratic circle. Delphine has just given a dowry to her remote cousin Matilde de Vernon, whose mother, Sophie, has a strong hold upon Delphine through her worldly grace and charm. In spite of this, even before she has ever set eyes upon him, our heroine falls in love with Matilde's intended husband, Léonce de Mondoville, and he comes to return her passionate attachment. Though Delphine wants to explain to Mme de Vernon that this has happened, the older woman constantly and skillfully puts her off. When, finally, Delphine insists and manages to tell her of her love for Léonce, Sophie appears to embrace her feelings fully, even promising that she herself will go to Léonce and speak to him on Delphine's behalf. Meanwhile, Delphine has compromised her reputation by harboring in her house a friend, Thérèse d'Ervins, whose lover, the Italian M. de Serbellane, has come to say a final goodbye. In the midst of their interview, Thérèse's enraged husband arrives and there is a duel in which M. d'Ervins dies. The news that Serbellane has killed Ervins for Delphine's favors rocks

8. Albert Guillois, *Etude médico-psychologique d'Olympe de Gouges* (Lyon: Rey, 1904), p. 75.

Paris. Léonce de Mondoville, as it happens, is a man whose greatest defect is his dependence upon public opinion, and he cannot help suspecting Delphine. Perfidiously, Sophie has only to play upon this tendency to induce Léonce to pursue his original plan of marrying Matilde. As Léonce later discovers that he has been tricked, his marriage becomes hateful to him. Inconsolable, he tortures the gifted, beautiful, virtuous Delphine by insisting that he cannot live without continuing to see her; however, he will not renounce Matilde out of fear for his reputation. Delphine, on her side, is too good-hearted to wish to make the innocent but highly disagreeable Matilde unhappy. A phase of anguish over the physical deprivation of Léonce's passion for her ends in Delphine's contracting brain fever. Subdued, Léonce accepts a platonic relationship, and the "pure" liaison continues, tongues wag, and Matilde must be the only woman in Paris not to know of it. When Matilde is about to give birth to a child, she learns from Delphine herself of her continuing love for her husband. Once again the too-soft-hearted heroine had given shelter in her home, this time to an unwanted suitor, M. de Valorbe, a man in danger of political arrest. The ever-suspicious Léonce and he have been seen quarreling before her door, and this tale circles the town. Her love having been revealed to Matilde and her reputation at low ebb, Delphine flees Paris for Lausanne so that her lover will not find her.

Valorbe follows Delphine who, to save herself from him, goes to a Swiss nunnery whose Mother Superior is Léonce's aunt, Léontine de Ternan. The villainous Valorbe tricks Delphine into coming out of the convent to save him from imprisonment and compromises her reputation. His threats enable the wily Mother Superior to force Delphine to take her nun's vows. Both Matilde and her child having died, Léonce hastens off to seek Delphine, but finds her too late to prevent her from taking the veil. In the original ending Mme de Staël gave to her novel, Léonce runs away to war and Delphine, breaking her vows, follows him, eventually taking poison just before he is shot by a firing squad. In an alternate ending Mme de Staël later affixed to the work to replace the original and much condemned suicide, Léonce and Delphine instead go off together, despite her vows, to Mondoville, Léonce's ancestral home. There he cannot bring himself to marry the runaway nun and thus dishonor the family's name. Delphine, sick at heart, dies, and Léonce goes off to battle to let himself be killed.

Dichotomies and Questions

The apologia that is *Delphine* evolves out of a series of attempts to confront basic questions. The prime one is the nature and role of woman in society, but linked indissolubly with it are questions concerning the character of love; of marriage and divorce (developed both novelistically and didactically through the actions and expositions of several couples); of evil and good, guilt and innocence; of reason versus passion, repression versus freedom; of Catholicism versus natural religion; and, last, the question of suicide.

Mothers and Daughters

Society expresses itself in the world of the salon in *Delphine*, and the world of the salon for Mme de Staël was originally, and was to remain for her, her mother's world. *Delphine* is a work written deferentially, apologetically, in propitiation of Suzanne Necker: the calculation and moralism that reprove Delphine in the novel represent, for Mme de Staël, not only the reproof of society but her own mother's reproof of her. The self-containment and the repression of her vitality that society would have liked to impose upon Delphine to make her truly acceptable to it are the same correctives Mme Necker endlessly tried to influence Germaine to apply to herself.

The social sphere—that of interpersonal relationships—is the one in which women dominate, even though its edicts must conform to the masculine code. It is this code that is the boundary of *Delphine*: it decrees that there be no conceivable femininity other than that which accords preeminence to men. Within this compass, *Delphine* will present in her heroine Mme de Staël's own personal conception of femininity from her youth,[9] and yet challenge it many times over. The prime challenge comes from the hero, Léonce, who internalizes society's view of proper conduct,

---

9. Mme Necker de Saussure tells us this: "Corinne est l'idéal de Mme de Staël, Delphine en est la réalité pendant sa jeunesse" (I, ciii).

but each of the women in the novel can be seen to provide an alternative conception of the question central to it: how can a woman live her life in face of the rigidity of society's edicts as to what she must do and be?

Léonce cites Littleton's rather too well known *Monody* as embodying Delphine's character:

> Polite as all her life in courts had been;
> Yet good as she the world had never seen;
> The noble fire of an exalted mind,
> With gentle female tenderness combined;
> Her speech as the melodious voice of Love,
> Her song, the warbling of the vernal grove;
> Her eloquence was sweeter than her song,
> Soft as her heart, and as her reason strong;
> Her form each beauty of her mind expressed,
> Her mind was virtue by the Graces dressed.
>
> (IV, XXXII)

Such was the civilized eighteenth-century idea of woman; a harmonious blend it was, one that few could actually achieve, since any small thing might set it out of tune—a mind not exalted, a voice unmelodious, a form imperfect. Delphine was so composed by Mme de Staël that she very nearly *is* this perfectly good, graceful, noble, bright creature. But an ever so slight excess in her distinction of mind quite unbalances the entire picture: it makes her less than totally convinced by conventional ideas, which then lose their power to control her so entirely. This intelligent openness of Delphine's has its parallel in her active life, in the spontaneity and genuineness of her reactions, her anxiety, bordering on mania, to give aid, her passionate readiness to follow wherever love should lead.

From the outset, Delphine is portrayed as free in other ways. An orphan, she has a large fortune to dispose of as she chooses and can come and go at will. Adulated by society, she yet despises its praises, which "leave a feeling of coldness and indifference deep in my heart that no pleasures of self-love can altogether alter," but she cannot help enjoying society's life and the delights of a heightened sense of herself and of her powers of riposte that it gives to her. Matilde, her arid-hearted opposite, at the outset warns her prophetically against her too free ways: "Cousin, where would we be if all women took what they would call their own conscience as their guide? . . . those men who are considered in modern terminology to be freest from prejudice still do not want their wives to be liberated from all bonds" (I, II).

Arsinoé and Célimène

The pious Arsinoé in Molière's *Le Misanthrope* (III, v) attacks the worlding Célimène in a distinct parallel to Matilde's advice to Delphine:

> I visited, last night, some virtuous folk,
> And, quite by chance, it was of you they spoke;
> There was, I fear, no tendency to praise
> Your light behavior and your dashing ways.[10]

Matilde is more "sincere" than Arsinoé, whose self-interest is comically evident in her every unctuous word and gesture. Rhetorically asking why Delphine, though beautiful, gifted, rich, and successful is still not happy, she tells her benefactress (who had provided the dowry for her marriage to Léonce) that her very "independence in opinion and conduct, that perhaps gives your conversation so much more of grace and piquancy, is beginning to make people speak ill of you and sooner or later will surely harm your standing in society" (II, II).

Matilde, though a caricature and the least successful important character in the novel, is significantly the bearer of the most telling of all the female challenges to Delphine's way of being. Arsinoé's acid critique of Célimène is a scene of purest jealousy. Mme de Staël sets the confrontation between pious and worldly women before their rivalry in love, but it is nevertheless with love that they are concerned. It is Arsinoé's very cry, "it is not enough to live well for yourself alone," that Matilde turns upon Delphine. A

---

10. "Votre conduite avec ses grands éclats
  Madame, eut le malheur qu'on ne la loua pas."
Translation of *Le Misanthrope* by Richard Wilbur (New York: Harcourt Brace, 1954).

true woman does not step out of line: her egoism must never show. She must conform not merely to the norms of the world, but even to superstition if that be required for her to remain anonymously discreet. If she should not, no man would want her. We know that Alceste, a man of taste, prefers the delightful Célimène to the brittle Arsinoé, but in her refusal to be bound by his idea of her and to give up the world for him, she ends by being suspect in his eyes. So does Matilde preach at Delphine, "Do you think a sensible man would be in a rush to become tied to someone who sees everything by her own lights, submits her conduct to her own ideas, and generally disdains accepted wisdom?" Arsinoé does not precisely attack Célimène for independence, but rather for its corollary: a sensual love of pleasure. We see how closely the two are linked. Matilde indicts Delphine, ultimately, for loving excitement and for wanting to be the center of attention.

Célimène replies in her celebrated witty sallies by accusing Arsinoé of hypocrisy, aptly attacking the contorted jealousy of her that lies behind the latter's "helpful" advice. This is where we perceive Mme de Staël's distinctive sensibility and mentality. Though stung, Célimène makes marvelous light of Arsinoé's animus. Delphine, however, takes Matilde's criticism so earnestly that she is moved to anger. Unlike Célimène, whose pleasures in society are ephemeral and so make no serious claim upon her being—what she wants is to please and be pleased—Delphine's need of society is more basic: it is in fact a need for love. "I have but one goal; I have but one desire; it is to be loved by those with whom I live." She perceives that Matilde does *not* love her, but tries nevertheless to propitiate her and appeal to her sympathies. Why, Delphine reasons, should she fear the world? "I bear toward it only benevolent and gentle feelings; if I had lacked all forms of attractiveness I should perhaps have been unable to prevent myself from some bitterness against women who are lucky enough to please, but I hear about me only flattering words." This suggests something of Célimène's bite, but the knowing, mischievous Célimène would never have uttered this: "Why wish to afflict a creature as *inoffensive* as I, and whose wit . . . has no other motive than to be agreeable?" (II, III).

Delphine's "gift" is simply that of a superior conversationalist, and one who is exceedingly good to look upon, but her talent is an aspect of her being; it is not separable from it. The very grace that she brings to the salon she also brings to her friendships. In fact, Delphine, like Browning's *Last Duchess*, is indiscriminately loving and lovable. Spontaneity and naturalness are her gods. Restraint of any sort, particularly the Christian kind that Matilde entreats her to accept, would be felt by her as unbearable, as irrational constraint.

Matilde, as Sainte-Beuve noted, is portrayed with an intense, unconvincing bitterness from the outset, one that suggests the author's lack of control over her depiction. That Matilde is Mme Necker's grossly caricatured surrogate in the novel is suggested not only by the role she plays as pious, prudish, and narrow rival and critic of Delphine, but also by the later action of the novel when she becomes the wife of the beloved and loves him in return (her redeeming grace), bears him a child she kills through insisting upon "mothering" (breast-feeding) it, and is, despite our heroine's "kindness," scalded by unkind reproaches and injunctions from Delphine as she finally brings herself to renounce Léonce. Germaine's resentful jealousy of her mother, even to the conflict about nursing (Suzanne had valiantly tried it; Germaine considered it absurd) is given its properly intemperate echo in this loaded and cruel characterization.

Matilde, then, represents the caveats of society in their strictest and least attractive form. Raised consciously by her own mother, Sophie de Vernon, precisely to *be* narrow and satisfied with her lot, she is a sort of anti-Delphine, the archenemy of any woman who would at all be free. Matilde, so psychically rigid, so bound by churchly precepts of conduct, fails to show sympathy for the ailing Léonce and thereby alienates him before their marriage, whereas Delphine, who never thinks of the *qu'en dira-t-on*, impulsively tends his wounds and weeps for his suffering. Exposing again her arid heart, Matilde refuses even to help her desperately debt-ridden mother until her absent husband returns to approve her action. Delphine remonstrates with her and Matilde replies, "You apparently believe, cousin . . . that there are no fixed principles about anything; and what would become of virtue if we let it respond to all its impulses?—And virtue, said I to her, what is it but consistency in generosity?" (III, XXVII).

The Evil Mothers

The orthodoxy concerning woman's role represented by Matilde is shared by Léonce's mother, Mme de Mondoville; yet the older woman is both more personally antagonistic and more opposed theoretically to the existence of persons like Delphine than is Matilde. Mme de Mondoville, like the idea of woman she stands for, is a shadowy and unnerving enemy, whose outline waxes and wanes to conform to the exigencies of the wildly evolving plot. Her enmity is the backdrop of Léonce's own resistance to Delphine's ways, a curtain of unspoken reproof to the heroine for her heedlessness. Matilde and her mother-in-law reflect society's rule, but as a force in the novel their natures are too rigid, their views too inflexibly narrow and foolish, to truly challenge Delphine's far more supple style of femininity, which claims our sympathy. For example, the older woman questions the value of intelligence for women: "Our conduct is set out for us, our condition imposes our opinions upon us; what is the use of that spirit of inquiry that so turns people's heads?" Or, "We can never subdue these so-called superior spirits to the necessities of life; they constantly have to be making fresh judgments upon everything and to be developing their own principles on each question, which they call reason; this manner of being seems to me supremely absurd, especially in a woman" (V, IX). There is at such moments a touch of humor in the expression of ideas as foreign as these to the author's mind and so supremely absurd to her, but to say that this view is expressed without sufficient nuance in the characterization of those espousing it is not to say that we do not recognize it still as a widely shared sense of the way things ought to be.

This ideological bigotry of Mme de Mondoville's is interestingly combined, in her continuing rejection of Delphine as daughter-in-law even after Matilde's death, with a maternal correlate of oedipal love. "Léonce will love me more than anyone else if he is not married to a woman he is in love with and who absorbs all his affections; . . . if he takes a wife who has wit as well as youth and beauty, what will I be to him? . . . I feel hatred for whomever he loves more than me" (v, xxvIII). This syndrome, in which prolonged maternal fixation on the son is combined with its obverse, the narrowest of conceptions of feminine capability, is illuminatingly captured by Mme de Staël's penetrating understanding.

What Mme de Mondoville's villainy achieves is to compound the animosity of the mothers to Delphine's fulfillment, a pattern in the novel, for Léonce's aunt, Mme de Mondoville's sister, will join forces with her to prevent the union of this couple. But Mme de Ternan, the Mother Superior of the convent to which Delphine retreats, is of a very different nature. Hers is the most successful *portrait* (in the fashion of the seventeenth- and eighteenth-century salon) in the novel, one well worth anthologizing.

Mme de Ternan is a woman who at first meeting fascinates Delphine because, by one of those coincidences the novelists of her period did not in the least blush at, she bears a troubling resemblance to her nephew Léonce (her own name is Léontine). Mme de Ternan is a former great beauty, melancholically past her prime at fifty, who has lived successfully within society and still has her worldly wit and manners. What is startling is the motive given her by Mme de Staël for her resolve to bind Delphine to her: it is precisely because she is young and beautiful, as she herself once was. "She gives back to me some of the pleasures I have lost; she is unhappy, even though young and beautiful, and this consoles me for being old and sad; she must stay with me" (v, x). We see how Mme de Mondoville and Mme de Ternan are sisters: both are dedicated to the frustration of the course of youthful impulse. With no real concern or affection for Delphine, Léontine de Ternan is prepared—rather too nakedly—to sacrifice the younger woman's life for her own sake. Delphine understands this, for she says, "I do not know why the very pleasure she takes in seeing me does not persuade me that she loves me" (v, xI), and she finds in the personality of this curious nun "I know not what aridity that chills the heart even of one most disposed to attach itself to her." Delphine, unable to guess what has brought the Mother Superior to her present life, finds her upsettingly composed. Her suspicions of Mme de Ternan are confirmed by Delphine's young Swiss friend,

Mme de Cerlèbe, who warns that the Superior's haughty demeanor and imperious ways are not the result of a laudable self-mastery, nor of any genuine piety, but are only the effects of a frustrated self-love: "Self-love made her leave the world, self-love is still her sole guide in solitude."

However, in giving Mme de Ternan an occasion to present her own account of her life, Mme de Staël lends considerable substance to this woman. The effect of her narrative is in fact a highly unusual mitigated pathos. This is a portrait in eighteenth-century style, dryly recounted, but in its grasp of psychological and social criticism it seems far more modern. As Léontine describes her own life—once graceful, clever, and courted by society—she was as Delphine might have been: "Driven by a desire to please and the satisfying confidence of having been successful in doing so," she was inspired to express "a mass of ideas and epigrams that she had never since found the wit to invent." (Here Mme de Staël candidly explores the causal link between the drive to please and the stimulus of social intercourse.)

Léontine had married a good and reasonable man who loved her madly. Although her husband was constantly preoccupied with his affairs, she still remained faithful to him "more from pride than out of virtue." She gave her two children much care in their childhood and enjoyed their responding tenderness, until, in their sixteenth or seventeenth year, they began to grow beyond her. When, from the age of thirty, she began to feel her attractions waning, she despaired: "I feared the future instead of desiring it. I made no more plans. I held back the days rather than hastening them." She made no new friends and had no new hopes to buoy her existence. Whatever attempts she did make to connect with others were vain: "I did too much or too little for others. . . . " After some time in this limbo, she went to a ball at which she had the horrifying experience that "no man addressed any compliment to me on my appearance"; but worse, people spoke to her in strained tones of younger and more beautiful women and of graver matters. In mid-life, "I saw no future, not a hope, not a goal that could concern me. A man at the age I was then could have begun a new career; until the last year of a long life, a man may hope for an occasion of glory, and glory is, like love, a delicious illusion, a happiness quite unlike any that simple rationality offers us with its efforts and its sacrifices; but women, good God! women! how sad their destiny is! in the middle of their life nothing remains to them but insipid days that grow paler from year to year; days as monotonous as our material existence, as painful as our moral life" (v, xi).

The Delphine who is so unself-conscious, even of her beauty, who cares not so much to please as to be loved, and whose concerns are by no means so petty, is not emotionally akin to Mme de Ternan: hers is a dessicated egoism so palpable that it cannot quite be rendered sympathetic, even in her own account. Mlle d'Albémar, a woman devoid of that physical beauty that might have given her greater access to human relationships, is particularly acid concerning Mme de Ternan. Why, she asks Delphine, should she have shut herself away from the world? Having children, why did she not go and live with them? She is rich—why did she not effect some good with her fortune? "Had she been a man, she would have made others suffer; she is a woman and has suffered herself: but I see in her not a trace of goodness, and without goodness, how could sorrow itself inspire our interest?" (v, xxvi). However, the portrayal given here of woman's options in aristocratic society is so acute as to condition any negative judgment upon her with the sense that her limitations have been imposed. Imposed is the cult of beauty, the injunction to please. Imposed is the injunction never to grow older. Imposed is the requirement that she have no idea of self but that which she hears from other people's lips, so that when she ceases to be spoken of she feels she has ceased to be.

Compounding the social disaster are the temporal fortunes of motherhood, in that "we are the prime object of our children's affection at the age when we can also be that of our husband or of the lover who chooses us; but when our youth ends, our children's begins, and all the charm in life takes them away from us at the very moment when we need most to rely upon their feeling for us."[11]

---

11. What Mme de Staël makes less of in this fiction is the avidity of the younger woman for a part in life's drama at the very time when motherhood is

Mme de Staël touches here with equally bitter aptness on the failure of marriage to sustain a woman in middle life. As Léontine tries to turn toward her husband, she finds that he has simply lost the habit of being interested in her, and she asks plaintively, "What pleasure can you find in the company of a man to whom you are essentially unnecessary, who could as well live without you as with you and who takes less of an interest in your existence than you do yourself?" Finding no response to her need, she discovers that "the more a feeling, a pleasure, a goal, becomes necessary to us, the more it becomes difficult to obtain; nature and society follow this maxim as if it were in the Gospels: *they give to those that have;* but those who lose experience a contagion of troubles that rush in to succeed upon each other and are born one from the other."

Self-love is fed to woman as the sustenance of her life. Léontine de Ternan is a literalist whom it has completely dominated: "Self-love necessarily has great effect upon the happiness of women; since they have no business to attend to, no enforced occupations, they fix their attentions upon themselves and divide their lives into parcels. . . . " Although Léontine's ignobly selfish purview is given as extreme, it touches emotional verities both without and within the author. The Mme de Staël who in her twenties already dreaded ageing, who had been deserted by lovers several times over, was not mocking Mme de Ternan when she had her say that death begins "with the first affection that is extinguished, with the first feeling that grows cold, with the first charm that fades." All women who still live for love know some such dread.

If Mme de Ternan is wrong, according to Delphine, because she has allowed self-pity to make of her something of an unfeeling monster, the indictment of society nevertheless remains strong. It is that very narcissism so fostered in women that disables Léontine from being a "real woman" in her sentiments; that is, selfless. The challenge Mme de Ternan presents to the heroine is that of

---

apt to make her total participation as an individual more difficult and the paradox of an increased appreciation of maternity as it eludes her biologically. George Sand's life gives a fine example of this essential problem.

a woman whose narcissism is simply not counteracted by a sufficient love of others. This Mother Superior is a destructive mother, feeding on Delphine's youth and sorrow to compensate for her own emptiness. She has turned to the convent to assume "a way of life that, far from combatting her sadness, consecrates it . . . as the sole business of her life." *Schadenfreude* is her revenge.

A curious phenomenon is the power Mme de Ternan immediately assumes over Delphine, initially ascribed to her resemblance to Léonce but maintained through her own powers of personality. Delphine is just as submissive to older women of dominating demeanor as she is to her lover, but the most celebrated by far of all the mother-enchantresses in the novel is Mme de Vernon.

Talleyrand has often been given as the model for this character.[12] However, it is safe to assume that no reader unaware of Mme de Staël's life could conceive that this portrait of Mme de Vernon had been drawn after a man or a statesman. The sole importance Talleyrand had as a model for Mme de Staël was as an inspiration for the depiction of perfidy in a charming and dearly loved friend. Like betrayal in love, such flightiness was deeply puzzling and troubling to her in life. The assumption that Mme de Vernon *is* Talleyrand may amuse us, but a far more important source for the creation of Sophie is again to be found in Suzanne Necker.

In the relationship between Sophie and Delphine, Delphine is the suppliant whose warm and overt affection is returned, if at all, only by the cool and over-civilized forms of friendship. Sophie stands as a substitute mother to Delphine and is the younger woman's ideal. Mme de Staël was wont to say, "Never have I been loved as I love" (I, cclxvii). We are reminded of Mme Necker's old reproaches to her daughter for her "exaggerated" expressions of feeling when we hear Sophie tell Delphine, in explaining her betrayal, "I thought . . . I alone had really understood life and that all those who spoke to me of devoted feelings or exalted virtue were either charlatans or dupes" (II, XLI).

As was the case with Léontine de Ternan, Mme de Staël's

---

12. Béatrice Jasinski is probably correct in seeing elements of Narbonne's remote charm and his emotional betrayal of Mme de Staël in this portrait.

major achievement in this characterization is to be found in Sophie's "explanation," another first-person account, which exposes her background and the motives behind her actions.[13]

Although she has been warned by her sister-in-law, Mlle d'Albémar, that Sophie is manipulative and untrustworthy, Delphine is so enslaved by the delight of her company that she trusts, as is her practice, to her own impressions alone. Like Delphine, the reader is shocked by the revelation of her perfidy to so devoted and generous a young friend and waits for some clarification of her startling behavior. What impels Sophie to betray Delphine is precisely the latter's naïve assumption that Sophie will come to her aid and explain her dubious conduct to Léonce to enable *her*, rather than Sophie's own daughter, Matilde, to marry him. When Sophie acts according to her merely natural preference, Delphine concludes that the Sophie in whom she had had such absolute trust did not love her, and "if Sophie does not love me it must be true that I cannot be loved."

Mme de Vernon reminds us once more of Mme Necker as she says, "I am better off in every circumstance when I am self-contained, and emotionalism does me harm." It is to explain this (for Delphine) unnatural disposition—her unwillingness to feel or to love—that the dying Sophie recounts the story of her life. Her history, like Mme de Ternan's, is a penetrating critique of woman's lot in eighteenth-century France and, closely allied to this, of the spiritual climate of its society.

Sophie is at the last impelled to concede that Delphine is the only person ever to have loved her, and in retrospect she wonders why she should have been moved to turn her love aside. Orphaned at three, she was raised by an indifferent guardian who "considered women as toys in their childhood and in their youth as more or less pretty mistresses who should never be listened to concerning anything reasonable."

"I noticed quite soon that what feelings I expressed were

---

13. Sainte-Beuve, in fact, found this to be the best part of the novel. It bears some intriguing resemblances to the celebrated Letter 81 of Laclos's *Liaisons dangereuses* in which that novel's villainous Mme de Merteuil "explains" her own evolution.

turned to ridicule, and that I was not expected to speak my mind, as if it were inappropriate for a woman to have one." Her reaction was an age-old one: she remained silent about what mattered to her, and soon she would have been unable to say whether anything at all really did matter. What is more, she became quite magnificently artful at dissimulation, and it was her pride alone, of all the wells of passion, that did not die within her. If caught in a lie, she would never explain, but only withdraw into a sullen silence. Sophie's marked originality concerning her condition as woman is her lucid refusal to play against such odds: ". . . I found it rather unjust that those who counted women for naught, who accorded them no rights and scarcely allowed that they had any faculties, that these very same people then wished to demand of them the virtues of strength, independence, forthrightness and sincerity."

Forced by her guardian to marry M. de Vernon (her lack of a fortune giving her no alternative), she "firmly believed that women's lot condemned them to duplicity." For the unhappy slave any ruse is licit in dealing with the tyrant. Of her marriage, she says, "I made M. de Vernon do as I liked, and yet he always treated me harshly. He did not suspect I had any influence upon his actions, but in order to prove to himself that he was truly master, he always spoke to me roughly." Although unhappy, and both pretty and witty, she would not take a lover, for she was afraid of the power of love, sensing that it might undermine the shield that dissimulation provided her against feeling and suffering. "I was convinced, as I still am today, that women being the victims of all society's institutions, they are doomed to misery if they abandon themselves in the least to their feelings, if they lose control over themselves in any way." Status and the respect of those about her became her only interests. Sophie concluded that religion could be a way of reconciling a woman to her lot without destroying her sincerity, and this is why she gave her daughter Matilde the intensely devout upbringing that resulted in her becoming a bigot and a prude.

If we take Sophie's logic a step farther, we see that if religion failed her, a woman who was not a hypocrite simply could never be reconciled to her fate. Were she honest, she would have to be a rebel, albeit, as here, a covert one.

Mme de Vernon's challenge to Delphine is the challenge of a lucid but arid rejection of her society's conception of femininity. She realized that Delphine's virtues of openness and readiness to befriend and help others—the obverse of her own character—would make her an easy prey to the nastiness of the world: "The independence of your opinions, your romantic way of behaving and looking at things, seemed to me to contrast with the society in which your tastes, your successes, your rank, and your wealth would place you." Having herself "stifled the sensibility nature had given me," Sophie is repelled by her opposite, the Delphine who stifles nothing within, whose credo is like Blake's: "Rather murder an infant in its cradle than nurse unacted desire!" But Mme de Staël, prodded by the need to reconcile in fiction what was inadequately reconciled in life, makes Sophie, before she dies, succumb gratefully to Delphine's love for her and admit her as the sole trustworthy exception in all of wicked humankind. Since becoming acquainted with Delphine she has sometimes wondered whether her soulless system was correct, but concludes, "I still do not know whether it is not true that with any other person but you the only reasonable relations are calculated ones."

Sophie had surprised the credulous Delphine by showing her that the social graces (which the older woman possessed in abundance) are sometimes at the antipodes of virtue. The irresistible charm of society masks evil. Mme de Vernon's cynicism is that of eighteenth-century society, and in her own generation's revolt against it Mme de Staël excoriates the attempt, implicit in its praxis, to nullify the unselfish and spontaneously good side of man and, even more relentlessly, that of woman. The absurdity as well as the splendor of Delphine's attempt to be an *"honnête femme,"* reacting directly, *à la Rousseau,* to events themselves rather than to some public view of how they should be reacted to, emerges in the contrast with Sophie. Sophie's interpretation of the facts of woman's life had not been by any means erroneous, but Mme de Staël makes us cower at her willfully life-denying course. Had Mme de Staël been but a trifle more the artist and less the essayist, Sophie de Vernon would have been an immortal representation of the destructive force of the repressed female psyche. As it is, she is only an unforgettable one.

The Good Mother

The "good" mother, a pseudo-parent to Delphine, is Louise d'Albémar, her epistolary confidante. The sister of Delphine's "husband" in name only, Louise belongs to the generation of her parents. She embodies, as do nearly all the characters of the novel, certain aspects of the author's own nature, in this case that of the unbeautiful woman.[14] The case here is complex. An old maid of unprepossessing appearance and of great warmth and intelligence, Mlle d'Albémar has made a conscious decision to retire from society and to live quietly on her income. To Delphine's entreaties that she come and live with her, she makes this melancholy reply: "You know I have the most ungracious aspect in the world; my figure is awkward and my face has no good feature" (I, VII). Even as she had before, Mme de Staël places Louise's plight in the context of the feminine condition, as she makes her argue her reasons for her withdrawal. "Should I have gathered people about me to hear them tell me what others possess and what I lack?" Her youth had been a trial to her, and so, as she reached womanhood, she had concluded that "with my face, it was ridiculous to love." Men, she claims, can overcome ugliness through achievement, but "women have no existence except in love." Although she has an all-too-loving heart, Louise rejects a life of self-deception and in its stead chooses solitude.

Such a woman might seem on the surface to be the very soul of moderation. Her language is always affectionate and motherly and her comportment itself appears to represent a sage retreat from worldliness. Yet in one of the first letters in the novel she is already goading Delphine on in her affection for the Léonce neither of them has ever seen, as she writes, "You know it makes me virtually angry that you have arranged for Matilde to marry Léonce de Mondoville? I hear that he is so handsome, so lovable and proud that he seems worthy of my Delphine" (I, VII). This curious lack of moral propriety is continued throughout, for Louise constantly wavers. First she is the firm guide—"I will not preach to you about your duties, but I will say, think of Matilde; . . . will you abuse those charms nature has given you by taking from her a heart that God and society have given to her as support?" (II, XII). Then, in

---

14. We recall that Mme de Staël in childhood was called Louise.

a turnabout, once she has seen Léonce, she becomes almost the satanic prodder: "Delphine, after having allowed so much love to grow in Léonce's heart, it is the duty of a feeling soul to handle his passionate nature with the greatest delicacy; . . . after Léonce's marriage you should have separated from him, and yet now you must not break his heart by sacrificing it suddenly to some untimely virtue" (IV, VI). This is the oscillation that makes D. G. Larg call Louise d'Albémar the incarnation of "the wisdom of the lesser evil." If Louise is the elder, the chorus, the conscience of the novel, then its conscience is ambivalent, for she is not able utlimately to judge, either to praise or blame.

Mme de Staël had once said, "Women, all having the same destiny, tend to the same end" (III, 204). For this reason she has given her heroine's confessor characteristics that turn her away from that common destiny. The author's sympathy for the *ignorés et offensés* of the world enables her to enrich and make slightly more credible one of the least believable roles in literature—that of the confidante. If we are close to forgiving Louise her moral lapses, it is because we realize how much she lives vicariously through the adventures of her pseudo-daughter. And though she eggs her on, Louise also reminds Delphine that women should try not to be misled by the passions of youth into thinking that love is the whole of life. It is her own distance from the tyranny of love that permits her to think such a thought which, through her, is at least enunciated in this novel otherwise so unalterably love-obsessed.

Louise's challenge to Delphine is that of a woman who feels rejected by love, even as she accords it primacy. She is the polar opposite of Delphine, who was made for love. Through her character the love ethic itself is made to come under some critical scrutiny: its shallow values condemn large classes of clearly valuable people to outcast status, either to ill use at the hands of society or, fleeing it, to a frustration of their usefulness as people. Curiously it is Louise's lack of a lover that somehow makes her for Delphine and for Mme de Staël the ideal mother figure.[15] The Germaine who

---

15. The only genuinely "good" mother in the novel is the Swiss Mme de Cerlèbe, a woman also admired in the novel by Delphine for her qualities as devoted daughter; but again, although she has a husband, she is absolutely indifferent to him.

first wanted her mother for herself and then wanted to steal her father away from her finally has it her own way: Louise not only has no one to love but Delphine—"I live in you," she writes; unlike Mme Necker she espouses her daughter's questionable passions. In her fiction Mme de Staël thus wrests for her heroine surrogate that essential approval that she never knew in her own life.

Love and Marriage

Mme de Staël pursues her meditation upon woman into her invention of various couples who embody one or another conception of the love relationship. Love and life are indissolubly entwined in *Delphine*: life is described as a few brief episodes of love's intensity followed by long years of monotony, regret, decay, and demise. Love is a vital need, whose absence is a living death. Man needs hope, Delphine says, and already at twenty-five his yesterdays are better than his tomorrows: "he holds onto the top of the slope, attaches himself to each branch so that his steps might draw him less swiftly toward old age and death" (III, XIV). Delphine writes Léonce that love is the only antidote to such a fate: "The power of love makes me feel within myself the immortal source of life." Love alone allows us to hope, and the happiness it gives reconciles us to the Creation, to the Creator.

According to Delphine's verbal pronouncements, love, for a woman, is conceivable only in terms of a marriage of the most traditional stripe. We might as readily believe this passage from Mme de Belmont's remarks to have come out of Prudhomme's *Révolutions de Paris* as from Mme de Staël's novel:

> The first happiness of a woman is to have married a man she respects as much as she loves him; who is superior to her by virtue of his intelligence and his character, who decides everything for her, not because he oppresses her will, but because he enlightens her reason and supports her in her weakness. Even in those circumstances where she might have a different view from his, she concedes happily. . . . In order for the marriage to fulfill nature's intentions the man must have, in terms of his real worth, a true advantage over his wife, an advantage which she recognizes and enjoys: woe be to a woman who is obliged to manage her own life, to cover up the faults and pettiness of her husband, or to free herself and bear alone the weight of existence! The greatest of pleasures is that admira-

tion of the heart which fills our every moment, gives a goal to all our actions, a continual prod to our desire to be more perfect, and places by our side our true glory, the approval of the friend who honors us by loving us. Dear Delphine, do not judge the happiness or unhappiness of families by the vicissitudes of their fortunes; find out the degree of affection that conjugal love allows them to enjoy; and then only will you know their share of mortal happines. (III, XVIII)

Setting aside the protest of the *mal-mariée* Germaine de Staël to which this passage also gives voice, Mme de Belmont's commentary illustrates the primacy the author gives to intimate satisfactions in her scheme of things. True glory—this from a woman everywhere regarded as a glory seeker—is nothing but acceptance and confirmation from the beloved. Mme de Staël's "bartering strategy" of accepting male superiority to insure love to the female is patent here. Her ultimate soundness reappears in the lucid description she gives—out of her own want—of the confidence in being which love can bestow and which is, despite her craven bow to the man's dominance, obviously seen as a bond of reciprocity.

Although her jealousy of her parents' strong bonds and her own disappointing marriage made Mme de Staël view married love as an Eden, her attitude toward marriage is infinitely more complex than it would appear from her overt proclamations. Larg, for example, points out that in *Delphine* she approves of marriage and divorce simultaneously and for identical reasons: marriage when it represents the fulfillment of love, and divorce when it permits lovers to marry.

With seeming unconsciousness, Mme de Staël stands the idea of marriage on its head in her description of the Belmonts' ménage, given as the embodiment of marital contentment. The Belmonts live in the country, "relegated to a corner of the earth," well away from society, that enemy of private life. Belmont speaks glowingly to his visitors of the "charm of the affections" and the tone of the entire passage concerning this family is elegiac and blissful. It is far too blissful. "The Belmont household, like love in marriage, is a dream," writes a critic.[16] M. de Belmont is, to be sure, morally strong and admirable, but he is also blind. His blindness does not

---

16. Larg, *La Seconde Vie*, p. 73.

permit him to dedicate himself to any sort of career, and so his area of action is limited. Deprived of this sphere, he does not pine, but rather rejoices in his passivity and dependence:

I am pleased to think I cannot take a step without my wife's hand, that I could not even feed myself if she did not bring food to me as she does. No fresh idea would reanimate my imagination if she did not read me the works I wish to know; no thought comes to my mind without the charm her voice gives to it, all my moral life comes to me through her, imprinted with her being, and in giving me my life Providence left to my wife the task of completing the gift, which would be useless and sorrow-filled without her aid. (III, XVII)

Mme de Belmont is no ordinary wife to her husband, but a mother eternally needed by her "child." The wife here plays the combined role of lover, parent, and pedagogue whose august role is to put the finishing touches on God's creation. Not only is woman the giver of life (Mme de Belmont is also the mother of a family), she becomes the divinely ordained protector of its every phase. Despite the lip service to conventional matrimony, we have here most certainly a reversal of sex roles. In the "perfect union" of the Belmonts, the wife plays precisely the sort of role which society had always assigned to the male partner in marriage: she provides for his needs, and his whole life, intellectual and moral, is filtered through her. The completeness of this reversal is evident if one imagines the latter portion of the statement coming from a young wife of the period speaking of her husband—there would then not appear to be the least oddity in it. What Mme de Staël presents here as an ideal of marriage contains this curious component: the wife is the whole world to her husband, who needs no independent being outside her orbit. That this was not her explicit ideal does not detract from our impression that this is indeed her conception of the love relationship. Since we have seen and will see similar conceptions (*Mirza, Corinne*) in her works, we must assume that this is the counterstructure to the traditional conception of love that lay within her spirit.

The very extreme nature of this model of love suggests a more profound layer of need. In Belmont's expression, "How necessary the shelter of sure and constant virtue is to me, who could not conquer anything and had no hope of happiness except that which

might come and find me out" (iii, xviii), the passive role is, if
you will, given vindictively to the husband, who not only accepts
it in good grace but espouses it positively, quite contentedly living
as much in his feelings as women have always been exhorted to do
in theirs. Indeed, Belmont asks of other men, as any good *mère de
famille* might of other women, "How is it that all men do not seek
happiness within the family?" That the woman, the active partner,
is a mother figure, feeding, teaching, catering to the infantile needs
of her lover (the happiness that comes and finds him) suggests
that Mme de Staël plays back her own need to evoke love, not so
much into the commonplace mother-child relationship, where it
might have been absorbed less spectacularly, but into the love relationship. Here it becomes a total infantile fulfillment of the passive masculine partner by the active female one. Evidently arrested
in her jealousy of the omnipotent mother, Germaine in adult life
arrogates to herself this commanding role. If her reason could find
no condemnation of this altered structuring of the norms, it is because, using the stratagem of Belmont's blindness, she had con-
cealed even from herself her deep rejection of the laws of hierarchy
within marriage.

Prompted by her own unhappy marriage, by her Protestant and
anti-Catholic prejudices, and by "common sense," Mme de Staël
brought all her means to bear on a plea for an escape from the cruel
and strict marital customs of the time. (A divorce decree was passed
by the Revolutionary Assembly on September 20, 1792, but we
recall that the action of the novel is set just prior to this period.)
The arguments for divorce are the sole instance of a militancy directed to some specific end in Mme de Staël's fiction, which may
somewhat surprise us in works so infused with theses. It is of interest to note that her "daring" in this instance was not so great
as it might seem, for she spoke in favor of a social change that had
already taken place when she wrote, but that she now saw being
undermined by Napoleon's demand for a Catholic orderliness in
moral matters—on the part of others. Henri de Lebensei is Mme
de Staël's spokesman in this domain and he writes, "In forbidding
divorce, the law is severe only to the victims of marriage ... it seems
to say I cannot insure your happiness but I can guarantee the continuation of your despair" (vi, 319). Mme de Staël shows no pa-

tience here with the Catholic belief that through suffering one may achieve moral perfection, although she herself often gives signs of believing this. Her arguments for divorce, although coupled with praise of marriage ("the only joy that consoles one for living"), necessarily start from an attack upon that hallowed institution's horrors.

Elise de Lebensei had first been married to a cruel, slave-owning despot a good deal her senior. As in her other *portraits*, Mme de Staël has the subject herself make a critique of her education. Elise expostulates against the poverty of her own, having learned from the sourness of her experience that enlightenment is just as necessary "to charm, to independence, to the goodness of life,"— that is, to a woman's life—as to any other career. She was able to endure her wretchedness and maltreatment until she met and was loved by Henri, a Protestant nobleman from Languedoc with an English education. Henri's unflinching conviction of the rightness of the Revolution's ideas enabled him to feel quite detached from public opprobrium, and so Elise divorced her Protestant husband to marry him. But neither society nor her family have accepted their actions, and Elise counsels Delphine never to emulate her: "It is a great risk for a woman to run if she defies opinion; to dare to do so, she must feel, according to a poet's comparison, a triple ring of brass about her heart!" (II, VII). The less Pollyanna-like Elise is permitted to allude to an aspect of the question that Delphine is made "too modest" to avow: to renounce the world as she has done one "must not be gifted . . . with a rare mind or rare beauty which would make one regret successes forever lost. . . ." Neither marriage nor divorce are really feasible for the likes of Delphine, who has both.

Good and Evil

Delphine is a work remarkable as a novel of moral ambiguity written in a tone of moral certitude. *La Nouvelle Héloïse* had established this mode, so wildly successful with the public. As compared with Mme de Staël's, however, Rousseau's novel appears the work of a complacent author engaged in the delectations of nostalgic fictional invention: St. Preux's passion is a poetic peccadillo, after all. Mme de Staël in *Delphine* is, on the contrary, an author battling to justify her heroine-surrogate within a far more question-able supramarital relationship, and one for which women are tra-ditionally less readily forgiven. Delphine is a tractably naïve Rous-seauist who actually tries to function within that society whose pleasures she does not totally disdain, but whose values are at odds with her own.

Like Rousseau before her and Stendhal after her, it was to that portion of the public who see themselves as above society's laws that Mme de Staël had addressed her novel: "What all men feel in misfortune, tenderer souls feel habitually; for these, there can be no prosperity that renders them invulnerable, and even in the happiest moments of life, they know how necessary to them pity might well become." What marks her "happy few" is a kind of divine discontent: all distinguished beings, Mme de Staël believed, have felt life to be beneath their desires and feelings and have been impelled emotionally toward a higher life. Delphine herself cer-tainly embodies both this sensibility and this aspiration. These are the qualities primary to the author's notion of "goodness."

Good and evil in this novel are, on the face of it, set forth clearly enough, no doubt too tidily for the casual reader even in that time. Scrutiny reveals, however, that these categories, much as we might expect in the post-Revolutionary world, are scrambled, and that the moral world of *Delphine* is not merely ambiguous, as some critics have had it, but deeply ambivalent.

As Delphine represents the individual, Léonce is charged with representing society. Society is diabolical; the unspoiled individual, angelic. Though this is roughly the scheme, Léonce is made to be fiercely proud, a characteristic not given as hateful, even though it makes him needful of society's good opinion. It is Delphine who is so very attached to the world that she cannot help rejoicing at being nearly always in company.

Generous literally to a fault, Delphine lavishes her money on her friends as well as on herself: on Matilde's dowry; on Thérèse d'Ervins, whom she consoles and for whom she compromises her-self; on Mme de Vernon, whose debts she pays and who dies in her arms after the blackest betrayal. She cannot refuse aid even to her enemy, the villainous suitor Valorbe. Quite unmindful of conse-quences, she throws herself into these various events of her life.

Her attitude toward her suspicious and jealous lover is a constant, yielding submissiveness. How, we may wonder, can a character so marked with a cloying, stereotyped femininity represent individualism? The answer must be that Delphine's character is a defense of just this image of feminine goodness and finds its validation in the very intensity with which the character lives it. It is as if Mme de Staël were saying, "If this is your image of real femininity, I'll show you how splendid it can be, but how truly little it is wanted by your society if it is taken seriously as an ideal."

The author endowed her Léonce with considerable beauty and physical courage, but she bestowed upon him also, as a tragic flaw, her own unworthy weakness: subservience to the opinion of the world. Her own supersensitivity to the *qu'en dira-t-on* had been passed on to her directly by her father who wrote: "*They* blame you. *They* accuse you. *They* expect such and such an excuse or sacrifice from you. . . . What king is this 'They' whose authority is so frequently proclaimed? He is a king with no pomp, no visible throne and, even so, at the sound of his voice, all obey, all tremble. . . ."[17] Necker's was a perfect model of Germaine's own stance, resenting this voice, but heedful of it. In fact, because Léonce becomes society's mouthpiece, we may conclude that this hero owes not a little to Necker. The battle that raged both within Mme de Staël and between her and her *bien-pensant* father is repeated in the struggle between Léonce and Delphine. By making it impossible for Delphine to live up to society's expectations of her, Léonce still demands emotionally that she do so. His strong sense of propriety is also a legacy of Narbonne's: "Mme de Staël is, with all her wildness and blemishes, a delightful companion, and M. de N. rises upon me in esteem . . . : their minds in some points ought to be exchanged, for his is as delicate as a really feminine woman, and evidently suffers when he sees her setting *les bienséances* aside, as it often enough befalls her to do," wrote Fanny Burney's sister to her.[18] Fundamentally, the evil Léonce unknowingly enacts is that of pride.

---

17. Jacques Necker, "Mélanges," in *Oeuvres complètes*, 15 vols. (Paris: Treuttel et Würtz, 1821), XV, 257.

18. Frances Burney d'Arblay, *The Diary and Letters of Madame d'Arblay*, edited by her niece, 2 vols. (Philadelphia: Carey and Hart, 1842), II, 394.

At first Delphine's lover is presented as rather formidable, strong but moody, as befits the pre-Romantic mold; but Léonce also suggests the more traditionally heroic Cornelian source, uniting as he does, "in the highest degree pride, courage, intrepidity, all that inspires respect." However, it is rather as a wounded warrior, pale and Christlike, that Delphine first sees him and as the story progresses we observe that Léonce, despite appearances, is not strong at all: he is a weakling whose moral cowardice and bullying will in the end revolt the reader. He is a seducer: "Love me and be adored in the smallest detail of your charms," he will say, or that old reliable "Oh! Delphine, the laws of society were made for ordinary people" (III, I). Sometimes he threatens: "You will become hard and lose your perfect goodness" (III, III) if she does not give herself to him. He threatens her with the loss of her beauty: "It is your depth of feeling that gives a celestial air to your features." Finally, Léonce accuses Delphine of causing his wife, Matilde, pain by withholding herself from him: ". . . if I plunge the knife of pain into Matilde's heart, it will not be my maddened hand that will be to blame, it is coldness and tyrannical reason that will have deranged me" (III, v). Here, even Delphine loses patience and berates him for his moral blackmail, but this is not by any means the last time he will employ such a stratagem. Later he threatens to die if she should leave him: "No command of yours could make me bear life if I ceased to see you" (III, XXIX). At long last, Léonce realizes that his problem lies in his own personality. When he goes off to war he writes Delphine: ". . . is it not the most singular and frightful [torture] of all to find in our own hearts the tendency that parts us from the object of our love?" (VI, XVIII). There is a core of sadness in Léonce's rather violent nature that is intensified by his fear and uncertainty and his need to be right.

Again Mme de Staël's sense of character and her probing of herself to find elements of this hero triumph over her intent. She wished to create a fiery Spaniard, strong yet tender, but she makes him speak and act in such a way that her readers have found him perhaps believable, but certainly not admirable. We see him as cruel, immature, and neurotic, and wonder why the "gentle" Delphine continues to be taken in. If the character of Léonce is a strangely troubling and disagreeably convincing one, it is because it was Germaine herself, as much as it was Benjamin Constant, who was obsessed with her standing, if not her behavior, in the world and who was given, in the extremities of disappointed passion, to making low threats against her lovers. Mme de Staël rejects these unsavory parts of her own nature as imperfect and unfeminine and makes them adjuncts of the destructive male.

To the same degree that Delphine is selfless, Léonce is selfish. He is so exclusive in loving that he cannot bear even to share in the admiration others give to her. "I suffered from the agreement of all these minds with my own," he reflects as he sees her dance the polonaise at a party; "I would have been happier if I alone had been watching her" (I, xxvii). The heroine's love, Mme de Staël wrote in her reflections on the novel, is more perfect than the hero's: "this must be so, because she loves and is a woman."[19] To love "better" is to give oneself utterly to passion, and passion, in a logical extension of Rousseau's will so to believe, is necessarily good. In love, self is forgotten, the world beyond it melts, and the boundaries of the self become obscure. Evil is a force from without, one foreign to Delphine's intrinsic goodness. She asks: "Have you not yourself felt that there exist in us at times transient moods that are absolutely contrary to our nature? It is to explain these contradictions in the human heart that people use the expression: 'these are the devil's thoughts.' Good impulses spring from the bottom of our hearts; the evil ones seem to come from some foreign source that troubles the order and the coherence of our reflections and our character" (I, xii). This is not to say that Delphine has no self-doubts. Had she not written, "To keep the heart in all its purity, we must not shun to look within ourselves" (I, xii)? The pure heart is not the one that knows no fault, but the heart that comprehends its errors. Nevertheless, Delphine's self-searching remains mild: she usually finds herself innocent.

When Léonce has insisted that to save her reputation she attend a concert where she is disdained by all, she goes out into the open, distracted and dismayed: "Alone, on foot, in the wind and the rain, dressed as for a ball, without reflecting an instant upon what drove me there, I fled before malevolence and hatred." Lé-

---

19. Rousseau had held that women could not love as well as men: *Delphine* is a flat contradiction of that thesis.

once, remorseful, follows and offers to die with her if she wishes. Disheartened, she asks, "Am I still as I was?" She then decides that her plight is caused by "the others": "The wicked have finally given my soul a mortal wound" (IV, xxvIII). Her self-assurance begins to return. The error is not hers after all, only the hurt; society is in error in judging her ill. The incomprehension and absurdities of the multitude are to blame.

Evil is the shock that comes to the self, ever an innocent victim, in the form of the world's disapproval.

Liebestod

There is paradox here. The position of victim is one women have assumed and been made to assume so untiringly that it is considered by some as a natural disposition of their nature, and masochism is at times given virtually as Delphine's *raison d'être*. Indeed she has an urge, verging on delirium, to sacrifice herself. "An unspeakable emotion came over my heart yesterday, obscuring my reason, my virtue, all my strength; and I felt an inexpressible desire to restore your life at the expense of my own, to shed my blood so as to warm yours, and to give my last breath to warm your trembling hands" (III, xxIV). This passage recalls the frenzy of *Zulma*. A palpable sensuality, otherwise unavowed, obviously speaks in this desire. Delphine is anxious to sacrifice her life for love. Yet in another connection she says, "My character lacks the strength necessary to make sacrifices," and indeed she is markedly unwilling to sacrifice anything less than her life.

Mme de Staël is assumed to be, despite her varied amorous life, a fleshless author. It is held that there is in her work no overt expression of sensuality beyond that found in the nicest, most demure novels of the period—perhaps even somewhat less. Yet *Delphine* is a very *young* work, and so a strong sense of latent sexuality is present in it.

Having already been wounded in the intemperate defense of his family's honor before we first see him, Léonce de Mondoville is the image of the pale and vulnerable yet essentially proud and strong hero in Delphine's eyes. This physical weakness of his clearly has sexual force for the author. As the couple dance together in the early days of their love, the delight of self-abandon in the pleasures of rhythm and touch make them lose their sense of re-straint: "It seemed to me that her arms," wrote Léonce, "opened almost involuntarily to call me back, and that despite her perfect lightness, she was often pleased to lean upon me" (I, XXVII). They dance so intently they forget Léonce's serious wound, which then opens and becomes painful, occasioning Delphine, in the extremity of her concern for him, to compromise herself by showing how openly she cares.

The wounded hero is synonymous with the passionate hero in the physical stress of his desire, and the heroine who goes to his aid is exhibiting her ready responsiveness to him.

In the battle Delphine wages against Léonce to maintain her chastity, he often argues well for he defends the author's actual practices: "Believe me, Delphine, there is virtue in love, there is even some virtue in the total gift of oneself to a lover that you so condemn." Her counterargument is not a refusal of him, but of her own vilification: "Do you wish to degrade Delphine's image?" She is, of course, here giving voice to the argument of public opinion, but it is clear that Delphine overwhelmingly wants to give her-self: "I was born to obey him as much as to adore him. . . ." If she says she fears she will cease to admire and perhaps to love him if he forces her surrender, these concerns are clearly those of a self-love in conflict with her own will to surrender.

When Delphine hides from her violent lover, the merest sight of him in the courtyard becomes intensely sensual: ". . . never, I confess, have I found in your face and expression a seductive charm that more completely penetrated my being." The more his passion is sharpened, the greater his pain, the more seductive he becomes to her, despite her denunciation of his threats. When Delphine forces the reluctant Léonce to accompany her to the church where Thérèse has resolved to take her vows to warn them against her profane example, the couple, in their grief and love, are seized by that deep, oceanic feeling Mme de Staël so often speaks of. "I asked God if I might die in that state, it was so full of delight; I no longer imposed anything upon my soul, it gave it-self up to a boundless emotion; it seemed to me I would die weep-ing, and that my life was about to end in an immoderate passion of pity and loving-kindness" (III, XLIX). This climactic emotion is one of generosity, of an acceptance passing beyond the premises of all but the most primal duty, that of love. No wonder Mlle d'Albémar thinks of any "error" of Delphine's as "an error such as an angel would commit if it witnessed human weakness and suffering." Sensuality is an intrinsic part of this cult of loving kindness for Mme de Staël. It is fleshlessness, its opposite, as we have seen in the cases of Mme de Vernon and Mme de Ternan, that is evil.

Freedom

The rejection of limits has a face other than that of the sensual liberation toward which Delphine is drawn: it is the face of freedom. This is a heroine astonishingly and unwarrantedly independent in mind. "Why, lovely Delphine, why," her puzzled lover asks, "do you support opinions which arouse so much hateful passion and to which your class, perhaps rightly, has such an aversion?" Part of the answer lies in Delphine's upbringing which, no less than Germaine Necker's, was like Emile's. Her soul is free and natural, given to its own impulsions.

The very essence of Delphine's way of being is the liberal credo that truth is relative to the self, never absolute. A shifting relativism embraces all aspects of Mme de Staël's thinking, without, paradoxically, affecting her style or her depiction of character. It affects her conception of character, even though she does not herself fully realize this in fiction:

Alas! from one age to another there is frequently more difference to be discerned in a single person than between two beings totally different from each other; and yet the man of one day can enslave a whole life! what has the imagination not invented to give itself moorings! but of all will-o-the-wisps, eternal vows are the most unbelievable and terrifying. Our moral nature rises up at the idea of this total enslavement of our future, which was originally given us that we might place our hopes in it unbounded, and only crime could deprive us of it with no recourse. (VI, XII)

The love of freedom is not only an individual, but also a political cult, and Mme de Staël makes Henri de Lebensei say, in defense of the Revolutionary party, "Each time a nation strives toward freedom, I may profoundly condemn the means it uses; but it would never be possible for me to remain indifferent to its goal." For Mme de Staël, lightly as this is touched on in this particular work, Rousseau's model of progressive education and his belief in the cultivation of the individual judgment and conscience fuse with Montesquieu's conception of the enlightened state. The Revolution is for her the future. To crush it would be to stifle "all the ideas that for four centuries enlightened spirits have worked to gather together." The truth that is finally born to the conscience of a searching spirit is, or should be, in contrast to the shifting values it tests and sets aside, firm. Once Henri has resolved to help Léonce divorce Matilde so he can marry Delphine he proclaims, "No, let all the prejudice in the world arm itself against me, no matter! I know I do a good thing . . . ; I disdain any who would attack me . . . ; they will never shake that perfect conviction of spirit which is also a conscience for an enlightened man." In this independence of all but one's own lights we see Mme de Staël's ideal for the free man. As Delphine's evasiveness illustrates, this ideal is not deemed accessible to her, a woman.

Freedom, "the prime happiness, the only glory of the social order," is a kind of total *disponibilité,* an availability to experience. Its converse, rigid restraint of any kind, is wicked. We think of Blake's "Damn braces, bless releases." We might have predicted that religion would not have a place of honor in this scheme.

Faith

The author's outrage at the Church of Rome and its rigidities is embodied, in the novel, in a pointed contrast of death scenes. As representation of Catholic rites, we are given Matilde's death throes, during which her confessor, "a man filled with both fanaticism and ability," repeatedly brings her the crucifix to be kissed. Elise de Lebensei, outraged, writes to Delphine: "Is it right to surround our last moments with so sinister a panoply, to surpass death itself in frightening us . . . ?" (VI, IV).

In edifying contrast we had earlier been witness to the death of Sophie de Vernon which reflected Mme de Staël's attempt to grapple with her own conception of dignity in dying. Matilde is naturally anxious that her mother receive the last sacrament, but Mme de Vernon, in token of her change of heart, her conversion to Delphine's "religion" of sincerity, refuses. "Deceit has sullied my life; I do not wish my last act to partake of its character. I have always disliked the Catholic death rites; they have something somber and awful about them that does not accord with my idea of the goodness of the Supreme Being. Above all, I am deeply opposed to opening my heart to a priest, perhaps to anyone else but you . . ." (II, XLI). Of course it is Delphine she is speaking to and Delphine it is who undertakes to "play priest" to Mme de Vernon, or, as a wry critic of the era puts it, "the priest is packed off and Delphine mounts astride the sublime to lead the slightly blackened soul of Mme de Vernon to heaven."[20] This she does by preparing Mme de Vernon for a humanist's death by reading to her from the works of "some ancient and modern moralists, religious and philosophical, what was most meet to sustain a waning soul in the face of death's terror." The state of mind Delphine tries to induce in Mme de Vernon, as well as her means, give one an idea of her religion. Tranquility is her goal: ". . . never before had one been able to awaken deep within the heart those feelings and devout emotions that make us pass gently from the last glow of life into the pale glow of the tomb" (II, XLIII). It is those elements of the continuum of life and death that are sought out and looked upon as comforting. That melodrama so much enjoyed in the midst of life is shunted aside in favor of a meditative calm.

This peaceful female death scene is brusquely broken into by Matilde, who arrives with her confessor to plead that her mother accept the ministrations of the priest, that she might not suffer eternal damnation.[21] To this occasion Mme de Vernon rises, roundly sermonizing her daughter and the priest, assuring them that "no man can tell me if God has forgiven me; the voice of my conscience will inform me of that better than you" (II, XLI). In the voice of conscience, as always, we hear the call to insubordination.

Guilt

"Real" morality is natural; "sham" morality is that dictated from above or beyond the self. From this it follows that the indi-

---

20. F. (Fiévée?), *Mercure de France,* XI, no. LXXIX (Nivôse an XI—Jan., 1803), p. 78.
21. This scene is paralleled by Meursault's angry rejection of the priest in Camus's *The Stranger,* his only moment of passion in the work.

vidual is basically innocent and that Delphine is a martyred victim to her belief that virtue is "consistency in one's generous impulses." "Your grace is in your self-abandon and naturalness," her lover writes to her, ". . . you speak on impulse and this impulse is the true genius that inspires you; but just that quality that makes you charming for one who understands how to know you makes the conduct of your life dangerous for you" (III, XVI). Delphine is the protected young person who has never known between herself and others "any other relations than those of the services I might render them or the affection I might inspire in them." Unconsciously condescending, then, she is shocked out of her dream of oneness with the world by the hostility she meets.

Matilde's late entry onto the scene brings in a painful reality Mme de Staël had sedulously postponed to enable her lovers to maintain the semblance of a love without consequences to others. When Delphine weakly asserts, "Are you forgetting, Matilde, that our relationship . . . was never guilty?," Mme de Staël, whose sympathies are nearly all on her protagonist's side, is nonetheless unable to prevent Matilde from making an impassioned reply: "You call guilt only that last wrong that would have dishonored you; but what name do you give to stealing my husband's affections from me?" Delphine has seen Léonce every day for a year and pretends not to be guilty. "What innocence, merciful heavens!" cries the outraged wife.

As Matilde angrily demands that her rival depart without further ado, Delphine agrees to do so, but in the moment of giving up Léonce she feels justified: "my soul, in its sacrifice, became superior to hers" she claims. "I have more than expiated my sins; I believe myself to be above those women who would not know the feelings over which I triumph" (IV, XXVII).

Delphine's vigorous rejection of guilt, far from being a shadowless protective screen, as the novel's detractors tend to see it, is more truly a pompous defensive posture adopted after an unhappy self-examination. We see how, in her removal from society, Delphine questions herself and wonders first if she is not demented: "Is it possible that an enthusiastic and passionate nature is a step [sic] closer to madness?" She decides in the end that her folly is not of that order. "No, my plaints are not justified," she admits, but only to her own journal. "It is vain for me to hide it from myself. I do not suffer for my virtues, but for my faults; have I respected morality and virtue in all their compass? There was nothing of wickedness in my heart, but was there nothing guilty?" This guilt is unbearable, and Delphine again appears to admit her fault only to find in herself some higher virtue: "The soul that is tenderest and purest is punished for the least of faults because it has felt and fought against them, because it has *sacrificed its ethic to its passions*,[22] whereas those who are never warned by their own hearts live without reflecting and degrade themselves with no remorse . . . my regrets are heaven's punishment!" (v, fragment vi).

All of her superiority can give Delphine only momentary comfort, and the cult of individual morality is just as unforgiving in time of stress as it had been indulgent in time of prosperity. "I give in to unconsidered impulses; my best qualities draw me further on, and my reason intervenes too late to hold me back. . . ." This rooting of events in character sounds lucid enough, but it is a truth that cannot be borne plain. If Henri de Lebensei, the free man, is able to accept this truth ("Is the source of good ever entirely pure?"), Delphine, the woman who has been deluded into thinking herself free, is totally undone by the revelation of moral ambiguity. Accused by Matilde, unable to accept guilt, Delphine wants only to die, and she accepts the living death of the cloister. When Henri suggests to the newly free Léonce that Delphine renounce her ill-advised vows and marry him, the proud hero swoons and Delphine once more feels her openness of character as a curse. "You see, I bring him death: I do not know what kind of being I am; I bring woe wherever I go . . ." (vi, x).

Death apotheosizes guilt, absolving it. Failing that ultimate, suffering may suffice. An inexhaustible dolorism permeates the latter part of the novel. "In no work do I see, before [Mme de Staël's] own, such concentrated attention given to the ultimate tortures that completely alter the moral ambience, afflict the very sense of being, and end in a sort of doubling of vision, as if an excess of

---

22. Italics mine.

wretchedness made us unrecognizable to ourselves: 'It seemed to me that it was my phantom that walked among the living.' "[23] This *doppelgaenger* effect is unbearable to Delphine. To survive oneself, one's own vitality, one's powers to love and to act, is to *live* no longer so that the only appropriate issue becomes a willed death.

Suicide

For Delphine, by virtue of her independence of character, love is an act, not a surrender. As her acts of defiance of society's law turn one by one into provocations of disapproval and pain to others and to herself, her freedom is reduced to nothingness. The only gesture of freedom left to her is that of suicide, but this suicide, to be valid, must be witnessed by the beloved. Delphine agrees with Montaigne's dictum that "the most willed death is the most beautiful one," and we have seen her help Mme de Vernon gain control over that passage. Nevertheless, Delphine's suicide is portrayed, in the novel, as an act of despair, only partly as one of reflection: she resolves to die because she is about to lose her "only love." It is *survival* that would be felt by her as sinful,[24] perhaps the greatest sin. For a woman to outlive love, the ultimate value of her existence, would make no sense. This is the *reductio* Delphine portrays.

"People only kill themselves if, in some sense, they have always been outside of everything. It is a matter of an original unsuitability that we may be unaware of. The one who is *called* to kill himself belongs only by chance to this world; at bottom he belongs nowhere."[25] Delphine's "new" original sin lies in her having the wrong character for a woman and being, in her readiness to defy opinion, not of her world, indeed of none, as her sense of being a phantom at the ball suggests. Mme de Staël's own constant threats of suicide certainly demonstrate this truth: "The obsession

23. Joachim Merlant, *Le Roman personnel en France de Rousseau à Fromentin* (Paris: Hachette, 1905), p. 221.

24. See Jean Starobinski's discussion "Suicide et mélancolie chez Madame de Staël" and also Jean-Albert Bédé's excellent study, "Mme de Staël, Rousseau et le suicide," *Revue d'Histoire Littéraire de la France,* 66, no. 1 (1966), 52–70.

25. E. M. Cioran, *Le Mauvais Demiurge* (Paris: Gallimard, 1969), p. 73.

with suicide is the characteristic of one who can neither live nor die, and whose attention never wanders from this dual impossibility."[26] The author, cursing in her letters her inability to suppress her instinct to live when her lovers fail her, yet withal vibrant and responsive to life, is hung on this dilemma. Like the unhappy Léonce bewailing the fate that saved him from drowning, Mme de Staël would cry, "Danger retreats from the unhappy; it leaves all to the will . . ." (1, 26).

Delphine's suicide sublimates the suffering and the guilt, but it is also an act, and that is its psychic importance to the novel. "To kill yourself is, in fact, to compete against death, it is to show you can do better than it, play it a trick. . . . I say to myself: 'Til now unable to take any initiative, I had no esteem for myself; now all is changed: in destroying myself, I destroy in this stroke all my reasons for scorning myself. I regain confidence, I am someone for all time."[27]

The suicide that completes the work is its essential ending, and the later substitute, despite some merit, can never be considered one with it. The too-gifted Delphine dies to prove the totality of her impasse and to make herself "someone for all time." Mme de Staël has her die to destroy that impasse in herself, to enable her to bypass the murderous paradoxes of love and opinion in her own life. Rising to an unexpected height of courage and self-abnegation through her death, Delphine becomes heroic. Mme de Staël leaves the pathetic wraith, superior but guilt-ridden, tucked between the inside pages of her book.

The Novel

Mme de Staël wrote her novel for those "gifted with a critical mind, and with a heart that suffers from the verities the mind uncovers to it." In *Some Reflections on the Moral Goal of Delphine*, she argues with a putative opponent who might say to her, "There is real danger in your novel: you celebrate only youth and love in it, depicting its problems alone; you fail to show life's serious and dutiful aspect; you make us disgusted with the grave, cold ex-

---

26. Cioran, *Le Mauvais Demiurge*, p. 87.
27. Cioran, *Le Mauvais Demiurge*, p. 75.

istence nature inflicts upon half of mankind and upon half our life span." To this she replies only that such a reproach is more to be directed against novels in general than against hers alone. Her argument then turns to an excellent defense of love itself. Love exists. As so great a part of existence it deserves our attention: ". . . the most happy marriages are those which, even in old age, rebound from memory to memory, back to love. We never say filial friendship, motherly friendship," she insists. For these feelings only the tenderest word will do. The word love is also that used to express our feeling for humankind. "The power of love is the source of all men have done that is noble, pure, and disinterested on this earth. I believe that works that develop this power with nuance and sensibility will always do more good than harm: nearly all the human vices presuppose hardness of heart."

This novel unfortunately does not always sustain her high aim. Aside from its inherent inconsistencies, it is derivative in its tone and method and, worse, it mimics the theatrical sentimental platitudes of its decade with painful fidelity. Its language is distinguished primarily by its imprecision and verbosity.[28] But if Mme de Staël chose inadequate models for her *Delphine* and was not quite enough the innovative artist to create new ones, the reason must be partially sought in the nature of her undertaking. Insofar as *Delphine* is a woman's novel, Mme Riccoboni's and Mme Cottin's works were as germane to its spirit and content as were Prévost's.[29] But the woman's novel was, all in all, a timorous genre, striving to score its points against a colorless facade of ordinary, readable niceness.

In its totality, then, *Delphine* is not easy to read, but no one denies that, in a thousand places within it, it succeeds. Mme de Staël's *critique mondaine*, for example, is shrewd though it plays only a minor role in her novel. Delphine writes of Mme du Marset, who had taken an intense dislike to her because of her popu-

---

28. See Lucia Omacini's article "Quelques remarques sur le style des romans de Madame de Staël, d'après la presse de l'époque (1802–1808)," *Annali di Ca'Foscari*, X, fasc. 1–2 (1971), 213–38.

29. Le Breton in fact makes an extended parallel between *Delphine* and Mme Cottin's *Amélie Mansfield*.

larity: "For a while I tried to appease her; but when I saw . . . that since she could not create her life out of friendship she had taken the tack of doing so out of hatred, I resolved to disregard whatever was real in her aversion for me" (I, vi). Monsieur de Fierville is her admirer who has "more wit than she and less character, a circumstance that allows her to quite dominate him." Mme de Staël here skillfully and lightly illustrates the game of appearance and reality that is the subject of all commentators on the life of society. Her *portraits* are also fine, if frozen; but here we come to grips with the inherent difficulty of accommodating within a single work the conflicting manners of the eighteenth-century salon style of character description and the sheer melodrama of the novel's great scenes, and even of some smaller ones. When Delphine, after Léonce is married, goes to the theater to see Voltaire's *Tancrède*, she sees a dramatic figure of a man, draped in a cloak, weeping ostentatiously over Amenaïs's faithlessness and, overcome, stumbling from the theater. It is Léonce, of course. An ironic, sophisticated, contained salon spirit and a palpitating, soaring, liberating Romanticism jar each other painfully in *Delphine*, which in this respect gives itself away as a creation of artistic and spiritual irresolution.

Mme de Vernon's dying hours in Delphine's care partake of the ideologized prose-poetry of an Enlightenment meditation, but Romantic melodramatism erupts into it with the violent rejection of Matilde's confessor and then altogether engulfs the action when Léonce, upon learning of Sophie's perfidy and willfully ignoring Delphine's plea that the woman is dying, demands that she free him of his bond to Matilde. In a scene worthy of Donizetti's collaboration, Delphine takes it upon herself to assure the dying woman that she will protect her own rival's happiness. Stendhal tried to diagnose the trouble: "If Mme de Staël had not wished to be more passionate than nature and her early education had made her, she would have written masterpieces."[30] In some of the less fulsomely dramatic action, such as the wedding scene, or the

---

30. Victor del Litto, *La Vie intellectuelle de Stendhal; genèse et évolution de ses idées* (1802–1821) (Paris: Presses Universitaires Françaises, 1959), p. 279.

St.-Albe concert, or the masked ball, where we follow Delphine's consciousness as she passes through that dreamlike scene, the more the author contemplates, the more successful she is.

Accordingly, some of the finest passages in the book are descriptions of Delphine's anguish: of waiting, for a letter or a visit that seems never to come; of fear that Léonce does not love her; of bewilderment about the rightness of her course. And there is too a profusion everywhere of penetrating and felicitously phrased commentary that raises the work far above the level of apparently similar novels. The heroine will remark: ". . . we are content with none of our faculties, with none of our opinions, once they have been useless against the punishments of life" (v, III); or in a more analytical vein, when discussing Léonce's mania for honor, she has the sensible Lebensei write in a way that suggests our modern neuroses and the workings of the unconscious:

There is in nearly all men something that partakes of folly, a certain vulnerability that makes them suffer, a weakness to which they never confess and that has more power over them than all the motives they talk about; it is a sort of mania in the soul that the circumstances particular to each man develop in him; we must treat it in itself . . . we must avoid objects that would arouse the mania, make a new life and occupations, outfox the imagination . . . instead of trying to subdue it, for it influences our happiness even if we prevent it from dominating our conduct. (VI, XII)

Mme Necker de Saussure's remarks on the effect of this novel are, as usual, cogent. She writes that its impact is "powerful, and I am not sure that it is not especially so in its least stormy scenes. Perhaps her talent is most remarkable when it is least self-conscious, and when the author and the reader are not warned of its appearance. Mme de Staël was better equipped to depict love in its noble exaltation than in its fury. So it turns out that as an expression of passion itself, the pieces written by Delphine when she believes herself separated forever from Léonce are incomparably the most affecting ones" (I, cv).

This is the paradox in the composition of Delphine: the characters are well, even splendidly, drawn in themselves, in their own hopes, hesitancies, and failures. The author's moral imagination is, though wavering, credible. But when the characters interact, the believability they possessed in stasis fades. There is a further hiatus in tone between the bantering and worldly treatment of the minor characters and the sometimes grandiose melodramatism of the depiction of hero and heroine. The irresolution in the novel is patent even to its smallest formal detail, and it is certainly visible in the vicissitudes of its plot. In *Delphine* subplots are so intrusive that we sometimes have the impression we are juggling five works, not one: the novel of Delphine, Léonce, and Matilde; the novel of Delphine and Mme de Vernon (though these two are linked); the novella of Thérèse d'Ervins and M. de Serbellane; the novella of the Lebenseis; and the novella of the Mondoville family and Mme de Ternan. Even these hardly exhaust the peripheral occurrences of the work. As she confessed to Fanny Burney, Mme de Staël had difficulty imagining any new tale that would be ingenious and natural withal. It is as if, in her insecurity and ambition combined, she did not know when to stop.

This mixture of modes, the proliferation of side issues, the unwillingness to leave anything unsaid once it presented itself to her mind, all these factors combine to make *Delphine* very long and uneven. As was often the case with the rambling picaresque novel, which with its multitude of incidents it resembles, there is no intelligible curve to the intrigue: the author simply subjects her heroine to as many different trials by social pressure as possible. Delphine's dilemma itself, played out in all these *péripéties*, makes an ending implausible. Either Delphine sacrifices happiness and leaves Léonce, or she sacrifices virtue and lives with him. It is within Mme de Staël's power to make neither choice for her heroine. Clearly both must die, but how? From our own moral standpoint in the late twentieth century the suicide, over which so many contemporary readers wept, seems trumped up. For us, she might better have ended her novel where she began both denouements. At that point, Léonce, arriving too late to prevent Delphine from taking the vows of her novitiate, is prevailed upon by Henri de Lebensei not to consider these binding but to take Delphine away with him so that they may consider together their future course. This Léonce consents to do only so as not to ruin Delphine's life, though for himself he wants only to die. Delphine leaves the convent with him, and "their fate now depends upon themselves alone." An "ambiguous" ending at this point would have appeared consistent with the insoluble problem of the novel and would have accorded more with our modern sensibility. But the Romantic spirit operated in response to other imperatives.

> To be good only is to be
> As God or else a pharisee
> BLAKE

Lies, Evasions, Contradictions

Curiously it appears as if she preferred the role of victim to that of fighting heroine, as if tyranny were more atrocious when it was relentless in persecuting weaker beings.

Mme de Staël, this actor par excellence, this dominator by instinct, loves what is most "feminine" in women, most gentle; happiness is a dream of passivity. Even when they enjoy the greatest gifts of intelligence, the heroines of her novels submit to their destiny. She transforms herself in her *Ten Years of Exile* in the same way. She appears embarrassed to play a role in the book where she relates the story of a writer mixed up in politics. She is no more than a rather innocent woman, at the most inconsequential and in any case not responsible, just like other women, conforming to the role the society of her time assigns her.[31]

The fascination of Delphine the heroine lies in her dissimilarity to her author. Meek and meltingly beautiful, her only apparent pretension is to please. She is intended to be the eternal woman as man seemed to wish her, living by and for love. "I am proud of my passion for Léonce," writes Delphine; "it is my glory and my destiny, all that is in harmony with it gives honor to me in my own eyes . . . I give myself to it as do believers to their faith. I am nothing except through Léonce" (VI, XIII). But, as we have established, what is the novel *Delphine* but the demonstration of the nonviability of such a femininity?

Delphine exhibits the author's pull toward immanence, toward that fullness one can find within the confines of existence, in which one is altered but does not materially alter the other. Prudhomme, the misogynist, said of Portia, that model of woman-

---

31. Simone Balayé, introduction to *Dix Années d'exil* (Paris: Bibliothèque 10–18, 1966), p. xviii.

kind, that she wrote no books. The cedar, he claimed, was built to brave the winds, but the rose knows only breezes: "Nature never made women to reflect, but rather to love and to be."[32]

One of the novel's more cutting critics mocks the heroine: "It must be seen with what amorous anxiety . . . Delphine makes herself into a housewife, sets the fire, prepares a supper with her own hands, one of two eaten in the novel, where the characters usually go without food. She demonstrates that in 'these good and simple attentions it is sometimes pleasant to find how in one's home' an intelligent woman, 'even the most remarkably beautiful and witty one' acquits herself better, infinitely better, than a stupid woman."[33] What appears to be ridiculous to him is the pretension both to the simpler and to the more complex gifts, and yet how is this drive to "be feminine," to occupy herself with her interior, its appointments, its comforts, any different from that of the modern woman executive who must be an exquisite cook, bake bread, and demonstrate flawless taste in her ingeniously decorated home to be considered feminine? Woman has been imprisoned in immanence, but it would be an absurdity for her to turn her back upon it, for it has been the sole important area in which her creativity has been welcome, and we are only beginning to realize how crucial the creative contributions to our intimate lives have been to our evolution as people, intimacy having been carefully abstracted from our understanding of history. If Mme de Staël is drawn to the immanent role, it is not alone because it is the only truly acceptable social role for woman in her time, but because she perceives its inherent worth, as is shown by her admirative portrait, in the novel, of Mme de Cerlèbe, the woman fulfilled as mother and daughter.

But what is perplexing is not so much her admiration for a kind of being she does not emulate, but her frenzied will, as expressed in *Delphine*, to embrace it, to be engulfed by love until death.[34] For Mme de Staël the ending of love is the greatest evil,

32. See Lacour, *Les Origines*, p. 265.

33. Larg, *La Seconde Vie*, p. 51.

34. Pierre Fauchery's study is illuminating here in demonstrating the omnipresence of the love-victim aura in the vast majority of the feminine novels of the period.

and even death is deemed good if it forestalls this horror. "Ah," cries the dying Delphine, "from what evil does death save me!" Denis de Rougemont has written of the chivalric ideal as a progression toward the death in which Tristan is purified. In Tristan and Iseult's tale the obstacle to love, rather than its fulfillment, actually becomes the goal. "And passion has only played a purifying role, one might almost say a penitential role in the service of that transfiguring death. . . . The love of love itself hid a much more terrible passion, a deeply inadmissible will. . . . Unknowingly, the lovers, despite themselves, never desired anything but death! Unknowingly, passionately deceived, they never sought anything but salvation and revenge for 'what they had undergone'—the passion awakened by the philter."[35] Delphine's *Liebestod* little resembles the enchantment, the waking dream of the philter, even as she most aspires to this magical state. She finishes her existence only when all her strength is wasted; "her theatrical death is prolonged through several scenes and she ends her existence in an apotheosis."[36]

Moreover love itself is experienced by the heroine as violence. First, Delphine's heart is tortured by her lover's "unworthy threats"; then she is made to go with him to the church where he had married Matilde, only to hear him cry, "Swear to your lover you will be his or I will break my head upon these stones before your very eyes and my blood will be upon you" (III, LXIX). Delphine, shamed and abased, begins to despair. In a strikingly cinematic description, she recalls her dismay in the scene at the concert where she was treated as an outcast in an episode such as that Mme de Staël had herself endured:

. . . no woman offered me a seat next to her, no man rose to give me his. I began to see things double, my agitation increased at each useless step that I took; I felt as if everyone were looking at me, even though I dared raise my eyes to no one; as I went forward, they withdrew from in front of me; men and women stepped aside to let me pass, and I found myself alone in the midst of a circle, not as a queen would be, surrounded by respect, but like a criminal, to whom any approach would have been fatal.

---

35. Denis de Rougemont, *L'Amour dans l'occident* (Paris: Plon, 1939), pp. 36–37.
36. Merlant, *Le Roman personnel*, p. 225.

In my despair I noticed that the door of the salon was open . . . ; this exit that opened before me seemed to me an undreamed of escape and in a confused state resembling madness I went from that chamber, descended the staircase, crossed the courtyard, and found myself in the midst of the Place Louis XV . . . ; alone on foot in the wind and the rain, dressed in the apparel of a ball, without having reflected a moment as to what drew me on, I fled before malevolence and hatred as if before sword's points that pressed me ever farther. (IV, XXVIII)

We recognize the old theme of exile, but here we perceive that this hatred on the part of society is an effect, though not an immediate one, of love.

This pathos of victimization is metamorphosed into a wrath and violence that achieve their most sinister effect, in *Delphine*, in the story of the judge's pardon. Léonce having been imprisoned at Chaumont, Delphine goes to the judge to plead for his release, making a long and tormented argument for judicial charity. The judge is sympathetic. He is himself convinced that Léonce's motives were apolitical, but other members of the jury are sure to condemn him. When the judge's wife enters the room to speak to him of their sick child, Delphine cries out this warning to him: "If you give Léonce over to the court, your child, that which is most dear to you, will die! he will die!" (old conclusion). The wife, terrified, pleads with her husband to release Léonce, and intimidated by this vile bargain, he signs the release.

This passage strikes a curious note: the mild "victim" Delphine has within her the untamed passions and the cruelty of a wild beast. Though it is scarcely Mme de Staël's intent, this incident reflects the darker side of a human nature that takes only itself as arbiter of right, whose will to power is so thwarted that it is tempted to arrogate divine attributes of destructiveness to itself. The poison Delphine takes is her final violence, a punishment, like Werther's of Charlotte, of the inadequate beloved. Delphine's glorious death is supposed to show Léonce in his last moments just what he had squandered in his abject slavery to the world's good opinion.

There is truly no death wish here, but rather a warped will to live. Rougemont's hero is quintessentially male, consumed with guilt over illicit sexual longings. The chivalry Léonce espouses is a masculine *Gestalt*. Mme de Staël uncovers its cruel inadequacy as a code conceivable for a Delphine, notwithstanding her determination to be self-abnegating. Woman, Delphine, does not necessarily feel her own sexuality as guilty. She is often perceived by the man as arousing a passion she may not in the least be aware of, so that her own stance is that of a surprised innocent. Experience decreases her "innocence" and if she then insists too much upon it, she acts in bad faith. An essential falsification of *Delphine* is that the heroine, unlike the novelist, is chaste. The psychological truth the novel exposes is that Mme de Staël, unchaste, did not *really* feel guilty—"nothing in me warns me that love is a crime." Confined to the role of passive, immanent object of another's desire, could women ever be deemed guilty? Mme de Staël, active in love as in everything else, still thought of herself in the passive, masochistic mode, and her ideal of woman and of love embodied this posture.

The scurrilous personal attacks of the left and the right and the reiteration by the Revolution of the ancient prejudices against woman have visibly done their work upon this woman's spirit. In the image of the compromised, trapped, encircled Delphine whom no one will approach in society, we discern how Mme de Staël has distilled the sense of her unacceptability to others. This work consecrates her post-Revolutionary understanding that she may not present herself or any woman much resembling herself as a heroine, and so Delphine is very much an underground self-representation.

What are those explosive matters which have been denied reality, but which nonetheless emerge in the violent and vengeful mood at the end of the novel? The first of these is the problem of talent in woman. When Delphine swears that she lives only for her lover, that her powers of expression and mind are to be used for his delight, Mme de Staël deforms a heroine we see at first as the adornment of Parisian society, but she does so convincingly. After all, women *are* so deformed by their need for love and by the assurance they receive from childhood on of their relative incompetence. "I have no confidence in my own strength; I have to call upon a protective arm. ... I can do nothing for myself; what people are pleased to call my superiority is nothing but vain praise given to a few brilliant and useless gifts; my soul is weak and trembling. . . ." Mme de Staël thus purposefully abases, within her own novel, even the gift that allows her to write. Delphine's distinction of person is allowable only in the realm of sensibility, the realm of immanence. Even in thus limiting her, Mme de Staël transmutes all her distinctions—her intelligence, liberality, enthusiasm—into fatal flaws that, depriving her of love, eventually kill her. This, obviously, is a severe repression of the more powerful statement she would have to make if her heroine were, like herself, a woman of action.

The second question the novel frustrates of its full expression is that of free love. Well before the Revolution the rights of free love were becoming a literary commonplace.[37] Pope makes his Héloïse intone:

> How oft, when pressed to marriage have I said,
> Curse to all laws but those which love has made!
> No, make me mistress to the man I love . . .
> Oh happy state, when souls each other draw
> When love is liberty and nature law.

The theme that occupies Mme de Staël is quite respectably old even in the novel, for Mlle de Gournay, Montaigne's godchild, published in 1594 her *Proumenoir de M. de Montaigne* in which an unmarried girl risks her life and reputation to follow a man she loves.[38] We have witnessed how the conservatism of her parents seems to have inhibited Mme de Staël from admitting the existence of extramarital passion with openness, but it is also true that she herself felt serious ambivalence concerning marriage.

Another essential question repressed in this novel is that of woman's relation to the transcendent: "If I believe my heart, women cannot exist alone in that active, sustained, busy life that makes the world and its interests go round; they need something exalted, enthusiastic, supernatural which carries their spirit off to ethereal regions" (II, XXVI). The question appears to have been

---

37. See Paul van Tieghem, "Les Droits de l'amour et l'union libre dans le roman français et allemand—1760–1790," *Neophilologus*, XII (1927), 96–103.

38. See Marjorie Henry Ilsley, "New Light on the *Proumenoir de M. de Montaigne*," *Modern Philology*, LII, no. 1 (Aug., 1954), 1–11.

raised only to be put to rest. But it does not rest, as we see in the outbreak of Delphine's will in threatening the judge's child with death and in her own suicide. The effect of all this subjugation of instinct, of generosity, of gifts, produces a potential for rage, a will to act even if it be in destruction, wild megalomaniacal flights to insure to the heroine a validation via the imagination that the author felt was denied her in life. In accepting the values of the traditional woman's yoke—marriage, motherhood, and filial piety —*but not for herself*, Delphine illustrates, within her love, an unmistakable will to power. As against the spun-sugar bride and groom she describes near the novel's end, he "calm and tender" guide and support, she "as confident of him" as if he were the "sovereign of her heart," going forth together like Adam and Eve in the Garden of Eden, we have the astonishing letter (III, XVI) from Léonce to Delphine in which he overturns Milton's words of Eve to Adam: "God is thy law, thou mine," by addressing them to his mistress. Delphine it is who becomes lawgiver (she preaches a good deal to her wavering lover), quasi-divine, the "most perfect of [God's] creatures." Here her active, as some will inevitably say "masculine," aspirations crop up, as they do too in Delphine's demonstration of courage before death. But Léonce's adulation has as much the quality of a precarnal courtly paean as of that mirthless homage paid by Milton's Eve to her mate. Mme de Staël's need to be loved *and* admired has forced her to this "absurdity" of making her heroine rival man. It will go much farther in *Corinne*.

A related hypocrisy is Delphine's inability to express the political ideas she professes to believe in. These are instead all stated by Lebensei, who has the organs requisite to pronouncing himself on politics. Of course it was innovative to make Delphine a woman with any ideas at all, but Mme de Staël could not go so far in a novel as to let her state them. The closest she comes to a statement of principle is revealing in terms of its division of labor: "I have no destiny save that of pleasing you . . . ; but if I were a man, it would be as impossible for me not to love liberty, not to serve it, as to close my heart against generosity, friendship, all the truest and purest feelings" (III, XXXIII). Mme de Staël herself of course spoke and published her mind on whatever questions— political or ideological or literary—struck her as requiring her utterance. Though her stance might be muffled by the effects of prejudice, she was no shy Delphine.

Woman's power is licit in *Delphine* only when expressed via man. Her conception of the power to charm a man is, interestingly enough, not a magical one. It is a power consonant with the author's view of freedom. She must enlist the love of a free man through her genuine qualities of charm, wit, and loving-kindness. These powers are not used to bend another's will. Delphine disagrees with Léonce's conservative political views but she does not try to press her own upon him, though she lightly argues against his lack of conviction.

Delphine, an act of expiation of Mme de Staël's own experience of love, is also an assertion of love's limits. Men do not need love as women do, she argues. Having other concerns, they are able to escape the full brunt of its consequences. *Delphine* is an outcry against the injustice that "puts women, by order of society, in the noble impossibility of escaping from the miseries caused by their failings." It is a novel that adopts a "posture of submission" like those that a cornered beast enacts, in the hope of obtaining from the other a sign of nonaggression. In the face of the virulence male-dominated society had shown her, this was a not unnatural course for Mme de Staël to pursue.

Despite her exploration in *Delphine* of the terrain of woman's capacities and their repression, more thoroughgoing and complex than had been seen in any novel before her time, Mme de Staël ultimately lacked the courage to defy opinion openly on their, or her own, behalf. The novel curses their common fate: it does not confront it, except by indirection. Nevertheless, even in its timidities, in its fear of angering the men and their satellite women, it is a document in women's struggle for freedom and her own.

The novel *Delphine* is a protest of a woman against the rules of love and their enslavement of the character of woman. Delphine's tragedy is that of having accepted the rules of the game.

CHAPTER 5

Corinne—Origins

> If anything could disarm my enemies it would be
> this harmless book.
>
> GERMAINE DE STAËL
> MAY 7, 1807

Corinne appeared in print in late April, 1807, in both Leipzig and Paris. Napoleon, who with his police and spies had been quite effective in keeping Mme de Staël away from the capital and who finally had exiled her from France altogether, found himself powerless to prevent everyone from talking about her and her book. "There was but one voice, one cry of admiration in all of European letters; this phenomenon was an event everywhere" (I, cxxxix). The sensation caused by the book was far from being one of praise alone. Bonaparte himself, according to Villemain, attacked the work in the *Moniteur*, stressing the unpatriotic treatment of the Frenchman Erfeuil.[1] But Mme de Staël was not much hurt by even so high-placed a cavil for, as Blennerhasset puts it, "Her success was such that a few isolated criticisms did not injure her in the least."[2] In fact, it was this novel that marked the turning point in her fame.

Whatever virtues *Delphine* may possess as a work of literature, they are surpassed in *Corinne*. One critic looks upon *Corinne* as a retraction of *Delphine* while another thinks of the two volumes as constituting but one novel between them. Both views contain some truth; the second work is in part a continuation of the first, yet in some sense a retraction of it. But it is far more: it is the culmination of Mme de Staël's long meditation, begun in adolescence, upon woman, upon love, upon herself. Mme de Staël's

---

1. Abel François Villemain, *Cours de la littérature française; tableau de la littérature au XVIIIe siècle,* 4 vols. (Paris: Perrin, 1891), IV, 356–57.
2. Blennerhasset, *Madame de Staël et son temps,* III, 197.

cousin-biographer gives us her own telling contrast between the two novels:

> It is simple to see that the fundamental idea in *Delphine* and in *Corinne* is the same. There is in both a woman gifted with superior faculties who cannot bend herself to following the path that public opinion has traced for her, and who is soon prey to the cruelest sufferings because she has departed from that path. . . . The heroine in *Delphine* is exceedingly witty, but she does not have any extraordinary talents to justify her; she has neither complete innocence nor outstanding fame, and nothing detracts from the painful impression she creates. Corinne is presented with more grandeur. . . . For her the struggle is one between marriage and death; there is dignity in this alternative. She is not prey to remorse or to humiliation; she is at odds with the nature of things, with misfortune, and her genius exalts her. (I, cxxxvii-cxxxviii)

Three events of capital importance had transpired between the writing of the two novels: Mme de Staël's first trip to Germany in 1803–4, and especially her stay in Weimar; the death of Necker, which occurred during that trip; and her subsequent voyage to Italy in 1805.

In Germany she had learned from her earnest conversations with the Schlegels, Goethe, Schiller, and Humboldt about a vast new world of thought and feeling. The impact of the German experience has at times been overrated as having wrought a total revolution in Mme de Staël's conceptions.[3] As much as it was an introduction to ideas new to her, her interaction with the Germans gave her the impulse to reassess and select anew from among the views she already held; it had the effect of making her harden and deepen her thinking. It was somewhat as if Kant had provided a rationalization for Rousseau. What more precisely excited Mme de Staël in Germany was not only the dialectic itself but also the dialectical mode of apprehension in which German culture was

---

3. The idea that Mme de Staël underwent a complete transformation in Germany is upheld by Paul Gautier in his *Madame de Staël et Napoléon* (Paris: Plon-Nourrit, 1903) and by Blennerhasset. It is Larg who takes issue with this view, basing his disagreement on the fact that until his time a true biography of Mme de Staël had not been written, but only the biography of the author of *On Germany*. One must agree with him that the perspective on the importance of this voyage has been skewed. This pilgrimage, like the subsequent trip to Germany, tended primarily to confirm and deepen some trends of Mme de Staël's nature. True conversion is rare in human experience.

expressed. The dialectic was a positive delight to this mind that had never been appeased altogether by *la clarté française* and had taken pleasure in exploring apparent contraries, like that of the relative *Weltanschauugen* of the North and of the South (in *On Literature* [1800]). The infinitely greater readiness she found in Germany to engage in metaphysical speculation, of which she was a bit suspicious but which far from displeased her, did in fact change the cast of her mind, but not her beliefs. The mentality of the woman who had conceived the novel *Delphine* was quite different from that of the author of *Corinne*. The pat conventional assumptions concerning good and evil that the author of the first had struggled to uphold, even as she rebelled against them, were now abandoned to her more supple understanding. Germany's bombastic artistic climate, which she had been tempted, Parisian fashion, to ridicule for its grotesque theatricalities, would nevertheless reach a deeper chord of her being in its attempt at poetic flights and its willingness, its anxiety, even, to contemplate mystery.

But it was only after *Corinne,* on her second trip to Germany, in 1807, that Mme de Staël came more completely under the spell of that nation's ethos. In 1803 and 1804, suffering from the thoroughness of Napoleon's ban upon her reappearance in his capital, she was perhaps more taken with the effect she herself produced in Germany than with Germany's effect upon her, and this was more germane to the writing of *Corinne* than all of Kant's philosophy. She wrote to her cousin from Weimar on January 31, 1804: "I have acquired [here] perhaps a rather bad trait: it is the confidence to acknowledge my singularities; for everyone who writes four lines together has so many that I can certainly say what I think. . . . There is more eccentricity here than in France and on account of this my pleasure in the country is all the greater. It also greatly pleases me that they sense a thousandfold more what I may be worth."[4] Received as a celebrity, dined by princes and poets, treated in general like a distinguished exile from a nation that had failed to appreciate her gifts, Mme de Staël felt her self-esteem increase and her personality expand. "There is a current of good nature and admiration for superiority that releases one from being

---

4. Letter 201, *Choix de lettres*, p. 250.

continually on guard, as people habitually are in France."[5] She began, in this exceedingly favorable atmosphere, to lose her sense of self-constraint and wrongness and to reveal, especially to herself, who and what she really was and wanted to be.

This realization was heightened and tragically deepened by the death of her father, on April 10, 1804. She had undertaken her voyage knowing him to be ill, but had acceded to his protestations that she should go. Despite his age, his daughter was in no way prepared for his death, nor could she ever have been, in view of the nature of her tie to him. Her grief was unbounded, for in losing him she lost the purpose of her being, which was to prove her worth to him, the most truly loved one. She gloried in the "insidious sorrow" of her mourning, and it is this somber glorification that colors the novel she wrote in reaction to his death. Dead as alive, he was the greatest force in her life. Old men became a cult for her, and "even as true Christians see Jesus in every poor creature, she saw her father in all old men" (I, ccxxxv). She became increasingly devout out of a longing to find him again beyond the life of the flesh. Some impute the ardor of her dedication to remorse, saying she went to old men seeking "their absolution, to obtain that last blessing she had been unable to deserve."[6] Was her sense of guilt occasioned by the last thoughtless farewell she took from her father, or by her whole (to him) shameless life? Of course these took their toll, but Mme de Staël's greatest remorse, to judge by the novel *Corinne*, was caused by her sense of not having measured up to her father's ideal of womanhood, as her mother had. Caught in a struggle between the will to be free, to be her own unorthodox self, and a will to be loved, to be yielding, gentle, moral, like those women traditionally given fealty by men, she had found herself an ever-aberrant being. This is the great conflict that is at the center of the second novel. And, as *Delphine* was the novel that confronted the mothers and their complicity in woman's fate, *Corinne* will be Mme de Staël's "novel of the fathers."

During this same period Germaine's relations with other men, with her lovers, were equally stormy. Her liaison with Constant,

5. Letter 221, to Mme Necker de Saussure, *Choix de lettres*, p. 267.
6. Larg, *La Seconde Vie*, p. 235.

which he had been wishing intermittently, at least since 1803, to terminate, but which caused him aching doubt—not to mention fear of the unmanageable passions of "Minette"—was still in the balance. Involved with Charlotte von Hardenberg whom he thought he loved and who was ultimately to be the instrument of his liberation from the "too famous" Germaine, Constant wrote of her in wrath on January 1, 1807, "She is the most egotistical, frenetic, ungrateful, vain, and vindictive of women. . . . Even if I had broken with her 8, 7, 6, 5 years ago, had I broken off a year earlier . . . I would have been better off. . . . She is odious to me, hideous, unbearable. I must break it all off or die. . . ."[7] Their almost daily scenes were highly painful to both, but excruciating to Benjamin, who desired calm above everything whereas Mme de Staël appeared to get at least some sadomasochistic gratification from her melodramatic outpourings. It is told of her that one day she cried out before her children, "Here is the man who proposes your ruin or my death. You will be ruined if I marry him, and if he leaves me I'll die."[8] The partners in this unquiet union had long since tired of each other, though never quite entirely, and had sought love elsewhere. Her evident Don Juanism made her restless prey to a need for other, younger, more physically comely lovers, and her emotional state was one of constant alternations of exaltation (as she hoped) and abject dejection (as she despaired), in none of which did she have Constant present in her preoccupations except as an epiphenomenon. She wrote her friend Bonstetten during her Italian voyage, "Alas! As long as I've been alive, this is the first time I've spent two months without a *premier ami*, and I am looking to the heavens here to provide me with one."[9] They were provident: Don Pedro de Souza, Duke of Palmella, briefly became the object of her passionate attachment, but before *Corinne* was finished others (the Austrian Maurice O'Donnell and the Swiss Prosper de Barante) would also attract her. Germaine and Benjamin were irresistibly and cruelly tied by a durable intellectual attraction

7. Henri Benjamin Constant de Rebecque, *Journaux intimes*, ed. Alfred Roulin and Charles Roth (Paris: Gallimard, 1952), p. 130.

8. Marie-Louise Pailleron, *Madame de Staël* (Paris: Hachette, 1931), p. 147.

9. Letter 253, *Choix de lettres*, p. 303.

and by an old and passionless affection. Both inclined to be honorable, they went on thinking from time to time that they should marry, though neither really wanted to. Constant's most believable statement about their relationship is this: "Mme de Staël certainly has many good qualities, but I could never be the center of her life. There would never be any rest."[10]

The emotional ferment of both was such that each wrote a novel, and *Adolphe* and *Corinne* are both fruit of the year 1806.[11] Mme de Staël's work was already in process when Constant began his, and it seems plausible that he felt the need to interrupt his own work on the history of the religions because he wished to give his version of the truth in novel form.[12] Since Mme de Staël's own work was largely completed when she first knew Constant's, she could answer him only in Oswald's tale, which is the exact complement to *Adolphe*, a tale of temporizing and failure of duty.[13]

Synthesizing these currents in her life, the prime source for her novel lay within the novelist, in her ardent drive for self-realization. Healthy at the core, unaffected, amazingly alive, she yet remained unhappy and unreconciled. In Germany she had taken a first step and had admitted to herself that she was simply unlike the generality of women. Though Bonaparte had proven, in exiling her, that he took her seriously—"He fears me, it is my

---

10. Constant, *Journaux intimes*, p. 304. This statement is paralleled by one of her own: "I am a person others can neither live with nor without, not because I am despotic or bitter, but because I seem to everyone to be something odd, worth more and less than the habitual." From a letter to Mme Récamier cited by Henri-Frédéric Amiel, "Madame de Staël," in *La Galerie suisse* (Lausanne: Georges Bridel, 1876).

11. Larg affirms that Constant read his novel to Mme de Staël in November, 1806. There is an entry in Constant's journal for December 28, 1806, stating that he had read the novel to De Boufflers. Because of his notation, "Scène inattendue à cause du roman—Unexpected scene about the novel," we may suppose Mme de Staël to have been present, or at least to have heard details of this reading.

12. See both Larg and Christopher Herold for their able accounts of the parallels between the two. See also Paul Bénichou's admirable synthesis of the character of Ellénore in his "La Genèse d'*Adolphe*," *Revue d'Histoire Littéraire de la France*, 54, no. 3 (1954), 332–56.

13. However, the portrait of Oswald is, even in Oswald's tale, by no means that of Constant alone. Others played their part in its origin, as did Mme de Staël herself. Geneviève Gennari has traced the links of other lovers and friends to the portrait of Oswald as we find it in the novel.

joy, my pride, and it is also my terror"[14]—Napoleon in fact took special pains to humiliate and to ridicule her. He spoke of her as a mere gossip who concerned herself with things beyond her understanding, telling her to go back to her household, her tapestry, her knitting (!). "In 1802 she had written *Delphine* because she had been attacked in her honor as a woman and in her feelings. In 1807, attacked for her intellectual superiority and, so to speak, in the sex of her genius, she published *Corinne*."[15]

The Italian ethos acting upon this injured pride brought *Corinne* into being. Corinne is a Germaine de Staël with a difference, garbed in elegant Roman simplicity, enhanced by the blue and gold aura of Italian sky and sun. The city of Naples cast an even more immediate spell over her. There the power of beauty, before her sojourn a largely theoretical force to Germaine, began to reveal itself to her, causing the neatly bound world in which she had always lived so clumsily to expand its shell and crack. The ease, serenity, and liveliness of Italy wrought deep changes in her moral outlook. Corinne observes to herself that "reason does not consist in triumphing over oneself according to the rules, but however one may manage it" (VI, I).

Byron is supposed to have said of Mme de Staël that "she was goodness itself, and that no one was ever more witty or amiable than she, but that she was spoiled by her desire to be . . . she knew not what."[16] *Corinne* in fact shows us that she did know. She aspired to fame, to glory, and these goals were simply deemed absurd ones for a woman, becoming the more absurd the more outspoken she was in seeking them. Here is the revealing and self-revealing interpretation Constant gave to Mme de Staël's dissatisfaction: "Accustomed early in life by the weakness of her father and later by the flattery of her circle to finding all her resources and amusements outside herself, she retained from her too auspicious and far too brilliant debut in life the fatal habit of depending for her happiness upon others and of considering their support as her due."[17] But was hers anything more than a more

---

14. See Eaubonne, *Une Femme témoin de son siècle*, pp. 5–6.
15. Le Breton, *Le Roman français*, p. 137.
16. Quoted by Sainte-Beuve, "Dix-neuvième Siècle," p. 173.
17. Constant, *Journaux intimes*, p. 173.

exacerbated instance of a dependency all women are encouraged to espouse? *Corinne* is, to be sure, a return in some sense to the great success of her childhood, where she was the "little muse" of the Necker household. Yet, although it relies upon her unwonted childhood experience for its assertiveness, it is not by any means a childish look backward, a regression. As Mme Necker de Saussure saw it, the heroine Corinne was Mme de Staël's ideal in maturity: "I am not Corinne, but if you like, I shall become her."[18]

Even as it smote her with pain and guilt, her father's death released her. She needed no longer minimize to herself or to others the fact of what she was: that she wrote, thought, acted, loved out of the common run. Her novel was the instrument by which she would try to free herself from the straitjacket of opinion her father symbolized for her. *Corinne*, a personal document as well as a novel, was written to cast off all shackles, to repudiate the conformity and the conflict that make *Delphine* so ambivalent a work, to affirm Mme de Staël's full stature as person and as artist. Freed from parental reproof and the fear of it, after twenty years of equivocation about her own nature, she here dares to assert her whole amazonian self.

The Story

In the novel, Oswald Lord Nelvil, a noble young Englishman, is traveling in Italy to assuage some personal grief. In Rome he attends a celebration at which the poetess and improviser Corinne is crowned with laurel at the Capitol. Oswald is captivated, and Corinne notices him. Her crown falls and Oswald retrieves it. She thanks him in the purest of English accents, which perplexes him.

Invited by Corinne, he becomes part of her circle, and she volunteers to show him Rome. This she does at length, going to St. Peter's, St. John Lateran, the Catacombs, and the Forum, among other places, and lecturing Oswald on Italian music, art, and letters, in sections so elaborately developed as to constitute a travelogue in themselves. Oswald and Corinne love one another, but both have stories about their past they find it difficult—and undesirable—to divulge, and so they go on, filling up the present with pleasures. Corinne recites, acts, receives a large company of Roman notables

---

18. Larg, *La Seconde Vie*, p. 277.

—this is her Roman life—and Oswald usually observes it all appreciatively, but sometimes argues for the superiority of his England.

They then go to Naples together, in a voyage that is destined to either seal their love or break it. Oswald there relates his tale to Corinne. While he was in France he had been tricked by a charming and seductive Frenchwoman, sister of his best friend, into staying there rather than returning to his ailing father. When he finally understood her deception and went back to England, his father was dead, and Oswald is tormented with a sense that he has both betrayed and been betrayed. After Corinne's improvisation at Cape Miseno, she recounts her own tale to Oswald. Her family and Oswald's have been allied, for she is the elder daughter of Lord Edgermond, the older Nelvil's closest friend. Her mother had been Italian, and she had lived in Italy until early adolescence when her mother died. Lord Edgermond, who had remarried, then brought Corinne to Northumberland, a place in which she felt deprived of air. The society and temperature of England were alien to her. Her stepmother's coldness to her and to her gifts for music and conversation made her feel an outcast. Only her father and her pretty little half sister, Lucile, had made life tolerable. When her father died, Corinne, with her faithful Italian maid, had run away from England. Independently rich, she became a poetess and now lives freely, taking and leaving lovers, being idolized. Then she met Oswald, the only man she has truly loved.

Oswald, unsettled by her English connection, gradually begins to think of returning to his duties and his nation. They go to Venice, where Oswald finally takes his leave to join his regiment, but he gives Corinne his ring, thinking he will return. In England he learns his father had once written to Edgermond concerning the young Corinne, whom he had met and considered as a possible match for his son, but whom he had rejected, saying she was unsuitably dominant because of her character and her talents and could never be happy in domestic life. Gulled by the second Lady Edgermond, who wants him to marry Lucile, Oswald is increasingly drawn to her youthful blond beauty. Corinne, despairing of Oswald's return as the months go by, goes to England and sees Nelvil with her sister. She feels inferior and unworthy and, at a ball where she is a hovering outsider, sends Oswald his ring, freeing him. She returns to Italy and declines. Her art is dead; she is dying. Despite the birth of their daughter, the reserved Nelvils are not happy, since they never impart their secrets to each other. They travel to Italy where they are witness to Corinne's lingering death.

Some Literary Echoes

Chateaubriand, whom Mme de Staël admired inordinately, contributed much to *Corinne*. The figure of René and the tradition that lay behind it, that of the languid, sorrowing Hamletic hero, seems to have played a part in the creation of Oswald's character. The whole mood of *René* resembles that of the English episodes of *Corinne:* the shadow of mourning falls upon René and Oswald alike; both, like Werther before them, are afflicted by an obscure and hopeless sense of guilt and the wish, so powerfully single-minded in the post-Revolutionary decades, for death.

The framework of *Le Génie du Christianisme* itself is not un-related to that of Mme de Staël's novel. Like the treatise on the *Passions*, with its Zulma episode, *Le Génie* embodies a novel in an extensive and categorized study of a larger subject. *Corinne* turns the emphasis around and puts the novel aspect first, but its travelogue and its studious abstractions are a major feature of the novel. *Corinne* shows us conclusively that Mme de Staël has abandoned her battle with Chateaubriand over *Le Génie*, for in her work she has taken from his defense of Catholicism insights into the nature of Christianity and its power over the imagination and conscience of man.[19]

Chateaubriand's letter from Italy to Fontanes, published in the *Mercure* in April, 1804, had an even more direct influence. "This fine letter produced a whole school of painters, a school I will dub *Roman*. Mme de Staël was the first to be smitten by it. . . ."[20] Inspired by the Pantheon, and the Coliseum as seen by moonlight, Chateaubriand wrote: "Rome sleeps amidst its ruins.

---

19. For an insightful discussion of Mme de Staël's Christianity, see Frank Paul Bowman's essay, "Madame de Staël et l'apologétique romantique," in *Colloque de Coppet*, pp. 157–70.

20. Sainte-Beuve, "Dix-neuvième Siècle," p. 214.

This star of the night, this globe one imagines as finite and deserted wanders in its pale solitude over the solitude of Rome."[21] *Corinne* appropriates its mood. The moon, so evocative for Chateaubriand, will have its portents for Oswald and Corinne. Mme de Staël's entire experience of Italy, in the voyage she undertook in 1805, was colored by Chateaubriand's letter, read before she set off. During her sojourn in Rome she wrote a friend: "To stay in Rome, as Chateaubriand says, calms the soul. It is the dead who live in it, and each step one takes here is as eloquent as Bossuet on the vanity of life. I will write a sort of novel that will serve as framework for a trip to Italy and I think many thoughts and feelings will find their proper place in it."[22]

Parallel to and of equal importance with this altogether literary influence of Chateaubriand's was one of a more intimate nature. In 1803 Pauline de Montmorin de Beaumont, who had been Chateaubriand's mistress, died in his arms. She had followed him to Rome where he had left her, but orphaned and alone in that foreign place in her last days, she aroused Chateaubriand's compassion and he returned to comfort her in death. Later he raised to her memory a sentimental monument that still stands. The same age as Mme de Beaumont, Mme de Staël had long been fond of her. Their fathers had been associates and her admiration and affection were such that Germaine felt her loss acutely. That Corinne's plight was born out of and identified with that of the beloved friend, a victim of love, betrayed and dying in pathetic solitude in a foreign land, is confirmed by a notation in Mme de Staël's *Travel Notebooks*. After making her pilgrimage to the tomb of Pauline in the year preceding the writing of *Corinne* she wrote: "Tomb of Mme de Beaumont because she was no longer loved. Corine."[23]

21. François Auguste René de Chateaubriand, *Oeuvres complètes*, 12 vols. (Paris: Garnier, 1859–60), VI, 292.

22. Letter 257, to Suard, Apr. 9, 1805, *Choix de lettres*, p. 306. Bossuet was the seventeenth-century priest, orator, and confessor to Louis XIV, of a legendary eloquence.

23. This parallel, developed by Geneviève Gennari in her book, was confirmed by Simone Balayé in her edition of *Les Carnets de voyage de Madame de Staël* (Geneva: Droz, 1971), p. 251.

As for her introduction into the particulars of Italian geography and history, Charles-Victor de Bonstetten's work, *Voyage to the Scene of the Six Last Books of the Aeneid, Followed by Some Observations Concerning Modern Latium,* published in Geneva in 1805, made a considerable impression upon Mme de Staël. Bonstetten had long been an intimate at Coppet, and Mme de Staël had presented an extract of this work before the Coppet assemblage in August, 1804. Ponderous and learned as it was, it gave her essential background for her trip and for her novel, and it must be counted among the models for the descriptive passages.[24]

Corinne owes a great deal, too, to other novels of the period—some would say too much. Mme de Staël was not a highly inventive artist, but she had an inventively eclectic mind and borrowed elements from numerous sources in weaving her novel. A popular work which offers intriguing similarities to *Corinne* was the German Heinse's *Ardinghello* (1780), an Italian travelogue novel with a seer–artist enthusiast hero and at least one female character, Fiordimona, who combines robust beauty and vigor with artistic talent. Corinne would seem to be a blend of Fiordimona's qualities and Ardinghello's, but we have no evidence that Mme de Staël knew Heinse's work. She did know *Wilhelm Meister's Travels,* Goethe's Italian travel diary of an artist's initiation. Closer to her own tradition, Madame de Krüdener's *Valérie* bears strong resemblance to *Corinne* in that it too has a luxuriant travelogue. Otherwise, it is quite unlike Mme de Staël's work, being far more intimate and conventional. Mme de Krüdener's art is more picturesque and less philosophical and moral than Mme de Staël's, and the kinship between the two works has perhaps been overstressed. Mme de Staël decidedly disliked *Valérie,* finding it a "caricature" of the novel genre, and hopelessly vague to boot, but since it was only a week after reading it that she resolved finally to write *Corinne,* hers was a fruitful annoyance.

A genuine precursor of *Corinne* in many ways was Mme de Charrière's *Caliste.*[25] The two novels present, on the surface, some

---

24. Simone Balayé (*Les Carnets de voyage,* p. 100) also mentions the travel books of Dupaty and de Brosses as source materials.
25. Belle de Zuylen, a beautiful, noble, cultivated Dutchwoman, had, like

disturbingly strong resemblances. In each the hero is a British offi-
cer, ill and in mourning, and the heroine is a gifted woman rejected by society, whose love is both a glory and a torment to
her. Both heroes are compelled to marry women of their fathers'
choice, and a little girl is born to each union. In both works the
heroine dies in an apotheosis of love and grief. Caliste is English,
and the problem of nationality does not enter Mme de Charrière's
novel, whereas it is crucial to that of Mme de Staël.

The spiritual resemblance between the two women authors,
who were not ever to be friends, but rather antagonists, was considerable. Both were highly independent natures chafing under
different sorts of repression barely tenable to them. Both were
foreigners living on Swiss soil. Both found in Constant their *ami
de coeur.* It is not too surprising that they created heroines who
love, suffer, and die in much the same fashion, especially since
Mme de Staël had read and been much taken with *Caliste,* a
beautifully wrought brief novel, when she first read it in 1794.
Luckily Mme de Charrière had died in 1806, the year before *Corinne's* appearance, or else she might have felt that not only her
lover, but her novel as well had been appropriated by her rival.

However, the resemblances make us slight the differences,
which are capital. *Corinne* is the novel of the love of a female genius: *Caliste* is the far more conventional tale of the love of a good
and very gifted, but fallen, woman. There can be no comparison of
scope, for as one Swiss critic has aptly put it, "*Caliste* is a jewel,
the very model of an exquisite genre . . . *Corinne* is a monument.
I have read and reread *Caliste* with a delectation Mme de Staël
has never, in any of her works, given me. But I must agree that
Corinne towers over this fragile episode. We may prefer the Lake
Leman to the sea, but we know that the sea occupies more space in
the world."[26]

Mme Necker, been courted by Boswell, but finally married the undistinguished
M. de Charrière and buried herself in reading and writing and, eventually, in
her friendship with the young Benjamin Constant, then fresh from the folly of
his first marriage. An older and wiser head, she had great influence upon Constant's style of being. A writer whose almost caustic honesty and classical purity
were unstinting, she apparently found in Constant a ready pupil. See Geoffrey
Scott's charming *Portrait of Zélide* (New York: Charles Scribner's, 1927).

26. Kohler, *Madame de Staël et la Suisse,* p. 217.

Rousseau, whose ethos was so important an influence upon *Delphine,* had little traceable effect upon *Corinne,* and this indicates the spiritual withdrawal from the Rousseau aegis which progressed throughout Mme de Staël's career.[27] A far more imposing literary mentor for *Corinne* was Jean Racine. *Andromaque* and especially *Phèdre* were great favorites at the amateur theatricals engaged in so enthusiastically at Coppet. "Above everything else, the playing of tragic roles, exciting others in speaking a language made sublime by its profundity of feeling, putting herself so in touch with the state of mind of a numerous company that a look, a gesture, a vocal inflection might resound in every heart, this was for Madame de Staël an extension of being, an exalted and empathetic joy that nothing else could match" (I, cccxxxv). During the summer of 1806 while *Corinne* was being written, Mme de Staël played *Phèdre,* and Benjamin records notes such as these in his journal: "*Phèdre* performed. Mme de Staël played admirably." Or, "Rehearsal of *Phèdre.* Mme. de Staël performed beautifully, but it is not that talent in a wife that makes a husband happy."[28]

By 1806 the experience of being a "woman scorned" had seeped deeply into the author's conscience and the person of Corinne herself is a vaguely pietized but still recognizable Phèdre, sentenced by destiny and yet saying to herself, "il y a dans mon sein des orages que ma volonté ne peut gouverner" (I, cxxxix). It is Phèdre's quality of fury that is passed on to Corinne. In Corinne's picture gallery at Tivoli is a painting, actually Guérin's showing Phèdre, Hippolyte, and Thésée (Plate 3). Corinne comments to Oswald, "Phèdre wears upon her face an anguish that chills us with horror" (VIII, 332). Phèdre's legend had clearly come to belong to Mme de Staël's own collection of significant tales.[29]

Even if it were not true that *Phèdre* and *Corinne* are related in particular ways, it would still remain true that, in a larger sense, Racine's power in dealing with a woman's passion is nowhere

---

27. See my article "Mme de Staël, Rousseau and the Woman Question." It could be argued that *La Nouvelle Héloïse's* impact is still observable here in the resemblance between Lauretta Pisana's tale and Corinne's.

28. Constant, *Journaux intimes,* p. 283, 353.

29. See my article "Mme de Staël's Debt to *Phèdre: Corinne.*"

3. From Corinne's picture gallery. *Phaedra and Hippolytus*. Guérin. Musée du Louvre. (Photo from Réunion des Musées Nationaux, Paris.)

better respected than by Mme de Staël's *Corinne*. We may imagine her steeped in the Racinian heroine's violent sorrow and wrath and trying to achieve herself—whether consciously or not—Racinian effects of horror and sympathy.[30] If in her language she fails abysmally to match Racine's genius, in her characterization she achieves a measure of success.

Simone Balayé has elegantly reconstructed another, earlier, literary origin for *Corinne* from the retrospective account Mme de Staël gave in *De l'Allemagne* (*On Germany*) of a German play, *The Nymph of the Danube*. This play, as Balayé indicates, repeats "the theme—most precious of all to Mme de Staël—of a man hesitating between two women, one worldly and prosaic, the other of superior essence; like Oswald, the knight reveals himself incapable of living the fullness of an extraordinary love." Hulda, his unearthly love, queen of the nymphs, withdraws from the world, concluding its creatures are unworthy of her love. Mme de Staël had first known this legend in Weimar in 1804 as the comedy of the *Saalnix*, and she was so taken with it—it does, after all, recapitulate her own *Mirza* and *Zulma*—that she wrote her father on February 2, "Yesterday I made a new outline for a novel, while seeing a quite remarkable play of fantasy and imagination."[31] But though the theme of the play as later recounted by Mme de Staël in *On Germany* is identical with that of *Corinne*, the treatment of the two is quite different. The mood of the *Saalnix* is comic: separated from her lover, who makes an earthly marriage, the Saalnix pursues him with her arts and "every time he begins to settle down in his marriage," she unsettles him with her enchantments of flowers, music, or dance. Finally an accommodation, in which the

---

30. Mme de Staël had withheld an unstinting admiration from *Phèdre* in the *Passions*, claiming that the play was a failure in that its "*verve poétique*" was too overwhelming for the drama and its characters too bound to the yoke of an unrelenting fate. In *On Literature* (IV, 295) she had in fact compared *Phèdre* unfavorably with Voltaire's *Tancrède*: "*Phèdre* inspires us to astonishment, to enthusiasm; but her nature is not that of a delicate and feeling woman." This is the precise and problematic combination she will try to achieve in Corinne. Essentially, it is the hopelessness of Phèdre's situation that made her rebel over Racine's play: "What can Phèdre, unloved, have to lose in life?" (IV, 390) Nonetheless, she pays glowing tribute to Racine the poet (IV, 249).

31. Balayé, *Les Carnets de voyage*, p. 195.

lover is allowed to spend three days a year with his Saalnix, is worked out.

It was the skeleton of this, to her, eternal triangle, then, that was fleshed out by life, and by other literary analogues, during the subsequent voyage to Italy.

Italy and Personal Liberation

Aside from the storminess of her sentimental life during the time of *Corinne's* composition, Mme de Staël's social situation was still a thorny one to her. Maintained as she was in impotent exile from her beloved Paris, her second novel was a renewed challenge to the tyrant who denied her access to her native city. Switzerland and her Swiss acquaintances held no rival charms for her: Coppet was the quintessence of the stagnant life in her eyes, a lovely prison from which she ceaselessly tried to escape. She had sampled English life during the Revolution and, much as she admired English political institutions, she could not help being depressed by English indifference to her. Italy was a land she had never much admired. Its population was poor, ignorant, and Catholic, its governments corrupt and under foreign domination. It appealed neither to her French, Protestant, self-righteous nature, nor to her conception of the enlightened state; but after her father's death, needing to separate herself from the place where he had lived and died, she nevertheless decided to spend the winter there. "I am curious about things Italian, if ever I can be curious about anything besides my own sadness," she wrote.[32] On her voyage in Italy she was accompanied by August Schlegel, whom she had met and become fascinated with in Germany and enrolled as tutor to her children. She was attracted by his vast classical culture and by an aesthetic refinement in him which was not otherwise to be found in her circle; both of these were areas in which she was herself consciously deficient. With his help, she saw what she had never noticed before: analogies of style; historical filiations; detail in artistic creation, especially the visual, and its relation to the whole.

Geneviève Gennari has given a painstaking account of the

---

32. Larg, *La Seconde vie,* p. 297.

trip to Italy and the people Mme de Staël met there, and Simone Balayé has edited her travel notebooks; both works add much to our understanding of the ties between the novel and the voyage. Actually she was bored a great deal during the trip which was, after all, a voyage of mourning during which her emotions were still drawn within. She was parted from her lethargy only periodically in Italy—during her visits to Rome, to Vesuvius, to the countryside near Naples. It was only upon her return to Coppet, in the summer of 1806, that her vision of her experience crystallized and she was seized with enthusiasm for things Italian, read Dante and Roscoe's life of Pope Leo X, sought out the company of Italians, and steeped herself in correspondence with her new Italian acquaintances, especially the poet Vincenzo Monti whom she bombarded with requests to visit her at Coppet. But, as her travel notes illustrate, the idea of the novel had been already in her mind before she undertook her voyage, although its growth took root in the sights seen and people encountered in Italy. By August, 1806, she was ready to read portions of the work to her friends.

Nature itself had never before aroused Mme de Staël's spontaneous enthusiasm. In this, as in other major respects, she remained an incomplete Rousseauist. The arts, still largely conceived of as imitative of nature in her formative years, appealed to her even less. "Love of the arts was always something acquired, exotic, for Mme de Stael, like a potted plant that has never known the real soil."[33] Goethe wrote to Zelter that "literature, poetry, philosophy, and all that relate to them touch her more than art." Mme de Staël was so little moved by the natural beauty of land or sea that she could write that "nature, never saying anything except vaguely, does us no good when any positive disturbance possesses us" (IX, 193). Italy, with its heady abundance of visual delights both natural and man-made, went a long way toward changing this. The refinements of Schlegel's knowledge and taste, Mme de Staël's flirtation of mind and heart with the poet Monti, and her own intellectual curiosity and emotional susceptibility made her Italian travels an apprenticeship that gave her real insight into the world of art.

---

33. Sainte-Beuve, "Dix-neuvième siècle," p. 62.

Music was the only art besides literature for which she had had any true feeling before. She had a beautiful singing as well as speaking voice, loved song, and found in music a tranquility she found in nothing else.[34] Yet, even in this realm, "learned music, music of the mind, did not reach her," her cousin tells us.[35] Only the lyrical drew her with immediacy. Of all the arts, painting appealed to her least. Like Corinne, she would develop more feeling for architecture and sculpture, the more grandiose forms. Even as we salute the increased awareness of art Corinne displays, we must admit that it remains true of Mme de Staël that "she is concerned more with the *good* than with the beautiful" and that she "examines all with the eye of the moralist and makes light of the beautiful if it opposes the good."[36]

The stately art of the city of Rome, so bound up in humanity, was the ideal entrée to the realm of art for Mme de Staël. Schlegel was her guide to the city, just as Corinne would be Oswald's. The moralist would never quite overcome her natural deficiency, however: the appearance of things simply was never as meaningful to her as the essences she ceaselessly sought to distill from them. "The representation of a secret of the soul, a way of suffering less or of being loved touches me a thousand times more than those beautiful feet, those beautiful hands they go on talking about all the time," she wrote Monti.[37]

The Sibyl and the Italian Air

Mme de Staël found in Italy a freedom of atmosphere and a gift for eloquence she had never expected to find. Her ignorance

---

34. For a discussion of music in *Corinne,* see Simone Balayé's "Fiction romanesque de la musique et des sons dans *Corinne,*" *Romantisme,* 3 (1972), 17–32.

35. There were exceptions. In a letter to her cousin from Germany she wrote, " . . . on Good Friday there is a cantata sung on the death of Jesus Christ that moved me more deeply than anything of this kind has ever done: I will bring this cantata to you. . . ." Letter 221, *Choix de lettres,* p. 269. It remains true that an extramusical association (in this case, the Passion) was necessary to draw her into art.

36. Geneviève Gennari, *Le Premier Voyage de Madame de Staël en Italie et la genèse de Corinne* (Paris: Boivin, 1947), p. 168.

37. Gennari, *Le Premier Voyage,* p. 91.

of and indifference to Italy had in fact been so extreme that she had been able to write of the Italians in *On Literature*, "When they try to abandon their true natural talent, for the comic, to attempt oratorical eloquence, they are nearly always affected" (IV, 232). Mme de Staël was astonished to discover the extraordinary expressiveness of ordinary Italians in their everyday speech. Particularly remarkable to her was the tradition of oral poetry and storytelling, an art still kept alive by the improvisers of the time, some of whom she was privileged to hear.[38] Though Monti openly expressed to her his scorn for this "debased" art, almost all aspects of it were bound to excite Mme de Staël's imagination.[39] Here at last was a form in which women were allowed to excel, in which their capacities were given free rein, and in which they could attain more than mere celebrity—true fame, *gloire*. And clearly the link between improvisation and Mme de Staël's own undisputed gift *par excellence*, that of conversation, was very close. After all, she inspired a myriad of comments such as this one by her own power of speech: "There was in her something of that power that Alcibiades, in *The Banquet*, attributes to the word of Socrates."[40]

Mme de Staël seized upon this art form for her *Corinne* and embellished it, for Corinne would not be merely an improviser: she was poet, too, sibyl and muse. We remember that already in adolescence Germaine Necker had been characterized as a sibyl

---

38. She heard the Abbé Biamonti in Bologna and, in Rome, Isabella Pellegrini; in Florence, Mme Mazzei and La Fantastici (whose name she later used in a playlet). She also heard Amarillis Etrusca (Teresa Bandinetti). It was the already legendary Maria Madellena Morelli (Corilla Olimpica—1727–1800) who was an important model for Corinne, having been, like her, the most celebrated poetess of her time, crowned at the Capitol with the *laurea capitolina* of Tasso and Petrarch.

39. A visual analogue to verbal improvisation was the great popularity at just this time of the *tableau vivant*. The ravishing Emma, Lady Hamilton, was the foremost practitioner of this minor art or parlor game (one wag claiming that she chose this specific form because she was so vulgar once she opened her mouth) and she was much admired for her skill at dramatizing and costuming scenes from history and literature. She, too, was painted in 1794 as a sibyl, after Domenichino's, by Rehberg, one of Mme de Staël's favorite artists. See Kirsten Cram-Holmström, *Monodrama, Attitudes, Tableaux-vivants, Studies in Some Trends of Theatrical Fashion, 1770–1815* (Stockholm: Alquist and Wiksell, 1967).

40. Karl Ritter's testimony, quoted by Amiel, "Madame de Staël," p. 16.

by Guibert, and the memory of it haunted her. In the period when this novel was written she seems to have been particularly imbued with the idea, for she wrote to the young Don Pedro de Souza, "Do not forget that sibyl whose heart was prophetic. . . ."[41]

Important representations of the sibyls abound in the Renaissance art Mme de Staël saw in her travels, for although their origin is pre-Christian, they were supposed to be bearers of the predictions of Jesus's coming and are incorporated into Christian iconography. We find them glorious overhead in Michelangelo's Sistine Chapel and handsomely subdued underfoot in the tiled floor of the Duomo in Siena. Like the improviser, the sibyl is one of the few licit images of female genius, even though she represents possession by the inchoate power of prophecy. We recall Diderot's evocation of the Delphic sibyl as properly representing female genius, possessed by an alien power, an other. In a significant distinction Guibert had drawn between the sibyls and Germaine, he had written in his early portrait of Germaine as Zulmé: "Once I had seen the Delphian Pythia, and I had seen the Cumaean Sibyl: they were lost; their movements had a convulsive air; they appeared less to be filled with a godly presence than devoured by furies. The young priestess [Germaine] was animated without undergoing any change, and inspired without drunkenness" (I, xxxix). Mme de Staël, similarly, blends her sibyl with a muse who is no demonic force, but one possessed of her own powers alone. After reading in Rome Propertius' verse in which he praises young Cynthia,

> and when she strikes up a tune
>   with Aeolian plectrum
> her lyre equals a goddess's, a muse by her fountain;
> Her graven verses rival those
>   of Antique Corinna . . .
>   (II, 3)

Mme de Staël appropriated the name of Pindar's rival in poesy.[42]

---

41. Quoted by Gennari, Le Premier Voyage, p. 125.
42. Les Carnets de voyage, p. 105.

But even after we have assayed all these sources and echoes, biographical or literary, for the light they shed on the origin of this work, we have still failed to account for the very extravagance of this vision of the priestess of Apollo *cum* sibyl we find at the outset of the novel, borne in on a chariot led by white horses. Even as we recall the exalted poetic gifts of Zulma and Mirza in their varying exotic settings, we witness here an augmentation, a progression in the delusion of grandeur proposed, for the magnitude of this project has repercussions that overflow the margins of the work.

Steeped in the neoclassical taste that informs the works of her time, and receptive to its pieties, Mme de Staël presents to us her own "natural" goddess in the form of a nike.[43]

The nike, or winged victory, had become under Napoleon, who was so excessively fond of cameos and friezes, a highly popular theme in Empire art, used repeatedly in emblems of Napoleonic victories, as for example in the decorative friezes of Percier and Fontaine, official decorators to the court. Its omnipresence had an evident impact upon the conception of Corinne, for the conventions of representation of the *nike* are scrupulously adhered to in our first revelation of her: the demigoddess wears a white tunic, carries in one hand a crown, in the other a palm, and rides in a chariot led by a team of horses.

The usual conception of the nike in decoration, at the turn of the century, was apt to be rather pallid, but what had revivified her in the popular mind, and most assuredly in Mme de Staël's, was her fusion with another female goddess: Reason. Jules Renouvier long ago wrote illuminatingly about the evolution of this figure, whose initial avatar he thought he had found in the frontispiece of the *Encyclopédie* (1751). At first (as there) she is a baroque allegory, but little by little she assumes a new Revolutionary form and we find her as the embodiment of Reason, or as the Republic, on

---

43. The following ideas are more fully developed in my contribution, "Madame de Staël et l'esthétique du camée," to the "Colloque de Clermont sur le préromantisme" (June 29–30, 1972), which was published as *Préromantisme: hypothèque ou hypothèse?* (Paris: Klincksieck, 1970).

4. *The Celebration of the Supreme Being.* 1794. Artist unknown. Bibliothèque Nationale, Cabinet des Estampes.

5. *Freedom* or *Death*. Regnault. Courtesy of the Hamburger Kunsthalle.

6. *Winged Victory*. Cartellier. Bas relief from Palais du Louvre. Musée du Louvre.

7. *Liberty Leading the People.* Delacroix. Musée du Louvre. (Photo from Réunion des Musées Nationaux, Paris.)

8. *Peace Led by Victory*. Boizot. Biscuit des Sèvres. Musée National de Céramique, Sèvres. (Photo from Réunion des Musées Nationaux, Paris.)

thousands of tracts and posters of the Revolutionary period. "Beneath their ancient dress, their Phrygian bonnet, their Athenian helmet and their Roman diadem; with tunic, peplum, or chlamys . . . ; seated or standing, winged and radiant; . . . amidst sheaves of wheat, cornucopias or oak boughs—one always sees the same woman, whose eye is illumined and whose arm stretches forth to the new beginning"[44] (see Plates 4–8). The worship of this goddess as Reason, by the Revolution, was consecrated in mass celebrations in 1793. The enthusiasm and future-ideal–oriented quality of this goddess, a quintessentially alive representation of woman whose ultimate expression is probably Delacroix's *Liberty on the Barricades* of 1830, are reflected in Corinne's physical and spiritual nature. But the very timeliness that made it possible for Mme de Staël to capitalize on the omnipresence of these female figures in popular taste to create her remarkable heroine has eroded our ability to apprehend the magnitude of the chosen symbol, goddesses having receded once more from popularity.

A further strand drawn from the mythic representation of the time that Mme de Staël will utilize is the softening, subsequent to Thermidor, of the bellicose air of the goddess, whose aspect now becomes gentle and full of a pity and sentiment that had been felt as cruelly deficient in the excesses of the Terror (see Plate 8). Often she will lose her godlike attributes to take on the aspect of a Grecian-draped woman in a relaxed, melancholy pose, seated sighing by a tomb, with book or stylus in hand.[45]

These mythic figures, made available to Mme de Staël by the vicissitudes of history and of taste—nike, goddess of the Revolution and embodiment of sensibility—are combined by her with her own personal sibyl-muse myth in the person of Corinne.

Italy further complicated the already troubling problem of nationality for Mme de Staël. Essentially she used Italy for its soothing powers, but she would use it also, less pacifically, for her own grandiose purposes in her battle against the Emperor. "Like Bona-

---

44. Jules Renouvier, *Histoire de l'art pendant la Révolution* (Paris: J. Renouard, 1863), pp. 402–3.

45. Renouvier marks this change in his *Histoire de l'art pendant la Révolution*. It recreates the elegiac mood of the Greek and Roman funeral stele.

parte, she was content to proclaim: Here I am! Like him she had herself crowned. . . . A whole people at her feet; and all *that,* people were made to see, cost not a single death, not a tear. . . . the kingdom of Corinne was that of the Spirit. If Corinne was right, the Spirit, too, was a force."[46] Against the absolute ruler who mocked her pretensions to a place in this world, Mme de Staël raised the figure of the woman of art, peace, love, and a freedom transcending worldly ambition. To maintain the parallel, Mme de Staël made her fictional heroine Italian like the live hero who was her enemy.

---

46. Larg, *La Seconde Vie,* p. 276.

CHAPTER 6

Corinne—The Frozen Vision and the Thaw

Novel and Travelogue

A poem is what Vinet called *Corinne;* Sainte-Beuve, too, referred to it as a *roman-poème,* but even though this novel was intended by its author to be a *roman-poème,* simply, it defies classification because of its ambitious, multiple nature. Blennerhasset said of it, "Its principal claim to enduring fame as a work of art is . . . that the multiplicity of its concerns does not detract from the unity of its composition, and our sympathies remain fixed upon the noble figure of the woman placed at its center."[1] Yet, despite this generous estimate, which remains valid in a general sense, the work presents us with serious stylistic inconsistencies not altogether foreign to those of *Delphine.*

The plot is one that fits E. M. Forster's description: "It is the novel in its logical intellectual aspect: it requires mystery, but the mysteries are solved later on."[2] But then what are we to say of the travelogue, that series of friezes, or engravings? Despite the fact that Mme de Staël was by no means the first to interlard her novel with a voyager's observations, her travelogue is at once more extensive and more integrated with her plot than had been the case with similar works. At least some contemporary readers found them fine: Mme Necker de Saussure felt that the plot and the descriptive passages were indissoluble, and the *Edinburgh Review* insisted that "the narrative of Mme de Staël is as lively and affecting as her descriptions are picturesque and beautiful."[3] Larg, a century later, was less convinced that the two genres present a seamless web, and he wryly remarked: "When in Rome Don Pedro had said to Mme de Staël: 'I must leave'; she had replied:

---

1. Blennerhasset, *Madame de Staël et son temps,* III, 186.
2. E. M. Forster, *Aspects of the Novel* (New York: Harcourt, Brace, 1927), p. 144.
3. *Edinburgh Review,* XI (1807–8), 183.

'Let's see the Vatican museum!' As soon as Oswald begins to have his doubts, Corinne uses the same tactic. This is why the table of contents that ends the book has such a fine look of objectivity. Between crises, the heroine prescribes to the hero a strong dose of ancient culture."[4] Brunetière pointed out that Corinne invoked Italy to dissipate Oswald's melancholy, but he objected, "far from being a merit in Mme de Staël's work, it is what displeases us in *Corinne*. The link is truly too frail and, above all, it is too artificial, between the descriptive parts and the novel proper."[5]

There is no one who would claim that the two genres are completely integrated; they are, however, ingeniously, though not always skillfully, dovetailed. Mme de Staël has achieved this interlocking of parts by choosing to unfold her mystery in those places most appropriate to the mood of the narrative at a given point. And by giving to Oswald her own skepticism concerning art and making Corinne its enthusiastic advocate she succeeds in creating some tension between plot and description; but this frail tension never could bear the weight of the quantity of information Corinne pours into the ears of the compliant hero.

To plot its geography and risk marking out what James called "frontiers as artificial . . . as any that have been known to history," *Corinne* is a work in five "acts" or "movements" and twenty books that may be arranged as follows:

1. Oswald: Introduction to Italy (Book I).
2. Corinne: Italy, its art, history, religion, mores (Books II–X).
3. The voyage of the lovers: the revelation of their secrets and their parting in Venice (Books XI–XVI).
4. Separation: England, Scotland, Florence. Oswald's evolution, Corinne's adventures in Britain and her return (Books XVI–XVIII).
5. Corinne's vengeance: Oswald's return to Italy and Corinne's death in Florence (Books XIX–XX).

So it is that places are to some extent integrated with the plot, but

---

4. Larg, *La Seconde Vie*, p. 303.
5. Ferdinand Brunetière, "Les Romans de Madame de Staël," *Revue des Deux Mondes*, 3 (1890), 686.

no outline could pretend to contain the travelogue, because it is everywhere in the work. If we think of the great cities alone, Mme de Staël has been truly skillful in depicting something of their spirit. Rome is the place of triumph; Naples, flower of the south—"that happy countryside"—is the place of love's fulfillment, but Vesuvius is there at hand to threaten it; Venice is the frayed grandeur of a noble but fragile past, a fittingly melancholy setting for the parting of the lovers; and Florence, barely breathing in its quiet contemplation of its violent history, is an appropriate frame for Corinne's death.

In her attempt to reanimate the disheartened hero, Corinne tries to pique his curiosity and draw out his opinions, to engage him in that dialogue that was an essential component of Mme de Staël's conception of love. Their visit to the Coliseum, in all its architectural splendor, is the occasion of one of their characteristic differences of opinion. Oswald "could see in these places nothing but the love of luxury of the masters and the blood of their slaves and was angered by the fine arts, which never concern themselves with ends and are prodigal of their gifts, no matter the nature of the object. Corinne strove to argue against his state of mind" (IV, IV). Their natures unfold to some degree in such exchanges; but Mme de Staël often goes very far afield, making the reader virtually despair of ever finding the story again. Aside from the fact that this is an author who tends constantly, in speaking of art, to transpose from the aesthetic to the moral plane, often leaving us wandering in a field of prosey and cliché-ridden abstraction, we are frequently disappointed as we see the relatively interesting dispute between the lovers jettisoned in favor of a monologue by Corinne. In this way a meditation or an essay is merely grafted onto the novel; but the leisurely and lengthy consideration of ideas we are willing to accept as a successful mode in *On Literature* or *On Germany* is simply out of kilter with the required tightness of a work of fiction.

As Corinne discusses the mores and character of Italians she seems more at home. When Oswald ungraciously attacks Italian marriage, saying tactlessly that "even infidelity is more moral in England than marriage is in Italy" (VI, II), Corinne is of course mortally offended and refuses to see him for awhile. For once, here, action and description are linked, but Mme de Staël's handling of this conflict turns painfully artificial and didactic. Oswald, in his turn, posts a long and moralistic letter to Corinne (probably containing a good part of the author's own reservations about the Italian character), in which he excoriates Italian morality and praises the English.

After they are reconciled, Corinne goes on to an examination of literature and the graphic arts. Despite Mme de Staël's high regard for the natural eloquence of the Italians, she felt that it was somewhat frozen by their literature. Her critique is arresting so applicable is it to her own works: "Their very eloquence, so lively when they speak, has no spontaneity when they write: one might say that they grow cold as they write" (VII, 1). This dynamic of freeze and thaw is central to Mme de Staël's aesthetic understanding. The chapter on Italian literature has been looked on as the cornerstone of the "novel of Italy." Everyone is there, Oswald, Corinne, Erfeuil, Castelforte, and Mr. Edgermond (a remote relation of the two English families), so that this becomes an international conversation, a genuine discussion instead of the rather arid teacher-pupil didacticism with which the overinformed Corinne plies an ignorant Oswald. Literature was the sole art in which Mme de Staël could really claim authority, and it cannot surprise us that the literary debate has so much more life and meaning than the treatment of the other arts: ". . . she *isolates* Italian literature from its great French rival; she sets it up as a threat to it; she presents it to Europe via Corinne's voice; she places Count Erfeuil in a dangerously exposed position. Such is the goal of her argument: the overthrow of classical tyranny and the renewal of national literatures."[6] The debate is crowned by a supreme performance of *Romeo and Juliet* with Corinne as Juliet, a triumph of English genius on Italian soil.

But as we pass to the graphic arts, the vivacity of an exchange of views is again jettisoned, as the lecturing tone is resumed: "You, dear Oswald, do not care for the arts in themselves but only for their connections with feeling and thought. Only that which reminds you of the heart and its pain is moving to you. Music and

---

6. Gennari, *Le Premier Voyage*, p. 202.

poetry are appropriate to such a temperament, whereas the arts that speak to the eyes, even though their meaning is in the realm of the ideal, can please us only when our souls are tranquil and our imaginations free." The static, frozen quality of these discussions *within a novel* rob the whole of it of forward movement, but within even this evidently pat, cool discussion it is the volatile question of emotivity that is being raised: the visual arts simply fail to satisfy Oswald by their inability to evoke immediate warmth of response in troubled souls. The culminating section on the arts of painting and sculpture is a stroll through Corinne's picture gallery at her villa in Tivoli. Again the author strives here to unify her travelogue with her novel by making this visit an illustration of Corinne's taste and artistry. But as she goes on to have her discuss her paintings—all of them anecdotal and in high neoclassical style—purely from an interpersonal standpoint and divorced from all concern with plastic values, a sense of fixity, of remoteness, once more descends upon the text. The substance eludes the form.

The chapter devoted to popular festivals and music manages to be more effective and evocative as Corinne speaks of *la musique bouffe,* the gay popular music: "At the core of the pleasure it gives us are poetic sensations, a cheerful dream world that spoken pleasantries could never call up. . . . There is no more void, no more silence about us, life is full, the blood flows quickly" (IX, II). It is this desire for plenitude that mirrors Corinne's criteria for aesthetic realization. The immobility and silence that embalm and chill the *style Empire* are basically repudiated in favor of sound, fullness, beat, movement. Such joyous music has power to stop, momentarily, the old emptiness so dreaded by the Staëlian heroine.

In the author's treatment of religion, descriptive and narrative forces are once more joined together. The opposition between Nelvil's rigorous and artistically restrained Protestantism and Corinne's merciful and artistically cluttered Catholicism is made to act as a factor that will eventually part them. Oswald sees Corinne at St. Peter's and does not speak to her, "thinking thus to respect the religious meditation he believes her to be engaged in," but as she catches sight of him, she approaches him gaily and is soon prattling vivaciously to all her friends in the midst of the magnificent cathedral. Oswald is appalled: he "was seized with a feeling

of scorn for the lightness of spirit she must be capable of" (x, ɪv).
Corinne, perceiving his amazement, takes him aside to discourse
on the difference between their two religions, and their conversation, long and didactic though it is, illustrates Oswald's deep repugnance for the ostentatious faith of his beloved, a difference between them that grows with time. Mme de Staël rejects for her
heroine the relative rigidity of the English faith, here identifiable
with a neoclassical aesthetic, for a more affective and mobile, even
though Catholic, Romantic Christianity.

The lovers then embark on the fatal voyage which is to end
in their parting. On approaching Naples, "you feel a well-being so
perfect, so great a sense of kinship with nature, that nothing can
change the delight it evokes in you" (xɪ, ɪ). This essentially idyllic
mood of their visit is significantly marred by the moon's passage
beneath a cloud, interpreted by Corinne as a sign that Heaven condemns their love. It is upon this ground, made radiant by the sun
and sea, that the lovers finally feel sufficiently free to confess to one
another their past experiences. But from this point onward the
novel will be nothing but decline: Corinne is taken with the
plague that infests Rome upon their return, and Oswald nurses
her back to health; they then go to Venice in flight from that
awful malady. Venice, with its still waters and its brilliant facade,
is portrayed as a city of melancholy, an effect only heightened by
Corinne's great triumph there, playing in *La Fille de l'air*, Gozzi's
fantastic comedy. Afterward, "the parting in the midst of the
night, surrounded by the silence and mystery of the Venetian
capital, is highly pathetic, and worked up with all the adventitious
circumstances that can be supposed to aggravate the pain of
separation."[7]

It is only after Venice that the plot holds sway uncontested.
Book XVIII tells of Corinne's arrival in Florence. She finds the city
dull: "People promenade every afternoon along the banks of the
Arno and in the evening ask each other if they've been there"
(xvɪɪɪ, ɪɪ). Here we find the most credible combination of Corinne's
sentiments with the author's observations of Florence, largely because the latter are slight. This section is superior in that it does

---

7. *Edinburgh Review*, XI (1807–8), 187.

not attempt to do justice to the real beauties of the city, but slurs over these in favor of the inner reality of the heroine.

Books XIX and XX are the finale of the novel, and we find in them only the barest minimum of description. The Nelvils' dramatic crossing of Mont-Cenis is recounted with great vividness and blends with the unspoken anguish of the couple. The trip through Turin, Milan, and Bologna is the merest sketch—it is as though Mme de Staël felt compelled to throw in some words about the north of Italy, also—and this artifice again momentarily distracts us, but the pace is faster now, and the reader does not feel as before that the plot has been betrayed or arrested. Finally, in Book XX, the denouement is played out uncontested by decor, and Corinne is permitted her last agonies without benefit of recondite references to her surroundings. But the last chapters overflow in a different fashion: here is a convergence of emotional excess we have seen only intermittently in the rest of the work. Mme de Staël was unable to put her story to rest. We sense that her imaginative powers were incapable of sustaining her tale *qua* fiction to the end. The emotional origin of *Corinne* lay in a personal agony that was far from over. She was unable to transcend her own anguish sufficiently to be able to give her heroine a fate more consistent with traditional novelistic necessity.

In our attempt to understand what has gone wrong in this often highly impressive novel, Edwin Muir's distinction between the dramatic and the character novel can be illuminating: "... the imaginative world of the dramatic novel is in Time, the imaginative world of the character novel in Space. . . . On the one hand we see characters living in a society, on the other figures moving from a beginning to an end. These two types of the novel . . . are rather two distinct modes of seeing life: in Time, personally, and in Space, socially."[8] Mme de Staël's novel confuses these two modes and even more numerous genres, though fewer than in her *Delphine*. A similar confusion in point of view—of the social and the timeless with the individual and the perishable—is to be found in all of Mme de Staël's other works to varying degrees, often, in

---

8. Edwin Muir, *The Structure of the Novel* (London: The Hogarth Press, 1946), pp. 62–63.

fact, enriching them by her attempt to fuse distinctive modes. Here she has written a novel of sentiment of considerable power, but she has willed that it be entwined with Italy so that considerations of place are omnipresent. The drama of Oswald and Corinne's encounter is rightly free in time, but space—or place—is constantly being asserted—this museum, that mountain, this city, that sculpture, this book, that nation. The effect of it all is a dwarfing of the characters by the subordination of the personal to the social or, at the very least, to the impersonal. Complex though the dovetailing of the plot to description may be, hard as Mme de Staël has worked to fit all the manifold elements into a clever whole, organically the work does not succeed because of this contradiction at its core.

I believe that this confusion arises from her woman's uncertainty (and the more in a work questioning woman's nature) as to the true distinctions to be made between social and individual spheres, stereotype and truth. Place in *Corinne* confers authenticity (Italy) and place (England) withdraws it. Unable to hew to the tighter compartmentalization of a *Tom Jones* or a *Nouvelle Héloïse*, both of which she much admired, Mme de Staël was forced by the form in which the novel presented itself to her to break into a rocky, resistant, untrodden path. She made place a metaphor for sex, and sex for character, all to the end of expressing, in Romanticism's fashion, an individual's tragic dilemma.

The Whole and Its Parts

Notwithstanding these difficulties, Mme de Staël managed to capture the imagination of her readers by the pure grandeur and daring of her venture. Sainte-Beuve, in his later appreciation of her works, remarks on their having faded in his lifetime and notes that "the stronger part of their charm is in their totality, and one could scarcely detach a single page from among them. Sentences themselves scarcely hold together, looked at closely; they cannot be taken out of context. . . . Sometimes the vagueness of expression is to blame, sometimes an inappropriateness of terms or the lack of aptness in an analogy."[9] Mme Necker de Saussure, admitting

---

9. Sainte-Beuve, "Dix-neuvième Siècle," pp. 119–20.

that her cousin's work contained some faults of style, attributes this to the rapid flow of her ideas.

Even here we have ambiguity. Brunetière wrote that if Mme de Staël's works succeed "it is because while writing badly, Mme de Staël thinks well; that is, she thinks wittily, as she doubtless must have spoken; because her wit excites, illumines, warms us."[10] We observe the vivifying verbs he uses to express the effect of her work. This warming undercurrent accounts for the fact that another critic can see *Corinne* as "a work full of life, a work full of passion, that hides behind a single tonality, a variety of harmonies."[11]

It is altogether natural that Mme de Staël's writing should have been compared with her remarkable conversation. Aphorism, for which she had the gift, is in quintessence a momentary verbal command of the world, compressing reality into compact but novel mini-revelations. "She never hesitated in speaking. The word which best conveyed her meaning always came uppermost, without effort," says one witness; another, "her conversation was never tainted with pedantry or obvious preparation. . . . Its dominating feature was its perfect naturalness, and she could talk of dress with as much interest as of the institution of a state."[12] A modern critic comments that in "writing she still spoke. Her finest pages are selections of worldly eloquence or the best moments of a serious conversation. She strews them with incisive or brilliant or touching remarks."[13] In *Corinne*, Mme de Staël strove hard to press her ebullience into a form, and the habitual meandering of her non-fictions is somewhat lessened. We must certainly imagine there was some intent on her part to transmute her own conversational genius into Corinne's art, that of improvisation.

The improvisations in *Corinne* are certainly the most am-

---

10. Brunetière, "Les romans de Madame de Staël," p. 684. But in opening his treatment of the novels one of the very first things he says is that if we read them no longer it is because they are badly written.

11. Gennari, *Le Premier Voyage*, p. 10.

12. Constance Hill, *Maria Edgeworth* (London: John Lane the Bodley Head, 1910), p. 270.

13. Kohler, *Madame de Staël et la Suisse*, p. 690.

bitious poetic task Mme de Staël ever set for herself.[14] There is certainly a paradox inherent in attempting to seize and transfix not only genius, but a particularly spontaneous species of genius. That Mme de Staël should have wished to do so is an index of her dissatisfaction with the unspontaneous and fixed art around her. We sense her straining, in this enterprise, after an Ossianic mood that could convey Corinne's regenerative powers, a gift of the word resembling that of Blake's bard:

> Hear the voice of the Bard!
> Who present, Past and Future, sees;
> Whose ears have heard
> The Holy Word
> That walk'd among the ancient trees,
>
> Calling the lapsed Soul,
> And weeping in the evening dew;
> That might controll
> The starry pole,
> And fallen, fallen light renew!
>
> (Songs of Experience)

All the genial Corinne requires for her spirit to engage in such creation is the suggestion of a subject from her audience. There are but two proper improvisations in the novel, one at the Capitol and one at the Cape Miseno. Both are crucial for the novel: the first must establish beyond question Corinne's eminence; the second is the exalted cry of Corinne's genius as prelude to her destruction.

The subject of the first improvisation is "the glory and bliss of Italy." It is all sun and serenity:

It is not merely with vine-branches and sheaves that our nature adorns herself, but she bestrews beneath man's feet, as in a sovereign's path, an abundance of flowers and ornamental vegetation which, designed to please, does not debase itself by serving us.

---

14. Balzac, in his *Illusions perdues*, set himself a similarly impossible task of describing the work of an artist—in his case, a painter—who has a sublime artistic secret. Balzac "solves" the problem by making his man's work an apotheosis, whether a glorious swindle or a transcendence of painting we never know. Mme de Staël was more ignorant, more innocent, and braver.

Delicate pleasures, cultivated by nature, are enjoyed by a nation worthy of perceiving them; the simplest dishes suffice to it; it does not besot itself at the fountains of wine abundance has prepared for it: it loves its sun, its fine-arts, its monuments, its countryside at once ancient and spring-like; not for it the refined pleasures of a brilliant society or the gross pleasures of a greedy people. (ii, iii)

The prosaic quality of the passage is painfully evident. The syntax is flat; passives make the stanzas static; there is a nearly total and murderous absence of imagery. Utilitarianism does not help: for Mme de Staël, nature cannot long retain its aspect as the magical ornament and terrible mystery that it is; it becomes chiefly a useful adjunct to the lives of virtuous men. What she achieves here is a tenuous elegiac mood altogether analogous to that conveyed by an 1806 frieze. Here is an acceptable rather than an exceptional utterance, carrying little of the pulse of poetry, but at least not utterly destructive of the author's attempt to establish her heroine as extraordinary.

How different an image of abundance this is from the fresh and blithe one, even in its moralism, found in James Thomson's *The Seasons,* much admired by Mme de Staël:

> Oh, stretched amid these orchards of the sun,
> Give me to drain the cocoa's milky bowl,
> And from the palm to draw its freshening wine;
> More bounteous far than all the frantic juice
> Which Bacchus pours. Nor on its slender twigs
> Low-bending, be the full pomegranate scorned;
> Nor, creeping through the woods, the gelid race
> Of berries. Oft in humble station dwells
> Unboastful worth, above fastidious pomp.[15]

There is nothing but a vague kinship of feeling between Mme de Staël's own improvisation, stamped with the impress of the Enlightenment, and the poetry that touched her. Hers is an awkward blend of pulpit rhetoric with the mild poetic impulse of the eighteenth century. Concern for the social ideal is never absent,

---

15. James Thomson, *The Seasons and the Castle of Indolence,* ed. J. Logie Robertson (Oxford: The Clarendon Press, 1891), p. 83 (*The Seasons,* "Summer"), lines 676–84.

and her thoroughly ethical sentiments do not seem to her, any more than they would have to a Voltaire or an Abbé Delille in whose tradition she writes, to be in the least misplaced in a poetic improvisation.

The greater is the paradox in her choosing *poetic* creation to be the quintessence of Corinne's genius. "Man's genius is creative when he senses nature; imitative when he believes himslf inventor of it," she says at the Miseno. With this Romantic proclamation she enters upon an improvisation on "the memories recalled by this place." Her voice is troubled, her soul distressed, and this anxiety is expressed in her performance. The contrast with the first improvisation is complete and, as everywhere in the novel, neoclassic and Romantic elements press hard upon each other. "If you strike this ground, the heavenly vault resounds. One might say that the inhabited world is nothing but a shell ready to open. The Naples countryside is the image of human passion: sulfurous and fertile, its dangers and pleasures seem to be born out of these inflamed volcanoes which give the air so many charms and make the thunder growl beneath our steps" (XIII, IV). The more intense and powerful poetic feeling of this passage is achieved through its ideas, and in spite of the manner of their expression. The comparison of this seething land with human passion touches the imagination, but the author, with clumsy, prosaic locutions like "if you strike" or "one might say that," erects barriers in her own way. This, at best, is a lofty prose, not poetry: we are hard put to conceive of its being sung to the lyre as Corinne, like the Corinna of antiquity, is supposed to have sung hers.

In her attempt to create poetry Mme de Staël was twice cursed: by the times and by her impatient nature. Her vocabulary is all abstraction, the plague of eighteenth-century poesy in France —"Love, supreme power of the heart, mysterious enthusiasm which enfolds within it poetry, heroism, and religion!"—and her unsettled and ultimately timid temperament would not allow her to pause long enough to find the appropriate concretion for her exalted notions. For this reason Corinne's improvisations are, in terms of craft and of the task she set herself, the poorest part of Mme de Staël's novel, and the irony of the greatest conversationalist of her age failing to render the pulse of live improvisation is fully realized. She erred in believing it so simple to produce a beauty "at which a novelist should never aim, though he fails if he does not achieve it."[16]

Since the improvisations decidedly fail to give us an idea of Mme de Staël's own conversation, one might logically turn to dialogue as another vehicle that might convey her genius. We are less disappointed here, although there is regrettably little conversation in *Corinne* and a great deal of monologue. The author scores a decided success, for example, in recreating the graceful banter, devoid of substance, of the Count Erfeuil. In the celebrated conversation of the English ladies at the tea table in provincial Northumberland Mme de Staël's perception of cultural patterns is given play. "One woman was saying to the other: My dear, do you believe the water has boiled sufficiently to pour it over the tea?—My dear, replied the other, I do think it would be too soon, for the gentlemen are not yet ready to come in.—Will they stay long at table today? said the third; what do you think, my dear?" (XIV, I). The author's sharp ear has caught the banalities of provincial conversation, but she ironizes over them rather than rendering them. Her skill understandably was not admired by the *Edinburgh Review*, which held that "the coldness of the manner in the English ladies, their reserve and want of animation, are painted too harshly."[17]

The finest conversation in the novel is the one that takes place in Naples, between Oswald and Corinne, after she has told him her story. It renders economically and eloquently the confusion and distress of both. Corinne starts:

". . . speak, then, and tell me what you have determined to do."—Oswald, frightened by the sound of Corinne's voice, which betrayed her inner feelings, knelt before her and said: "Corinne, your lover's heart has not changed; what have I learned that could make me love you less? But hear me out—" And as she trembled all the more, he began again more resolutely: "Listen to me without fear, for I cannot live if I know you to be unhappy." "Ah!" cried Corinne, "it is my happiness you speak of; you speak no longer of your own. I do not reject your pity at this moment, for I have need of it: but do you think that I could wish to live on your pity

---

16. Forster, *Aspects of the Novel*, p. 133.
17. *Edinburgh Review*, XI (1807–8), 193.

alone?" "No, we will live, both of us, by our love," said Oswald; "I will return. . . ." "You will return," interrupted Corinne; "ah! then you wish to go?" (xv, 1)

The genuine distress of the trapped Oswald, hounded by the alarmed and wretched Corinne, is nowhere better rendered in the novel than here, in this moment of dramatic validity. Yet, though the author's theatrical flair erupts at some such points into effective dialogue, her chief means as a novelist lie elsewhere.

Despite undoubted flaws in her narrative, Mme de Staël reveals herself in *Corinne*, when not bogged down in excesses of exposition, to be an excellent storyteller. In the "tales" of Oswald and of Corinne (their written, first-person confessions) there is not the slightest lag of interest. Oswald's story, in fact, is so complete a little eighteenth-century novella, replete with unprincipled villains on the Lovelace model and an innocent victim, in this case the hero, that it seems rather out of place in the work. The inherent conflict in this tale between the cynicism of Laclos and Restif and Romantic innocence is portrayed very deftly, and a sense of intrigue is captured. Mme de Staël's *gaucherie* falls away from her at such moments when she is busily engaged in narration, and we at last have the sense that her own voice is being heard. Her style then is direct, even terse, whereas it is always overblown in the self-conscious descriptive or poetic passages.

While the tale of Oswald hearkens back to the eighteenth-century novel, that of Corinne stands fittingly at the center of the work, fully in character and suggestive of the psychological novels that are to succeed it. The moody tale of the misfit girl, her strict stepmother, the "cold and humid temperature" of the northern setting, the boredom of the heroine, and her finally triumphant revolt are the core of an almost modern novel. The author comes swiftly and pithily to her end—"Neither Europe nor posterity could make us indifferent to the misbehavior of the neighbors next door; and whoever would be happy and develop his own gifts must, above all, choose carefully an atmosphere in which to live" (xiv, 1).

A feeling for distress, as in the description of the crossing of Mont-Cenis, strikes a deeper chord of eloquence in Mme de Staël. In Venice, after Oswald has left her, there is a great storm, paralleling the heroine's storm of spirit. Cruelly agitated, "Corinne walked along the narrow stone path that separates the canal from the houses. The storm worsened continually and her terror for Oswald's safety increased each moment. She called out to the boatmen who took her cries for the calls of distress of unfortunate travelers capsized by the tempest, and yet no one dared approach, so stormily fearful had the waves of the Grand Canal become" (xvi, iii). This highly pathetic, Romantic scene of dismay works to reinforce the sense of abandonment of the heroine. It is in such passages that the Empire style, stasis, yields to passion. Mme de Staël writes most effectively when she speaks of motion and emotion and renders her sense of the transitoriness of life, of the chiaroscuro of our illusions.

But it is when she truly gives full play to her observations of a general order that she most convinces us. She will write, for example: "Passion makes us both more perceptive and more credulous. In this state it would seem that we can see only with supernatural vision. We uncover the hidden and delude ourselves about the evident; for we are repelled by the idea that we suffer to such a degree without extraordinary cause, or that such despair could result from ordinary circumstances" (xvii, ii). The author's intensive knowledge of the pangs of passion adds cogency to her story. There is much in the manner and substance of the novel to raise questions in the reader's mind, but the general comment, in the supple wisdom of its accuracy, reassures and restores our confidence in it.

Out of the evolution of post-Flaubertian fiction, there arose the belief that a third-person narration achieves authenticity only when the author has not so completely identified himself, "as narrator, with his hero that he can give him no objective weight whatever." Only if distance is maintained can he "allow him some of the value of a detached and phenomenal personage like the rest of the company in the story. . . ."[18] It is plain that Mme de Staël could achieve such detachment only with her secondary characters, never with her protagonists. Not a single one of her heroines has autonomous being, and the authorial voice, despite its medi-

---

18. Percy Lubbock, *The Craft of Fiction* (London: Jonathan Cape, 1957), p. 260.

tative quality, is never entirely disjoined from either defense or advocacy of their course. The calculated aloofness of the author from the major figures in the novel that one finds in *Madame Bovary* was certainly outside Mme de Staël's ken. But we are constrained to see that Mme de Staël's very lack of detachment and even her lack of patient artistry give another sort of value to her novel. There is a fundamental difficulty in discussing any of her works in terms of style understood as the art of language. To her, "the word is nothing but an instrument; and although her expression of it is nearly always felicitous, her merit is related to what she is saying, rather than to the words themselves" (I, ccvi). The language used is in fact very ordinary,[19] full of clichés and, as Goethe noted, of "*mais*—buts," thus of qualifications, as well as frequently clumsy in its searching after the right expression of feeling or thought; and yet the tone is infused with a living presence and intellect.

"*Corinne* alone, among Mme de Staël's works, seems to me the work of an artist."[20] This is palpably so despite the work's defects, because of its carefully premeditated form and because its characterizations are consistent and well drawn. Yet whatever the strength of the images conveyed to us in its pages, it springs primarily from the vibrancy of Mme de Staël's wit and her penetration of the mood of sorrow. She could write only out of felt emotions, not imagined ones. The abandoned Corinne, when she attempts to compose some lines, finds that her sorrow has stopped her creativity:

Feeling herself incapable of turning her thoughts from her own situation, she depicted what she suffered; but it was no longer of general ideas that she wrote, these universal elements that find answer in all men's hearts; it was a cry of pain, a cry in the end monotonous, like that of the birds of night; there was too much fire in the expression of it; too much impetuosity, too little nuance; it was sorrow, but it was not talent. To write well, no doubt, a genuine emotion is required, but that emotion must not be destructive. (xviii, iv)

---

19. I refer readers again to the study by Lucia Omacini, "Quelques remarques," which treats specific criticisms directed against Mme de Staël's novelistic style during the period of their publication.

20. Vinet, *Etudes*, p. 188.

This quotation demonstrates that precisely what is sometimes thought to be the prime flaw of the novel must be viewed as its greatest force and originality. It is precisely that expression of un-refined grief which Corinne thought should be contained if art, as Mme de Staël understood it, were to be served that is its strength. When it is hidden, the novel becomes sometimes a feeble thing, but when the towering passion and anguish are expressed (as in Corinne's meditation [xviii, v]), a note of terrifying melancholy majesty is struck. It is as though Mme de Staël's *Corinne* were an exception in art to the "rule" of submerging the artist's self: in the measure that her own energy and passion are expressed here, her novel is a great one; in the measure that they are betrayed, by false aestheticizing or by conventional melodrama, the novel fails.

Even as Corinne, as we see her first before her crowning at the Capitol, had attired herself in picturesque fashion yet "without departing so much from established usage as to be thought af-fected," so had Mme de Staël conceived her novel in "female" timidity. It was to be in Empire style, full of cameo scenes of Co-rinne and Oswald at the Forum or in the Campagna. It was to be the novel of the woman of genius, but her genius must be re-assuringly tempered, not presenting the terrors inherent in female revolt, but tamed by the passive voice, by geometric line, by an embalmed, controlled eighteenth-century rhetoric. It is not, I think, absurd to seek the cause for much of Mme de Staël's timidity in her conception of *Corinne*, even in its language, in a fear of offend-ing taste as well as sensibility while protesting against the given order.

The torment of Corinne, the self-appointed priestess of Apollo who is also a natural, artless woman, wrenches the novel free of its frozen frame. The angry and avenging heroine of the end of the work is an analogue no longer to a frieze by Percier and Fon-taine or Prud'hon's celebration of Bonaparte (see Plate 9). In the struggle against that view of the world which, as Coleridge wrote, "presents everything as lost or gone or absent and future," Co-rinne's disposition to be concerned with present raptures and griefs confronts and accuses the arid postures of the aesthetic of the time. A more appropriate analogy to the Corinne of the last books of the novel must be Prud'hon's allegorical painting, *Justice and*

Vengeance Pursuing Crime (Plate 10). Here metaphysical concern, movement, uncertainty have replaced elegiac stasis. Skies move, color and line flow, shadow replaces unbroken light, sorrow and wrath replace a counterfeit serenity.

Somewhere within the tortuous coils of this style, Romanticism has come to life.

9. *Triumph of the Consul Bonaparte*. Prud'hon's frieze-like celebration of Bonaparte's assumption of power incorporates its neoclassical themes—cupids, goddesses, equine splendor, and martial victory sung by bards—in a sensuous procession of graceful line and shadow that yet remains mute and still. Musée Condé, Chantilly.

10. *Justice and Vengeance in Pursuit of Crime*. Prud'hon. From the Salon of 1808. Musée du Louvre. (Photo from Réunion des Musées Nationaux, Paris.)

CHAPTER 7

Corinne—The Prophecy

With woman dependency is interiorized.
She *is* a slave even when she acts with
apparent freedom; while man is essentially independent and his bondage
comes from without.

SIMONE DE BEAUVOIR

Un Coq ayant trouvé un diamant, dit: "J'aimerais
mieux avoir trouvé un grain d'orge."
Ainsi jeune beauté, mignonne et délicate,
Gardez-vous bien de tomber sous la patte
D'un brutal qui n'ayant point d'yeux
Pour tous ces beaux talents dont votre esprit éclate,
Aimerait cent fois mieux
La moindre fille de village
Qui serait plus à son usage.[1]

CHARLES PERRAULT

Megalomania versus Nothingness

When Oswald, far into the novel, finally reads Corinne's confession, he is distressed and full of pain: he is dismayed at the
thought of Corinne's past suffering, induced by the incomprehension of his countrymen and women; he is assailed by doubts she
can ever be happy in simple domesticity; he is torn over his father's
role in the story. He goes out into the airless and torrid Neapolitan

---

1. A cock, finding a diamond, says: I would have
    preferred to find a barleycorn.
    So, my fetching, delicate beauty,
    Take care never to fall into the hands
    Of a brute, who having no eyes
    For all those fair talents that gush forth from your wit,
    Would prefer a hundred times more
    The least of the village girls
    Who would be more to his purpose.

midday sun. Corinne, unable to bear the stress of waiting any longer to hear his response, goes to his room and, learning he is gone out toward Portici, herself runs out on foot.

She had no idea of going to Portici, but she went on, ever more quickly; suffering and distress quickened her steps. No one was to be seen at that hour on the main road, the very animals hide themselves away; they fear nature.

From moment to moment Corinne felt she was about to fall; she found no tree to lean upon, and her reason wandered in this inflamed desert; she had but a few steps to go before she would come to the king's palace, within whose portals she would find shelter and water to refresh herself. But her strength failed her; she tried to walk, but in vain—she could see the road no longer; a vertigo hid it from her and made a thousand lights, brighter than the day's, shine; and all at once a cloud came up, following the lights, and hid her in stifling darkness. A burning thirst devoured her. She met a lazzarone, the only human creature who would brave the rigors of the climate at such a moment, and begged him to go and fetch her a sip of water, but this man, seeing a lady so striking in her beauty and the elegance of her dress alone on the road, was convinced she must be mad, and ran away in terror. (xv, 1)

Like Delphine, wandering through the ball in isolation, and fleeing it into the storm, Corinne finds herself brutally separated from the normal course of life. But in *Corinne* the heroine's solitude is far more intense. Nature itself is inimical to her impatience and her passion, to her unwonted and brazen activity in seeking her lover under a sky that man (and, more's the reason, woman) defies at his peril. Her solitude, the passion that impels her on against all logic, are here equated not merely with independence or idiosyncrasy, but with downright madness. She feels engulfed by darkness. The reaction to her of a being from the normal world is nothing less than one of horror and flight.

"The fear of disappearing, of dissolving, is the profound dominant note in this existence, experienced with a searing intensity and expressed throughout Mme de Staël's Work."[2] Corinne is a heroine stranded between a fantastic megalomania and its opposite, nothingness. It is in the abyss between the two that the terror of madness lies.

---

2. Simone Balayé, "A propos du préromantisme: continuïté ou rupture chez Madame de Staël," in *Préromantisme: hypothèque ou hypothèse?*

Megalomania has exposed the heroine, as well as the author in her Corinne *persona* ("You may call me Corinne"), to this belittling taunt: the character of Corinne is nothing but a monstrous absurdity. A promise of ridicule is attached of necessity to a dream of self-fulfillment so blatant, so patent as this. Constant acidly commented, concerning his embattled mistress, "I know of no woman and even of no man . . . more convinced of her immense superiority over everyone else and who can yet manage so little to make others share in that conviction."

This is the kernel. The capacious ego, which had never been and perhaps never could be appeased, here grants to itself its own deepest desires. There is a touching, foolish innocence in Mme de Staël's so open, obvious, vulnerable self-exposure.

Born into the Enlightenment, temperamentally attuned to the modern rather than the ancient, Mme de Staël must have been at some loss as to where to find appropriate models. No modern heroine existed that even suggested what she had it in mind to portray: feminine genius.[3] She had to invent such a vision herself and yet endow her with the density of a tradition. To accomplish this she would not hesitate to go against the grain of the spontaneous and the immediate, to borrow from everywhere—from antiquity, from the faddish and flat classical revival in whose style she wrote, and from republican art. She willed her *Corinne* to be a myth-making novel, and she drew her principal mythical model from what Phyllis Chesler, in *Woman and Madness*, has called the Daughter-Woman: the chaste, self-possessed, adventurous goddess, or the seer-priestess, possessed of higher, visionary powers. But she did not settle for this model alone, and we find elements both of Demeter and of Athena in Corinne, as well as of the muses, the sibyls, and the demigodlike Nike. Even so, the desire for contemporaneity would win out. Corinne's story is conceived as a modern one, yet its heroine seems to stand out of time, timeless. Intended as fable, as parable, the dream that this novel enacts is a

---

3. Learned or literary ladies like Héloïse, Louise Labé, Pernette du Guillet, Marguerite de Navarre, and others existed in some numbers, but where had there been one who, like Corinne, was the glory of her nation and her age?

fantasy of the self magnified, and the magniloquent heroine is the stuff of myth. Such is the mad, the grand, the megalomaniacal aspect of *Corinne*. But equally important, it is countered, checked everywhere in the novel by apprehension and doubt. The poetess is, despite the notoriety of her courageous unconventionality, assailed by a deep and convincingly modern uncertainty. When we and Nelvil see her first,

She was dressed like the sibyl of Domenichino, an Indian shawl circling her head, with her hair, of the fairest black, braided through it; her dress was white; a blue drapery was tied beneath her breast; and her costume was very picturesque without, however, departing so far from accepted taste as to be guilty of affectation. Her posture in the chariot was noble and modest: one could tell that she was happy to be admired; but a feeling of timidity was mixed with her joy, seeming to ask forgiveness for her triumph; the expression on her face, of her eyes, of her smile, made one interested in her, and Lord Nelvil's first glance made of him her friend, long before any deeper feeling had subjugated him. Her arms were of a dazzling beauty; her tall figure, somewhat full in the manner of Greek statuary, was redolent of the energy of youth and happiness; her look held something inspired. One perceived in her manner of greeting and of acknowledging the applause she received a kind of naturalness that heightened the aura of her extraordinary situation; she gave at once the impression of being a priestess of Apollo going toward the temple of the Sun, and of a woman perfectly simple in the daily occupations of life; in fine, all her motions had a charm that excited interest and curiosity, astonishment and affection. (II, 1)

Megalomania is tempered here. A dichotomy is everywhere apparent: this is a grandeur that needs to plead in its own favor, to pray to be excused; indeed, to resemble ordinariness as much as it can—while yet remaining grandeur. It is, in fact, a higher grandeur that, in conformity with the dictates of Enlightenment canons of taste, contains its opposite and reproaches pomposity. Corinne is genuinely delight-giving to those about her. She is a far from marmoreal goddess. The electric charge of admiration given, she returns, enhanced, to the giver.

Priestess of Apollo, "daughter of the Sun," so attired, so treated by the multitude: this is the solar vision that surrounds the Corinne of the book's opening. Madness and destruction, reinforced by images of shadow and phantoms, characterize its ending, completing the dualism inherent in Staël's vision of her heroine's destiny.[4]

Yet at times the megalomaniacal impulse seems to slip out of the author's control. When Corinne performs in public as Juliet (in her own translation of Shakespeare's play), she claims it is for her lover's sake alone that she plays her balcony scene, and she becomes the only player on the stage. Her greatest happiness is not solely an intimate one; it is powerfully linked with a public enactment. In showing her perfect *command* of feeling, in acting, "she knew, at the price of her repose, that delight of the soul that she had wished for in vain before, and that she was to regret forever after." Her need for recognition is wedded to the genuine achievement of her performance: it is not at all a pure—that is demented—megalomania, but Mme de Staël here muddies and combines the two, confounding our sense of what it is that Corinne is after. At a concert she and Oswald attend, the crowd fawns upon her and Corinne responds excitedly to its plaudits. Oswald huffily departs, muttering that he would not want to take her away from such adulation since it makes her heart beat quite as hard as does love. His jealousy robs her of all pleasure in the occasion, since she has a need for him "to be witness" to her success. Here again is an obvious reversal of sex roles: the man who needs the public witness of the woman to feel his triumph complete. We may ask just how it is that a similar impulse comes to appear megalomaniacal simply because it appears in the other sex. Mme de Staël has revealed the truth of this possibility, the universality of this need for confirmation of the self in the eyes of the beloved of either sex, by setting it forth here. But she is by no means as entirely confident of our acceptance of it as she tries to appear, and in her apprehension that her own view is "mad," she exaggerates the evidence for her heroine's gifts and popularity, hoping to force our accord.

The conception of Corinne as a sibyl, as possessed of near-supernatural powers of utterance, links her not only to Virgil's wild, will-less sibyl, but, once again, to the seer that Diderot saw

---

4. See Maya Lehtonen's articles on the imagery of *Corinne*, which are illuminating, but which regretfully, because of the focus of this volume, could not be given the attention they deserve. "Le Fleuve du temps et le fleuve de l'enfer, thèmes et images dans *Corinne*," *Neuphilogische Mitteilungen*, 68 (1967), 225–42, 391–408; 69 (1968), 101–28.

in woman. Of course, in a male artist genius can be conceived of as possession by another power without its visitation appearing to deprive him of his integrity. The male artist's frequently female muse withdraws from him, leaving him intact and, indeed, enriched. The same visitation in a female genius, it would seem, immediately takes on the cast of rape: the woman's genius is male, invading her loins, depriving her of her feminine subjectivity by bringing a foreign, active component to bear on her ostensibly inert person. In this sense, the sibyl is truly mad, possessed of an incomprehensible (to her) utterance, of which she is but the vehicle.

Mme de Staël does lend her Corinne some aspects of the sibyl, speaking her poetry in the manner of one possessed; but she corrects this image of "madness," of possession, by giving her an Apollonian, civilized character quite at variance with that of the "feminine" improvisers who played so important a part in her delineation and who exploited the permission accorded to women to make inspired utterance as long as it appeared to be "mindless" and of divine rather than personal origin.[5]

The madness with which Corinne is threatened is a terror of invisibility. In all the scenes of despair in Mme de Staël's work, it is nonrecognition of the heroine *as herself* by the beloved, and through him by the world, that is the cause of the trauma. It is the ultimate lack of seriousness in the quality of attention that is accorded woman by man and by society that calls up this fear of nothingness, cause of so much genuine, nonfictional madness in women. Roger Bastide has written of madness that it is a "ritual of rebellion that fails."[6] The *Corinne* fiction reflects just such a dumb-show of revolt. For the author herself her novel was a hubristic display ending in a failed ritual of rebellion, its heroine's

---

5. What increased respect do Sylvia Plath, Virginia Woolf, and now Anne Sexton inspire in us for becoming "mad" and "possessed" and succumbing to suicide? Theirs is the "correct" posture of suffering and discomposure before a genius held ultimately to be alien to woman. They are "feminized" or weakened by their plight and so rendered pathetic, sympathetic. The equal but resistant greatness of an Emily Dickinson or a Willa Cather, non-suicidal artists, renders them, comparatively, merely cold rather than, were they men, noble.

6. Roger Bastide, *Le Rêve, la transe et la folie* (Paris: Flammarion, 1972), *passim*.

defeat resulting from the author's need to force upon her the world's feminine ideal, that of self-immolation.

Mme de Staël's failure of nerve and her reluctance to do open battle clearly had their origin in her old filial piety. What had made her feel she might be "mad" was the war between her lifelong fear of nothingness, the possible remnant of her mother's conditional love (surely reinforced by her ceaselessly replicated experiences of abandonment by men), and that enormous zest and talent which pressed her forward in her will to power as well as in her need to become the worthy heir of her obsessively loved father. But Necker was a man who, like Diderot, approved of women in their (female) spontaneity, not in their (male) artistry. He admired Germaine's conversational gifts, her immanent art, inordinately, overtly, unsparingly. Toward the writer she wished to be and, underlying this, her drive to transcendence, he was unfailingly sarcastic.[7] The author of *Corinne* embodies this split in her novel in a number of ways, the most rigid of which, to a modern reader, is her division of the novel into national categories: England becomes normalcy, continuity, immanence; Italy stands boldly for art and its triumphant victory beyond personal mortality.

The Italy of the Spirit

The late Christopher Herold, Mme de Staël's biographer, scarcely ever able to resist one of his own witty sallies, said of *Corinne* that it is *On Literature* in novel form. In point of fact it is, on the contrary, a complete reversal of the stand of the earlier work that we find in *Corinne*, for that long essay had argued the superiority of the North and its Christian mysteries over the paganism of the South. *Corinne* holds, conversely, that only the South, the Mediterranean with its pagan appetite for the unforeseeable and its rooted acceptance of a mortality that it thereby transcends, is congenial to art. A tremendous alteration in Mme de Staël's values is apparent in this reversal, for her, of the meaning of North and South. Corinne is of an Italian mother (the author

---

7. See Béatrice d'Andlau, "Journal de jeunesse," *Occident et cahiers staëliens*, Oct. 15, 1932.

discards her own and reinvents for her heroine a kinder and
warmer-blooded one who, having taught her art and grace, tact-
fully dies) and of a devoted but weak English father, soon controlled
by the chilly domineering of his *bien-pensante* country-English
second wife (Mme Necker recurs after all).

Mme de Staël, the distillation of her era, though permeated by
Enlightenment *clarté*,[8] is irresistibly attracted by the enigmatic: it is
unlike her and draws her beyond herself, where she always wished
to be. "Voyager est, quoiqu'on puisse dire, un des plus tristes
plaisirs de la vie—Travel, whatever one may say, is one of the
saddest pleasures in life." It is Oswald, miserable and believing
his life has been a betrayal of his father, who expresses the author's
état d'âme at the outset of the novel, that melancholy Germaine
herself had felt after her father's death, when Italy's spirit could
not pierce through the layers of her grief. Oswald's puzzlement is
all the greater, for Italy's mystery could be apprehended "by the
imagination rather than by that spirit of judgment that is particularly developed by English education." Oswald's incapacity to
be deeply touched by the Italian spirit is Germaine's own former
blindness of *On Literature,* and Corinne herself is emblematic of
the tantalizing mystery it represents for him. "Corinne's poetry
... is a sort of intellectual melody that can alone express the charms
of the most fleeting and delicate of impressions" (II, II). The truth
of Jean-Albert Bédé's assertion is visible here: that Mme de Staël
moves toward obscurity, "at least toward that obscurity which
results from a need to translate the untranslatable."[9] Italy, then,
means something new here, but what?

Italy, Art, Woman

Italy, Corinne's chosen nation, is the symbol of a teeming,
multifaceted mystery. It is made to stand not merely for art, but
for individualism and for woman. Contemporary Rome, with its
glorious past, now fallen, "is the asylum of the world's exiles; is
Rome itself not dethroned? Its aspect consoles kings dispossessed

---

8. See Roland Mortier's excellent summary of this side of Mme de Staël in
his "Madame de Staël et l'héritage des lumières," *Colloque de Coppet,* pp. 129–44.

9. Jean-Albert Bédé, "Mme de Staël et les mots," *Colloque de Coppet,* p. 329.

like itself" (IV, I). A fallen grandeur is akin to woman's, which either is lost in prehistory or has never yet risen. The incoherence of the peninsula's odds and ends of antiquity, its cities' rises and falls from political power, combine with its other greatness in the arts and sciences to give Italy the nonlinear temporal quality Mme de Staël wishes to associate with Corinne's genius. A rich mass of intuition linking past and present is a ground of Romanticism, and Italy represents Romantic fullness as against the "masculine" linearity of Enlightenment England. So Corinne will insist, in speaking to Oswald, that the unknown has primacy over the known, thus rejecting the power of the mind as ultimate. "What we know is just as inexplicable as the unknown; but we have . . . become accustomed to our habitual darkness, whereas new mysteries terrify us . . . " (IV, I). If Corinne stresses this, it is to heighten our sense that her tale is intended as testimony to the inexplicably complex nature of things, not as a simple nostrum.

Mme de Staël, even in creating the audacious Corinne, did not dare to depart altogether from the idea that improvisation was somehow more acceptably "feminine" than deliberate art. Her heroine's poetry is "comme une conversation animée—like animated conversation," and she feels often that "what speaks in me is better than myself" (the sibyl's curse once more). But she presses beyond this as she asserts, "I feel myself a poet." It was Italy that enabled Mme de Staël to set this astonishing assertion upon her heroine's lips. In some basic and crucial way, the Italian experience, perhaps even more than the German, had emboldened her to feel and to invent her own creative powers. The spontaneity for which she was famous and infamous in France and Switzerland there became a mere natural phenomenon among a people as naturally spontaneous, voluble, and impulsive as she.

When Oswald attacks Corinne—"You are an unbelievable person, deep in your feelings and light in your tastes; independent in your pride of soul and yet enslaved by the need for distraction; capable of loving one alone, but needing all. You are a magician who alternately disturbs and reassures. . . . Corinne, Corinne, one cannot help but fear you, even in loving you."—it is for her differences with the Englishwomen who are his model of femininity. Corinne's defense is in part a direct attack on this more contained idea of woman: "The Englishwomen's reserve, so full of virtue, and the artful grace of Frenchwomen, believe me, often serve to hide half of what occurs within the spirits of both: and what you are pleased to call magic in me is but an unconstrained nature which sometimes reveals its divergent feelings and opposing thoughts, without a care to setting them in harmony; for that harmony, where it exists, is nearly always false, and most true character lacks consistency" (VI, III).

Corinne is a woman unbent by a distorting social order, where all women must tend to a single ideal, measure themselves against it, "understand" themselves through its reflection of their nature, denying any other. A child of two cultures, Corinne escapes the grasp of both to some degree, but espouses the more life-giving, accepting, Italian mode. In Italy she has been allowed moral space to discover her own nature and not to worry whether others think it fitting or proper that she be as she is. Corinne warns Oswald against the nexus of hidden feelings—the resentments stifled, the opinions suppressed, the "unacted desires"—still alive under the cover of their mannerliness, in those seemly and self-contained women. Her Sophie de Vernon in *Delphine* and the Lady Edgermond of this novel are dramatic representations of the devastating effects of such repression upon the characters of women. Corinne's openness is an exact mirror image of their closedness: she is alive and determined to avoid spiritual death; they, as we see them later taking tea at Lady Edgermond's, bored and perpetually exhausted, have long since, in childhood, consented to abdicate all need to feel alive.

Italy is not merely "woman's" country but the homeland of Corinne's mother, a homeland to which she had been so passionately attached that "my aunt often repeated to me that it was her fear of leaving her country that made my mother die of sorrow." The bond of this freer, more "natural" land is thus extended to the generation of the mother. We remember Mme de Staël's ambivalence of feeling toward her own mother. She here conquers some of the anger that dominates the portrayals of all the biological mothers of *Delphine* and now espouses a positive bond with the dead mother, making Corinne a sort of Persephone-Kore who "belongs" to her Demeter-like Italian mother, but who is arbitrarily severed by her fate from the earth and spirit that would truly nurture her.

As Corinne defends her country to Oswald she does so in terms that are just as apposite to woman's fate as to Italy's. "I am not sure whether I err in this, but the faults of the Italians inspire in me only a feeling of pity for their lot. Foreigners have conquered and laid waste this beautiful country, the object of their eternal ambitions, in every age," she says, and yet the same foreigners reproach her for having the "faults of a nation defeated and torn." Women too are often held, like Italians, to be childlike, indolent, frivolous, and volatile. Mme de Staël sees such traits as a consequence of the internalized habit of dissimulation imposed upon the defeated. She reveals the unspoken basis of this analogy more plainly, as she comes closer to her theme, in saying that the other nations, having received the gifts of arts and letters from Italy, now try to turn them against her, and "often contest her the last glory allowed nations deprived of military strength and political freedom, that of the arts and sciences."

So we grasp that Corinne is laying claim for herself as woman and genius to a right to that previously uncontested rule by man over the realm of the spirit. Like her nation powerless in temporal terms, she craves, "at the least," a spiritual power. The singularity of this novel, as against the range of achievements in art by other women in other times, is that *Corinne's* preoccupation is with a kind of power and with its absence. Corinne is an embodiment of Italy's natural physical loveliness, of its uncontested primacy in the creation of the visually beautiful, and of the splendor of its poetry. Setting aside Rome's hegemony, and the Pope's, and Venice's—the temporal successes of that nation—Corinne, a modern heroine, takes to herself only the pacific victories. Modern Italy is a country radically stripped of all power save that of its artistic and spiritual traditions. In these achievements Mme de Staël recognizes the raw materials, scorned by the world which dances to the temporal tune, that can be identified with and made available to women. To "useless" art, *Corinne* is, therefore, a poem of praise. If enthusiasm, art, affect can be seen as "feminine," Corinne will make them into instruments of her female powers and be, not a lady dilettante, dabbling in her boudoir, or even an Elisabeth

Vigée-Lebrun executing her formidably graceful portraits, but a self-conscious poet, one who will attempt to rival no lesser poets than Virgil and Tasso, who will strive to create at their level of poetic statement and who will expect, too, the rewards of the poet: the laurel wreath, applause, adulation, fame.

Yet the very breadth of this vision of the woman poet seeking power through her art, identifying with an old and great nation, is constantly undercut and diminished by the author's own uncertainties. Corinne *as poet* is no dilettante, yet she is a dilettante painter (she draws perfect likenesses), musician (she plays the harp), critic. The author's will to power is hungry. She heaps upon us unwelcome evidence of this superabundance of gifts, and irritation and incredulity begin to weaken our awe and admiration. The novel totters between the two, constantly losing credibility through excess and then regaining it with some sharp psychological observation or intriguing critical perception.

We understand that basically it is the novel as an act, not the poetry of the *belle Romaine,* that propels this work. Mme de Staël wrote of Alfieri, with whom there is in this respect a complete identification, that "né pour agir, il n'a pu qu'écrire—born to act, he was allowed only to write" and that his style and his tragedies mirror this constraint. It is such an electric charge of temporal power displaced that puts Corinne on her pinnacle and permits the author, by the grace of Italy, to make of her a free woman.

The young Corinne, returned to her English home, surviving her father's death, lived on there in an appalling constriction of feeling. The sorrow of exile—so acutely a part of Germaine's experience—is echoed by Corinne's: "I could not recall without emotion the kindly expressions of my country. *Cara, carissima,* I would say to myself while walking alone, to imitate to myself the friendly greetings of Italian men and women; I compared these with the greetings I was receiving" (XIV, III). Instead of the bird calls of Italy, she hears only the crows croaking in the English countryside; instead of blue sky, she finds only fog; instead of ripening fruits, pale flowers languidly growing.

The human warmth, the sense of possibility inherent in the southern climate, the colors of sky, fruit, sea, combine to draw Corinne back to her homeland, away from the denial of all of these that England is for her. Italy is her predestined element: she prospers in it, fawns on it. When Oswald, not the first of her lovers, becomes the focus of her life, she nevertheless does not want to marry him, and "believing herself loved, she was happy, for she did not clearly know what she desired besides" (VII, III).

Italy, sated by its too turbulent past, is the country of the unforced present, contrasted with the still puritanical, history-obsessed England of the novel, still dreaming of past and future conquest. Corinne is a free woman who wants only to live fully. All she asks of Oswald, probably all she ever wishes of him, is that "you not leave me." Even as she recognizes intellectually that life does not belong entirely to love, the perfection of their affection and regard for each other makes Corinne cry out for stasis, for time to stop, for other concerns to cease importuning them and let them be. Though she does not detail the terrors that marriage conjures up for her, we understand them perfectly well. She is free; she would not then be free. She comes and goes at will; she could not. She receives whomever and whenever she likes (she is very rich); she no longer could. She writes and speaks as she pleases; a husband would assume the power at the least to make observations, at the most, to censure. Her creative life would die under such scrutiny. No, far better not to worry about marriage, even with a man fondly loved.

Italy embraces Corinne, rejoices in her enthusiasm and spontaneity, allows her to be.[10] She receives from it that sustaining response that allows her to become a creator. "You have allowed me glory, oh liberal nation that does not banish women from its temples, you who do not sacrifice immortal talent to passing jealousies, you who ever celebrate the expression of genius, victor without victims, conqueror without spoils, drawing upon eternity to enrich time!" (xx, v). We may well wonder at this Italy that "does not banish women from its temples": it is scarcely the Italy we know. Mme de Staël has presented Italy to us as a utopian Arcadia

---

10. "Italy is much more than the setting; for the attention given to its nature and its art, it is one of the principal characters of the novel." Francisco Romero, "Mme de Staël en la revolución feminina del siglo XIX," *Cuadernos Americanos*, CVII, no. 6 (1959), 159.

with respect to the place of Corinne in its society, but for the rest she painstakingly strives to maintain a sense of its reality, idealizing it only lightly. "Here sensation blends with idea, all of life drinks from a common spring, and the soul, like the air, fills the confines of earth and sky. Here genius is at ease, because dreams are gentle; as it becomes agitated, they calm; if genius mourns some loss, dreams gift it with a thousand chimeras; if men oppress it, nature is there to succor it" (II, III).

Italy, then, stands for the free woman Corinne herself, for her love of art, for her liberality of spirit. If it sometimes takes on the aspect of Circe's enchanted island, with Corinne as Circe, it still bears so many marks of being the "real" Italy that we tend to forget that its reality has been blended with an ideal one. Mme de Staël's pleasure in her own creation mollifies her former reserve toward that nation and impels her to make of it a place beyond time, severed from history, symbol of life and love untrammeled. "If men were ever to meet together stripped of the tyranny of the many, what a pure air would breathe into our souls: how many new ideas, how many genuine feelings would revive us" (XVIII, v). Corinne's pacific Italy, as celebrated in her poetry of freedom, is the Staëlian analogue of Blake's New Jerusalem: it is there our fairest dreams may be realized.

England—Land of the Past

If Italy is the Present, England is both the Past, ignorant of present time, and the Future, in that it represents an idea of futurity subordinate to the Past. Italy is Romanticism, England the Enlightenment. And as Italy is woman's country, England is man's.

The very place where Corinne has been so confined and wretched is the place to which she must return, once love has brought her low. There can be no more striking juxtaposition of megalomania with nothingness than that of the glorious Corinne we see on the Capitoline with the anonymous one in Hyde Park, dressed in black, hidden in a coach. Never one to fail to turn the dagger in the wound, Mme de Staël emphasizes this: " . . . no, it was not thus," thought Corinne, "that I went to the Capitol when first I met him: he has thrown me from my triumphal chariot into the abyss of despair" (XVII, VI). It is not by the power of love that this has come to pass, but through the Englishman's defective conception of love. Corinne had foreseen all this, had told Oswald that in London there would be people to tell him that "promises of love do not bind one's honor" and that hordes of Englishmen had loved and forgotten their Italian amours.

Mme de Staël's Anglophilia is well documented.[11] It can be felt still in this novel where *le beau rôle* has been accorded to Italy. Oswald is grateful, even in leaving Corinne, to rediscover, in comparison with the public disorder of Italian life, England's reassuringly hierarchical order. English institutions, despite their imperfections, were combined in Mme de Staël's mind, even as they had been in Voltaire's, with the most advanced ideas concerning political freedom, so that that nation appeared to her to be the best extant model of the enlightened state. But the conception of England we have in the novel is not that of an idealized state; it is rather an England of the emotions.

We recollect Mme Necker's romance with Gibbon and his subsequent friendship with the Neckers. We recall her attempts to marry her daughter to the younger Pitt, and the strong bonds of mutual sympathy between the Swiss and the English Protestants which, along with Suzanne Necker's own Anglophilia, made England, for both mother and daughter, the never-never land where the best and most distinguished suitors bloomed. His martial bearing and his pronounced aloofness from the affective life, in terms of taste and temperament, combined with his love of domesticity make the Englishman the most dashing conceivable prize to Mme de Staël. The man made to love despite himself has the mythical force of the convert: he testifies to the strength of a power he once resisted. English reserve, in Oswald's case compounded by his grief-stricken withdrawal from life, will accentuate the regenerative power of Corinne's love. Ever since Hamlet (a Dane, to be sure!), the melancholy Englishman had assumed ever greater romantic dimensions in the French mind.[12] The pathetic

---

11. See Robert Escarpit's *L'Angleterre dans l'oeuvre de Mme de Staël* (Paris: Didier, 1954).

12. Examine, to take two widely spaced examples, *Sidney* by Louis Gresset (1745) and Victor Hugo's Gwyneplaine, hero of *L'Homme qui rit* (1869).

appeal of this kind of figure is at its apogee, now acculturated like Werther to the various nationalities, as we see in Chateaubriand's René, Senancour's Obermann, and Constant's Adolphe. Mme de Staël maintains her hero as English because the proud, insular soldierliness of Oswald, his stock heroic physical courage (proven in the very first chapters of the book, as he saves others from drowning and from fire) is essential to her idea of the hero. Despite his abject moral suffering, this hero (in contradistinction to those imagined by the male writers of the period) can act, has an ideal of self-abnegation, and is not yet so self-engrossed as to be beyond noticing (and trying to alleviate) the pain of others. Action, for Mme de Staël, is a good. A hero totally incapacitated from acting would for her have no heroic dimension.[13] Furthermore, England alone among the nations remained, politically, as a viable realm of masculine activity for Mme de Staël. By 1806 Napoleon had deprived most of remaining Europe of that imaginative possibility.

Just as essential to Mme de Staël's choice of England as the term opposite to Italy in her scheme of the novel is the highly developed conception of domestic felicity for which it is celebrated. Mme de Staël was much taken with James Thomson's praise of connubial bliss in *The Seasons*, citing it in *Delphine*:

> Where friendship full-exerts her softest power,
> Perfect esteem enlivened by desire
> Ineffable, and sympathy of soul;

This inviting vision is augmented by our memories of rosy Reynolds ladies, dressed with flowery freshness, embracing their robust yet pliant children, with hair long and silken like that of their alert and healthy dogs. Mme de Staël, against her grain, not only worshipped this idea of marriage all her life but was drawn nostalgically to the myth of country pleasures in which it is embedded:

> An elegant sufficiency, content,
> Retirement, rural quiet, friendship, books,
> Ease and alternate labour, useful life,
> Progressive virtue, and approving Heaven.

---

13. Oswald can be thought of as just as Byronic (before the fact) as he is Wertherian.

The country mouse/city mouse struggle we recall from the earliest works remains undissipated in Germaine's mature years. A comforting image, this is also, simultaneously, a despised one. It remains an ideal of the heart that, *but for the lack of the truly complete partner,* might have been realized. But he never was, and the rural myth (at Coppet as elsewhere) always failed Mme de Staël.

With Oswald, Corinne visits an English ship that is lying at anchor in the Bay of Naples for the Sunday morning religious service. "The subordination, the seriousness, the regularity, the silence that could be observed on that vessel were the image of a severe and free social order in contrast with that city of Naples, so lively, so passionate, so tumultuous" (XI, III). Naples here is the final antithesis to England. The Englishwomen are surrounded by their children, "fair as the day, but as timid as their mothers; and not a single word was exchanged before a new acquaintance. This constraint, this silence, made Corinne quite sad; she raised her eyes toward beautiful Naples, toward its flowery coast, toward its animated life, and she sighed." English life, with its hierarchy, is for Corinne worse than a prison: it is a well-kept cage whose dimensions, like those of the ship's cabin, confine the mind, the spirit, the very body of a woman.

The England of *Corinne* bears a strong resemblance to Mme de Staël's conception of her parents' Switzerland: Italy, to her own France. For her, Helvetia was the land of exile, where narrow, devout, earnest, well-intentioned people simply bored to lingering death people of talent, wit, temperament, and ambition like herself. France, in her experience, was the brilliant stage of life where her being took on meaning and effectiveness, where she was someone to be reckoned with. In this novel's England we have an affective recollection of that bittersweet period of Mme de Staël's English exile at Juniper Hall, where she enjoyed the forthrightness of English manners, but could not have enjoyed the sting of the delightful Miss Burney's having been made to quit her company, as being unsuitable to a maiden lady. England and Switzerland are spiritually blended here to become a Staëlian brew of national repressiveness of feminine talent by hostile social pressures.

England symbolizes the belief that the interests of society must take precedence over those of the individual. Society must be preserved; ergo, marriage and the family. Much as Oswald appreciates Corinne's talents, her genius, he believes more "that the relations of social life ought to be prime, and that woman's destiny, and even man's, lies not in the exercise of one's intellectual faculties but in the accomplishment of one's duty" (XIII, III).

The Conflict: Talent versus Society

The duties enshrined in the *bienséances* of English life are portrayed primarily in the character of Lord Edgermond's second wife (Corinne's stepmother), the dry, even-tempered, heartless (to Corinne) Lady Edgermond. If we set her alongside Mme de Vernon, Lady Edgermond emerges unquestionably as the fuller, the more realized villainess. Mme de Vernon's depiction is lively and filled with credible elements, but it is at first all charm, then all evil, and, finally, all forgiveness, while Lady Edgermond's temper is consistent throughout: not entirely blameworthy, not entirely praiseworthy, even as we see how she is destructive to the protagonists. The equilibrium Mme de Staël achieves here is the more notable if, as I believe, Lady Edgermond is modeled essentially after the author's mother. As Mme de Staël describes Lady Edgermond—"A passionate person, beneath a cold exterior"—she summons to mind descriptions of Suzanne Necker, who "never lost an opportunity of expressing her rather severe religious opinions," by her daughter's own account, and seemed to be "guided only by her conscience and listened to it alone."[14] Like Mme Necker, who had never liked Paris, Lady Edgermond "loved only the province in which she was born, and my father, whom she dominated, had sacrificed a life in London or Edinburgh to her" (XVI, I). The Mme Necker who had insisted on keeping Necker in her province had likewise deplored her daughter's sexual conduct, her tastes, her style of being.

The lifelong struggle of personalities between them had left the daughter feeling somehow accursed. "Has God's curse, my

---

14. Anne-Louise Germaine Necker de Staël, "Madame Necker," *Biographie universelle*, 21 vols. (Bruxelles: H. Ode, 1843–47).

mother's, been called down upon me?" she wrote to her father in his last illness,[15] wondering whether her voyage had brought some terrible punishment to her. Mme de Staël makes Lady Edgermond, Corinne's father's second wife, a rival for the love of the father whom it is licit to hate without the need to feel guilt. The vivid description Corinne gives of Lady Edgermond, and that lady's reactions to the heroine, are clear transformations of that troubled bond. The stepmother is "a cold person, dignified and quiet. . . ." According to Corinne, "she had made a promise to herself to change me if she could" (xiv, i).

Lady Edgermond's opposition to Corinne's talent has the support of religion and the social conventions, and so it is virtually omnipotent. Corinne had warned Oswald:

. . . a redoubtable enemy threatens me in your entourage: it is the disdainful mediocrity, the despotic severity of my stepmother. She will say all she can to blacken my past life. . . . The talents I may have, far from being an excuse in her eyes, will be considered, I know, my greatest wrong. She understands nothing of their value and sees only their danger. All that does not agree with the destiny she has traced for herself she finds useless, and all the poetry of the heart seems to her nothing but an importunate caprice that arrogates to itself the right to scorn all reason. (xvi, iii)

Lady Edgermond is that sort of domineering domestic woman who, feeling in duty bound to maintain what she deems to be the best interests of her sex, construes herself to be womanhood's highest expression and rejects, with all the confident authority of one whom society approves and respects, any deviance, no matter how fetching, from her own highly successful model of feminine subservience.

The passage above reflects Corinne's view of Lady Edgermond. Oswald's feelings toward her are quite different, far more generous. To him, it seemed when seeing her again after having heard Corinne's tale "that there was more feeling in Lady Edgermond than Corinne granted her, and he concluded that she simply had not, as did he, the habit of reading contained faces" (xvi, iii). So he is inclined to peer beyond her silence and reserve and to guess at the meaning of it. In the end, Oswald comes to admire her:

---

15. Larg, *La Seconde Vie*, p. 203.

Lucile's mother deserved respect and obtained it; she was someone who was still more severe toward herself than to others. Her limitations had to be attributed rather to the extreme rigor of her principles than to any lack of natural intelligence; and in the midst of all the bonds she had imposed upon herself, all her acquired and natural stiffness, there was a love for her daughter all the more deep in that the bitterness of her character arose out of repressed feeling that gave new force to the only affection she had not extinguished. (XVI, III)

Compassion here somewhat counterbalances Corinne's more acid view. But Lady Edgermond is a menace because she rationalizes her own narrow nature by prescribing limits to female comportment. Corinne wittily decries those like her: "One would say to hear them that duty consists in the sacrifice of whatever exceptional talents one might have and that the possession of wits is a sin to be expiated in leading exactly the same life as those who have none" (XIV, I). Yet Mme de Staël relents at the end and takes care to soften her a little: "The defects of her character were dissipated at the very moment when her deteriorated state might have made them seem more excusable," and Lady Edgermond's last wish is to unite her daughter to the husband she had won for her by sacrificing another.

This lady's actions and views are made to conform to a single end: to deprive Corinne of her powers. In a sense the stepmother is the touchstone of the novel in that she is the emblem of convention. Were she not credible, the story would have been considerably less effective. The specific claims society makes upon women, which are so firmly expressed in her defense of them, have no other strong exponent in the novel to counteract Corinne. We are aware how much ambivalence Mme de Staël herself felt concerning these claims and that she could never bring herself to deny their validity for most women, but that for herself she felt them to be murderously repressive. The author's skill in creating such a woman as this proper English dame, a woman Corinne's exact opposite in character, and her ability to sketch the dynamics of their mutually distrustful relationship while seasoning her portrayal with a few grains of mercy constitute no small novelistic achievement. Once again, as in *Delphine,* Mme de Staël shows herself to be a superior portraitist of women.

When Corinne, at her first dinner under her stepmother's roof, tries to speak chaffingly some graceful love lyrics to the gentleman beside her, she finds the company abruptly dismissed, the ladies separated from their male companions. Her stepmother, in kindly fashion, reveals to her her faux pas. First, the young ladies are not to speak until spoken to; and further, the word *love* must never pass their lips. Then Lady Edgermond tells her to forget Italy, where none of this "unseemly" behavior had ever been taken amiss, for "it is a country it were better you had never known." In the England of her youth, as later through Nelvil's rejection of her *for* England, Corinne is made to wonder if she is not mad, "if it was not I whose way of thinking was folly and if that solid existence that avoids sorrow as it does thought, feeling as it does dreaming, was not more worthy than my way of being." But her healthy self-esteem preserves her from this: "What use would such a sad conviction have been to me? It would have made me regard my faculties as an affliction, whereas in Italy they were thought of as a gift from heaven" (xiv, 1). So Corinne resists the aridity of her English life, keeps to her room, and cultivates her skills. "What good is all that to you," asks Lady Edgermond, "will it make you any happier?" in the age-old effort to pull down the plucky girl who does not know her place. In *Corinne* it is not the end of the argument: it is not society that has the last word about woman's place, but Corinne. "What is happiness," she tells herself, "if not the development of my faculties? Isn't physical suicide the same as moral suicide? And if I must snuff out my mind and my soul, what use is it to keep the miserable remnant of life that troubles me in vain?"

The England of Corinne's tale is the land that must be fled, because it is a domestic trap, filled with nice, but silly and empty people whose lives are a horror of sameness and emotional dreariness. The women in their little circle continue a conversation "that differed from that of the day before only by virtue of the date on the calendar and the trace of the years which came eventually to imprint itself upon the faces of these women just as if they had lived during that time."[16] Corinne is pitiless. A mechanical doll,

---

16. The aptness of Mme de Staël's cutting perceptions of Englishwomen is

slightly improved in its workings (an image she uses a number of times to express female emptiness) might easily have replaced her in that circle, she notes. She sees that some women there do indeed have wit and reflective spirit: this they repress. " . . . one would have appeared a hothead, a woman of doubtful virtue, had one spoken openly or revealed herself in any way; and what was worse than all these discouragements was that there would be no advantage in having done so" (xiv, 1).

Surely few women writers have written so scathingly and accurately of the feeling of social reproof that women have felt and often go on feeling even now, much as this iceberg of repressiveness has dissolved. Corinne's tale is one of triumph, of a woman's escape from a world closed against her, one that would treat her talents, her personality, "as a malady."[17] The argument Mme de Staël advances in her "wayward" heroine's defense is that of Aristotelian reasoning (though Aristotle himself would have disapproved!) that potentialities ought to be fulfilled, and that society—English society is here made to bear the brunt for them all —in morally killing the potential of its women kills all but the most meager part of their being. Corinne, in escaping, frees herself and becomes a radiant counterexample of woman. She could do this only by leaving England behind, but it catches hold of her again when she loves and is touched by man.

Fathers

Corinne's tale of her youthful escape is one of woman's triumph, but the novel in which it is set is the tragedy of woman. Its tragic outcome is predetermined, in an almost ludicrously accurate confirmation of contemporary feminist theory, by the role

---

corroborated by Mary Wollstonecraft: "The conversation of French women, who are not so rigidly nailed to their chairs to twist loppets, and knot ribbons, is frequently superficial; but, I contend, that it is not half so insipid as that of those English women whose time is spent making caps, bonnets and the whole mischief of trimmings, not to mention shopping, bargain-hunting, etc., etc." *A Vindication of the Rights of Women* (1792) (New York: Source Book Press Reprint, 1971), pp. 96–97.

17. Sigmund Freud's diagnosis of feminine discontent and aspiration as penis envy falls under this rubric. One wonders what further shapes the need to believe this may assume in the future.

patriarchy plays in Corinne's fate. In this, *Corinne* caps a tendency of the eighteenth-century novel: ". . . the despotic father overflows the dimensions of a simple individual; he is God, he hallows the virile constraint that he colors with tenderness, thus paralyzing all powers of resistance."[18]

As we and Oswald meet Corinne she, significantly, has neither a patronymic nor any family bonds anyone knows of. Her extraordinary status as a free woman is obviously buttressed for Mme de Staël by precisely this lack of ties. She is bound by no one's expectations, and only because she is not so bound has she been able to achieve the status of artist, both intrinsically, in that she has been able to devote herself wholly to poetry, and socially, in that her pretensions to the role of poet are accepted and allowed free rein. As long as she remains, in the novel and for Oswald, that phenomenon of nature, a free woman, he is unable to categorize her, and he continues to love her, even as he blames himself for doing so, wondering if she is some species of anomaly, a freak, and not the delightful and fascinating woman she seems to be. But once Corinne tells her tale, we learn that she is the daughter of an Englishman and we see her as wayward runaway child, as half sister of Lucile, as renegade woman, and as rebel against English life and the structure of patriarchy, her love having been cursed by the paternal order even before it came into being.

The fathers of the novel are its chorus as well as its gods. It scarcely needs to be repeated that the cult of her father was one of Mme de Staël's chief characteristics. "L'ange gardien des enfants, c'est leur père—The guardian angel of all children is their father," says the poet Corinne. We see in Oswald's remorse and mourning the same cult. "Never have I loved anything more deeply than my father," he tells Corinne. The mystic love father and son bear one another impels the father to entreat Oswald to abjure the Frenchwoman, Mme d'Arbigny, and return home, or else he will cause his parent mortal injury. Indeed, when Oswald finally does return, he learns that his father has died. Now the paternal claims are rendered all powerful, as the son vainly tries to fulfill his dead father's vision of him. He finds a manuscript that had been written

---

18. Fauchery, *La Destinée féminine*, p. 515.

by the elder Nelvil (actually a page from Necker's *Cours de morale religieuse*) in which are outlined the duties of children to parents:

Honor therefore thy fathers and mothers, honor them, honor and respect them, were it only for the sake of their past reign, for that time when they alone were master and which will never come again. . . . this is your duty, presumptuous children who are so impatient to run off alone along the road of life. They will disappear, doubt it not, those parents who dally in leaving you their place; this father whose speeches have a quality of strictness that wounds you . . . and you will seek for better friends in vain. . . ." (xii, i)

On reading this, the guilt-ridden Oswald cries, "Corinne . . . do you think it was against me that he wrote these eloquent complaints?"

In his letter to Lord Edgermond about Corinne, Nelvil expresses himself without Oswald's mediating presence, and here the effect is rather different. The father appears as narrow and uncompromising in character, a personification of all one is made to hate in the novel, obstinately opposed to any but the traditional mold for women, chauvinistic, and dictatorial with regard to his son's future.

When Corinne tells of her past and the relation between the two families is bared, we discover that though their fathers were fast friends (allies in her undoing?) Corinne, when first she met Lord Nelvil, had perceived immediately that her vivacity was displeasing to him. Corinne's own father had gently remonstrated with her when she first came to England, saying, "You must not struggle against the customs of the country you live in. . . . " "My dear child," he goes on, "it is not here as it is in Italy: women have no other vocation among us than domestic duty; your talents will lighten your boredom in solitude; perhaps you will find a husband who will be pleased by them . . ." (xiv, iii).

Fathers represent not only public opinion and conscience, but seemingly fate itself. A father is a gentle spiritual blackmailer whose power, seeming to inhere in nature, cannot be called into question. Fathers love us, but they cannot approve of what we do. In acting, we inevitably impugn the purity they have instilled in us and decreed us to enact in our lives. Inevitably we betray their love, even as we go on loving them. Though they die, their hopes in us remain with us, commanding us not to destroy even the memory of them by our acts. *Memento mori*, they live on in our anguish: " . . . had I but seen him a moment before his death, if he had only heard from my own lips that I was not unworthy of him, if he had believed it, I should not still be wracked by remorse like the most criminal of men." Oswald and Corinne both share, eventually, this sense of having deeply disappointed the established order of the world and of deserving its curse. Corinne in Scotland, standing in the park outside the house where she believes Nelvil to be happy with her sister, recalls Mr. Dickson's statement that Oswald's father "forbids him to marry that Italian, and it seemed to her as if her own father had joined with him and that *all of paternal authority* condemned her love."[19] Her reaction? It is a perverse masochistic pride: she is "proud to immolate herself so that Oswald might be at peace with his country, with his family, with himself."

That distant English cousin, Mr. Edgermond, the first father surrogate we meet in the novel, occasions on the part of the narrator a general observation: Mr. Edgermond "had those principles and prejudices which serve in every country to maintain things as they are; and this is a good, as long as things are as good as human reason allows: in that case men like Mr. Edgermond, that is, partisans of established order, even though they may be strongly attached to their habits and their ways of seeing things, must be considered as enlightened and reasonable people" (vi, iv). The sophistry is patent. England, to Mme de Staël's mind, was the most politically enlightened nation of Europe and yet, at the same time, the most patriarchal and alien to the very idea of freedom for women. Its benevolently despotic liberalism maintained power largely where it had always been, permitting it to be wrested only in violent spasms of outrage by the lower orders. The rich heiress Staël espouses, on this score, its politics. But she has raised, amazingly in her time, the question of whether the condition of woman in that "enlightened" state is in fact "as good as human reason allows," suggesting, though in convoluted fashion, that it most certainly was not.

---

19. Italics mine.

The power of the fathers in *Corinne* is victorious; their pre-eminence reasserted. The heroine is defeated. Mme de Staël was not able, ultimately, even as she saw so clearly what power it was that was inimical to Corinne, to reject it openly. Her lasting love of her father would never allow such a break, and so it is rather as we scrutinize the fine grain of Nelvil *père's* bigotry, or Lady Edgermond's arrogant limitedness, or the author's caustic contempt for the quality of ordinary English life, that we distinguish her anguished wrath against a patriarchy that could never accept her.

> What loss would a woman of high attainments and of genius have, in a man of character so low as to be afraid of the perfections of the woman who would give him the honour of calling her his?
>
> SAMUEL RICHARDSON

Oswald—The Sibyl's Muse

Shrouded in melancholy, obsessed with death, Oswald yields only slowly to Corinne's beneficent love. He is so dispirited that even in the early phases he cannot be said positively to love, but rather to receive Corinne's advances. It is Corinne who declares her love first and Oswald, in response, does not accept it assertively, but merely fails to reject it: "No, Corinne . . . no, I will not turn away from this beam of happiness that perhaps my tutelary angel has sent to shine upon me from the high heavens" (IV, III). He behaves, as has been observed with shock often enough, like the traditional girl in love, hanging on every word of the beloved, opening himself to her every mood, every gesture. "He never looked at her without emotion; in the midst of a party he could scarcely separate himself even for a moment from the place where she was seated; she uttered no word that did not move him; there was not a moment of sadness or gaiety for her that was not reflected upon his own face" (VIII, 186).

Mme de Staël renders her hero's vapors more credible by making them a function of his situation. Indifferent to life, Oswald must be charmed back to it, comforted, nursed, and mothered. Like Tristan or Hyperion, Oswald is the wounded hero (as was Léonce in his day). His actual cure is symbolized within the novel when he goes to save a drowning man and is in consequence almost drowned. He is taken home by Corinne who nurses him back to health, but, like Iseult the Dark, despite her steadfastness she loses her cured and forgetful lover to Iseult the Fair.[20]

But Nelvil's weakened spirits and health are not the only factors that make him subordinate. He is, like Constant with respect to Mme de Staël, slightly Corinne's junior in age, and vastly so in experience. Through Oswald's tale we learn that he has had but one (to be sure rather trying) crisis in his life, whereas Corinne has been transplanted in childhood, run away from her second home, become a famous personage, and had several lovers. Aside from his dearth of experience, Oswald simply is Corinne's inferior in knowledge, strength of character, and human quality. Fascinated by her powers, he is vastly more ignorant than she and becomes her pupil. Mme de Staël makes absolutely no allowance, in depicting Oswald, for the masculine vanity of male readers. Her hero's "manliness" lies entirely in his reckless courage and in the stubborn affirmations of his rather schematized, philistine English tastes, his pragmatic ideas.

A kindred spirit to Chateaubriand's René, Oswald is so full of feeling he is devoid of will. Once he has learned that his father, through the inexorable coincidences of Romantic convention, has disapproved of Corinne, he longs for chance to provide him with a a way out of his predicament: "He would have been willing to see her compromise herself for him in the eyes of the world so that her very error might put an end to his uncertainty" (VIII, I). Oswald is moved far more by what others think of him than by what he himself thinks. "Tear Corinne's heart apart or fail to honor his father's memory—this was an alternative so cruel that he asks for death a thousand times . . . ; in the end he did again what he had done so often, he put off the moment of decision" (XVII, II). When he finally receives the external pressure he has longed for and is called up by his regiment, he still wavers, reluctant to go:

---

20. Oswald returns this care, for later, with great solicitude, he nurses Corinne back to health from severe illness. We see the author's belief in the ideal of parity in love in this exchange of devotion.

"Oh Lord, oh my father! do you demand this of me?" "Go," Corinne tells him, "you must" (XVI, III). So it is she who forces him to leave her simply by being firm and recognizing tragic necessity, a thing which he cannot do.

In her *Passions* Mme de Staël had written, "Love is more smitten by what it gives than by what it finds . . . man delights in the superiority of his nature, and like Pygmalion bows down only before his own works" (III, 152–53). This perception appears to be belied for a time by Oswald, so full of loving admiration is he for the independent Corinne. Yet, predictably enough, in the long run he follows Pygmalion's path and turns to the unformed Lucile: "He still felt sure that Corinne was not the weak and timid woman, in doubt of everything excepting her duties and her feelings, whom he had chosen in his imagination to be his life's companion; and the memory of Lucile, as he had known her as a child of twelve, harmonized better with that idea: but who could be compared to Corinne?" (VI, IV). Corinne, enchanting as she is, is the antithesis of all which he himself, his father no longer there, considers a wife should be. Even were a wife to be gifted, should she not conceal her gifts modestly from the world and display them only in the intimacy of the home? "He would have wished to be alone to know her wit and charm; he would have preferred that Corinne, timid and reserved as an Englishwoman, nevertheless possess for his sake alone all her eloquence and genius. However distinguished a man may be, perhaps he can never unreservedly enjoy the superiority of a woman; if he loves her, his heart is troubled; if he does not love her, his self-esteem is offended by her" (VII, II). In this way the author charts the conflicts that female gifts evoke in the male psyche.

Vinet has argued that Oswald is not reprehensible, merely egotistic. "But for a man to be egotistic concerning the woman he loves, for his love itself to be egotism, is this exceptional? and in his role as the hero of a novel, did Oswald have to be something more than a man? I think not."[21] This critic underscores the truth of the novel by confirming that Oswald's need to privatize Corinne, his preference for Lucile-Galatea, is far from exaggerated. If Os-

---

21. Vinet, *Etudes*, p. 98.

wald in love is reprehensible, it is a quality he shares with many men. His meanness and vanity are far from extreme; in fact, he is rather good. But Oswald is weak. He never loses the character of son, and his stiffness and unbendingness, even stuffiness, spring from his subjection to a past that puts its death-grip upon his ability to accept experience openly.

"Mme de Staël," wrote Albertine Necker de Saussure, "divided herself between her two principal characters. She gave to one her eternal regrets, to the other her fresh admiration: Corinne is enthusiasm, Oswald grief" (I, cxx–cxxiii). We must carry her insight a step farther. Oswald is the heroine's *Doppelgaenger.* He embodies the internalized self-destruction inherent in Corinne's daring stance: he is her alter-ego, the other through whom she is destroyed, but with whom she herself cannot help identifying.

Woman as she has been known to us so far, if she would live with man, has always had to embrace his world view as her own. Mme de Staël strives to separate Corinne from Oswald, gives them separate nations as signs, makes them radically disparate persons. But for the bond they discover between them to appear— and be—a deep one, for their love to be more than one of mere surface glitter, she gives them a common origin; and that common ground, England, from which their tragedy arises is not hers but his. Corinne indeed says, when Oswald regrets their difference in faith, "Do not our hearts and minds share a single fatherland?" She means to refer to a higher realm than that of nation, but even that realm is the "fatherland" of Christianity.

If Nelvil "fails" Corinne it is because, ultimately, he will not sustain her aspirations, for it is no less than this that she asks of him. But then, neither can she herself sustain them, once he has made her doubt their value, and he is able to do this not so much by virtue of any act, but simply by being the representation of another order that she is compelled, by her love, to take into account. Another way in which she is induced by her own tendencies to be drawn into his orbit is to be found in their exchange of moods. Oswald is elevated, made drunk by that contagious enthusiasm that is her mark. Yet Corinne herself, once Oswald has gone, suffers all the ravages of *his* "natural melancholy," as if it were he who had infected her with his malady. For all her charms and powers, she cannot finally infuse his life with buoyancy. His simple rejection disallows her all effectiveness.

Oswald's doubts as to her "normality," her acceptability, then, become Corinne's own, and the chief source of contention between the two is, finally, centered on a difference in their conceptions of love. Perfect love is conceived of, as ever before in Mme de Staël's works, as a restoration of nothing less than a primal wholeness. The heroine laments the elusiveness of the communion from which Oswald has fled in her puzzled question at the book's end: "How can it be that two beings who have blended their most intimate thoughts, who have talked together of God, of the immortality of the soul, of suffering, can become all at once utter strangers to one another? An astonishing mystery is love; a feeling either admirable or negligible; as intense as the faith of martyrs or colder than the most uncomplicated friendship!" (xviii, v). As of yore in *Zulma*, "the beloved, or the image of the beloved in the heart of the one who loves," is "the miraculous agent of a universal coherence," writes Starobinski.[22] Zulma herself had said, "For me the link among all thoughts and the connection among all objects was Fernand." Corinne similarly proclaims, "It would cost me even more to renounce my admiration for you than my love . . . I would flee the sight of a human face; it would evoke terror in me if Lord Nelvil were capable of betrayal" (xvi, iii). It is evident that the lover, the male order, is held responsible for maintaining the moral—even the metaphysical—order of the world, since it is subject to laws that he has enunciated.

Oswald is a needed double for Corinne, but by his very character he is not susceptible to capture and refuses that role. "The gift doubled by a capture" is the way Jean Starobinski characterizes the dynamic of Mme de Staël's vision of love. But surely hers is simply the traditional romantic view, intensified, taken seriously, and turned about. "I give that great prize of myself to you if you consent to be mine alone" is the ancient formula of love, with man the prize and the captor. This is the role Corinne would play, but Oswald instead wants this trophy to preside over his hearth and Corinne, taking his view too late, wonders what glory there could

22. "Suicide et mélancolie chez Madame de Stael," p. 247.

be to compare with being Oswald's "respected wife," *his* captive.

Finally, we see that in confirmation of her love for Oswald Corinne is compelled to recognize what she had refused to see before. "Lady Edgermond's severity and the boredom of a small provincial town had deluded her cruelly concerning all that was good and noble in the life she had renounced" (xvii, iii). Even her preference for Italy flags, as the very terms of love force her to embrace her lover's ground rules, to be the captive of his conceptions now, in preference to those she had held by herself.

Many a biographical original has been adduced for Oswald, of course. Perhaps, since Oswald is the fullest portrayal of the fatal lover in Mme de Staël's fiction, we can see in him also much of her greatest love, Jacques Necker. Reserved, Protestant, courtly, dutiful, earnest, patient, conscientious, Philistine—the ideal husband—it is possible Oswald resembles Necker in character more than do the other models, who are more akin to Oswald for their analogous role of unreliable lover in Mme de Staël's life. Necker is recalled from the start by such a remark as "what made his situation wretched was the liveliness of his youth united with the thoughts of another age" (i, i), for Necker's daughter paid repeated tribute to her father's perennially youthful spirit into advanced years. It is true that in the first description of Oswald we also see a good deal of Constant: "At twenty-five he was discouraged with life; his wit judged all things ahead of time, and his wounded sensibility no longer entertained any illusions of the heart" (i, i). He is a devoted, disinterested friend like Benjamin, and, again like him, nothing gives him any real pleasure, not even the services he renders. Sorrow has robbed Oswald of the power to hope. He is himself a victim. It is this quality that draws Corinne to him. He is vulnerable man, not armored within his self-sufficiency against the encroachments of woman and thus impervious to feeling, but suffering and seeking. This kind of man, apparently "weak," is Corinne's "other," her soul's complement, the muted masculine component of her nature: her suffering victim, the muse that drives her to utterance, is male.[23] He it is who gives ex-

---

23. I am indebted to Annis Pratt's remarks re her own muse, at an MLA workshop in 1970, for this insight.

pression to that dark fatality that frames the novel, opening and later closing it. As we see Oswald first, peering into the sea's eddies, he meditates on death, which "inspires a kind of scorn for human destiny, for the powerlessness of grief, for all those vain efforts that will be broken upon necessity" (1, 1).

The workings of necessity suggest that Oswald's order is his not very much more than it is Corinne's after all, for both can be destroyed by it. By consenting to live in accordance with the code of a dead forebear rather than following his inclinations, Oswald loses his own integrity, just as he compromises Corinne's. Mme de Staël had learned that the reluctance of a Constant, or a Barante, or a Don Pedro to follow her star was in some degree a capitulation to their need to appear to be free masculine agents, choosing and not chosen, and so she claims in her novel that this is not an authentic choice but only an abdication to a rigid idea of the social order, mere subservience to an ideal that enslaves both sexes. Oswald has been forced by his experience to sell out the youth in himself to the old man that already at twenty-five he has internalized. How long, the author seems to cry, must this form of murder go on being the law of society?

France and Revolution: Rupture

Corinne is set during the years 1798 to 1803 and, in its tales, harkens back to the first years of the last decade of the eighteenth century. The Revolution was to its contemporaries not a series of breaks with the past, but only an exhausting, chaotic continuum. *Delphine,* though set in the period of greatest upheaval and though it bears the mark of upheaval in its style and its stance, is, in its sensibility, though published in 1803, still essentially a pre-Revolutionary work, whereas *Corinne,* in its somber negativity, bears far more clearly the mark of that great rupture with the past that the Revolution came to be.

Three nations, not just two, are at war in *Corinne:* if Italy represents beauty, art, higher morality, and England, the good, the real, the ethical realm, then France upholds, if that can be the word, amorality, self-interest, self-love.

Mme de Staël's ire toward the French is expressed nowhere more openly than here. Certainly she must have felt considerable emotional justification for painting so arid a picture of the French character. Her quintessentially French *ancien régime* lover Narbonne had caused her the most decisive sentimental defeat of her life; France had mercilessly slandered and excluded her. "To be born French," Mme de Staël wrote, "with a foreign character, to have French habits and tastes and northern ideas and feelings is a contrast that ruins your life."[24] Although the ideas and feelings of the author are transposed southward in *Corinne,* her habits and tastes remain decidedly French.

The cutting portrait of Erfeuil, the traveling Frenchman of the novel, created quite a hubbub in France, as Mme de Staël undoubtedly hoped it would. Frivolity, a quality his originator did not esteem, is the keynote of Erfeuil's nature; but it must not be thought that her treatment of him is mere caricature. Nelvil thinks a good deal about Erfeuil and his "singular combination of frivolity and courage, his scorn for misfortune, which would have been more praiseworthy if it had cost him more effort, that would have been genuinely heroic, if this scorn for danger had not sprung from the same source that made him incapable of any deep affection" (I, III). The only thing Erfeuil is serious about is his love of self. This being so, Mme de Staël tells us, he was "worthy of being loved as he loved, that is like a good companion in pleasure and peril; but he understood nothing of a sharing of pain. He was bored by Oswald's melancholy, and through goodness of heart as much as from taste, he would have liked to dissipate it" (I, III). Erfeuil is an amiable and fatuous fellow. He performs genuine services to Corinne, accompanying her on her trip to England when she is distraught and weakened, but cheerfully and callowly jollying her with his urgings to forget "that cad," Nelvil. As he takes leave of her, the narrator's voice comments on such as he: "Shallow feelings are often of long duration; nothing breaks them because nothing deepens them; they follow events, disappear, and return with them, whereas deep affections are broken off without ever coming back, and leave in their place only a painful wound" (XVIII, I). The light-hearted and the level-headed are despised for their cool blood, their lack of depth, their unwillingness to suffer.

---

24. Merlant, *Le Roman personnel,* pp. 228–29.

It is not just any idea of France that Mme de Staël attacks in Erfeuil, but that of the high society of eighteenth-century France,
with its materialism, its love of pleasure, and its commonsense
negation of the values of mystery and suffering. These latter begin
to be perceived by the post-Revolutionary generation as essential
questions rejected by the cowardly rationalist mentality of their
forebears.

In Oswald's tale we find a more searching layer of discussion
of the French. It must be remembered that the only too political
Mme de Staël obscurely hoped that *Corinne* would seem sufficiently harmless to the Emperor that he might permit her return
to Paris, and so she allowed herself to indulge in no overt political
statement in her novel. Napoleon nonetheless interpreted this
novel as an assault against his regime. It was not primarily such
an act of partisanship, however, but rather a probe, at a deeper
level of politics, into the influence of nations upon private life.

Going to Paris against his father's wishes (it was the time of
turmoil), Oswald initially found French society delightful: "I was
astonished by the simplicity and the freedom that reigned in the
salons. . . . Everything in Paris was perfectly combined to favor
external happiness" (XII, 1). Ego, Nelvil will discover, is never
manifest in the forms of French life; rather it saturates its core.
Enchanted with the friendship of Count Raimond, a man who
combines grace with gravity, and seduced by the exquisite manners
of his sister, Mme D'Arbigny, he stays in France to be with them
even though the Revolution's dangers threaten vaguely in the
background. Spurred by Raimond, who fears his calculating sister's
power over the guileless Englishman, Nelvil returns home to Scotland. Raimond, proscribed as an aristocrat, is massacred while
trying to escape from France with his fortune. It is his violent
death that causes Oswald's subsequent troubles. Raimond's murder is symbolic of the destruction of the older social order with its
kind of integrity. Now the Mme d'Arbignys and the M. de Mal-
tigueses of France can make innocents like Nelvil their prey. The
lady seduces him in fact, and when he becomes conscious that
he must leave to fight for his own country, by then at war with
France, she claims, falsely, that she is pregnant. Her suitor and co-
conspirator Maltigues, whom Oswald detests, is always about. A

petty and self-engrossed man, he whines to Oswald that it is the Revolution that has made him cold and unfeeling, and that although he is a born enthusiast, his experience of people during this time has undeceived him: he no longer has faith in anyone or anything. "Nowadays, when everyone is being tortured, the scoundrels along with those we've agreed to call honest folk, there is not a difference in the world except that between birds caught in the net and those that have escaped." Oswald is revolted: "I thought . . . that the goal in life of an honest man was not a happiness that serves himself alone, but a virtue that serves others" (xii, i).

The Enlightenment's pursuit of happiness, after the Terror and in its wake, has proved to be illusory. Mme de Staël, in the midst of this quite private novel, takes up new ground, as did her generation, in Republican virtue. Sickened by the pent-up passion for egoistic excess that the Revolution's aftermath had released, she makes Oswald, in this context, her spokesman, the English citizen-subject. The supposedly "apolitical" Corinne herself echoes him in her improvisation at the Cape Miseno when she decries the end of the Roman Republic: "The crime of the triumvirs goes on; it is still against us that their murder was committed" (xii, iv). Napoleon was not wrong to see in this a reference to his own destruction of the French Republic. Though Corinne is careful to make her allusions to the martyrdom of Cicero and others by despotism a function of their search for a truth higher than the temporal, the implicit reproach to those who repress our pursuit of the ideal in the real is plain; it is, for Corinne, an outrage she feels still, across the centuries, as an offense against humankind.

But the clearest mark of the Revolution's rupture in *Corinne* is at the center of the work, in Corinne's fate as she describes it in her last poetry recital. It moves from a pre-Lapsarian statement: "What confidence nature and life once inspired in me! I believed that all sorrows came of not thinking enough, of not feeling enough, and that even in earthly life we could taste in advance that heavenly lucidity of enthusiasm unending and constancy in love." There has been a breach of faith. Mme de Staël has reached middle years, Oswald has abandoned Corinne, love has proved unfulfilling, and the world has lost all meaning. All of this is distilled in the post-Lapsarian summation: "Hope, youth, longings of the heart, all this is ended. Far from me, all illusory regrets: . . . were I to try to seize life again, it would quickly turn all its swords against me" (ix, v).

The personal conviction that something radical has changed and can never be again is thus played out in *Corinne*, despite Mme de Staël's continuing attempt to maintain the values prized in her youth. In her latter-day Promethean anguish, so unlike the early Apollonian optimism, we hear the overtones of the Revolution that failed.

The Two Sisters: Sibyl and Madonna

An astonishing feature of this novel is the praise the previously anti-Catholic author makes her heroine utter of the Virgin Mary. "Sometimes God seems too imposing to mere man," says Corinne to the Protestant and skeptical Oswald, and at such moments, "is it not sweet that a woman may be considered as intercessor for sinful humans!" (xv, iv). Corinne herself obviously means to be something like an intercessor to Oswald, and it would seem she gives some theological validation in this way to her own public role as poetess-priestess. But Mary, as the author well knows, is no priestess but the image of Mother, loving and forgiving.

Two portraits are contrasted in the novel, that of the celebrated and now unhappily deteriorated Coreggio fresco in the Parma museum, the *Madonna della Scala* (Plate 11), and the far less well beloved but very rich, graceful, and elegant painting of a sibyl by Domenichino (Plate 12) which hangs in the Galleria Borghese in Rome. The madonna is intended to be the emblem of Corinne's half-sister, Lucille; the sibyl is emblematic of herself. "Lucile and Corinne," writes Mme Necker de Saussure, "are also generalizations; they are England and Italy, domestic happiness and the pleasures of the imagination, the brilliance of genius and a modest and severe virtue. The pleas for and against these two styles of existence are equally powerful . . ." (i, cxx–cxxviii). The choice of those portraits shows us the fairness and wealth of this contrast: a madonna in the most supple and charming of her guises, whose whole bodily conformation is gentle embrace and receptivity, whose baby, even to its clutching of her long, loose

11. *La Madonna della Scala*. Coreggio. National Gallery, Palazzo Pilotta, Parma. (Photo from Photographic Archives, National Gallery of Parma, Italy.)

12. *The Sibyl*. Domenichino. Galleria Borghese, Rome. (Photo from the Gabinétto Fotografico, Rome.)

hair, is hers symbiotically, in its very curves and folds, even to making for her the outward glance that focuses the work dynamically, and that she, in her modestly downcast, Da Vinci–smiling, enigmatic way, is too shy to make; a sibyl just as gracious, but self-contained, singular, alone. Instead of a child, she holds the linear musical scroll and book which are emphasized by the grace of her hands; it is she herself who looks out from wide eyes beyond us to some unseen realm of thought or art; her head, not her figure (as in the madonna) is the focus of the work, elaborately emphasized by her turban (here a tamed and civilized expression of hair) that draws us to her eager, alive, about-to-speak expression; the sculptured head on the viola da gamba gazes, like us, at her. Both Lucile, the yielding, lovely, mysterious, and conventional mother-woman, as man has wanted her to be, and Corinne, woman given over to her own light—exciting, stimulating, demanding—love Nelvil. He is their judge. "Either one must have," muses Oswald, "a genius like Corinne's, that passes beyond the powers of the imagination, or those mysterious veils of silence and mystery that allow each man to project upon them the virtues and feelings he wishes to find" (XVI, III). Oswald's masculine ego makes the choice for the latter because to choose the former would be to choose a world in which he might himself be dominated, or in which he might have to struggle to avoid domination.

Domenichino's painting presents an impressive resemblance, not to the coloring or features of Germaine de Staël, but to her beturbaned aliveness of expression, to the parted lips, the bright eyes, the full bosom, the graceful hands so many of her observers remarked on in the author. As the visual metaphor of Corinne, Domenichino's sibyl reveals to our eye that precise blend of singularity—in the sense that commerce with one's own spirit and the practice of an art make one oneself—with an external grace of form and style Mme de Staël strove to express by her invention.

It may be that we feel some surprise at the strength with which the author depicts her opponent, even to the choice of a symbolic portrait so profoundly appealing.

Corinne, what Phyllis Chesler (*Woman and Madness*) would call the "daughter-woman," and Lucile, the "mother-woman," are half sisters: but rather than viewing them as "other," as additive, complementary (though sometimes warring) selves, which is the sense in which I see Oswald as Corinne's alter ego, the sisters rather represent an internal schism, aspects of a woman's nature seen as a diptych, the divided parts of what ought to be a unity.

Despite what appears initially to be a simple, externalized divorce between domesticity and achievement, Corinne is quite lucid about the underlying complexity of this schism: ". . . it is only in domestic life that it can be good to feel dominated by a single affection. I who need my talents, my wit, my imagination to sustain the brilliance of the life I have chosen—it pains me, and much, to love you as I do" (VI, I), Corinne tells Oswald. Accentuating the tumultuousness of her conflict, she dances—like Ibsen's Nora—a tarantella, and in it she falls on her knees as the man dances around her. In the author's narration here, there are two moments: first, one of adulation of her adulation—"comme à genoux elle était souveraine!—how sovereign she was on her knees!"; and then, as she plays her instrument, the worship is mitigated as the surface meaning of her triumphant gesture of self-abasement is questioned:—". . . she seemed animated by an enthusiasm so filled with life, youth and beauty that one could only be convinced she needed no one to make her happy." "Alas!" the author comments, "it was not so; but Oswald feared it. . . ." We are made to wonder if Corinne is so singular, so dissimilar from other women, that vast pool of the ordinary with their ostensibly simple needs, or if, in fact, she resembles them. And if difference there be, what does the author think of it?

Immanence

Corinne's proud claim is that she is more valuable than the woman who lives only to create an ambience for life, even on the latter's own ground. In *Delphine*, too, we observed the heroine's arts of conversation, of creating beautiful interiors, of orchestrating celebrations, all richly explored. Corinne is a hetaera even more splendid than she: her "ravishing" house at Tivoli, in a place consecrated to the sibyl, reveals her "rare understanding of happiness." Aeolian harps sing in her garden; her paintings are handsome images of profound and touching themes; her conversation, though sometimes tedious to us, delights Oswald. When he is ill, she cajoles, nurses, feeds, entertains him by reading and singing to him and sometimes, "in a conversation in which she alone spoke, animated herself, alternately in light and serious vein, with sustained interest" (VIII, 1). So perfect is her comportment that Oswald comes to think that "domestic life with you is made up of continual enchantments, and you differ from other women only in adding to all the virtues the prestige of all the charms." The completeness of the delights she here presents to her lover may well summon to mind those of the "Lady of the House of Sleep" of legend, that "paragon of all paragons of beauty, the reply to all desire, the bliss-bestowing goal of every hero's earthly and unearthly quest. She is mother, sister, mistress, bride."[25]

What Mme de Staël strives to heal here is the traditional split in the female image. Corinne, visibly, is as virtuous as the "pure" woman—devoted, interested in others, ready to take pains for them. Her talents are no hindrance to her in this, but tend only to augment her virtue. Art for Mme de Staël, and here she is served by her inbred woman's sense that ambience matters greatly, over-flows from transcendence to immanence. Corinne as artist is at one with Corinne as woman. We remark this in her improvisation at the Capitol, when she speaks of Dante: "At his voice, all the earth is turned to poetry; objects, ideas, laws, phenomena become a new Olympus of new divinities. . . . The magic words of our greatest poet are the prism of the universe; all its marvels are reflected there, divide themselves, recompose; sounds imitate colors, colors blend harmonically; rhyme, sonorous or bizarre, quick or drawn out, is inspired by this poetic divination; supreme beauty of art, triumph of genius, that reveals all those secrets of nature enfolded in man's heart" (II, III). Her conception of art does not split our intimate world from the objective one but, in Romanticism's way, strives to harmonize the two. The synesthesia of Dante's poetry is echoed in Corinne's garden, where aeolian harps mingle their sounds with delicate perfumes. In fact, Mme de Staël is presenting in Corinne a case for woman's superiority precisely in terms of her mastery over immanence, as we perceive in the

25. Joseph Campbell, The Hero with a Thousand Faces (New York: Pantheon, 1949), pp. 110–11.

consciously androgynous comment made by the prince, Castel-Forte, Corinne's friend who, in his greeting to her at the Capitol, lauds her, saying, "Look at Corinne. Yes, we would follow in her footsteps, we would be men as she is a woman if men could, as women do, create a world in their own hearts, and if our genius, necessarily dependent upon social relations and external circumstances, could be illumined by the flame of poetry alone" (II, III). Poetry, the very distillation of the world of the self, is for Mme de Staël cultivated naturally by women in their own spirits and lives, and by men rather for the world's sake.

Art's transcendence is reflected in its intimations of sublimity; but for Corinne, preoccupied with greatness and antiquity though she may be, these are not separable from the life she is in the act of living. *Corinne* can and should be read as a novel advocating life as art, as an eloquent argument that art's liberating influence is feared by Nelvil, by society, precisely because of the danger of its potential polymorphous perversity of sensation invading our ethical preserves, its seeping into our sensory lives. Mme de Staël's is, then, a unitary view of art that gives us pause in our rigorously dichotomous insistence on higher and lower realms, higher and lower arts. It is love itself that introduces the element of hierarchy into this unitary dream. Though Corinne is free, and determined to remain so—"I always hoped to escape from the absolute power of an attachment"—as the tarantella has shown she *can* be on her knees, and the author suggests a play between dominance and submissiveness within her character that bypasses the frozen postures to which we still wish to confine ourselves, denying the supple vicissitudes of our turns of need and mood. Corinne can play at being submissive to Oswald without feeling debased: in fact, it is he who becomes distressed. "In vain did Corinne, out of love, make herself his slave; the often unquiet master of this queen in chains did not enjoy his conquest in peace" (VII, III). Oswald cannot believe in her subservience, having known her mastery, and he is uneasy and unconvinced by her attempt to enact her new pose of supplicant. For Corinne does indeed, her love notwithstanding, equate domesticity with slavery: ". . . take me with you as your wife, as a slave. . . ."

Her sister Lucile, the incarnation of patriarchal woman, never becomes for Corinne a hated rival, as sibling or in love; rather, the elements of rivalry between the two are muted and suppressed. Indeed, the bonds of sympathy that arise between them are the most arresting aspect of their relationship.

In *Corinne*, Mme de Staël has divided between her dark and light ladies her own wish to be beautiful and dependent (a choice nature had deprived her of) and her drives toward achievement and power. Of course Corinne, too, must by convention be beautiful, but again according to convention her beauty will not be of that sort that men prefer in a mate, because it is linked, like the beauty of Domenichino's sibyl, to those talents which devalue her as an appealing woman, making her less than absolutely beholden to love. When Corinne saw Lucile, now a young woman, at the theater in London, "She compared herself in her mind with her and found herself so inferior, so much did she exaggerate the charm of that youth, of that whiteness, of that blond head, of that innocent image of the spring of life, that she felt almost humiliated by talent, by wit, by, in a word, acquired gifts or at least perfected ones, as against gifts bestowed abundantly by nature itself" (XVII, III). Nearly thirty, "at that time when youth's decline begins," Corinne feels her sister's radiant natural superiority over her as a rival in love. In comparison with this girl she loves who has but one hope in life, that of being Oswald's wife, Corinne, who has equivocated concerning this boon, feels unworthy. She sends back Oswald's ring, freeing him. Megalomania's other side is upturned: despair appears.

To Lucile, a fantasy creature epitomizing the good, beautiful, submissive, dutiful daughter all women have been taught to wish to be, Mme de Staël now gives the prize: the contested man.

Why does she do this? Yes, *Corinne* is in this wise a masochistic fantasy, but we are constrained to recognize here a tribute to the thing forsaken, offered not merely in a spirit of rue and spite, but also in sagacity and praise.[26] We see this guilty affection

---

26. Mme de Staël's sympathy for Lucile is another expression of her feeling for her much-loved cousin Albertine Necker de Saussure: "She has all the talents I am supposed to possess and all the virtues that I lack." See Constance Hill's *Maria Edgeworth*, p. 273. She always felt that the intelligent woman who had tamed her talents was a better, less self-indulgent woman than she was.

in the subsequent development of Lucile's character in the work as, like the Sleeping Beauty, she comes to life only after marriage. Far from being the permanent enigma of Oswald's imagination, we discover that she has critical perception and a good heart. Remembering her sister with warmth, she learns of Oswald's defection with dismay.

Oswald has treated her like a child-wife who must be spared all deep care, ignorant and unsuspecting of her depth. Her pride becomes increasingly bound up in concealing herself: "She had been convinced that she ought not to reveal what she felt, but she took no pleasure in expressing anything else" (xix, iv). So does Mme de Staël describe with great accuracy the etiology of the repressed woman's emotional *atonie*. Like George Eliot's Dorothea, Lucile has "shut her best soul in prison, paying it only hidden visits, that she might be petty enough to please." This is not what Oswald really desires, but what both of them believe he must desire. His and the narrator's judgment upon her become bitter: Oswald "did not do justice to his wife's mind because it was sterile, and was useful to her rather in finding out what others thought than in interesting them in her because she herself thought" (xix, iv). This is the most hostile sentiment expressed toward Lucile in the novel. As in *Delphine,* Mme de Staël always ends by embracing another woman's plight imaginatively.

But it is in her treatment of the Coreggio madonna that we divine Mme de Staël's deeper love for Lucile. In Parma where they see the fresco, Oswald notices its resemblance to Lucile, as she picks up their daughter Juliette to gaze at it. "The veil he [Coreggio] throws over her glance does not detract in any way from feeling or thought, but gives them an added charm, that of a celestial mystery" (xix, vi).

For Germaine de Staël the Coreggio madonna was not a symbol of the inferiority of sainted motherhood, as compared with the sibyl that represents her heroine. The cult of the virgin, which had never attracted her before, in Italy underwent a metamorphosis: now she saw it as "united in some way to all that is purest and most affecting in our affection for woman" (x, i). I believe that the physical warmth and emotional relatedness of the madonna to her child, and symbolically to all children, very much drew Mme

de Staël, a woman of expansive emotional disposition. Mlle Gérard's portrait of Germaine de Staël and her daughter Albertine is
certainly a graceful celebration of the mother and child theme.
Curiously, it is one of the most flattering and "pretty" of the
author's portraits. The incident of the Nelvils' crossing of Mont-
Cenis recreated in the novel was actually drawn from the real
terror Mme de Staël experienced for her daughter and herself in
her own crossing of the Alps.

"All that is purest and most affecting in our affection for
woman"—this suggests the nurturing embrace, the bonding of
persons to others that woman alone has come not only to symbolize
but actually to project in the world. If Mme de Staël grants to this
domain and to Lucile a place of equality with Corinne's in her
novel, it is because she is aware that Corinne's egocentrism, generously devoted as it is meant to be to humankind (and we have here
a conception of art that is perhaps marked by the female struggle
in its insistence that it must "serve"), may be limiting to her own
self-realization. Aside from the tragic central fact of the novel, that
the realization of love is made impossible for her, her choice of
self before others deprives Corinne of maternity. Mme de Staël
made little capital, in her works, of her own maternity,[27] but was
as devoted to her children as to her friends. Agape, as well as Eros,
called forth a strong response in her. Like other women of her time,
she conceived of maternity rationalistically, largely as an educative
activity.[28] Yet the idea of the Virgin, abandoning self to child, held
obvious power for her. In some sense it may have recalled that
oceanic longing for union with the beloved we remember from
her childhood, a longing denied in love to Germaine, yet still
achievable for woman at least in the infancy of her own child. The

27. In her distress over her daughter Albertine's illness in Germany, Germaine wrote her father, "No one should deprive a mother whose child is ill of
prayer. Such a predicament would make us discover faith even if no one had
ever spoken to us of it." Quoted in Balayé's edition of Les Carnets de voyage,
p. 50. Balayé also underlines the paucity of maternal expression in Mme de
Staël's works, except for Hagar's prayer for the prostrate Ishmael in her play
Agar dans le désert. La Sunamite, another of her plays (discussed below), is her
most direct treatment of maternal feeling.

28. The sole intellectual labor of Albertine Necker de Saussure, the friend
and cousin for whom her daughter was named, was an important treatise,
L'Education progressive (Paris: A. Sautelet et Cie., 1828–32).

attachment for Albertine, a greater one than that she displayed toward her sons, demonstrates her will to enact with the child of her own sex the fulfilled maternal relationship she felt she had been denied. It would seem that Mme de Staël knew, from her own experience, some such intense maternal rapture as is portrayed in the Coreggio fresco. She was unwilling to sacrifice her woman's bond with that great creative force, physical and spiritual, nature has given woman as her portion, but she appears to have viewed maternity as only the latency phase of female powers, a source of relatedness and vitality that must yet be mined and refined by the woman's mind and will. Immanence is not rejected in *Corinne*, but the cult of immanence is superseded by a richer sense of female humanness.

Despite Corinne's inability to countenance the self-destruction inherent in marriage, the author gives her a surrogate maternity. The child Juliette remarkably resembles her aunt Corinne, and when the Nelvil family comes to Florence to visit the dying Corinne and she refuses to see Oswald, he sends his little daughter to see her, unbeknownst to Lucile. Moved by the sight of her, Corinne consents to teach her: "The child made unbelievable progress in all areas" (xx, iv). Whatever else we may think about these lessons, they show a feeling for the place of generativity in existence. (We recall a similar "adoption" of a child, Mme d'Ervins's Isore, by Delphine.) We sense here that Corinne's life is made more complete, less tragic, by this fruitful encounter with childhood.

But this pedagogic incident will have a grim use, too: it is made to emphasize the pathos of youth and health in an encounter with death and decay.

All talent has a propensity to attack the strong.
GERMAINE DE STAEL

The Revolt

Corinne embodies, perpetuates, revolt. We have it from Napoleon himself that Mme de Staël was far too unsubmissive in her nature to be acceptable to him. He wrote, "[She] has wit, a great

deal of wit, but she is unaccustomed to *any kind of subordination*."
This insubordinate woman created an insubordinate heroine, free
of all ties, self-contained, answerable to no one. Like that of Mirza
singing in the mountains, hers is a song in praise of freedom. In
England, surrounded by the repressed ladies, oppressed by tedium,
depressed by her father's capitulation to this life, Corinne feels
her soul, as do all of those women who must stifle their spirit and
gifts, "tormenting me like a useless flame that consumed me, having nothing outside itself on which to feed" (xiv, i). When Lady
Edgermond proposes to match this untamed Italian girl to her own
brother, a handsome, high-born fellow, rich and of good character,
despite his "desirability" Corinne is horrified because young Mac-
linson is "so perfectly convinced of a husband's authority over his
wife and of her submissive and domestic destiny that any doubt on
this score would have revolted him as much as to put honor or
honesty in question" (xiv, ii). A friendly and witty woman takes
Corinne aside (as we see the author testify to a complicity of interest and of generosity between women) and tells her, "If you
must live here, submit; leave if you can; there are but these two
possible courses open to you." Again Corinne illustrates her own
and the author's guilt by commenting that she had a far greater
respect for that woman than for herself, because "with tastes similar to my own, she had known how to resign herself to a fate I
could not bear; much as she loved poetry and ideal enjoyments
she was an even better judge of the way things are, and of the
obstinacy of men" (xiv, ii).

Corinne, less wise, takes the more courageous course—that
of flight. What astonishes us now, more than 150 years later, as
women still agonize about the place their personal gifts should
play in their lives, is the exultation of that flight and the completeness of her antidomestic revolt. She knows she is leaving the
order of home, harmony, and family for another kind of order, and
when she hears Monti's song, *Bella Italia*, she falls into a sort of
"drunken state, and everything that love makes one feel I felt for
Italy; desire, enthusiasm, regret; I was no longer mistress of myself" (xiv, ii). It is an orgy of unity. In a nearly mystic ecstasy, she
marries herself to her own fate—as poetess of Italy—instead of to
that of a man. Her subsequent freedom and success delight her:

"My independent existence so pleased me that after long irresolution and painful scenes, I twice broke off bonds that the need to love had made me contract, and that I could not resolve upon making irrevocable" (XIV, IV).

Corinne's love for Oswald finally impugns her integrity, forcing her to choose "the one I prefer to the independent destiny that gave me so many happy days" (XV, IV). Loving becomes, as it was for Phèdre, a fatal flaw for women: Corinne the poetess-seer is diminished to the ranks of ordinary, suffering womankind by its ravages. The more Oswald longs to leave her, the more she clings tightly to him. She revolts less and less and pleads with and threatens her would-be master more and more insistently. There is a scene intended to be pathetic but actually comic. The people Oswald has saved from fire in Ancona recognize him when he returns there and kneel before him respectfully; so does Corinne. Oswald is furious with her: it is *he*, he insists, who worships *her*. Does she think him so overbearing, he asks? "No," she replies, "but I was suddenly seized by the feeling of respect a woman always feels for the man she loves. Eternal homage is given to us; but in truth, in nature it is the woman who profoundly reveres the one she has chosen to be her defender" (XV, V). Comedy arises out of the incongruity in their quarreling over who is to be more servile. Mme de Staël has tinkered too openly with the secret of courtly love— that only the lover is free, while the beloved is entrapped by worship in an impotent immanence. Kneeling, too, is an act.

We see, though, that Mme de Staël, despite her obvious pleasure in Corinne's independence, believes with nearly equal strength that women owe fealty in love. She understood clearly that the remnants of courtly tradition surrounding women were so much dross, that man did not *admire* woman, but woman, man. The sense that woman must submit, even though she be enthroned, is for her a truth as strong as nature. She is ineradicably patriarchal in this insight, but it is not with this capitulation that she ends her novel. Far from it.

Lord Nelvil had written to Lord Edgermond concerning Corinne, "Your daughter is delightful; but I seem to see in her one of those lovely Greek women who enchanted and subdued the world" (XVI, VIII). He identifies Corinne with danger and represents her as siren, enchantress, wicked witch. That decent, respectable old man would not have his son, a proud Scot, reduced to being a mere *cavalier servente* to his wife, and his word is final. Once this sentence has been pronounced, the novel becomes unrelievedly crushing. Corinne, always the superstitious Italian—a cliché which Mme de Staël could not resist tagging even on her enlightened heroine—becomes haunted by grief. The last dim hope she might have entertained is extinguished at Hyde Park as she sees Oswald look in admiration at Lucile, in a scene that recalls vividly that of Zulma's accidental sight of Fernand at the feet of another as well as her reaction: "I live so powerfully in my own being that to be shown another is beyond my endurance." No irony is allowed to escape the reader's attention. The novelist virtually rivets us to Corinne's fate: "The wretched woman knew these looks; they had been turned upon her" (XVII, VI). The terror of invisibility that ravaged her in her English youth becomes reality. Dressed in widow's weeds, she follows Oswald but misses every opportunity to be reconciled to him. If Oswald has looked upon another, she does not deserve even to be seen. "Sorrow had defeated her; is it not fated that sooner or later the most rebellious bend their heads beneath its yoke?" (XVIII, I).

The implication that Corinne is resigned to her fate will be repeated, but it will constantly be given the lie by her behavior. Claiming she does not blame Oswald, still she asks, "Oh why did Oswald destroy the gifts I had received from heaven . . . ?" (XVIII, III). Corinne's independence is grounded in her art: as her art declines she complains that "talent requires an internal freedom that true love never allows" (XV, IX). Torn, depleted, wretched, she feels herself no more the radiantly confident artist, but fate's puppet. Simone de Beauvoir has abstracted this state of mind:

The abandoned woman no longer is anything, no longer has anything. If she is asked how she lived before, she does not even remember. She let her former world fall in ashes, to adopt a new country from which she is suddenly driven; she foreswore all the values she believed in, broke off her friendships; she now finds herself without a roof over her head, the desert all around her. How begin a new life, since outside her lover there is nothing? She takes refuge in delirious fancies, as formerly in the convent; or if she is too strong-minded for that, there is nothing left but to die; very quickly, like Mlle de Lespinasse,[29] or by inches; the agony may drag out interminably.[30]

Too troubled to create, for the mind of a poet, as Virginia Woolf wrote, must have "no obstacle in it, no foreign matter unconsumed," Corinne comes to think of detachment from life as her goal and looks upon a statue of Niobe, that image of female self-abnegation, with interest, for it reflects a calm and a dignity maintained "through the depths of suffering." But she is not comforted, for like Niobe, Corinne in her sorrow has no place to turn but toward heaven, and there too she finds only enmity. In the culmination of her tragic musing, Corinne sees her lover as her murderer and invokes the angel of death: "and he is an angel, but an angel armed with the flaming sword that has consumed my fate. The one we love is the avenger of the sins we commit on this earth; the Deity lends him his power" (xviii, v). Love is transmuted into pietized masochism: Corinne seems to wish to die of the pain inflicted by her lover. Only in such a paroxysm would their relationship endure, at least until death.

In the *Passions* Mme de Staël had written of vengeance, "If there is one passion whose ardor is awesome, it is vengeance. There can be no question of any positive good to be obtained by it, because it owes its origin only to a great sorrow that one imagines can be pacified by making the one who caused it share its ravages. . . . Surely we bear with difficulty, at first, the idea that someone who has plunged us into despair can be happy. . . . The contrast between our pain and the felicity of our enemy produces a real rage in the blood" (iii, vi). Of envy, she had said that it "originates in that dread reaction that makes the spectacle of a happiness a man does not have so hateful to him, that he prefers equality in hell to the hierarchies of paradise" (iii, vi). In Corinne's discussion of the painting of Phèdre and Hippolyte in the gallery

---

29. Mlle de Lespinasse (1731–76) was the natural daughter of an aristocratic lady who became the companion of the celebrated but failing Mme du Deffand and later, through the generosity of Mme Geoffrin and others of her *mondain* friends, a great *salonnière* in her own right.

30. Simone de Beauvoir, *The Second Sex*, trans. H. M. Parshley (New York: Bantam Books, 1971), p. 627.

of her Tivoli villa, she comments, "A wronged woman can curse the one she loves in his absence; but when she sees him, there is nothing left in her heart but love" (VIII, IV). There operated in Mme de Staël's character a very powerful taboo against vengefulness but, though she rejects *lex talionis,* she shows such a marked understanding of the motives of envy and vengefulness that it is plain how very much these passions moved her.

Juliette, the Nelvils' child, "had the hair and eyes of Corinne: Lord Nelvil perceived this and took her to him, embracing her tenderly. Lucile saw in his gesture nothing but a remembrance of Corinne and from that moment forth she could never take an unmixed pleasure in the affection Lord Nelvil showed to Juliette" (XX, IV). No witch could have cursed the Nelvil family more successfully than the author. Lucile's own child is somehow made to seem not hers, but her rival's, a blight on her union with her husband. When Nelvil advises Lucile to take more interest in conversation, she is sure he is comparing her unfavorably to Corinne and "feels wounded, instead of benefiting" from his observation. The reader disengages from the author's point of view here as we see, as she does not, that as Lucile's suspicion is warranted, so is her sense of injury.

It is through the agency of the poetess's friend Castel-Forte that the author makes those overt accusations she cannot allow her heroine to make. When Oswald asks Castel-Forte if he thinks him guilty, that Roman replies:

Will you allow me to say so? I believe that you are. . . . The wrongs one incurs in dealing with a woman cause us no harm in public opinion; these fragile idols, adored today, can be broken tomorrow without anyone's taking up their defense, and for that very reason I respect them more; for as far as they are concerned, morality is defended only by our own hearts. A knife wound is punished by law and the ripping to shreds of a feeling heart is the mere occasion for a jest; we would do better to simply allow ourselves the jest. (XX, II)

Readers may feel that Oswald has been chastised and now understands: still the author is not appeased. Castel-Forte shows Oswald two portraits of Corinne, one as Juliet, radiant and fulfilled, the other a recent likeness, where she is portrayed dressed in black, inscribed with the line from *Pastor fido:* "A pena si puo dir: questa fu rosa—Scarce could one say: this was a rose." To Oswald's plea that he be allowed to see her, Corinne makes this scorching reply: "There is nothing in this world that has not been poisoned by the memory of you. The sole aim of existence is to make oneself worthy of eternal life. . . . Happiness, suffering, everything is but a means to this end; and you have been chosen to uproot my life from this earth: I held on to life too intensely" (xx, III).

What Corinne gives expression to here is a wrath of heroic proportions, barely tempered by the language of piety and resignation. She thunders at Oswald, reminding us of Zulma: "Will you find anything better than my love? . . . Do you know I would have served you like a slave . . . if you had truly loved me? . . . Lay no more claims to happiness; do not offend me by your hopes of still finding it. Pray, as I do, and let our thoughts meet in heaven" (xx, IV). Wretchedness drowns out love and pity. Her own pain obliterates Oswald's. The phase of submission to love has given way here to one of protest against fate. At the end, Corinne resumes the offensive, of which her vulnerability to love, like Atalanta's fondness for apples, had deprived her.

Since the posture of open hate and revulsion is too repellent to our erstwhile Apollonian heroine, both intellectually and aesthetically, to be openly assumed, a pose of fate-erinnye will be the mediating role she adopts instead. Lucile, going to Corinne in anger to protest her theft of husband and child, is appalled by her sister's state and, with her goodness of heart, ends by embracing her. Lady Nelvil then goes every day to Corinne for instruction and strives "with a truly amiable modesty . . . to resemble the woman Oswald has most loved." It is as if Mme de Staël were promoting her own model of womanhood and Lucile had to "go to Corinne's school" to become fully human, to learn from her not merely the arts, but a sense of self. Corinne tells her sister, ". . . as I must soon die, my sole desire is that Oswald should find in you and in his daughter some trace of my influence and that *never will he enjoy a sentimental pleasure without remembering Corinne*" (xx, IV).[31] A singular bond of complicity is created between the two women which, though it is pretended that its aim is Oswald's contentment, seems far more like a pact against him. So it is that Corinne

---

31. Italics mine.

seizes and enchants all three Nelvils, relieves them of their own personalities and wills, and fills them with her own ideas, talents, and manner of being, making them think only like her and of her.

At the somber final recital of her poetry, although her last words there are intended to imply acceptance—"The great mystery of death . . . must quiet us"—her accents are still despairing, and her spiritual rebelliousness escapes her as she cries, "Fair Italy! You promise me all your charms in vain, what power have you over an abandoned heart? . . . Would you recall happiness to me only to make me revolt against my fate?" (xx, v).

Corinne is dying. Feeling calm before God and death, she still refuses to see Oswald, who, she fears, would rob her of what peace she has achieved. In a last moment of clairvoyance, she speaks: "I never avenged myself for the evils done to me; . . . my faults were those of my passions, which would not have been culpable by themselves if pride and weakness had not combined their horror and excess with them" (xx, v). In the end she asks for the comfort of the cross: "Place upon my heart the image of him who came to earth not for power, not for genius, but to suffer and die." Oswald enters the room, but she can no longer speak. As a cloud comes to cover the moon as it did in Naples, cursing their fate, Corinne points to it, "and with her last sigh her hand fell."

The epilogue of the story relates Nelvil's derangement and illness after Corinne's death, and the book ends with the narrator's musings on Nelvil's fate: "Did he forgive himself for his past conduct? Did the world, which approved of him, console him? Was he content with his ordinary life, after such a loss? I do not know; I have no wish on this score either to blame or to absolve him."

In life, Mme de Staël had written Narbonne at the end of their love affair, "If a single one of my friends should see you again, I will never speak to you again as long as I live, and I will die of rage, hating, pursuing what I loved with a passion."[32] Of course she never did manage to go on hating her former lovers, but in the first anguish of loss passion turns from love to hate. Emily Dickinson gives us the essence of this distorted love:

---

32. Staël, *Lettres inédites*, pp. 166–67 (Sept. 21, 1793).

And were you—saved—
And I—condemned to be
Where you were not—
That self—were Hell to me—

#640

The raging self will often turn its rage upon the world, and Corinne's curse eats at Oswald's very heart. If the critic Gautier found
in the novel's last words a certain grandeur, it cannot be the
grandeur of acceptance, but rather the grandeur of gall: it is the
noble, bitter wrath of a disappointed love, which may fall alike
on man or woman.

The only sense in which one might say that the ending of
Corinne expresses resignation is if we believe, despairingly, that
for the author death for love can be the only apotheosis of a
woman's life. Curiously, most critics have found Corinne resigned
to her end. "The opposition between society and the heroine remains, but it is conceived of as fatal and inevitable. There results
in Corinne not a bleak despair, but the resolve not to place her
happiness in that impasse. Whatever happens, Corinne is Corinne
and her essential duty is to her genius."[33] Corinne does prefer her
genius to the stultifying bonds of marriage, but that is not to say
she thereby renounces happiness. On the contrary, it is her wish
to be happy, that is to be herself *and* to love, that kills her.

This is what the author confessed to herself, sighing all the while . . . but
this avowal, alas! is that of a soul that could not resign itself to choosing,
and whose heart was equally drawn to the happiness that lies in the affections and to those emotions that are satisfied by talent and glory. . . .
Corinne is not a treatise, but a work of enthusiasm and suffering. *It disa-
vows nothing, condemns nothing, at least distinctly;* Corinne has the right
to be Corinne; but she cannot lay claim to Lucile's happiness.[34]

Ah, but it does condemn. The *Edinburgh Review* saw that the interest of Mme de Staël's fictions was "founded on the inherent and
almost inevitable heartlessness of polished men. The impression
which they leave upon the mind is both painful and humiliat-

---

33. Larg, *La Seconde Vie*, p. 282.
34. Vinet, *Etudes*, pp. 96–97. Italics mine.

ing. . . ."[35] *Corinne* condemns the incapacity of men to integrate their emotional life and their moral imagination. It condemns the reserve that makes a gulf of a small breach between people and especially between couples. It condemns the constraints that "good" society puts upon its members. It implicitly condemns passivity in women, their acceptance of defeat, and their whole-sale acceptance of the male assessment of them. Corinne may be forced to admit that she cannot have Lucile's happiness, but she loathes this very admission. Hers is a masochistic solution we are led to abominate. Mme de Staël may well have written, "In study-ing the small number of women who have had true title to glory, we can see that this effort of their nature was always made at the expense of their happiness" (III, 1); all the same, Corinne can-not resign herself to this. She accepts her end, not as a player in a necessary fate, but as a martyred victim. Her fury at the end of the novel maintains the intensity of our image of Corinne the enthusi-ast, now turned to gall and evil. By turns muse, seer, and siren, "enchanting and subjugating," and the Medusa with vipered hair, turning to stone all who come in contact with her, she takes from Oswald what she had originally restored to him: his love of life. Oswald, Juliette, and Lucile are all scarred by the hand of death that Corinne, in her black garments, puts upon them, saying like Dido, "remember me."

We recall her telling Oswald that when she was a young girl, "I had great hopes for myself; is that not the first and noblest illusion of youth?" The juxtaposition of the buoyant girl, the fully realized woman and artist, and the shell of a destroyed life, the three images taken together, melodramatically confirm the heat of unrepressed anger in the heroine's heart.

Corinne's myth is that of a rebellion that fails. Her megalo-mania and her self-destructiveness both veer toward madness. But the readers are not reconciled to the inevitability of this failure: rather we are led to feel its utter evitability and wastefulness. *We* are invited to rebel against what has crushed Corinne: the terror of a woman's partner before the idea of her superiority.

---

35. *Selections from the Edinburgh Review* (London: Longman, Rees, Orme, Browne, Green, and Longman, 1833), p. 211.

This is a novel that rails impenitently against women's destiny. The very madonna-sibyl (or Demeter-Persephone) opposition, so carefully constructed, is not truly maintained within the novel, except as a handsome image of the world's schizophrenia concerning woman. Lucile and Corinne begin to resemble each other more and more as the former cultivates herself and the latter acknowledges her need of love, and they are seen in the end, not as antitheses, but as sisters. The parts of our natures are not so obediently discrete. The two women, made of the same matter, need, though in differing proportion, both love—connectedness—and a sense of self. When Oswald and Corinne visit Venice, they hear guns announcing a nun's taking of her vows, and Corinne tells her lover that the warlike thunder is "a solemn sign a resigned woman makes to those who still struggle against fate." It is the unregenerately rebellious heart of Corinne that is the final symbol of this novel, the one which criticism and posterity have declined to take seriously.

Corinne, a novel of revolt, was for Mme de Staël in some ways a propitiatory work as well, offered up to still the gods, to please the public, and to quiet her own soul. In it she punished her father by making his limited view of woman's role the cause of her heroine's tragedy. She punished Narbonne, Constant, and her other defecting lovers by making their betrayal of her the ugly thing she felt it to be in life. She passed beyond her sense of guilt at being the woman she was by inscribing her rebellion within the pages of her novel, thereby becoming a victorious "Corinne" in life. (See her triumphant depiction in this role in Gérard's painting of the scene at Miseno, Plate 13.) The book provided, momentarily, the sense of triumph that life had insistently denied her. If, as Albertine Necker de Saussure found, she made it one of the strongest counsels of her next work, *On Germany,* that we "place moral dignity in resignation rather than in revolt," her later equanimity would probably not have been achieved had it not been for the great but defective imaginative effort she made in inventing the embattled but sublime Corinne and in composing her lament that man's love for woman does not encompass her freedom, as hers is supposed to embrace his. And that was a prophetic complaint, worthy of a sibyl.

13. *Corinne at the Miseno*. Gérard. Courtesy of the Musée des Beaux-Arts, Lyon.

CHAPTER 8

What Was *Corinne*?

> We are ourselves at the end of life; we no longer seek
> to please; and the desire to do so ebbs along with the
> capability.
>
> SUZANNE CURCHOD NECKER
>
> My defense is the stir I create.
>
> GERMAINE DE STAËL

Life Follows Art

Mme de Staël's was an unquiet and questing life in which *Corinne* was but a momentary resting place. Coming as it did after banishment by Napoleon and the waspishness of public judgments against her *Delphine* for defending divorce, free love, and suicide, the response to the publication of *Corinne* was a longed-for confirmation of her claim to public attention. The reaction of officialdom, which denounced the novel as anti-French, merely increased its celebrity, and Goethe himself led in paying to it the tribute of the world of letters, hailing it as new and fresh. Even an ego as demanding as her own could not help but be quieted by such an adulation as then flowed toward Mme de Staël. People began to call her Corinne, seeing right through the thinness of the fictional gauze draped over this elaborate wish-fulfillment novel. She did not reject the appellation, saying only, "I am not Corinne, but if you like, I shall be."

She was. In despite of her emotional setbacks, her capacity to be interested in others, her intense and generous sociability flourished still, and Coppet with its marathon conversations assumed near-legendary status as a place of choice to all of lettered Europe, comparable to Weimar or to Ferney. Even though her hasty and guilty work habits did not entirely disappear—the Countess de Boigne records she never did have a study for work and wrote by placing a little writing case of green morocco containing her work and correspondence on her knees, carrying it from room to room, often surrounded by people—Germaine de Staël consciously adopted the *persona* of the woman of letters and, even though it gave her anguish, slowly began to assume her consequent autonomy. In the hectic melodramatics of Constant's break with her in the years following *Corinne's* publication, Mme de Staël had tried to deny to herself that a "Corinne" capable of liaisons with Maurice O'Donnell and Prosper de Barante really might not need the monogamous dependency that the link with Constant meant to her. Her grandiose displays of grief in losing Barante and Constant did not prevent her from engaging in enthusiastic rounds of amateur theatricals, for which she wrote a set of short plays, or from writing the imposing *On Germany* (1810), her most ambitious work, conceived before *Corinne*, but written mostly in late 1809. In this period a childhood friend wrote of her, "All I can say is that she is as lively and brilliant as ever—which proves the advantage of organizing one's heart in a system of multiple hiding places."[1]

A return to the analytical essay approach of *On Literature*, *On Germany* was also, like *Corinne*, an attempt to synthesize for the French reader a foreign nation's whole cultural range, by abstracting and speculating upon elements of its religion, philosophy, art, customs. Even though it suffers, as do all Mme de Staël's works, from didacticism, diffusion, and prolixity, in its sweep and pertinacity it is a testimony to the confirmed sense of self *Corinne* had left with her. *On Germany* had originally been conceived of as a novel. There is little doubt that, had it been written in that genre, the woman author's fantasies would have devalued her commentary, as was to be the ultimate fate of *Corinne*. Instead, *On Germany*, a "neutral" nonfiction, is that work of Mme de Staël's recognized as the most influential of all her writings in the etiology of Romanticism. The first printing of this aggressively pro-German work, celebrating the worth of a culture other than her own, was seized by the phobic Emperor ("I do not want to hear any more about that miserable woman or her book"),[2] whose police crushed

---

1. Catherine Rilliet-Huber to Henri Meister, quoted in Herold, *Mistress*, p. 401.

2. Herold, *Mistress*, p. 407.

it into pulp. It was not republished until 1813, after Napoleon's defeat, and then in London.

At forty-five Mme de Staël, who had more and more frequently taken young lovers, usually at her own initiative, was besieged sentimentally by a twenty-three-year-old wounded hussar named John Rocca. The jealous August Schlegel, her children's tutor, nicknamed him Caliban, but the name did him no harm at all, as he persisted, against her initial indifference, to plead his affection for Germaine. At once embarrassed and enchanted by the professions of passion of this dashing but not very brainy youth, she ended, in May, 1811, by promising before a Protestant pastor to marry him "as soon as circumstances allowed." In April of 1812, after months of pretended dropsy which in the end degenerated into real illness, she gave birth in secret to a son, Louis-Alphonse Rocca. The prefect of her Swiss canton, Capelle, quoted in his report to Paris this epigram circulating in Geneva:

> Even her dropsy, O woman ingenious!
> Will live to perpetuate her name.
> Astonishing woman! How fertile her genius!
> Whatever she makes is destined to fame. . . .

In this chaffing way, her physiological nature was made to serve as a relentless reproach to her "higher" claims. But, rich and independent, she could cast off this accident of fortune. A brief month after his birth, giving her infant out to be raised, she went off in her carriage dressed as for a little outing with her daughter Albertine and fled on a two-year journey to Austria, Russia, Sweden, England, and, at last, her beloved France.

The liaison with Rocca endured and in 1816, again secretly, Mme de Staël and he were married. As had ultimately been true in the case of Constant, it was even more true that in marrying Rocca she had no desire to lessen her own independence and autonomous standing. Paradoxically, Rocca was the only man in her life to have given her something akin to sentimental equality, by giving her his love freely and so relieving her of the humiliation of being ever the overwrought supplicant.

The triumphant renewal of her salon in Paris and the writing of the apologetic histories, *Considérations sur la Révolution fran-*

çaise (Considerations on the Principal Events of the French Revolution) and *Dix Années d'exil (Ten Years of Exile)* filled Mme de Staël's last years. Chronically ailing for some time and more and more reliant upon opium to ease her pain, in the end she collapsed and her body became paralyzed. Four months of suffering ensued and, on July 14, 1817, at fifty-one, she fell into her last sleep, as she said, "heavily, like a big peasant woman."

The last novel, *Corinne*, evidently cauterized the wound that femininity had dealt to her claim to greatness by its simultaneous assertion of her pain and her transcendence of it through art. She would never be serene—though she feverishly sought serenity in both Christianity and the use of opium in the late years—but she passed beyond her fears that as a woman of letters she was a monster. This relatively self-acceptant calm, coming in tandem with the banked fires of middle life, made possible the volume of untraumatized writing of the last decade, written without the need for fictional mediation.

The late playlets are a last revelation of her inner life. *Hagar in the Desert* (1806) confirms the mood of that year, when *Corinne* was also written, as a time filled with guilt over wanting both to "please and to reign" and failing, and of being unwilling to "survive what one loves." Hagar's sole sense of reality is derived from others, and their defection is spiritual death. But here we have, for once, a child present and another love, the maternal, expressed. *Geneviève de Brabant* (1808) carries on the theme of maternal love (the author needed to create parts for her daughter to play) and pays tribute to the child's power of restoring the mother's existence, rent by suffering from love, and to the mother's loving purpose in protecting the child against harm. Insistently, Mme de Staël probes other sides of the female condition in these wispy works, but *Geneviève* is imbued with the reaction Mme de Staël suffered, after *Corinne*, against the open expression of female self-will. After the terrors attendant upon the creation of the myth of the free woman, even one brought low by fate, she took refuge in a deepening patriarchal piety, as her last will attests:

I commend my soul to God, who has lavished His gifts on me in this world and who has given me a father to whom I owe what I am and what I have, a father who would have saved me from all my errors if I had never turned away from his principles. I have but one counsel to give to my children, and this is to have ever present in their minds the conduct, the virtues, and the talents of my father, and to imitate him, each according to his calling and his strength. I have known no one in this world who equaled my father, and every day my respect and love for him become engraved more deeply on my heart.[3]

The Shunamite (1808) is a curious reworking of come aspects of the *Corinne* themes. The Shunamite is a mother (the heroine role passes unobtrusively from Persephone to Demeter) so enchanted by her daughter's charms and talents that she forgets her oath to Elisha, the priest who had prayed for her birth (in the Bible, of course, it is a son that is delivered to her!), to dedicate the child to the Lord. The Shunamite argues that such gifts as those of her child, the most charming in the world, should not be hidden in obscurity, but spread abroad "like the perfume from the lemon trees"; she hopes her daughter's playing of the harp will rival David's in beauty. Pure at heart, the girl wants none of her mother's illicit plans for her, but she dies, innocent victim of a maternal affection that was a "fatal trap" the heavens laid for the Shunamite's "unhappy heart." So contrite is the mother, so powerfully does she sorrow, so fervently does she swear to yield her daughter up to heaven if only she is restored to her that Elisha's prayers bring her to life anew, a life now to be lived in unremitting piety.

We may read here Mme de Staël's pulling away from the now-achieved fame and a guilt projected back upon her own ever-available mother, perhaps at last sympathized with in some small measure, as she herself knows conflict concerning the fate of her own daughter. The Shunamite's pagan way, Germaine's, is defeated. All pride must be subdued. In this mother-daughter myth the mother adores the "false" goddess of feminine power and asserts her own claim for life, openness, and pleasure as against priestly male renunciation and the repression of female gifts. In the end, her gifts, like Corinne's (though more directly) bring death to Semida. Only in her abandonment of her powers to God (man and society) can Semida be allowed to live at all, and even then, only "in the shadow of the tabernacle," which alone gives

---

3. Herold, *Mistress*, p. 467.

protection against the dangers of the world. Necker's power over his daughter's spirit remained undimmed.

However, as all is alteration in Mme de Staël, excepting only her love for her father, the three comedies that end her imaginative *oeuvre* give us an unexpected and bracing change. *Captain Kernadec* (1810) is a delightful little spoof that pits the military against the poetic mentality. It gives us, as do few others among her works, some genuine feeling for the simple pleasure of Mme de Staël's good-humored company. The *Signora Fantastici* (1811) shows us a kind of comic side to *Corinne.* The elder son of the Kriegschenmahl family, Licidas, has met the Signora and her daughter and has been enrolled by them in their acting troupe. His parents are appalled: "It's good for a woman to play act, but a man must make war, always war." The Signora ends up by enlisting them all, despite their repressions, the bailiff thereby getting the power he doesn't quite have in fact, and without incurring any danger, and Frau Kriegschenmahl the chance to play (in prefiguration of Jean Genet and Harold Pinter) women of ill-repute, as she has always secretly wished to do. La Fantastici is a sort of pied piper representing the exact reverse of that renunciation of pleasure that was preached so solemnly in *The Shunamite:* "One has only to tear men away from their habits. We have to make them see the interest of a new life, the insipidness of their own. We have to arouse their self-love, excite their imaginations, and they are ours." Poetry leads us on the path to pleasure, and pleasure, to a better world. The Signora herself is a comic incarnation of the Romantic prophetess, and this little work shows us explicitly Mme de Staël's conception of the role of the imagination in liberating some of what we now think of as unconscious energies.

Sappho (1811), a small and painful drama that mirrors the love intrigue of Corinne, reenacts, as Jean Starobinski has seen, the suffering caused to the woman of genius who is unable, despite her gifts, to "capture" the beloved for herself.[4] Phaon remains free. A callow youth, like Oswald, Ximéo, Fernand, his gaze comes to rest elsewhere, and his love for Sappho ends with a blink of the eye as he sees young Cléone. Sappho becomes calm as she resolves to

---

4. Starobinski, "Suicide et mélancolie chez Madame Staël."

throw herself from the rocks into the embrace of the sea that knows no rejection. As Starobinski notes she is as calm as was Delphine once she had poisoned herself, for only in the *act* of dying can she be restored to the sense of self she had lost in love. This critic charges that Mme de Staël, unlike Balzac or Flaubert, is, here and elsewhere, unable to immolate herself to the substitute world of literature because she could never disengage herself from the dream of personal happiness.

This illusion (men do not live by it primarily) is the companion of woman, and of women writers as disparate as George Sand, the Brontës, George Eliot, and Doris Lessing. It has been concomitant with the unfreedom of women to conceive of themselves as alone. How is woman to imagine a destiny without "capture" of the male as long as her destiny is held to be meaningless or devalued without him, her worth problematic? Happiness is the promised reward for the assumption of secondary status by woman. This status she has assumed resignedly, even gaily, while she has hoped to achieve completion through another. Only if she were to cease to be obsessed by sentimental happiness—though, it may be hoped, not indifferent to it—could she be free, and so melt altogether into her works, as such authors as Colette, Virginia Woolf, and Nathalie Sarraute have shown us.

The last of the comedies, *Le Mannequin* (1811), called a dramatic proverb, is a slight, charming, highly anti-French, and very feminist work. The German girl Sophie is in love with Frédéric Hoffman, a painter, but her father, M. de la Morlière, even though his family has been settled in Germany for a hundred years, remains a Francophile who wants Sophie to marry the snooty and impecunious French nobleman, Count d'Erville. The count dislikes witty, outspoken women, however ("M. d'Erville would like to reduce women to the least of possible roles"), and really only cares for Sophie because of her money. She and Frédéric, interpreting his position as emblematic, rig up a mannequin and take d'Erville to meet it, introducing it as an heiress cousin of Sophie's. The count is enchanted by this attractive creature, who is so shy she does not utter a single word! (The conspirators claim she speaks no French.) At the denouement, Sophie explains: "I was annoyed with you for not caring for wit in women and criticizing those who were remarked about in society. Isn't it true that your talent for scorn has been exercised a hundred times over against people like me?—Yes.—Well, then, I wanted to have you meet one who did not stand out in any way at all, who could not fail to be agreeable to you in any fashion, in fact a real cardboard doll, not too different from a lot of living ones. Forgive me my little vengeance" (xvi).

"Forgive me my little vengeance" might be the distillation of Mme de Staël's fiction: tales of an embarrassed, guilt-laden vengefulness against social patterns and forces that depress the spirits and talents of all lively women. In this giddy little play we finally find the poetic pacification of a comic statement, coming at the last to temper so many anguished ones. Mockery, rather than pathos, becomes the apposite feminine response to the moral tyrannies of the male-ruled world. As comedy can be achieved only by a spiritual renunciation of passion's hold, a withdrawal from its toils to a plane above, Mme de Staël's final fictional statement illustrates the removal in middle life of her own, and woman's, moral battle to that Olympian terrain where ridicule alone kills. Revolt, as such, had died in her. She said to Byron near the end of her life, "You should not have warred with the world— it will not do—it is too strong always for any individual. I myself once tried it in early life, but it will not do."[5] It is, I think, important that her Sophie is not a genius, like Corinne, but only a spirited woman, like Delphine. This comic offensive is waged to claim a right to freedom of personality, a basic not an exceptional right, one that is everyone's due and simply not to be thwarted by shallow, preconceived ideas, like those of the d'Ervilles of this world, about woman's place. Mme de Staël's last fictional statement thus sidesteps special pleading and strives, modestly, to be universal.[6]

---

5. Quoted by Robert C. Whitford, "Mme de Staël's Literary Reputation in England," *University of Illinois Studies in Language and Literature,* IV (1918), 44.

6. In my article "Mme de Staël, Rousseau and the Woman Question," I try to show a parallel emotional disengagement in the second preface (1814) from her *Lettres* on Rousseau (1788). Both *Le Mannequin* and this preface illustrate a drier, more disabused, an illusion-free, view of woman's lot as compared with earlier statements, one not less but rather more confidently assertive, even though she still hedges about her views on the "normal destiny of woman."

Palazzo: a sibyl by Domenichino of the greatest beauty,
her turbaned coiffure, her red mantle.

GERMAINE DE STAËL

The Corinne Myth

Corinne's publication had established Mme de Staël's reputation: it was an act. This work above all the rest consecrated her
identity as an artist. In writing it, Mme de Staël had wrung out of
her spirit a new myth. But a myth, as Elizabeth Janeway has observed, if it is to deserve the name, must meet some ready collective
understanding,[7] and the Corinne myth stands radically apart from
ordinary experience.

The classic hero of monomyth "ventures forth from the world
of common day into a region of supernatural wonder: fabulous
forces are there encountered and a decisive victory is won: the
hero comes back from this mysterious adventure with the power
to bestow boons on his fellow man."[8] Such a heroine is the gifted
Corinne who leaves England for Italy. Her mythic adventure contains a sea journey (to England) and is marred by an encounter
with a dark power that prevents her triumphant return from the
"kingdom of dread." There could be no mythical resolution in
sacred marriage, nor through any ritual of father atonement in the
myth of a free heroine (in contrast to that of the hero), as Mme de
Staël saw: the errant daughter remains unwed and unforgiven.
The sole remaining mythical ending possible is that of apotheosis.
The gods must be seen to embrace what men are unable to understand, and Corinne is, at last, acceptable to the heavens. Only by
virtue of some such elevation through death can this myth be
salvaged from chaos and some boon to humanity be revealed in
its heroine's odyssey. Northrup Frye has written that the central
myth of art is the quest for the vision of the end of social effort,
the innocent world of fulfilled desires, the free human society. The

---

7. See Elizabeth Janeway, *Man's World, Woman's Place* (New York: Morrow, 1971).

8. Joseph Campbell, *Hero with a Thousand Faces*, p. 30.

Italy of *Corinne* partakes of the nature of such an earthly paradise and its ethos enfolds her apotheosis.

The Corinne myth is not one of a dying god, but of a dying goddess, isolated and sacrificed by the order of the world. In giving to her Corinne, as John Florio expressed it, all "three good things in a woman, the riches of Juno, the wisdome of Pallas, and the beautie of Venus," Mme de Staël was also exploiting her remarkable moment of history. The fall of the *ancien régime* toppled all institutions including the Church. Into the breach caused by the abolition of the forms of faith, the Revolution, without recking what it did, threw goddess worship: Reason, personified as a Demeter, replaced the dying God upon the altars. As she saw all about her such embodiments in her own sex of divine attributes previously reserved, in their highest sanctity, to the other, Mme de Staël seized the occasion to espouse a counter-patriarchal, feminine cult of transcendence through art. This is the revolutionary aspect of *Corinne*. Of course, patriarchy was soon reborn, if indeed it ever died, and in the nineteenth centry goddess worship, except that of Mary and Victoria, was banished.

Germaine de Staël did not scruple to capitalize on the existing myths of female power, alien as some of these might have been to her conception of female genius. In the eighteenth-century novel, woman, despite her ambiguous status, was often venerated as a "fecund power. She is Cybele, Pomona, Ceres, all the divinities of the harvest and of fruitfulness."[9] Mme de Staël, as we have seen her constrasting her Corinne with her Lucile, strove to blend the traditional, purely biological, nurturant powers of a Demeter, a Ceres, or a Mary with those of an Athena, a Persephone, an Artemis —the wise and solitary virgins. Her "virginal mother" Lucile is solitary and learns wisdom, and her wise and gifted Corinne is also generous and loving. But Corinne, while incorporating the Demetrian myth of female sacrifice, also undermines it by railing against its murderousness.

In the novel of the Enlightenment "woman is Protean, she incarnates not peace but instability, becoming, uncontrolled adventure; she is Circe, Armida, Calypso. Her essential foreignness thus confronts man's imperialism of 'knowledge,' it defies attempts

9. Fauchery, *La Destinée féminine*, p. 555.

to reproduce it, it implies inaccessibility. Woman is transfixed beneath a layer of ice."[10] Mme de Staël embraces this Protean concept, espoused more generally by male novelists, and makes Corinne a diverse and remarkable woman of many moods and gifts, a "natural" sorceress who virtually enchants her lover. The *Machtfrauen* of the German *Sturm und Drang* are, like Corinne, demigoddesses who are sensual, gay, witty, gifted, and strong-minded.[11] With the nikes and the vestals, they had their share in brewing the essence of the sibyl of 1807, Corinne.

Mme de Staël had herself, in *On Literature*, written some troubled paragraphs about force and grandeur in women: "The appearance of malevolence makes women, no matter how distinguished they may be, tremble. Courageous in misfortune, they are timid in the face of enmity; thought exalts them, but their character remains weak and sensitive. Most of those women whose superior faculties have inspired in them a desire for fame resemble Herminia armed for the battle: the warriors see the helmet, the lance, the radiant plumage; they think they are faced with force, and with the very first blow they strike to the heart" (II, IV). She clearly tries to mitigate whatever illusion of strength a woman may project by this allusion to her vulnerability; nevertheless, it is her capacity to be strong, to be seer and poetess, rather than her weakness that seems to call for explanation. For Freud, femininity is founded in a latent sexuality that only sexual congress with the male can fulfill. For Mme de Staël, femininity is rather a narcissistic polymorphous perversity feeding both on itself and on others. It finds something in itself of worth, something that can either receive or be deprived of validation by the "other." This is the core of the myth of *Corinne* that needs to be reckoned with.

We may want to view this polymorphism, as is so often done in the case of *ego* in woman, as mere narcissism. "At once priestess and idol, the narcissist soars haloed with glory through the eternal realm, and below the clouds creatures kneel in adoration; she is God wrapped in self-contemplation. . . . "[12] Beauvoir's characterization in some ways fits the megalomaniacal Corinne only too well.

---

10. Fauchery, *La Destinée féminine*, p. 531.
11. Fauchery, *La Destinée féminine*, p. 616.
12. Beauvoir, *Second Sex*, p. 595.

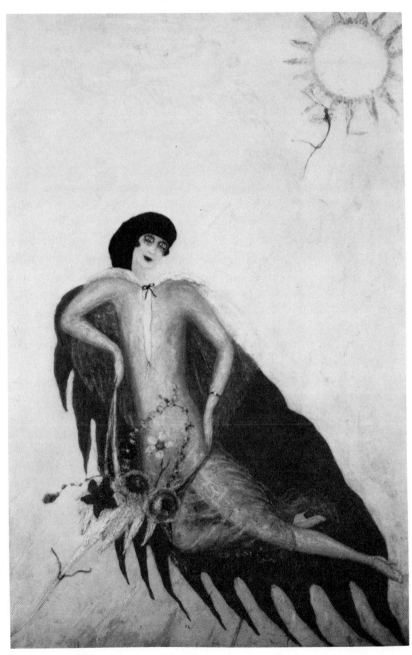

14. *Self-Portrait.* Florine Stettheimer. Courtesy of Columbia University, bequest of Ettie Stettheimer.

There is no question that *Corinne* is a myth of female narcissism, a dream any woman might offer herself passingly, of a magical ruling destiny of the spirit. Narcissism has been traditionally the sole licit form of female self-gratification, but what we have in *Corinne* is not sheer self-worship: it has a social dynamic. It is not merely an invitation from the woman to others to certify her charms; even more, it is the stance of the self-contained woman, expansively flaunting her charms and inviting the world to share in the pleasure she herself takes in her being. She arouses in others a heightened sense of themselves. Such is the Corinne of the Capitol. The effect she creates is curiously paralleled in a highly stylized realization of the same form of eroticized female self-love by the twentieth-century painter Florine Stettheimer, in her dramatic self-portrait (Plate 14). The woman's magnetic power is supremely that of subject, not of object. In the very "outrageousness" of the conception, as in that of Corinne, there is an assertion of female power. Hilton Kramer wrote of it that it is "ornamental and jewel-like, painted against an ice-blue background, with the figure of the artist reclining with a bouquet of red flowers on a red couch. Everything is exaggerated and outrageous—a little campy, a little bizarre, yet extremely powerful in its pictorial effect."[13] Stettheimer the painter paints herself as a dazzling palette: she adorns her art and is adorned by it. A similar campiness attaches also to the figure of Corinne, a similar use of the vagaries of the vogue of the period —here of the flapper, there of the goddess—toward a fuller assertion of personal force. And it is possible to see in this phenomenon an avatar of specifically female narcissism, as distinct from the manifold forms it takes in the male.

Of course, as Beauvoir has admitted, "when a woman succeeds in producing good work, like Mme de Staël . . . , the fact is that she has not been exclusively absorbed in self-worship. . . ."[14] Her biographer supports this: "Her object was not merely to exhibit or justify herself; rather it was to criticize a society that stifled generous impulses and that discouraged half of mankind (the feminine half) from developing its gifts."[15] What

13. *New York Times*, Feb. 20, 1973, p. 22.
14. *Second Sex*, p. 599.
15. Herold, *Mistress*, p. 199.

she has posited in *Corinne* is not only female self-love, which is important enough, but a related female autonomy and self-belief that actually allow the heroine to put her talents at the service of her society. Corinne's condition, at the novel's beginning, is that remarkable state for any woman in a novel: it is health. Like Beauvoir's intelligent hetaera (and here we fully comprehend the bond between woman's sensuality and her creativity) she resorts to "a more or less fully assimilated Neitzscheanism: she will assert the rights of the superior being over the ordinary, the elite over the vulgar herd. Her person seems to her a treasure the mere existence of which is a gift to humanity, so much so that in being devoted to herself she will claim to serve society. . . . If she sets great store by her renown, it is not for purely economic reasons— she seeks in fame the apotheosis of her narcissism."[16] Staël's megalomania is sheer overcompensation for the fear that her whole structure will be rejected. When the Nietzschean impulse originates in a woman, it automatically becomes ludicrous, and Corinne's plays against our full acceptance of her destiny as inherently tragic. "Destiny, in the nineteenth century, is principally male." In woman, greatness is felt to be at the least a social error, at worst a flaw, and the hypothesized greatness of a fictional female character by a female author is, for her time, presumption twice over: "The victorious woman . . . is surrounded by a décor of illusion that is at once jewel box and prison."[17] But in spite of this, even though trapped in its very presumption, the myth of Corinne took hold and lived for the nineteenth century.

The Dark Lady

The quality of Mme de Staël's heroines is her most singular contribution to the novel. Both Delphine and Corinne are prey, in their varying degrees, to what Adler called (he could find no other word for it) the "masculine protest." And both are forced, by characters at odds with their possibilities, into a destructive role culminating in death. But even so, the destructive bent is turned

---

16. Beauvoir, *Second Sex*, p. 541.

17. Jean Starobinski, *Portrait de l'artiste en saltimbanque* (Geneva: A. Skira, 1970), pp. 69–70. The quotation preceding this one is also from this source.

less without than within. Mme de Staël's preoccupation with suffering, the black goddess of sorrow that her Corinne becomes at the end of her novel, links her heroines unmistakably to the *femme fatale* or *fatal woman* Mario Praz has described in his *Romantic Agony*. The dark and dominant Corinne and her palely hesitant Oswald are well matched with Praz's description of the young and passive lover and his exuberant, superior, and demanding mistress. The demigodlike Corinne paid her full tribute to the Romantic's sense that beauty and death are sisters.

The struggle between the dark heroine and the fair ingenue is a commonplace of eighteenth-century male novelistic practice. "How many novelists are bigamists in their dreams,"[18] exclaims Fauchery, citing Rousseau's blonde and placid Julie and the brunette, mettlesome Claire. The dark and foreign women introduced into the novels of the time served the end of shaking up commonplace notions concerning woman and of representing transgression, whether happy or ill-starred. Mme de Staël gave this dark-light dichotomy considerably greater depth than was usual by granting to each term of this opposition some of the power of the other, thus complicating the split. Her attempt at depth was immediately dissipated by a work like Durdent's *Adriana, Passions of an Italian,* published in 1812. Seeming to derive directly from *Corinne,* the story is of a fiery and exalted Italian, Adriana, rival in love of the fair, gentle, modest Emmeline. The tragic Adriana withdraws from the struggle, believing that only Emmeline can bring their lover happiness. "This moral is rather distant from the sense of *Corinne.* It was not admissible that a woman of superior gifts might have the right to develop herself outside the limits of social prejudices and against them. . . . "[19] This critic perceived that even in "imitating" *Corinne,* a novelist would betray the intent of Mme de Staël's own idea of the dark-light dichotomy, and substitute a flat, traditional moralism for her raging irony. So it is that while the dark and sorrowing, passionate and exotic heroine was to be re-created many times in the course of the nineteenth century, there is no echo of the tragedy of the woman of genius, except if that genius

---

18. Fauchery, *La Destinée féminine,* p. 91.
19. Merlant, *Le Roman personnel,* p. 246.

be one of character alone. The noose of immanence tightens.

An arresting aspect of Mme de Staël's performance in *Corinne* is her own appropriation, at the novel's end, of the black role of preying mantis, of fatal, destructive woman. The vampire was a figure familiar to Mme de Staël who, fascinated by it, had, in Weimar in 1804, translated Goethe's *Bride of Corinth*, a rapturous gothic ballad of a ghostly bridal.[20] In her account of this narrative poem, which deals, in symbolic form, with Christian and pagan rivalry, Mme de Staël tells the tale of the dead Corinthian bride, promised an Athenian youth, who appears to him at night—a ghostly but beautiful visitor whose cold body he tries to warm with his ardent young passion. "There is a sort of funereal pleasure in this scene, where love makes an ally of the tomb, where beauty itself is a frightening apparition."[21] A fascinating excision from Mme de Staël's narration of this poem is her omission of the entire stanza in which Goethe's bride tells how she has been "urged forth from her grave to rediscover the joys of life, to love again the man I had lost and to suck his heart's blood. When he is gone, I must go on to others and young men shall feel my fury." What attracted Mme de Staël in this poem is its mystery, its poetry "more inward and more purifying than any other."[22] The image of the doomed heroine and her struggle to be alive, to be revived by the young blood of her groom, has an erotic, necrophiliac appeal for her, perhaps not unrelated to her love for her dead father, but her omission of the vampire element suggests that she could not morally accept what all the male poets, Goethe, Keats, Gautier, Baudelaire, revelled in: the leechlike destructiveness of the veiled and sorrowing fatal woman.

In the rejected stanza the inference is clear: the vampire feeds on man's substance. As Leslie Fiedler writes, "The Dark Lady with her luxuriant flesh is a bearer of poison. In such a symbolic world, sex and death become one."[23] Or, as Mailer's Rojack muses, "All

---

20. See *Les Carnets de voyage*, pp. 77, 81. Mme. de Staël also gives a lengthy account of this work in *De l'Allemagne*, ed. Mme de Pange and Simone Balayé, 5 vols. (Paris: Hachette, 1958–60), II, 202ff.

21. *De l'Allemagne*, II, 207.

22. *Les Carnets de voyage*, p. 81.

23. *Love and Death in the American Novel* (New York: Criterion Books, 1960), p. 280.

women once long ago were killers."[24] These are masculine meta-
phors, expressed by male artists. It is conceivable that their origin
is organic; the drama of detumescence is a constant of male existence, whose only analogue in woman is post-partum exhaustion
and depletion, often attended by depression. For woman, sex—
whether negatively, as violation, or positively, as pleasure—is not
so much death as life. Mme de Staël significantly rejects this identification of woman with murder, even as she embraces the "darkness" of the fatal woman. For her, the veiled figure is the scape-
goat, the butt of men's anger and fear, and if she assimilates this
symbol of the Dark Lady to her Corinne, it is in wrathful sorrow:
her Dark Lady is not destroyer, but destroyed. And yet her anger
holds some menace, whether she wills it or no.

Keats, *On Melancholy,* sings:

> She dwells with Beauty—Beauty that must die;
>   And Joy, whose hand is ever at his lips
> Bidding adieu; and aching Pleasure nigh,
>   Turning to poison while the bee-mouth sips:
>
> Ay, in the very temple of delight
>   Veil'd Melancholy has her sov'ran shrine,
> Though seen of none save him whose strenuous tongue
>   Can burst Joy's grape against his palate fine;
> His soul shall taste the sadness of her might,
>   And be among her cloudy trophies hung.

Into the very raptures of sexual delight an apprehension of its
transitoriness brings a terror of annihilation. Keats lets us glimpse
the hidden power in this sorrowing allegorical figure. Her sexual
nature, so overpoweringly projected in Romantic anguish as an
alien force, is only an image, fundamentally, of her generalized
power. The masculine spirit reduces it to its sexuality, the only
sphere in which this power is inescapable to him. But "Veil'd
Melancholy" can also be construed as subdued woman whose
terrible anger at the privation of her birthright, felt intuitively as

---

24. In connection with male phobias concerning woman of which such
imagery is an expression—though surely not merely that—H. R. Hays's intriguing
but uneven book, *The Dangerous Sex,* and Wolfgang Lederer's interesting
but ultimately misogynistic *The Fear of Women* (New York: Harcourt, 1967)
seem to me especially illuminating.

just by men, has been turned within. Her Medeaesque fury is estimated by the emotions as a charge of huge dimensions. The depth of her sorrow is the negative of her explosive potential. If she were to come to want pleasure for herself, actively, she would become a menace, not alone for sexual reasons, but because she would no longer be *object,* an aspect of man's being, but a subject being in her own right, her shadow yielding to a terrifying substance that the higher realms of male consciousness have not yet labored at meeting.

The undercurrent of fear of a generalized freeing of female power inherent in the fatal woman myth becomes more evident as we look at the witch Matilda in Lewis's *The Monk* (1795). Her physical charms are augmented by magical powers (she is a minion of Satan), but it is her strength of person that makes her so formidable: "Her eyes sparkled with terrific expression; and her whole demeanor was calculated to inspire the beholder with awe and admiration." When she comes to the monk Ambrosio's cell, "in her right hand she held a small book, a lively expression of pleasure beamed upon her countenance—but still it was mingled with a wild imperious majesty, which inspired the monk with awe. . . . 'I have renounced God's service, and am enlisted beneath the banners of his foes. . . . Abandon a God who has abandoned you, and raise yourself to the level of superior beings.' "[25] Naturally, Ambrosio hastens back to the fair and restful Antonia.

The fatal woman is an anti-Christ, a disturber of order. Her every feature, her potions, her wild hair, her book, even her vivacity threaten. Lewis's novel preceded *Corinne* by a decade, and the latter work probably owes nothing specific to *The Monk,* but Mme de Staël's embrace of the dark heroine is the more striking because she saw clearly how the male mentality tarred it in evil, even as she attempted to assert it as a "good" female image, because, not in spite of, its sensuality and vitality.

Although Praz does not mention *Corinne* (1807) at all, he does speak of Velléda, the brilliant priestess of Chateaubriand's *Martyrs* (1809). This druidess, who tries to seduce the prissily Christian

25. Mario Praz, *The Romantic Agony* (London: Oxford University Press, 1933), pp. 193–94.

Eudore, also promises her prospective lover power in return for his love. Eudore, like Oswald, is bemused by her passion: "In truth I felt that Velléda would never inspire any real attachment in me: for me she lacked that secret charm that makes a destiny out of a mere life; but Ségénax's daughter was young, she was beautiful, she was passionate, and when burning words came from her lips, all my senses were disturbed."[26] Her active senses simply terrify her hero who cries out, "Oh unhappy Velléda! You speak of a husband, and you will never be loved!" This is once more Rousseau's old threat against the woman so presumptuous as to usurp, through mere reading and writing, the male prerogative to initiative. Velléda, indeed, is so negative a force, as the Christian hero's guilty conscience attests, that following upon his physical union with her she can only die so that Christian virtue may prevail.

Praz did not think there was "an established type" for the fatal woman in literature, as there was of the Byronic hero: "For a type—which is, in actual fact, a *cliché*—to be created, it is essential that some particular figure should have made a profound impression on the popular mind."[27] Harry Levin believed that it was Mme de Staël who "introduced the Byronic bluestocking" (*before* Byron?) and that George Sand "authenticated the *femme fatale*."[28] Surely, *Corinne* already combines the two, and if the Corinne type thus created does not generally receive the accolade of critics as a pedigreed type, it nevertheless had consequences. Levin, in fact, says that "Delphine or Corinne, the *femme fatale* of Mme de Staël, was presented as the feminine counterpart—and consequently, the moral superior—to the *homme fatal* of Byron and Chateaubriand."[29]

There are undeniable Balzacian offshoots from *Corinne*: *Sténie* and the nobly expiring Mme de Mortsauf in the *Lys dans la vallée*, as well as the flamboyant Fedora of the *Peau de Chagrin*. Balzac, of

---

26. Chateaubriand, *Oeuvres complètes* (Garnier edition), IV, 142.

27. *Romantic Agony*, p. 191.

28. Harry Levin, *The Gates of Horn* (New York: Oxford University Press, 1963). See also Ellen Moers's tribute to the influence of Corinne's myth in "Mme de Staël and the Woman of Genius," *American Scholar*, Spring, 1975, pp. 225–41, and her *Literary Women* (New York: Doubleday, 1976), published after this book was written.

29. Levin, *Gates of Horn*, p. 247.

course, embraced no form of dissent in woman, but he seized with zest upon the dynamic and sensual aspects of the Corinne personage. Sir Walter Scott, especially in *The Waverly Novels*, in his depiction of the brilliant Flora, and in his opposition of dark to light ladies, appears to have been touched to the point of admirative emulation by *Corinne*. Hawthorne, following Scott, created heroines even more reminiscent of the strong Corinne in the dark ladies of *The Marble Faun* (incidentally, an Italian travelogue) and the *Blithedale Romance*.[30] And George Sand's *Consuelo* takes over and even heightens the exoticism, the individualism, and the dolorism of Mme de Staël's *Corinne* in consecrating the female novel of comfort and compensation in private ecstasies.

For the male author, the vision of the lively Corinne is an invitation to repeat and justify her punishment; for the female, a spur to explore and sympathize with women more deeply. But, as the nineteenth century wore on, in its relentless way the angel-devil syndrome inherent in the light-dark dichotomy gained ground, and with the assistance of the most subtle and gifted of poetic iconoclasts, that somber image most at variance with the cloying public worship of the life-giving, loving mother, with her milk-flowing breasts—a murderous metaphor for woman—is the one given most exquisite expression.

> Je sucerai, pour noyer ma rancoeur
> Le népenthès et la bonne ciguë
> Aux bouts charmants de cette gorge aiguë
> Qui n'a jamais emprisonné de coeur.[31]

---

30. Perry Miller writes: "Hawthorne's creature of darkness and sex—clearly another Corinne—owed all her being to his imagining a Corinne in New England." Introduction to *Margaret Fuller, American Romantic*, ed. Perry Miller (New York: Doubleday, Anchor, 1963), p. xxiv. If Disraeli's *Contarini Fleming* (1832) owes as much to Goethe's *Wilhelm Meister* as to *Corinne*, George Meredith's *Sandra Belloni* (1864) seems to owe its being primarily to memories of Mme de Staël's novel.

31.   I shall suck, to drown my rancor,
     Gall and wormwood
     From the charming ends of that sharp bosom
     Which has never enclosed a heart.
Charles Pierre Baudelaire, "Le Léthé," in *Oeuvres* (Paris: Pléiade, 1954), p. 216.

Prophetess of Romanticism—The Positive Legacy

If Romanticism can be characterized as a dissent bathed in despair, *Corinne* is certainly one of its first fruits: "From Mme de Staël's portrait of Corinne, from her description of the true poet, to Hugo's pose as a latter-day Moses, bearing down odes and ballads instead of tablets of stone, was but a short step."[32] Corinne is the prophetess of a better, because gentler, world. Upon her mountain-top of Cape Miseno she prefigures Olympio's semidivinity, art now endowing its creator with a ponderous sanctity. Art and politics were not yet altogether discrete in the first half of the century, and the ideological impact of *Corinne* long remained as important as its aesthetic. In terms of aesthetic, the *foisonnement*—teeming quality—of the novel, the very superabundance and prolixity that seem to us so gauche, were elements appreciated in its time,[33] as was the much-adopted doctrine Mme de Staël expounded of the superiority of "inspiration" over workmanship. "The well-wrought book is annoying," she would say, or "praiseworthy proportion . . . can sometimes stifle the impetuousness of a thought." Somewhat in the fashion of the twentieth century's Artaud, who spits upon our former conception of art to renew and refound an art uncorrupted, Mme de Staël and those who followed her rejected outworn classical proportions, conventions, and vocabularies. In her own works there is much timidity as she goes about doing so, but she was certainly an instigator of the vague but suggestively inspired prose and poetry of the Romantic school. The single power with which Mme de Staël most strongly endows her heroine is that of enthusiasm, and she imbues this notion with something more of its etymological sense, that of possession by a god. Enthusiasm implies a spontaneous freedom in human nature—Rousseau's English garden as against the espaliered severity of the French *parterre*. "There is no variety but in nature; true feeling alone inspires us to new ideas," says Mme de Staël. Balzac's Sténie agrees: "Enthusi-

---

32. Maurice Z. Shroder, *Icarus: The Image of the Artist in French Romanticism* (Cambridge: Harvard University Press, 1961), p. 21.

33. In fact, George M. Ridenour, in *The Style of Don Juan* (New Haven: Yale University Press, 1960), presents an intriguing argument for Corinne's "*mobilité*" as a contributing factor in Byron's conception of his supremely mobile Don Juan.

asm is to the heart what the breath of life is to the body, this heavenly gift, the attribute of a few loved by the gods is taxed as madness by the mediocre. . . ."[34] The belief that intense and unfettered feeling raises one to sublime heights and just by itself makes one extraordinary warms and liberates the new art. As they opposed themselves to what would now be perceived as the arid rationalism of their fathers, this is the flame the Romantic generation took from Mme de Staël's work. The elegiac lyre of the poetess Corinne sent Lamartine away from his first reading of the novel "transported to another world, ideal, natural, poetic." This fire of enthusiasm scalds in Hugo, burns in Balzac, and flickers in Stendhal.

As a political, no less than an aesthetic, embodiment of freedom, *Corinne* was perhaps even more powerful. Its heroine, together with her author, came to stand, as Hugo later did on his rock in exile, for the spirit of liberty banished from Napoleon's armed camp of a nation. The realm of the spirit that the Italy of the novel represented was for the Romantics the counter to the temporal realm's perversion of the spirit, and Italy gained thereby in prestige, becoming more and more, for the times, the poet's and the free man's *pays d'élection*. When Lamartine recalled Lake Léman in his poem, it was to celebrate the free and ebullient exchange of ideas that Coppet came to represent in the embattled succession of revolutions endured by the next generation. The suppression of censure of *On Germany*, her exploitation of the role of exile ("I am the Orestes of exile," she would exclaim), her last political work, *Considerations on the French Revolution*, which espoused an English-style liberal monarchy, all tended to endear Mme de Staël to those who bewailed the loss of their freedom as the century wore on. Lamartine reflects the quintessential image that Corinne and her creator represented in the Romantic era, one that fused poetry and freedom into a single entity:

> Mme de Staël, a male genius in female form: a spirit tormented by the superabundance of its strength, mobile, passionate, bold, capable of generous and sudden resolve, unable to breathe in that atmosphere of cowardice and servitude, demanding space and air around her, drawing

---

34. Honoré de Balzac, *Sténie ou les erreurs philosophiques* (Paris: Librairie Georges Courville, 1936), p. 103.

towards her as if by magnetic instinct all who felt a feeling of resistance or concentrated indignation fermenting within them; herself a living conspiracy, as capable of high intellect or of inciting to riot against the tyranny of the reigning mediocrity as of putting the knife into the hands of conspirators, or striking a blow against herself, if she could thereby restore that same liberty to her soul that she would have liked to restore to the world! Elite and exceptional creature the like of which nature has not given us a copy, uniting within herself Corinne and Mirabeau![35]

The Prophecy to Women

This goddess of freedom on the barricades was a far cry from the emotionally torn and often timorous Germaine de Staël, but she gives a proper measure of how the moral portrait of Corinne, wedded with her creator's own struggles, seized the imagination of the Romantic era.

Of course the fact that this symbol was that of a demigoddess did not go unnoticed by women. It was in all likelihood they who read her books most tirelessly throughout the many printings of *Delphine* and *Corinne* that appeared, tapering off by the end of the century. Between 1815 and 1845 these novels continued to be extremely popular and to receive great notice from both critics and the public. No other novelist whose works were not currently appearing was the subject of as many articles during this period. "*Corinne* was commonly recognized as superior to *Delphine,* and was coupled with *René* as a lasting work of the Empire." It must be added here that "the space accorded Chateaubriand did not compare with that given to Madame de Staël."[36]

In Sainte-Beuve's 1851 essay on the poetess Delphine Gay he tells how in the 1820s this pretty young woman had had herself posed and drawn as a muse, spoke of herself as, and was spoken of incessantly as "Corinne." "Mme de Staël's Corinne *was then in fact the great ideal of all celebrated women.*"[37] In the aftermath of her pious pilgrimages to Rome and to the Miseno in 1827, Delphine Gay made vain efforts to become France's national occasional poet,

---

35. A. de Lamartine, "Les Destinées de la poésie," in *Oeuvres complètes,* 8 vols. (Paris: Hachette, Furne, 1856), I, 32–33.

36. These findings are from Marguerite Iknayan, *The Idea of the Novel in France* (Paris and Geneva: Minard-Droz, 1961), p. 31.

37. *Causeries du lundi,* 2nd ed., 15 vols. (Paris: Garnier, 1856–62), III, 387. Italics mine.

writing verse on the deliberations of the Chamber of Deputies and against the bloodthirsty General Cavaignac. If Delphine Gay enacted such fantasies, we may only guess how many less rich, less impulsive, less young and pretty female readers of *Corinne* quietly treasured this triumphant heroine, who formed so violent a contrast with woman in the society they knew. That they identified themselves as well with Corinne's downfall is clear, for did it not make their own toleration of their mediocre lives more bearable to see this genius even more vulnerable than they? But the impact of the popularity of *Corinne* lay in the visibly encouraging effect it had upon their self-image. The powerful, seductive, and ephemeral heroine who had fled a living death to find personal liberation was certainly, for many *of them*, the analogue of the Byronic hero.

The Sand heroine succeeds her and—though never directly— often pays her tribute. Sand's women, though pursuing personality and identity, are never (like their inventor) geniuses seeking their own path. It is the "wild girl" side of Corinne, an inheritance from the *Sturm und Drang's* impetuous women, that Sand seems to seize upon and exploit. In *Les Sept Cordes de la lyre* (*The Seven Chords of the Lyre*) she sings the essential Sandean complaint: "I am the daughter of the lyre, and I do not know you. You have long made me suffer by condemning me to do labors of the mind that are opposed to my faculties. But all your reasoning is not for me: the time to live has arrived; I am a free being; I want to live; farewell!" Sand sings of an almost Jungean difference of woman from the man's world, but not of the incommensurability of that world to her nature. The demented, overblown claims to transcendence of Corinne, who strives not only for experience but toward the infinite, is foreign to Sand's fiction.

Perry Miller tells us that "Isabel Hill's translation of *Corinne*, published in 1807, promptly became a troubling intrusion into all Anglo-Saxon communities. It was perpetually denounced from middle-class pulpits and assiduously read by middle-class daughters in their chambers at night."[38] In New England no less than in Paris,

---

38. Perry Miller, in introduction to *The Writings of Margaret Fuller* (New York: Viking, 1941), p. xxi.

Corinne's was for thinking women the new version of female virtue, one linked to accomplishment. Embodying, as Emerson put it, "tenderness, counsel," this new woman is "one before whom every mean thing is ashamed—'more variously gifted, wise, sportive, eloquent, who seems to have learned all languages, Heaven knows when or how. . . .' "[39] This is how it came to pass that in the Boston of the 1840s it was observed that the disconcertingly brilliant Margaret Fuller had some of the affected airs of a "Yankee Corinna." Fuller acknowledges her debt to the hilt, proclaiming that Mme de Staël's intellect makes "the obscurest schoolhouse in New England warmer and lighter to the little rugged girls who are gathered together on its wooden benches."[40] Corinna was a figure that a lively minded, plain little girl like Margaret could warm to, showing her as she did the value of the life of the spirit in a heroic woman. She would immediately bypass the histrionic narcissism, the absurdities of this figure, because she needed it, could use it to fabricate her own identity as a being moving toward transcendence. As a far-ranging intellectual as well as a creator, like Mme de Staël, of self-aggrandizing fantasies, Fuller imitated Staël: in one of her rhetorically inclined heroines Emerson found "a new Corinna with a fervid Southern eloquence that makes me wonder as often before how you fell into Massachusetts."[41] His intuition was solid, for in fact the South, with its tradition of eloquence, enjoyed an even more intense Corinne cult than the North, and more than a few Southern salons were presided over by a "Corinne."[42]

This cult of a feminine sensibility wedded to gifts and accomplishments could and did easily degenerate into a climate where sometimes pretentious coteries pursued the purely cultural goals of literate discussion or musical entertainment. Yet at the

---

39. Miller's introduction to *The Writings of Margaret Fuller*, p. xix. The inner quotation is from Emerson.

40. Miller quoting Margaret Fuller, in introduction to *The Writings of Margaret Fuller*, p. xxi.

41. Miller, in introduction to *The Writings of Margaret Fuller*, pp. xx-xxi.

42. I have long been indebted for this piece of lore to Professor Anne Firor Scott of Duke University. I only touch here upon a fascinating piece of social history that I hope will be developed by others.

same time it certainly encouraged deeper forms of self-development in women, urging their minds and fingers to do more arduous things and giving a greater acceptance to their new skills and learning.

Surprising evidence of this confirming presence of Corinne is found in an anthology, *The American Female Poets*, published in 1853. In it we find two poems that appear to reflect the interest the sibyl Corinne held for highly literate women striving for poetic expression. Elizabeth J. Eames's "On the Picture of a Departed Poetess" does not allude directly to Mme de Staël's heroine, but there is little doubt that this is she:

> This still, clear, radiant face! doth it resemble
>   In each fair, faultless lineament thine own?
> Methinks on that enchanting lip doth tremble
>   The soul that breathes thy lyre's melodious tone.
> The soul of music, O! ethereal spirit,
>   Fills the dream-haunted sadness of Thine eyes;
> Sweet Poetess! thou surely didst inherit
>   Thy gifts celestial from the upper skies.
>
> Clear on the expansion of that snow-white forehead
>   Sits intellectual beauty, meekly throned;—
> Yet, O! the expression tells that thou hast sorrow'd,
>   And in thy yearning, human heart atoned
> For thy soul's lofty gifts!—on earth, O never
>   Was the deep thirsting of thy bosom still'd!—
> The "aching void" followed thee here forever,
>   The Better Land thy DREAM OF LOVE fulfilled.[43]

And Mary E. Hewitt wrote a "Last Chant of Corinne," published in the same volume, which ends,

> And, like that nymph of yore, who droop'd and faded,
>   And pined for love, till she became a sound;
> My song, perchance, awhile to earth remaining,
>   Shall come in murmur'd melody to thee;
> Then let my lyre's deep passionate complaining,
>   Cry to thy heart, beloved! remember me![44]

---

43. In Caroline May, ed., *The American Female Poets* (Philadelphia: Lindsay and Blakiston, 1853), p. 259.

44. C. May, ed., *American Female Poets*, p. 345.

We grasp what these vapid poems allude to. The very icon of atonement for female intellectual beauty and of the demand that her lover never forget her sacrificial passage, Corinne has touched these women. The passionate strains of her plaintive lyre go on resounding in them.

What the examples of Margaret Fuller, Delphine Gay, and the other "Corinnes" show us is the hunger of the women for a heroic model from whom, despite continued defeats, they could extract some vital strength. The eclectic goddess did not lack for followers, but that such cults never amounted to much more than a social and cultural epiphenomenon is a consequence of the ultimately conservative, "tragic" nature of the defeated heroine who inspired them.

I am a worker, she is a professor, doctor, engineer, but she is a woman. I cannot forget it. She has a vagina and two feet, but no brain. When I look at her legs in the subway, she is nothing but a wound under the pleasuring knife. I am purified. She has leprosy inside and her creative activity is only a gigantic copulation.

ALAIN VIGNIER
Parapluie No. 1

The Decline of a Reputation

Mme de Staël's reputation as an important writer has remained, true enough, but she has markedly lost ground in the century and a half since her death, and in particular she has lost status as a novelist. Thibaudet remarked in 1936, "This work [*Corinne*] which today seems dead to us was one of the most glorified of works in its time."[45] He added that Mme de Staël wielded her very real power over people's minds more for her novels than for her works of ideas. *Delphine* and *Corinne* had a success and a popularity that were, simply, immense. *Corinne* alone was published in more than forty editions between 1807 and 1872. Critics have nonetheless generally found the fiction too time-bound to

---

45. Albert Thibaudet, *Histoire de la littérature française* (Paris: Librairie Stock, 1936), pp. 54, 51.

deserve our attention. The critical works have been re-edited in the twentieth century in important editions, but the novels are yet to be so republished. There can be no question that there has been a withdrawal of critical approval from Mme de Staël, and this critical course deserves examination.

Since the novels have been interpreted almost exclusively as fictional projections of self, Mme de Staël's personal reputation has had a decided influence upon that of her novels, and particularly that of *Corinne*. The dubiety of this reputation, which already existed in Mme de Staël's lifetime, was not so much a function of the worth of the works as of whether or not their author was perceived as "feminine" or "masculine," a problem that had already been raised in the impersonal debates concerning woman's nature before and during the Revolution and in the campaign of slander that preceded the writing of *Delphine*. If she was "feminine enough," we read her works without fear or constraint and find her to have been an extraordinary and admirable being (albeit irritating at times), though we wonder at her splendid powers "for a woman." If we think her "masculine," we find her a monster: we rebuke her and her kind, and we dismiss her works, especially her "pretentious" and "inflated" novels. Finally, it is possible to think her "too feminine," a man-eater, a voracious harlot of a woman who could not possibly have possessed a brain. If we could but apply this division of critical opinion systematically, the result would be very neat; the truth is that we find every kind of combination of these omnipresent and conflicting views. Mme de Staël clearly perceived and bewailed this extraliterary dimension in assessing female performance, for she lived always with it: ". . . opinion seems to discharge men from all sense of duty toward any woman who has been recognized as superior: one can be ungrateful, perfidious, nasty to her without inspiring any inclination on the part of opinion to defend her. *Is she not an exceptional woman?* Then all has been said; one abandons her to her own strength, lets her struggle with her sorrows" (*Litt.*, II, IV). That this was no persecution mania can be amply documented.

Our contemporaries Henri Guillemin and Anthony West, far from being new and daring in attempting to expose Mme de Staël's ambiguous attempts to curry favor with Napoleon as ridiculous, are merely continuing an old and honored tradition of raillery begun by Bonaparte himself. In his letters, the Consul and, later, Emperor referred to her as "crow" and "slut." Of course political opposition was deeply enmeshed with sexual prejudice in Napoleon's mind. He found Mme de Staël "very dangerous, because she gathered together in her salon . . . all the partisans, republicans, and royalists. She put them in each other's presence; she united them all against me. She attacked me from all sides. . . . Her salon was fatal. You know that at the party M. Talleyrand gave for me on my return from Italy, when she asked me which woman in modern times I most admired, I told her 'the one who has had the most children.' She was stupefied by my response."[46] In Bonaparte's straightforward misogyny there is no elaborate screen of polite pretense or rationalization covering his impulse to put this nuisance of a woman back into her proper realm—the predetermined sphere of her physiology. This attack was less brutal than another of the Emperor's positions regarding Mme de Staël, which was simply to deny that she was a woman. After describing his resistance to her supposed advances, he retaliated like Napoleon Bonaparte to her ostensible temerity in taking the offensive with him, saying: "The Empress Josephine and Mme de Staël were absolutely at opposing ends of the scale from one another. One was woman, from the soles of the feet to the ends of her hair, the other was not even a woman in her . . . [genitals]."[47] Then Napoleon went on to relate what Narbonne had purportedly told him: that she had a curious physical anomaly. He concluded, "She is a man." Another time, in a somewhat gentler vein, the Emperor told of asking Talleyrand in genuine disbelief, "What is this hermaphrodite?" Talleyrand, faithful for once to his old friendship with Mme de Staël, replied, "She is a very witty woman who writes just the way she speaks." Yet when *Delphine* was published, with its singeing portrait of the arch-hypocrite Mme de Vernon in whom all of Paris recognized him, Talleyrand could not resist that famous riposte that all of Paris delighted in, "It seems that Mme de Staël has written a novel in which both she and I are travestied as women."

The enmity of Napoleon and his suite and the misogynistic

---

46. Henri Gratien Bertrand, *Cahiers de Sainte-Hélène*, ed. Paul Fleuriot de Langle (Paris: Bonne, 1959), p. 530.
47. Bertrand, *Cahiers de Sainte-Hélène*, p. 329.

caste of that enmity had major repercussions, both positive and negative, upon Mme de Staël's reputation. It preconditioned the untempered mixture of irrational phallic criticism and the treatment of her as a pretentious fishwife by the supporters of the *petit caporal;* their outraged rejection of such attacks made her own zealous supporters and her family cultivate an equally extreme reverence and piety concerning her and her *oeuvre.* These forces, between them, all but extinguished a proper sense of this major figure's ambivalent energies.

Harpy, nymphomaniac, hermaphrodite, man: this is the choice of image Mme de Staël's detractors consistently proffer. It must not be imagined that such characterizations were by any means confined to the arsenal of the virulent attacker, nor to the remote past. We remember Benjamin Constant's jeer at her as an *homme-femme* and his remark that her troubles came of the fact that, although having a mind like a man, she still wanted to be loved like a woman. For even this intimate, it was her mind that disqualified her as a woman. Byron, merely her friend, confirmed this view, claiming that she should have *been* a man, but then reformulated Constant's conception: "She thinks like a man, but alas! she feels like a woman." (As for nymphomania, did not Christopher Herold's enormously successful biography of 1958 play on this theme in its title, *Mistress to an Age?*)

To Goethe, a less involved observer, "there was something ravishing about her person both physically and intellectually and she did not appear angered if one were sensible of it."[48] A closer companion, the author Simon de Sismondi, who had spent long periods in her company at Coppet, traveled with her, and fallen bootlessly in love with her, wrote, "Well do I know which woman is always a woman, even as she is as eloquent as an orator, as deep as a philosopher or as inspired as a prophet. . . ."[49] There were many men who, despite her commonly accorded lack of conventional beauty, were decidedly attracted by her person; so much so that we are unable to accord any credence at all to any idea of physical masculinity in her.

48. Quoted by Blennerhasset, *Madame de Staël et son temps,* III, 68.
49. Jean de Salis, *Sismondi* (Paris: Champion, 1932), p. 131.

Those who admired her still needed to categorize her as an exceptional being, hedging their praises with caveats. There were many, like Goethe, Humboldt, and to a lesser extent Schiller, who although prepared to accord her personal gifts and laud her remarkable conversational genius, refused to accord her works much in the way of literary value. This strain of criticism may be linked once more to that recurrrent theory that it is natural for women to put their genius into their lives, but not into art or into other forms of transcendence. Essentially, this was the covert reproach of Chateaubriand and Fontanes, as they attacked *On Literature* in the *Mercure*. "In writing, she thought she was still conversing. Those who hear her do not cease to applaud her; I, however, was unable to hear her when I criticized her work . . ." says Fontanes. And Chateaubriand puts it this way: "Sometimes, inspired by her natural feelings, she sets her soul free: but then *argumentation* comes in again and puts an end to the promptings of the heart." Arguments, for Chateaubriand, are both unfeeling and unfeminine. He concedes, in the end, her singularity: "You are without a doubt a superior woman. Your mind is strong and your imagination full of charm." "But," he pleads, "show more heart."

Of course her literary reputation could not hope to escape this sexual vise. A favorable critic like Vinet, in the first half of the nineteenth century, still compliments her on having "to a superior degree one of the graces of the feminine mind: direct intuition. Everything with her seems to be seized, carried off at first glance. She affirms more than she demonstrates, but her affirmations are as good as proofs. . . . She will remain immobile at the foot of the obstacle rather than turn it. The forms and artifices of the dialectic are foreign to her. Her mechanics remained . . . that of the earliest and most elementary machines, but she applied to it a skillful and powerful hand."[50] A powerful but "primitive" writer, thinks Vinet. Even in a laudatory context, we find the concessive, condescending attitude of the male master dialectician, who admires the vigor of female adolescent effort and gives grudging approval to her triumph over her "inherent" passivity.

Of the single most influential critic of the century, Sainte-

---

50. Vinet, *Etudes*, I, 184.

Beuve, it must be said that as Mme de Staël's mystique was still strong in his youth (he had been received in the salon of her reverent friend Mme Récamier), he praised and celebrated her generously, both literarily and politically—calling Napoleon Emperor of Matter and Germaine Empress of Mind. But a later critic comments that though Sainte-Beuve gives considerable importance to this celebrated woman of letters and "appreciates her talent and admires her ideas," he "doesn't especially like her. . . . there is something too virile about the author of *Corinne* for her to please Sainte-Beuve."[51] In fact, Sainte-Beuve in general "likes less women who were professional writers, heroines, strong-minded women, than those who gave themselves up to literature only occasionally under the influence of some emotion."[52] We see this general reflection supported in his remark about Corinne: "From the moment when she is seized with passion . . . I love her powerlessness to console herself, I love this feeling stronger than her genius. . . ." In a late and devastating footnote to a much earlier text on Mme de Staël, the Sainte-Beuve of the mid-century writes:

If I had a young friend to instruct with my experience, I would say to him: "Love a coquette, a grisette, a duchess. You will be able to tame her, subdue her. But if you are after any happiness in love at all, never love a muse. Where you think her heart is, you will find only her talent.

"Do not love Corinne,—and especially if she has not yet reached the Capitol; for then the Capitol is inside her, and on any pretext, on any subject that arises and even on the most intimate ones, she'll mount it."[53]

But it remained for Lamartine, in his last essay on Mme de Staël, to pull together the several strands of criticism against the woman and writer. These later remarks of his convey so basic a censure that one forgets what an effusive admirer of hers he had been in his youth. It must be admitted that Lamartine poses with perfect directness the central question of Mme de Staël's life: "Is it appropriate for women to write and to aspire to glory in the world of letters?" He rephrases it to reflect the extreme case, as

---

51. Juliette Decreus-Van Liefland, *Sainte-Beuve et la critique des auteurs féminins* (Paris: Boivin, 1949), pp. 20–21.

52. Decreus-Van Liefland, *Sainte-Beuve*, p. 190.

53. Decreus-Van Liefland, *Sainte-Beuve*, p. 75.

did Mme de Staël: "Should nature endow woman with genius?" He reviews her youth, and concludes, rightly, that her early exposure to the society of men of letters gave her an insatiable need to be one of them. He observes that she first tried her hand at verse, and that despite the fact that "woman is the most poetic of beings," no women, except for a few "minor poets like Sappho, have written verse worthy of being transmitted as a 'monument of human thought.' " Then he erupts in this astonishingly phrased question, a masterpiece of codpiece criticism: "Could it be that the prodigious tension of spirit necessary to the great poet for that passionate and reasoned ejaculation that is verse is in disproportion to the delicacy of feminine organs of thought?"[54] Here is a direct transposition from the organic to the mental and spiritual plane, a smug assumption that destiny, and the poet's gift, flow from sexual size, shape, and function. Lamartine goes on to survey what he concedes to have been genius in Mme de Staël, and yet concludes, altogether paradoxically, that it would have been better left unexpressed:

. . . the charming timidity appropriate to her sex and her age, that modesty of the soul, as blushing as that of the body, never came to light in her. The glare of publicity in her youth suppressed it. Only this grace was lacking to her spirit, but this grace would have meant that she would have remained silent. People felt the want in her of that innocence of the genius who does not know his own powers, and doubts himself: they forgot this in hearing the charm of her virile improvisations. For *she was no longer a woman,* but a poet, and orator.[55]

Only her immodesty allowed her to express her genius. Im-

---

54. Alphonse de Lamartine, *Souvenirs et portraits* (Paris: Hachette, 1871), p. 220.

55. Lamartine, *Souvenirs et portraits*, p. 226. Lest we be tempted to consider Lamartine's a hopelessly outmoded critical strategy, we note Mary Ellmann's comment on John Berryman's "shouting, all women poets are spinsters or Lesbians! But what does he care? What is the implied interdependence of good poetry and heterosexual experience? Does Mr. Berryman suppose the imprimatur of his own work is his own copulative history? But, of course, the most immediate means of aggrandizing whatever one does is to say the opposite sex could not do it. Each cries out for its own matchlessness. And it is this cry, that She cannot do as well as He, which batters the more ears—and which therefore, inevitably, discourages the commitment of women to our social professions." *Thinking about Women* (New York: Harcourt Brace and World, 1968), p. 180.

modesty is of course unfeminine: ergo, her genius is unfeminine. Having unsexed herself, she is no woman but only a sexless (that is, not male) poet. The poet Lamartine himself seemed able to maintain his own sexual identity. Why is this? Simone de Beauvoir points out that "in a man there is no hiatus between the public and the private life: the more he affirms himself in action, the more virile does he appear; in him the human and vital values combine; instead of which, the autonomous successes of the woman are in contradiction with her femininity in that it is asked of her that she make herself into an object, to be 'the other,' if she is to be considered a 'real woman.' "

Lamartine sounds almost as if he had read the twentieth-century woman's analysis as prescription as he concludes that Napoleon's reply to Mme de Staël's question, that the most superior woman was the one who had borne the most children, was, although cruel, just. He re-poses Mme de Staël's old dilemma this way: "Which is the greater, that noisy woman, or a silent one, veiling her soul with the chaste modesty of her sex. . . . If literary vanity hesitates to decide between them, common sense and virtue do not: *the greatest of these is the most feminine one, that is, the most obscure one,* for as an old saying has it, misplaced glory is only the greatest of all pettinesses. A woman in the spotlight goes against nature; celebrity for her is nothing but an illustrious exposure. What would that woman be upon whose tomb all one could write in epitaph would be the vain words: She shone?"[56] For all his praise of her genius, this is the epitaph Lamartine appears to intend for Mme de Staël.

So we see the course of Mme de Staël's critical reputation following that of the status of woman and of the vagaries of taste in succeeding times. The religious and filial pieties that (for us) flaw Corinne were nearly the only aspects of the novel that remained popular. As domesticity returned in tyrannical force, feminine initiative went out; as enthusiasm waned, cynicism returned. The advent of the movement for the political emancipation of women, in any case more repressed in France than in England or America, could not restore the reputation of Mme de Staël's novels. It is

56. Lamartine, *Souvenirs et portraits,* p. 300.

interesting, I think, to see that a major critical reevaluation of them comes precisely from England in 1894, from George Saintsbury. In his introduction to a re-edited translation of *Corinne,* he admits to having followed the popular snobbery in despising it in his youth and wonders if he likes it better because it appeals to middle age. He still mocks its didacticism and its "properties"; the "schall," Nelvil's "inky cloak," and the "queer half-Ossianic, half-German rants." But Saintsbury moves beyond these, saying they "matter comparatively little, and leave enough in *Corinne* to furnish forth a book almost great, interesting without any 'almost,' and remarkable as a not very large shelf-ful in the infinite library of modern fiction deserves remark. For the passion of its two chief characters, however oddly, and to us, unfashionably, presented, however lacking in the commanding and perennial qualities which make us indifferent to fashion in the work of the greatest masters, is *real.*" Saintsbury is not insensible to Corinne: ". . . it is not, I think, fanciful to discover in this heroine, with all her 'Empire' artifice and convention, all her smack of the theatre and the *salon,* a certain live quiver and throb. . . ." He sees it as an important document in literary history, "a guidebook by prophecy to the nineteenth century." He adds, "It has an immense historical value as showing the temper, the aspirations, the ideas, and in a way the manners of a certain time and society. A book which does this can never wholly lose its interest."[57]

Without particularly remarking on its feminist content, Saintsbury has given an entirely judicious assessment of *Corinne's* literary worth, and he did so perhaps as the reign of prejudice against female art and artists had finally begun to wane.

A truly extraordinary example of male bias in the criticism of Mme de Staël's novels is to be found at the end of André Le Breton's 1901 essay on *Delphine* and *Corinne.* After a lengthy, excellent, and penetrating discussion of both works, encompassing their social criticism as well as their literary defects and felicities, Le Breton evokes Corinne's triumphant first appearance in the novel and admits that he, like Oswald, does admire her.

---

57. George Saintsbury, introduction to *Corinne or Italy,* trans. Dennis Lawler, revised (London: Dent, 1894), *passim.*

But . . . with her . . . our admiration is often hesitant. It seems to us that, without stifling her genius, she might have been woman, more simply, more purely than she was either in her life or in her works; and even as all exaggeration provokes a contrary one, her noisy and theatrical dream of glory would lead us nearly to believe with Napoleon that the mission of woman is neither to bother with politics nor to triumph at the Capitol. A memory haunts us, troubles us as we read *Corinne*. We remember what was happening, in these first years of the nineteenth century, in a Burgundian village and in a peaceful corner of Paris. . . . Two women come to mind, so gentle, so modest, so simple, entirely absorbed in their functions of mother and teacher. One was Mme de Lamartine, the other, Mme Hugo; and noiselessly, without uproar, they created two immortal works that are worth something more than all the songs of Corinne: they created the souls of their sons.[58]

In a *reductio* as devastating as Sainte-Beuve's and Lamartine's, Le Breton follows the patriarchal imperative and in doing so mars his long and excellent essay.

A reviewer of the highly popular Christopher Herold biography of Mme de Staël was moved to remark that it is of that species of art that makes such abundant fun of its subject that the reader is made to feel highly superior to her.[59] Deep in Herold's frequently incisive chronicle of scandal and high life, there lies a small but precious concession concerning his too-juicy subject: "Had she been born a man, three-quarters of her talents would not have been spent in combat to hold affection and to justify her right to be herself; the role she played and the work she left, though remarkable, were only a fraction of the potential she could have realized without the handicap of her sex."[60]

Mme de Staël perceived distinctly the stir she created and the kind of anxiety it occasioned. In Italy, in 1805, she had written, "It is true I am treated very well . . . here, but this is because there is no clear idea of what I am. There is some confused notion in all of this located somewhere midway between admiration and fear, and if people were to say I was a devil it would go down very well!"[61]

---

58. Andre Le Breton, *Le Roman français*, pp. 148–49.
59. Jean-Albert Bédé, review in *Romanic Review*, no. 51 (1960), 66–69.
60. Herold, *Mistress*, p. 233.
61. Letter 253, to Bonstetten, from *Choix de lettres*, p. 303.

Sociology has given the name of "contravention" to the systematic use of mockery and denigration by one group in its efforts to hamper the progress of another.[62] I would submit that this word describes the treatment accorded Mme de Staël's novels in literary history and criticism.

"Vive Corinne! Vive le génie!"

Feminism and the Exceptional Woman

Were not the phallic critics overzealous in seizing so energetically upon Mme de Staël to belittle her and her works? Why ever did they bother? Perhaps she had, without their perceiving it, done their own task for them. Pierre Fauchery writes:

Her heroines, like herself, always plead guilty, implore forgiveness; haunted by the shame of a "difference," of a superiority that isolates them and that all the feeling part of themselves has no courage to carry out to the end. More and more plainly as they approach their author, they proclaim the misery of the exceptional woman, in her quest for an impossible conciliation of insubordination and obedience, law and the exception. The last of the line, Corinne, bends utterly beneath glory and the burden: first woman "of genius"—and conscious of being so—in the feminine novel, and at the same time . . . doubting her power, oblique in her source.

And, "She draws her consolation, she reconstitutes the magic illusion of power, the oxygen of women, only in negativity—extending to all who surround her the contagion of her ill-luck."[63]

This critic, after perusing hundreds of eighteenth-century novels, attacks Mme de Staël more directly still: "... it is not rare to see women, whose independence of mind *is as well known to us as*

---

62. See Helen Mayer Hacker, "Women as a Minority Group," *Social Forces*, 30 (Oct., 1951), 60–69: "Rather than conflict, the dissociative process between the sexes is that of contravention, a type of opposition intermediate between competition and conflict. . . . It includes rebuffing, repulsing, working against, hindering, protesting, obstructing, restraining, and upsetting another's plans."

63. Fauchery, *La Destinée féminine*, p. 846. Readers may want to consult Nancy K. Miller's incisive review of Fauchery's work, "The Exquisite Cadavers: Women in Eighteenth Century Fiction," *Diacritics*, 5 (Winter, 1975), pp. 37–43, a feminist linguistic analysis of this critic's assumptions.

the liberty of their morals, indulge in the most humiliating stereo-
types for themselves and their sisters: if one kept to her novelistic
efforts, we would have the right to accuse a Staël of cowardice in
regard to the responsibilities of genius."[64] His charge, not altogether
unwarranted, is that with Corinne's doloristic demise, the cage was
closed upon woman, insuring that a full century of heroines would
die tragically. Such a view sacrifices the impact of the work to the
impact of its ending. It is odd to see a moralistic sexual bias intrude
here in the thinking of a critic so pretentiously radical that he can
call for a Sadean "bloodbath" as more liberating for woman than
the Staëlian concern for female genius.[65] Fauchery is somewhat less
condescending and far closer to the truth when he remarks that
equality terrified the women of the Enlightenment (not to speak
of the men) and that the "woman author chastises in her heroine
the revolt that lay within her, and whose literary creation cathar-
tically soothes her."

If, as Fauchery contends, female authors—and Mme de Staël
not least, for we have seen how little she sought to be innovative—
"keep nearly always to the male lexicon," surely it is because they
lived and wrote in a profoundly misogynistic climate. Their efforts
to combat it could only have been limited, halting, and mitigated
by a self-doubt shared by their women readers, a doubt intensified
by the suspicions of the men.

I have tried, throughout this study, to suggest the climate of
pre- and post-Revolutionary opinion concerning woman's situation, the hopes briefly fired by the Revolution, and their extinction
in the Napoleonic reaction. No judgment of Mme de Staël's novels
as feminist statement should abstract them from this political
background, nor from that of the climate of artistic taste, steeped
in Ossianic messianism and neoclassical *kitsch,* nor from the
sentimental roles women were required to play as heroines, as
authors, as people.

As an overt feminist, overall, Mme de Staël was certainly
timid, and G. E. Gwynne is largely correct in asserting that she
shared in the caution of the second generation of ideologues and,

---

64. Fauchery, *La Destinée féminine,* p. 104. Italics mine.
65. See Fauchery, *La Destinée féminine,* p. 847.

like Destutt de Tracy and Cabanis, recoiled from Condorcet's courageous egalitarianism to a retrogressive assignment of a given sphere of life to each sex: to man, the public; to woman, the private. In truth her professions on this issue evolved with the generations, as she turned aside from her original egalitarian statements of *On Literature* (1800), a more cautious posture having become politic, and gave an ultimately conservative cast to the statements on women she made in *On Germany* (1811). But the question of her basic stand is far more complex than this evolution suggests, as the study of the novels shows. Certainly Germaine de Staël was not a "private" woman herself, and in casting about for a means of preserving her own personality and its passionate need for activity from the underground forces of self-hatred and self-destruction that give so much of her work a melancholy aura, she turned to the stratagem, first, of the novel of the woman of personality, then of the novel of woman as genius. Does this open her to the charge of having used the novel merely as a personal therapy? Not entirely, for in so doing, she gave, for one, a new and extremely important twist to novelistic intrigue. In her time novels almost universally revolved around a love foiled by some arbitrary obstacle like that of parental disapproval, or the presence of older sisters, or dying relations. Mme de Staël's lovers also must be parted, but in both *Delphine* and in *Corinne* they are separated by their characters, and above all by social conventions which are held to be at fault. Her novels constitute a fairly vigorous and articulate attack against convention, and there is no doubt that in this respect they represent a far stronger arraignment of society than those of other women novelists of the time. After 1815, the fate of lovers becomes not alone a personal but a social problem in the novel, and the social structure itself will be held responsible for individual suffering, as Balzac especially will illustrate.[66]

A very satisfactory statement of Mme de Staël's contribution to the novel and through the novel to feminine consciousness is this:

---

66. Some of these notions concerning social criticism come from an article by J. S. Wood, "Sondages dans le roman français du point de vue social (1798–1830)," *Revue d'Histoire Littéraire de la France*, no. 1 (Jan.-Mar., 1954), 32–48.

With her depiction or her light satire—sometimes even harsh—of the mores and absurdities of "society," it is Mme de Staël who first set out in the novel the complete biography of a woman. Until her time, woman in the novel occupied only the place it pleased men to give her. . . . It is also Mme de Staël . . . who first posed in *Corinne* and *Delphine* the question that interests all women: that of the right of a woman to live for herself. . . . That society should arrogate the right to punish in woman a superiority of mind it admires in man; that the world should honor in Léonce an independence of character it condemns in Delphine; that public opinion should make it obligatory for Corinne, in order to be happy, to annihilate or bury her personality in the sole love of Oswald, Mme de Staël's common sense might have been resigned to, but her heart, but the consciousness she had of her worth forever, protested. There . . . lies the key to her novels and that is their contribution.[67]

No, the critics were not in error. Here was indeed a real enemy: in fact, as they discerned, *the* real enemy, for all her defensive masochistic display, for all her disingenuous cries that love was woman's ruling passion. She herself can appear, as in Fauchery's contention, to be but a cowardly advocate for her sex or, in Le Breton's, to have missed the point entirely by her concentration on the problem of genius. "Yes, in some ways," Le Breton agrees,

Mme de Staël's second novel is a novel of female demands, affirming the right of woman to a more independent life, affirming her right to an intellectual life, and I even agree that the question of the woman lawyer, the woman doctor, or even the woman legislator is implicitly contained in it. But in contrast to what occurs with *Delphine*, here the particular case dominates the general idea, and darkens or falsifies it. The thesis is no longer "the woman victim," but "the woman of genius victim." Now, genius is a rare thing. Few people of either sex are called to know the torments of its elect, and when Mme de Staël describes those torments, we modestly reply, "this is not our business, and we run no risk."[68]

Genius has always been a rare thing, yes, but rarer still in woman. In the novel that she knew was her bid for immortality, Mme de Staël had the gall to aver that Corinne was of this rare breed: it is for this hybris that she would find so few to forgive her. If men fear the rivalry and demands of a female sex no longer beholden to them for their self-esteem, the mass of women fear and

67. Brunetière, "Les Romans de Madame de Staël," pp. 688–89.
68. Le Breton, *Le Roman français*, p. 147.

have often been even more hostile to extraordinary women. They withdraw their approval from, and shun, those individuals who reject the code, adhered to by the majority, of obeisance to male domination. Since whatever security women have is derived from this code, it is altogether understandable that they should be jealous and anxious about overturning it. And yet, their frequent invidiousness toward remarkable achievement in a woman is one of the gravest barriers to her advance and theirs. For only their approval and celebration of their sister can efface her terror of achieving too much, of being an anomaly, of deeply believing herself mad in her ambition and creative strength. This inner bondage upon the spirit of woman is the ultimate "reason" why, as the question is so often and so disingenuously phrased, "there have been so few great women." The seemingly remote question of genius is, therefore, not really so remote. What is being asked, in some sorry sense, is, "What is all the fuss about? If you women are not really capable of the highest, you are nothing but a band of accomplished drones. We always thought so." To affirm the capacity for genius in woman is to affirm her right to every degree of ability in the human range, even to the highest. This last term of the series is nothing more or less than the logical capstone of the argument for equality.

It would serve no purpose, save that of obfuscation, to minimize or deny the melodramatical theatrics of Corinne's self-serving postures, or to deny that they both weaken the credibility of Mme de Staël's narrative and annoy the reader. But why do they outrage us as much as they do?

From childhood on, her family and her entourage constantly asserted Mme de Staël's genius. Her brilliance, her awareness, her activity, her spontaneity, were a wonder. "The Staël is a genius . . . an extraordinary woman in all that she does. She only sleeps during a very few hours, and is uninterruptedly and fearfully busy all the rest of the time."[69] Even in a portrait of her (under the name of Dona Elvire) that contains many strictures, we read,

She has something far better than wit; she has genius, or to speak more plainly, she is herself a genius. Powerful genius, deep genius, fertile

---

69. Hill, *Maria Edgeworth*, p. 131.

genius, creative genius, genius of improvisation. . . . Finally a genius fair and good, for she is also the genius of goodness. . . . Dona Elvire is too lively for her head and her head is too lively for her reason. This devouring fire of sensibility and this novel of love without a specific object make her unhappy and a bit absurd; but it is redeemed by so many unforeseen, quick, and attractive things that one forgives in her what would be unpardonable in another. . . . not altogether a man, not altogether a woman, this is rather the most distinguished of beings.[70]

As they accorded her genius, people tended to withdraw from her their most basic acceptance: that of normal being.

While I am in agreement with Virginia Woolf and, following her, Carolyn Heilbrun[71] in believing that great art is androgynous, and even though Mme de Staël does decidedly possess that androgynous mind and spirit which give her work enduring value, I am compelled nonetheless to argue for the essential need for a confident sexual identity in the *artist*. Of course it is incumbent upon all artists to transcend their sexual identity if they can, but our sexuality is still a ground of our being.

Feeling herself to be capable of creation beyond both the biological and the minor aesthetic register then deemed appropriate to her sex, Mme de Staël risked being called virile, that is, having her sex, and hence her essential female potency, denied. Truly not "virile," not envying men their own forms of potency, she took a giant and oblique step in embodying that sense of power and freedom she coveted for herself and for womankind in the demigoddess Corinne. Throwing all the myths and images of divinity together as she did, Mme de Staël had no goal but to affirm that a core of vital creative power equal in value to that inhering in the male genius resided in her sibyl.

Jane Austen, no less than Mme de Staël, had to derive her creative power from a sure sense of sexed self, but she achieved this by re-creating, even as she transcended it by the art of her novels, an immanent domestic world. As Virginia Woolf remarked, she wrote "as women write, not as men write." She transgressed no law of the social order, but utterly integrated that order into the

70. Charles Joseph Emmanuel de Ligne, "Un Portrait inédit de Madame de Staël," *Occident et Cahiers staëliens*, 2 (Feb. 15, 1935).

71. *Toward a Recognition of Androgyny* (New York: Knopf, 1973).

consciousness of her characters, and made the drama of her work turn on struggles between the conservative consensus concerning the nature of taste and of private morality, and infringements against that consensus. Mme de Staël, not her half as a novelist, was attempting to do something utterly different, but no less estimable. She sought to move woman via the immanent to the transcendent realm and to lay claim to a place for her there. This was a very fragile enterprise, for it challenged every notion of woman's nature and her place and could only have been attempted by a gifted woman whom life had conspired to make more rich, spoiled, protected, and proud than she was apologetic and humble. Here is a statement that says, "Woman possesses genius." It is for this unspeakable pretension that posterity has never forgiven *Corinne.*

The Flame of Poetry

In the Prince de Ligne's portrait of Mme de Staël as Dona Elvire, he writes concerning her genius that "it is no fireworks display that ends up by being sad and dark: it is no volcano that flames up and consumes. It is the fire I believe she stole from Prometheus, who had, I believe, stolen it from heaven, and that ever lights and animates." Corinne, in the Naples *campania,* speaks of fire as "this devouring spirit that creates life and consumes it" and sees the troubled and fiery countryside as "the image of human passions, sulfurous and pulsating; its dangers and its pleasures seem to be born of these inflamed volcanoes which give the air so much excitement and make thunder grumble beneath our feet" (XIII, IV).

An intriguing parallel with this Promethean image is to be found in Erica Jong's treatment of a "cluster" of images she finds in Adrienne Rich's poetry

... of fire and burning. The speaker of the poems describes herself at one point as "wood with a gift for burning"; and women are often described in terms of fire imagery. . . . The survivor-poet burns, yet her burning leaves her unconsumed. The poet as sacred flame—one might almost say. The poet as hearthkeeper. The visionary who lights the dark world by her burning. Her burning, however, is never a destructive burning, never a vengeful self-immolation. . . . This burning is an affirmation. The fire is a temple—or a hearth fire. It might even be the sacred flame at Delphi which women guarded.

If you follow the fire imagery still more speculatively and try to see the old myths with an unjaundiced eye, you may even conclude that Adrienne Rich's survivor-poet is a kind of Prometheus.[72]

Erica Jong concludes that Prometheus must have been a woman. Mme de Staël had been asserting at the least that Corinne was his daughter. The filial piety is there, but so is the gift of the sacred flame. We remember Prince Castel-Forte's remark: "We would be men as she is woman, if men could, like women, create a world in their own heart, if our own genius, necessarily dependent upon social relations and external circumstances, could take its fire as completely from the sole flame of poetry" (I, II). Women may wish now to slough off the burden so eagerly taken up by nineteenth-century women of this "sacred flame at Delphi" that was given into their charge as the "heart" or "soul" of humankind— while man marched on, as in a Steinberg cartoon parade, under a banner lettered MIND. Yet they suspect that if they were to yield up altogether the treasuring of it, it might leave the world as if it had never entered it. Mme de Staël strove toward a synthesis new in the cultural history of woman: that of heart with mind, of human feeling with transcendent vision; the result is one who is "more than woman; it was a poet . . . " (Mirza). But when her heroine-artist and firebearer is destroyed, as the man she loves rejects her claim, as mere woman, to inspire human love, Corinne is vengefully immolated. Unlike Rich, Mme de Staël could not yet envisage woman's survival of love as a viable course: Corinne's love for Oswald is the very metaphor of her poetic fire, a fire of connectedness to him and, beyond him, to the world. And this sense of connectedness is here still steeped in the love mystique.

Linda Nochlin has seized with great accuracy the murderous effect of the feminine mystique upon genius in women: "Its ambivalent narcissism and internalized guilt subtly dilute and subvert that total inner confidence, that absolute certitude and self-determination (moral and aesthetic) demanded by the highest and most innovative work in art."[73] Mme de Staël's novelistic fantasies of

---

72. Erica Jong, "Visionary Anger" (review of Adrienne Rich's *Diving into the Wreck*), MS, July, 1973, p. 34. Jupiter, in Jean Giraudoux's *Amphitryon 38*, observes of Alcmene, "It is she who is the real Prometheus" (II, III).

73. "Why Have There Been No Great Women Artists?," in Thomas B. Hess

glory and of betrayal display the ravages of that mystique, even as she struggled to transcend it. But there are two faces to Corinne, her Promethean genius and her death: " . . . women, like men, have never had any trouble worshipping a victim 'they' have destroyed or, more particularly, in 'forgiving' a talented woman her talent— after her death."[74] If Mme de Staël has never been so forgiven, by either sex, it is in part because she appeared to the world to lack the requisite portion of female humility. There was surely no lack of anxiety in her, but her self-doubt simply appears less dominant than her sometimes raving self-love. Chiefly she is unforgiven because of her assumption of superiority, no matter what she suffered because of it or how much it was merited by her gifts. Such an arrogation of superiority, an attribute of power, was and still remains an unacceptable quality in a woman for us. Yet all she had done was to develop in all her fictions, from *Mirza* to *Corinne,* that kernel of a notion we find, all unsuspectingly, in Milton. Eve speaks:

> But to Adam in what sort
> Shall I appear? shall I to him make known
> As yet my change, and give him to partake
> Full happiness with me, or rather not,
> But keep the odds of knowledge in my power
> In Female Sex, the more to draw his Love,
> And render me more equal, and perhaps
> A thing not undesirable, sometime
> Superior: for inferior who is free?
> This may be well: but what if God has seen,
> And Death ensue? then I shall be no more,
> And *Adam* wedded to another *Eve,*
> Shall live with her enjoying, I extinct;
> A death to think.
>
> *(Paradise Lost,* IX, 816–30)

---

and Elizabeth C. Baker, eds., *Art and Sexual Politics* (New York: Collier, 1975), p. 36. Simone de Beauvoir puts it that "no woman has felt herself authorized" to "enact the fate of all humanity" as the male genius does. *Second Sex,* p. 641.

74. Phyllis Chesler, *Woman and Madness* (Garden City, N. Y.: Doubleday, 1972), p. 11, note.

If woman must fear in perpetuity to rise above man, whatever her individual nature or his, she never can be free. *Delphine* and *Corinne*, whatever their other characteristics, are both works that advocate woman's freedom to be superior, but see for it the same pitfall that Milton's Eve did: that such freedom might be punished and Adam go off blithely with a servile Eve. Mme de Staël sought to raise the spirits and ambitions of women with her heroine and stir the consciences of men in depicting her fate. The reception of her work and of her person was not such as to reassure succeeding generations, and George Sand writes, as if in reproof of the Staëlian pose of greatness, "Never have I said to myself: What would it matter if men are small to me who am great! On the contrary, I have felt this bitter truth resound in my heart: What would it matter to be great if I had no brothers? Let the muse go, then, and offer her sterile palm to those who beg for it. . . ."[75]

This ostensibly nobler and more generous and loving pose of Sand's than that of the woman author who seeks achievement and does not reject fame is also, let it be underscored, a renunciation, a withdrawal, a rout, not only for herself but for all the "little rugged girls" in New England classrooms and everywhere else. It is an evasion, under the circumstances of women's diminished status, of all claim on their part to effective influence in the world. As Mme de Staël can still be hated with a public venom that twentieth-century "advances" have scarcely diluted, it is as a woman who pleaded unambiguously for power—albeit a pacific one—in women.

Underscoring this problem is the harsh judgment, again of an excellent critic of the novels in this decade:

. . . it is not the virile or vulnerable Corinne, pioneer held back by the heel, who proposes to woman around 1800, if not a true chance for salvation, at least a provisional *modus vivendi*, but the "spinster" well ensconced in her comfort and her modest certainties: she establishes a position of reserve, of waiting . . . so as to spy out at her ease the transformations

---

75. George Sand, *Correspondance*, 11 vols. (Paris: Garnier, 1967), III, 791. Daring so grandly to conquer her own freedom, Sand did not grapple with the question of women's equality, conceding their inferiority.

which one day, perhaps, will liberate her sex . . . judging the master and master of him, insofar as one can at will show his absurdities and escape their grasp, laying his power open to question without ever contesting it squarely. What more flattering, more comfortable attitude could there be, since no risk is taken?[76]

Mme de Staël, still blasted as "virile" in the 1970s because she had the courage to envisage active genius for women must be seen, finally, on this score, as not inferior to Jane Austen. The private and, paradoxically, universal Austen world leaves woman *in the world* largely as it found her, only less bemused. Its import lies in its telling so much more truth about her nature and condition than had been exposed, or stated so concisely, before. This, one might say, is quite enough. But we do know that in the sense that life is not literature, the stance of Austen, the caustic spinster, was altogether agreeable, even delightful balm to the male ego, and as such a distinct female retreat.[77] Even Fauchery realizes that it is not possible for a woman writer, given the precariousness of woman's identity, to pretend to a genuine Apollonian calm. He concedes that all she *can* do, if she wishes to approach to this ideal of art, is to set aside risk. The universal mode in art conserves; it does not dare. If, as Virginia Woolf has said, in a comment that illuminates the Staël-Austen conflict, "the self-centered and self-limited writers [like Staël] have a power denied the more catholic and broadminded [like Austen]," this is because it is power that attracts them. And it is, insistently, the presence of such power in the works of women that seems to call for excuse, for illumination.

An extraordinary reflection of the bond that links woman's grief, her erotic life, and her creative power is to be focused in Denise Levertov's powerful "Lamentation":

---

76. Fauchery, *La Destinée féminine,* p. 852. Fauchery visibly condescends, albeit admiratively, to Austen here.

77. Charlotte Brontë commented, "Jane Austen was a complete and most sensible lady, but a very incomplete, and rather insensible (*not sense-less*) woman. . . ." Inga-Stina Ewbank, *Their Proper Sphere* (Cambridge: Harvard University Press, 1966), p. 164. Mary Ellman, in her passage on "Balloonism" in *Thinking about Women,* executes some marvelously deft pinpricks at Austen's deflationary tactics against feminine liveliness.

Grief, have I denied thee?
Grief, I have denied thee.

That robe or tunic, black gauze
over black and silver my sister wore
to dance Sorrow, hung so long
in my closet. I never tried it on.

　And my dance
was Summer—they rouged my cheeks
and twisted roses with wire stems into my hair.
I was compliant, Juno de sept ans,
betraying my autumn birthright pour faire plaisir.
Always denial. Grief in the morning washed away
in coffee, crumbled to a dozen errands between
busy fingers.
　Or across cloistral shadow, insistent
intrusion of pink sunstripes from open
archways, falling recurrent.

Corrosion denied, the figures the acid designs
filled in. Grief dismissed,
and Eros along with grief.
Phantasmagoria swept across the sky
by shaky winds endlessly,
the spaces of blue timidly steady—
blue curtains at trailer windows framing
the cinder walks.
There are hidden corners of sky
choked with swept shreds, with
　pain and ashes. *Grief,
have I denied thee? Denied thee.*
The emblems torn from the walls,
and the black plumes.[78]

Here the dammed grief, repressed in the daily round, in compliance, "pour faire plaisir," like a gust of destructive wind exposes the littered landscape of the woman's soul, uncovering a poverty that is reproached by its firm and sorrowful evocation. The poet's

---

78. Denise Levertov, "Lamentation," in "Eight Poems," *New Directions 19,* ed. J. Laughlin (New York: New Directions, 1966), pp. 77–78.

lament reveals what convention would conceal: the waste of emotive power in a repressive order.

Corinne's expression of outraged grief had to be denied validity because it challenged the assumption that women's erotic and creative powers are so mitigated as to be negligible. Part of the scandal lay in its open display of an "unseemly" lamentation, nakedly impassioned—hence embarrassing, menacing. For Corinne's is a willful self-destruction. Her sacrifice is not holy, brings no peace into the world, but only discord. She immolates herself out of her sense of the incommensurability of her amorous fate to her worth and gifts, and her death testifies, in grandiose fashion, to the millions of mini-immolations women have suffered as they have suppressed, often in a related spirit of masochistic pleasure, their capacities and desires. Such expressions of female rage as this —that might prove effectively subversive in helping to release all the pent-up energies of women—are inherently dangerous. One senses their "hysterically" rebellious quality without needing to elucidate it precisely. No one ever planned any strategy of devaluation to defuse such dangers. There is no need, for the arms against such protests are ready at hand in our customs and beliefs. Power inhering in such works is simply denied them. If Corinne claims genius, we merely smile. If she suffers, we say she exaggerates, is spoiled, absurd. If, even, she should die, we say she willed it to be so by not willing herself other. Yet she remains discomfitting, a rebellious victim. Our strategic response is to refuse pity to the woman who laments her lot. In the end, our distaste for the "scold," and our ready consignment of female plaintiffs to that category, is but fear disguised.

Virginia Woolf expressed a related concern for women's fiction: "It is fatal for a woman to lay the least stress on any grievance; to plead even with just cause; in any way to speak consciously as a woman. And fatal is no figure of speech; for anything written with that conscious bias is doomed to death."[79] Such bias inflicts serious

---

79. *A Room of One's Own* (London: Hogarth Press, 1929), p. 157. Note Patricia Meyer Spack's comment on this work: ". . . the essay's inadequacies are themselves revealing. Its author's evasions of her own anger, her effort to dismiss feminine anger as a limitation on women's writing, her aspirations to escape in writing the problems inherent in her own sexuality: these aspects of the

wounds upon Mme de Staël's novels. But while Woolf is surely right about the effect of bias upon what we deem the ultimate in fictional art in its mastery over tone and point of view, art has many faces, and one of them is that of myth-making, as such artists as Victor Hugo and Norman Mailer have demonstrated.

A myth, to deserve the name, must be consecrated by a human community. The Corinne myth, despite the imperfections of the text in which it appeared, was embraced in its time by many women. Margaret Fuller tries to sum up its inventor:

De Staël . . . could not forget the woman in the thought; while she was instructing you as a mind, she wished to be admired as a Woman; sentimental tears often dimmed the eagle glance. Her intellect too, with all its splendor, trained in a drawing-room, fed on flattery, was tainted and flawed; yet its beams make the obscurest schoolhouse in New England warmer and lighter to the little rugged girls who are gathered together on its wooden benches. They may never through life hear her name, but she is not less their benefactress.[80]

Even Fuller is too self-conscious about Mme de Staël's defects, her "outrageousness," and makes too many concessions.

The reason, as Fuller knew why she and the other women who have followed must be grateful to Germaine de Staël is for her heroic claim to the realm of culture as a province for women. In the salon culture of the eighteenth century, of which Mme de Staël's life is an ultimate expression, woman asserted her capacity for wit and cultivation, but her participation was that of a delightful guest at a feast prepared for centuries by men. The novel *Corinne* represents an assumption by woman of the host role at the banquet of culture, a groping attempt to give form to a womanly model of transcendence; as such it was an incursion for womankind into the sacred precincts of the highest realms of poetry, prophecy, and religion that man has always reserved to himself. Viewed in this way, we better understand how the sudden ascent to such heights could have caused dizziness, to herself and to others. We find one response to Corinne's flight in the culture

---

book, its logical failures, tell us as much as do its triumphs. *The Female Imagination* (New York: Knopf, 1975), p. 14.

80. *The Writings of Margaret Fuller*, p. 162.

madness of upper-class women in succeeding times; another, in the drive to achieve educational goals beyond the wildest fancies of women born in 1766. Still diffident over their right to be creators, initiators, the mass of women now press eagerly their right to be distinguished followers. Their grasp upon their own destiny is yet effete and tentative, lacking the boldness and courage of the poetess Corinne's.

The sibyl of Domenichino, Corinne's emblem, with her direct and intelligent glance, is the symbol of the woman who commands matter: she is not dominated by it. To make us love her, Mme de Staël added to the sibyl's brilliance Corinne's own personal warmth and visionary concern for humankind. A future-oriented prophetess, though ill-starred, was what the nineteenth century saw in Corinne. For us, it is her dimension as an extraordinary woman that now seems prophetic. Perhaps it is no longer too soon to hope that the Corinne myth, that of the woman as genius, can be returned to us from slander and defamation as what its creator wished it to be: a goad to women to be whatever they will, to belong to the world and not only to the domestic circle; a goad to men, too, to lay aside their fears and doubts and not to deny the human face of greatness should they meet with it in woman.

Bibliography

Abensour, Léon. *Histoire générale du féminisme des origines à nos jours.*
Paris: Leroux, 1923.

Abray, Jane. "Feminism in the French Revolution." *American Historical
Review,* 80, no. 1 (Feb., 1975), 43–62.

Albert, Pierre, and Fernand Terrou. *Histoire de la presse française des
origines à 1814.* Paris: Presses Universitaires de France, 1969.

Alembert, Jean Lerond d'. *Oeuvres complètes.* 5 vols. Paris: Belin, 1821–22.

Amiel, Henri-Frédéric. "Madame de Staël." Extract from *La Galerie suisse.*
Lausanne: Georges Bridel, 1876.

Andlau, Béatrice d'. "Journal de jeunesse." *Occident et cahiers staëliens,*
Oct. 15, 1932.

Arblay, Frances Burney d'. *The Diary and Letters of Madame d'Arblay.*
Edited by her niece. 2 vols. Philadelphia: Carey and Hart, 1842.

Arnaud, François-Thomas-Marie de Baculard d'. *Eustasia, histoire italienne.*
2 vols. Paris: André, 1803.

Aulard, Alphonse. "Le Féminisme pendant la révolution française." *La
Revue Bleue,* Mar. 19, 1898, pp. 362–66.

Balayé, Simone. Introduction to Staël's *Dix Années d'exil.* Paris: Bibliothèque 10–18, 1966.

————. "La Nationalité de Madame de Staël." In *Humanisme actif. Mélanges d'art et de littérature offerts à Julien Cain.* 2 vols. Preface by
Etienne Dennery. Paris: Herman-Spes, 1957.

————. "Absence, exil, voyages." In *Madame de Staël et l'Europe: Colloque de Coppet.* Paris: Klincksieck, 1970.

————. "Fiction romanesque de la musique et des sons dans *Corinne.*"
Romantisme, 3 (1972), 17–32.

————. "A propos du préromantisme: continuïté ou rupture chez Madame de Staël." In *Préromantisme: hypothèque ou hypothèse?* Paris:
Klincksieck, 1975.

Balzac, Honoré de. *Sténie ou les erreurs philosophiques.* Paris: Librarie
Georges Courville, 1936.

Bastide, Roger. *Le Rêve, la transe et la folie.* Paris: Flammarion, 1972.

Baudelaire, Charles Pierre. *Oeuvres.* Paris: Pléiade, 1954.

Beauvoir, Simone de. *The Second Sex.* Translated by H. M. Parshley. New
York: Bantam Books, 1971.

Bédé, Jean-Albert. "Madame de Staël, Rousseau et le suicide." *Revue
d'Histoire Littéraire de la France,* 66, no. 1 (1966), 52–70.

————. "Madame de Staël et les mots." In *Madame de Staël et l'Europe: Colloque de Coppet*. Paris: Klincksieck, 1970.

Behn, Aphra Amis. *Novels*. Edited by Charles Gildon. 2 vols. London: F. Clay, 1722.

Bénichou, Paul. "La Genèse d'*Adolphe*." *Revue d'Histoire Littéraire de la France*, 54, no. 3 (1954), 332–56.

Bertrand, Henri Gratien. *Cahiers de Sainte-Hélène*. Edited by Paul Fleuriot de Langle. Paris: Bonne, 1959.

Beugnot, Arthur Auguste. *Mémoires du comte Beugnot, ancien ministre (1783–1815)*. Edited by Albert Beugnot. Paris: Dentu, 1889.

Blennerhasset, Charlotte Julia von Leyden. *Madame de Staël et son temps*. 3 vols. Paris: Westhausser, 1890.

Bowman, Frank Paul. "Madame de Staël et l'apologétique romantique." In *Madame de Staël et l'Europe: Colloque de Coppet*. Paris: Klincksieck, 1970.

Brunetière, Ferdinand. "Les Romans de Madame de Staël." *Revue des Deux Mondes*, 3 (1890), 682–93.

Campbell, Joseph. *The Hero with a Thousand Faces*. New York: Pantheon, 1949.

Chateaubriand, François Auguste René de. *Oeuvres complètes*. 27 vols. Paris: Ladvocat, 1826–31.

————. *Oeuvres complètes*. 12 vols. Paris: Garnier, 1859–60.

Chesler, Phyllis. *Women and Madness*. Garden City, N. Y.: Doubleday, 1972.

Cioran, E. M. *Le Mauvais Demiurge*. Paris: Gallimard, 1969.

Condorcet, Marie Jean Antoine Nicolas Caritat de. *Lettres d'un bourgeois de New-Haven à un citoyen de Virginie (Mazzei), sur l'inutilité de partager le corps législatif entre plusieurs corps*. Paris: A. Colle chez Froullé, 1788.

Constant de Rebecque, Henri Benjamin. *Journaux intimes*. Edited by Alfred Roulin and Charles Roth. Paris: Gallimard, 1952.

Cram-Holmström, Kirsten. *Monodrama, Attitudes, Tableaux-vivants, Studies in Some Trends of Theatrical Fashion, 1770–1815*. Stockholm: Alquist and Wiksell, 1967.

Decreus-Van Liefland, Juliette. *Sainte-Beuve et la critique des auteurs féminins*. Paris: Boivin, 1949.

Diderot, Denis. *Correspondance*. Edited by Georges Roth. 5 vols. Paris: Editions de Minuit, 1955–59.

————. *Oeuvres complètes*. Edited by Jules Assézat and Maurice Tourneux. 20 vols. Paris: Garnier, 1875–77.

Eaubonne, Françoise d'. *Une Femme témoin de son siècle*. Paris: Flammarion, 1966.

Edinburgh Review, XI (1807–8), 183–95.

Selections from the Edinburgh Review. London: Longman, Rees, Orme, Browne, Green, and Longman, 1833.

Ellmann, Mary. *Thinking about Women*. New York: Harcourt Brace and World, 1968.

Escarpit, Robert. *L'Angleterre dans l'oeuvre de Mme de Staël*. Paris: Didier, 1954.

Ewbank, Inga-Stina. *Their Proper Sphere*. Cambridge: Harvard University Press, 1966.

Fauchery, Pierre. *La Destinée féminine dans le roman européen du dix-huitième siècle*. Paris: Armand Colin, 1972.

Fiedler, Leslie. *Love and Death in the American Novel*. New York: Criterion Books, 1960.

Forster, E. M. *Aspects of the Novel*. New York: Harcourt, Brace, 1927.

Fuller, Margaret. *The Writings of Margaret Fuller*. New York: Viking, 1941.

———. *Margaret Fuller, American Romantic*. Edited by Perry Miller. New York: Doubleday, Anchor, 1963.

Gautier, Paul. *Madame de Staël et Napoléon*. Paris: Plon-Nourrit, 1903.

Gennari, Geneviève. *Le Premier Voyage de Madame de Staël en Italie et la genèse de Corinne*. Paris: Boivin, 1947.

Géruzez, Eugène. *Histoire de la littérature française pendant la révolution*. Paris: Didier, 1881.

Godwin, William. *The Adventures of Caleb Williams; or Things As They Are*. London: Richard Bentley, 1849.

Goethe, Johann von. *The Sorrows of Werther*. London: Blake, 1825.

Goncourt, Edmond and Jules, de. *La Femme au XVIIIe siècle*. Paris: Didot, 1862.

Gouges, Marie Olympe de. *Déclaration des droits de la femme et de la citoyenne*. Paris: [1791?].

Graffigny, Françoise d'Issembourg d'Happencourt de. *Lettres d'une Péruvienne*. Amsterdam: aux dépens de la Cie, 1761.

Grunberger, Bela. "Jalons pour l'étude du narcissisme dans la sexualité féminine." In *La Sexualité féminine*, edited by J. Chasseguet-Smirgel. Paris: Payot, 1964.

Guillois, Albert. *Etude médico-psychologique d'Olympe de Gouges*. Lyon: Rey, 1904.

Gutwirth, Madelyn. "Madame de Staël's Debt to *Phèdre: Corinne*." *Studies in Romanticism*, III, no. 3 (Spring, 1964), 161–76.

———. "Madame de Staël, Rousseau and the Woman Question." *PMLA*, 86, no. 1 (Jan., 1971), 100–109.

———. "Madame de Staël et l'esthétique du camée." In *Préromantisme: hypothèque ou hypothèse?* Paris: Klincksieck, 1975.

Gwynne, Gruffed E. *Madame de Staël et la révolution française*. Paris: Nizet, 1969.

Hacker, Helen Mayer. "Women as a Minority Group." *Social Forces*, 30 (Oct., 1951), 60–69.

Haussonville, Gabriel-Paul Othenin d'. *Le Salon de Madame Necker*. 2 vols. Paris: Calmann-Lévy, 1882.

Hays, H. R. *The Dangerous Sex: The Myth of Feminine Evil.* New York: Putnam 1964.

Heilbrun, Carolyn G. *Toward a Recognition of Androgyny.* New York: Knopf, 1973.

Herold, J. Christopher. *Mistress to an Age: A Life of Madame de Staël.* New York: Bobbs-Merrill, 1958.

Hill, Constance. *Maria Edgeworth.* London: John Lane the Bodley Head, 1910.

Iknayan, Marguerite. *The Idea of the Novel in France.* Paris and Geneva: Minard-Droz, 1961.

Ilsley, Marjorie Henry. "New Light on the *Proumenoir de M. de Montaigne.*" *Modern Philology,* LII, no. 1 (Aug., 1954), 1–11.

Janeway, Elizabeth. *Man's World, Woman's Place.* New York: Morrow, 1971.

Jolly, Pierre. *Necker.* Paris: Les Oeuvres françaises, 1947.

Jong, Erica. "Visionary Anger" (review of Adrienne Rich's *Diving into the Wreck). MS,* July, 1973, pp. 30–34.

Kohler, Pierre. *Madame de Staël et la Suisse.* Paris: Payot, 1916.

Lacour, Leopold. *Les Origines du féminisme contemporain: Trois femmes de la Révolution: Olympe de Gouges, Théroigne de Méricourt, Rose Lacombe.* Paris: Plon-Nouritt, 1900.

Lamartine, Alphonse de. *Souvenirs et portraits.* Paris: Hachette, 1871.

———. "Les Destinées de la poésie." In *Oeuvres complètes.* 8 vols. Paris: Hachette, Furne, 1856.

Lambert, Anne-Thérèse de Marguenat de Courcelles. *Réflexions nouvelles sur les femmes.* Paris: F. Le Breton, 1727.

———. *Lettres sur l'éducation d'une jeune demoiselle.* Paris: Louis, 1811.

Larg, David Glass. *Madame de Staël: La Vie dans l'oeuvre (1766–1800).* Paris: Champion, 1924.

———. *Madame de Staël: La Seconde Vie (1800–1807).* Paris: Champion, 1928.

Larnac, Jean. *Histoire de la littérature féminine en France.* Paris: Editions Kra, 1927.

Le Breton, André. *Le Roman français au 19e siècle Ière partie: Avant Balzac.* Paris: Boivin, 1901.

Lederer, Wolfgang. *The Fear of Women.* New York: Harcourt, 1967.

Lehtonen, Maya, "Le Fleuve du temps et le fleuve de l'enfer, thèmes et images dans *Corinne.*" *Neuphilologische Mitteilungen,* 68 (1967), 225–42, 391–408; 69 (1968), 101–28.

Levertov, Denise. "Eight Poems." In *New Directions 19,* edited by J. Laughlin. New York: New Directions, 1966, pp. 77–78.

Levin, Harry. *The Gates of Horn.* New York: Oxford University Press, 1963.

Ligne, Charles Joseph Emmanuel de. "Un Portrait inédit de Madame de Staël." *Occident et Cahiers staëliens,* 2 (Feb. 15, 1935), 229–30.

Litto, Victor del. *La Vie intellectuelle de Stendhal; genèse et évolution de ses idées (1802–1821)*. Paris: Presses Universitaires Françaises, 1959.

Lubbock, Percy. *The Craft of Fiction*. London: Jonathan Cape, 1957.

Luppé, Albert Marie Pierre de. *Les Jeunes Filles à la fin du XVIIIe siècle*. Paris: Champion, 1925.

Mauzi, Robert. *L'Idée du bonheur au XVIIIe siècle*. Paris: Armand Colin, 1960.

May, Caroline, ed. *The American Female Poets*. Philadelphia: Lindsay and Blakiston, 1853.

May, Georges. *Le Dilemme du roman au XVIIIe siècle*. Paris: Presses Universitaires Françaises, 1963.

Mercure de France, XI, no. LXXIX (Nivôse, an XII—Jan., 1803).

Merlant, Joachim. *Le Roman personnel en France de Rousseau à Fromentin*. Paris: Hachette, 1905.

Michelet, Jules. *Les Femmes de la Révolution*. Edited by Pierre Labracherie, Pierre Dumont, and P. Bessand-Massenet. Paris: Hachette, 1960.

Miller, Nancy K. "The Exquisite Cadavers: Woman in Eighteenth Century Fiction." *Diacritics*, 5 (Winter, 1975), 37–43.

Moers, Ellen. *Literary Women*. New York: Doubleday, 1976.

———. "Mme de Staël and the Woman of Genius." *American Scholar*, Spring, 1975, pp. 225–41.

Mortier, Roland. "Madame de Staël et l'héritage des lumières." In *Madame de Staël et l'Europe: Colloque de Coppet*. Paris: Klincksieck, 1970.

Muir, Edwin. *The Structure of the Novel*. London: The Hogarth Press, 1946.

Necker, Jacques. *Oeuvres complètes*. 15 vols. Paris: Treuttel et Würtz, 1821.

Necker, Suzanne Curchod de Nasse. *Mélanges extraits des Manuscrits de Mme Necker*. 3 vols. Paris: Charles Pougens, 1798.

Nochlin, Linda. "Why Have There Been No Great Women Artists?" In *Art and Sexual Politics*, edited by Thomas B. Hess and Elizabeth C. Baker. New York: Collier, 1975.

Omacini, Lucia. "Quelques remarques sur le style des romans de Madame de Staël, d'après la presse de l'époque (1802–1808)." *Annali di Ca'Foscari*, X, fasc. 1–2 (1971), 213–38.

Pailleron, Marie-Louise. *Madame de Staël*. Paris: Hachette, 1931.

Pange, Jean de. *Madame de Staël et François de Pange*. Paris: Plon-Nourrit, 1925.

Poulain de la Barre, François. *De l'Egalité des deux sexes*. Paris: Jean Du Puis, 1673.

———. *De l'Education des dames pour la conduite de l'esprit dans les sciences et dans les moeurs*. Paris: Jean Du Puis, 1674.

Praz, Mario. *The Romantic Agony*. London: Oxford University Press, 1933.

Quotidienne, La, no. 468 (le 18 Thermidor, an V—Aug. 5, 1797), "Variétés."

Renouvier, Jules. *Histoire de l'art pendant la Révolution*. Paris: J. Renouard, 1863.

Riccoboni, Marie-Jeanne. *Lettres de Mistriss Fanni Butlerd . . . .* Paris: Humblot, 1759.

Ridenour, George M. *The Style of Don Juan*. New Haven: Yale University Press, 1960.

Rivarol, Antoine, and Louis Champcenetz. *Petit Dictionnaire des grands hommes de la révolution*. Paris: Au Palais royal, De l'imprimerie nationale, 1790.

Romero, Francisco. "Madame de Staël en la revolución feminina del siglo XIX." *Cuadernos Americanos*, CVII, no. 6 (1959), 147–66.

Rougemont, Denis de. *L'Amour dans l'occident*. Paris: Plon, 1939.

Rousseau, Jean-Jacques. *La Nouvelle Héloïse*. Edited by René Pomeau. Paris: Garnier, 1960.

Sainte-Beuve, Charles-Augustin de. *Causeries du Lundi*. 2nd ed. 15 vols. Paris: Garner, 1856–62.

———. "Dix-neuvième Siècle, Madame de Staël." In *Les Grands Ecrivains français,* edited by Maurice Allem. Paris: Garnier, 1932.

Saintsbury, George. Introduction to *Corinne or Italy*. Translated by Dennis Lawler, revised. 2 vols. London: Dent, 1894.

Salis, Jean de. *Sismondi*. Paris: Champion, 1932.

Sand, George. *Correspondance*. 11 vols. Paris: Garnier, 1967.

Saussure, Albertine Necker de. *L'Education progresive*. Paris: A Sautelet et Cie., 1828–32.

———. "Notice sur le caractère et les écrits de Madame de Staël." In Staël, *Oeuvres complètes*, vol. I. Paris: Treuttel et Würtz, 1820.

Scott, Geoffrey. *Portrait of Zélide*. New York: Charles Scribner's, 1927.

Séjourné, Philippe. *Aspects généraux du roman en Angleterre de 1740 à 1800*. Aix-en-Provence: Orphys, 1966.

Sénac de Meilhan, Gabriel. *Le Gouvernement, les moeurs et les conditions en France avant la Révolution*. Paris: Poulet-Malassis, 1862.

Shroder, Maurice Z. *Icarus: The Image of the Artist in French Romanticism*. Cambridge: Harvard University Press, 1961.

Sorel, Albert. *Madame de Staël*, Paris: Hachette, 1890.

Souriau, Maurice. *Histoire du romantisme en France*. Paris: Spes, 1927.

Spacks, Patricia. *The Female Imagination*. New York: Knopf, 1975.

Spitzer, Leo. "A propos de *La Vie de Marianne*." *Romanic Review*, XLIV (1953), 102–26.

Staël, Anne-Louise Germaine Necker de. *Oeuvres complètes*. Published by Auguste-Louis de Staël; preceded by an essay on the character and works of the author by Albertine Necker de Saussure. 17 vols. Paris: Treuttel et Würtz, 1820–21.

    I—(Notice sur le caractère et les écrits de Mme de Staël). Lettres sur le caractère et les écrits de J. J. Rousseau.

    II—Morceaux divers: Réflexions sur le procès de la reine. Rèflexions sur la paix addressées à M. Pitt et aux Français. Réflexions sur la paix intérieure. Essai sur les fictions. Trois nouvelles: Mirza, ou lettre d'un voyageur. Adelaïde et Théodore. Histoire de Pauline. Zulma, fragment d'un ouvrage.

III—De l'influence des passions sur le bonheur des individus et des nations. Réflexions sur le suicide.

IV—De la littérature, considérée dans ses rapports avec les institutions sociales.

V–VII—Delphine

VIII–IX—Corinne

X–XI—De l'Allemagne

XII–XIV—Considérations sur les principaux événemens de la révolution française.

XV—Dix années d'exil.

XVI—Essais dramatiques: Agar dans le désert. Geneviève de Brabant. La Sunamite. Le Capitaine Kernadec. La Signora Fantastici. Le Mannequin. Sapho.

XVII—Du caractère de M. Necker. Mélanges.

———. *Des Circonstances actuelles qui peuvent terminer la Révolution.* Edited by J. Viénot. Paris: Fischbacker, 1902.

———. *De l'Allemagne.* Edited by Mme de Pange and Simone Balayé. 5 vols. Paris: Hachette, 1958–60.

———. *Lettres de Madame de Staël à Ribbing.* Edited by Simone Balayé. Paris: Gallimard, 1960.

———. *Lettres inédites à Louis de Narbonne.* Edited by Béatrice Jasinski. Paris: Pauvert, 1960.

———. *Choix de lettres de Madame de Staël 1766–1817.* Edited by Georges Solovieff. Paris: Klincksieck, 1970.

———. *Correspondance générale.* Edited by Béatrice Jasinski. 5 vols–. Paris: Pauvert, 1962–.

———. *Les Carnets de voyage de Madame de Staël.* Edited by Simone Balayé. Geneva: Droz, 1971.

———. "Madame Necker." *Biographie universelle.* 21 vols. Brussels: H. Ode, 1843–47.

Starobinski, Jean. *L'Invention de la liberté.* Geneva: A. Skira, 1964.

———. *Portrait de l'artiste en saltimbanque.* Geneva: A. Skira, 1970.

———. "Suicide et mélancolie chez Madame de Staël." In *Madame de Staël et l'Europe: Colloque de Coppet.* Paris: Klincksieck, 1970.

Suleau, Francois Louis. *Journal.* Niewied sur le Rhin and Paris: rue de Seine, 1791–92.

Taylor, I. A. *Lady Jane Grey and Her Times.* London: Hutchinson, 1908.

Thibaudet, Albert. *Histoire de la littérature française.* Paris: Librairie Stock, 1936.

Thomson, James. *The Seasons and the Castle of Indolence.* Edited by J. Logie Robertson. Oxford: The Clarendon Press, 1891.

Tieghem, Paul van. "Les Droits de l'amour et l'union libre dans le roman français et allemand—1760–1790." *Neophilologus,* XII (1927), 96–103.

Villemain, Abel François. *Cours de littérature française; tableau de la littérature au XVIIIe siècle.* 4 vols. Paris: Perrin, 1891.

Vinet, Alexandre. *Etudes sur la littérature française au XIXe siècle.* 3 vols. Paris: Fischbacker; Lausanne: Georges Bridel, 1908.

Weightman, John. "Madame de Staël." *Encounter,* XLI, no. 4 (Oct., 1973), 45–54.

Whitford, Robert C. "Madame de Staël's Literary Reputation in England." *University of Illinois Studies in Language and Literature,* IV (1918), 1–62.

Williams, David. "The Politics of Feminism in the French Enlightenment." In *The Varied Pattern: Studies in the 18th Century,* edited by Peter Hughes and David Williams. Toronto: A. M. Hakkert, 1971.

Wollstonecraft, Mary. *A Vindication of the Rights of Women* (1792). New York: Source Book Press Reprint, 1971.

Wood, J. S. "Sondages dans le roman français du point de vue social (1789–1830)." *Revue d'Histoire Littéraire de la France,* I (Jan.–Mar., 1954), 32–48.

Woolf, Virignia. *A Room of One's Own.* London: Hogarth Press, 1929.

Index

HOWE LIBRARY
SHENANDOAH COLLEGE &
CONSERVATORY OF MUSIC
WINCHESTER, VA.

840.92
St13g

67129

GAYLORD   PRINTED IN U.S.A.